BELIZE

Adventures

DAT

D0071713

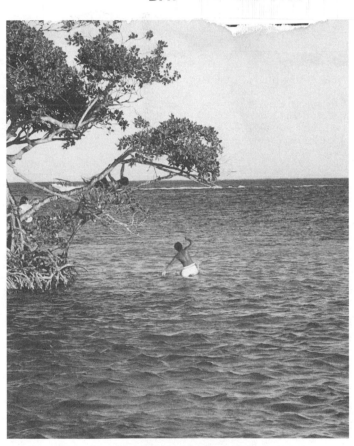

Richard Mahler

JOHN MUIR PUBLICATIONS
SANTA FE, NEW MEXICO

F
1443.5
.M34

John Muir Publications, P.O. Box 613, Santa Fe, New Mexico 87504

1999

Printed in the United States of America.
Second edition. First printing May 1999.

Library of Congress Cataloging-in-Publication Data
Mahler, Richard.
        Belize: adventures in nature / Richard Mahler. — 2nd ed.
                p.   cm.
        Includes index.
        ISBN 1-56261-431-2
        1. Belize—Guidebooks. 2. Natural history—Belize—Guidebooks.
        3. Outdoor recreation—Belize—Guidebooks. I. Title.
        F1443.5.M34 1999
        917.28204'5 —DC21   99-18072
                                                             CIP

Editor: Dianna Delling
Graphics Editor: Heather Pool
Production: Janine Lehmann
Design: Janine Lehmann
Typesetting: Kathleen Sparkes, White Hart Design
Maps: Laura Perfetti
Printer: Publishers Press

Title page photo: Richard Mahler—Caye Caulker
Large front cover: © Kevin Schafer—Belize barrier reef
Small front cover: © Jay Ireland & Georgienne E. Bradley—Jaguar
Large back cover: © Kevin Schafer—Karst hills
Small back cover: © Jay Ireland & Georgienne E. Bradley—Red-eyed tree frog

Distributed to the book trade by
Publishers Group West
Berkeley, California

CONTENTS

CONTENTS

ACKNOWLEDGMENTS

The author wishes to especially thank Rita Cadena for the inspiration to write this book and the warm, wonderful people of Belize for making it possible. I also thank everyone at John Muir Publications for their patience and assistance.

Special thanks go to (among many others) Wil and Susan Lala; Lionel "Chocolate" Heredia and Annie Seashore; Bruce Foerster and Neil Rogers; Alfredo and Yvonne Villoria; the Cesario Choco family; Ray Herbard and Clive Farrell; the late Stephen Smith; Jim and Marguerite Bevis; Charles Colby II; Lan Sluder; Mary Dell Lucas; Larry Feinstein; Therese Rath Bowman; the staff of the Belize Tourist Board; the Belize Tourism Industry Association; and last, but not least, my steadfast and supportive parents, Don and Mary Mahler. My deepest appreciation goes to Kate Droney, my favorite traveling companion and best editor.

For their gorgeous and informative photographs, my appreciation goes out to Kevin Schafer, Ricardo Castillo, Klaus Eiberle, Don Usner, Bob Mahler, Lighthawk, the Belize Tourist Board, Silckrock Adventures, International Expeditions, Jim Smith, Sue Dirksen, and particularly to Steele Wotkyns, without whom this book would not be possible. Thank you, Steele, for being a good friend, an excellent writer, and a staunch advocate for environmental preservation. Finally, my thanks go to Continental Airlines and the various hotels and outfitters (you know who you are) that generously extended courtesies during my research trips to Belize.

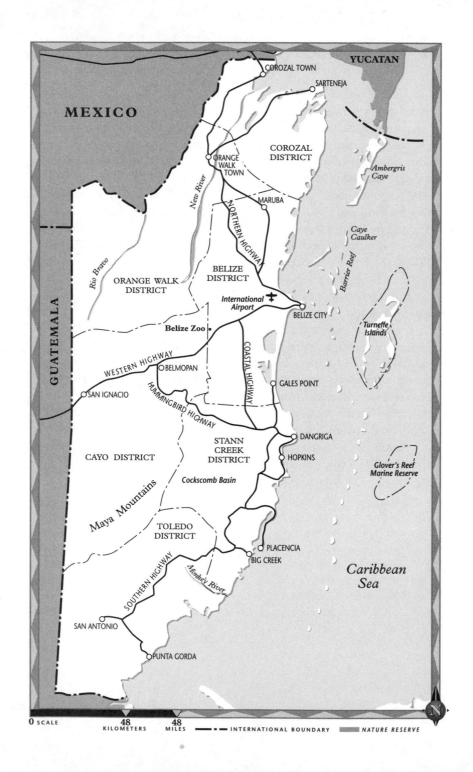

BELIZE: JEWEL OF THE CARIBBEAN

"Why would anybody want to go to Belize?" Chances are you'll be asked this question more than once before you get here. There are many answers, of course, and the one you select will depend on your interests and temperament. If you're a scuba diver, the offshore barrier reef is an obvious attraction. If you want to experience the unspoiled jungle, a trip to the interior of Belize makes perfect sense.

Perhaps the most obvious reason to visit Belize is to be able to experience the natural beauty and quiet ambiance of a relatively uncrowded and little-developed, subtropical destination. Whereas 80 percent of the native forests of Latin America have disappeared during the last two centuries, in Belize the opposite is true: nearly 65 percent of the original forest remains, and in a largely undisturbed form. Here you'll find hundreds of species of animals and plants that have largely disappeared from most of their original homes, yet are thriving in Belize. Offshore, meanwhile, one of the world's longest barrier reefs harbors exotic marine life in an underwater paradise unparalleled in the Western Hemisphere.

This sliver of Caribbean coastline remains the most sparsely populated nation in Central America, with less than 30 inhabitants per square mile. It is not the smallest country. With its 8,867 square miles, Belize is slightly larger than El Salvador. But whereas the latter is bursting with more than 8.5 million people, Belize had an estimated 1999 population of 255,000, about one-third of whom were crowded into a single town: Belize City. Stability is another obvious difference. Belize is a parliamentary democracy that has never suffered under the civil wars and dictatorships that have typified most other Central American countries. Belize enjoys a high literacy rate (93 percent of adults) and long life expectancy (73 years for women, 67 for men).

Belize is divided into six political jurisdictions that roughly correspond to states or provinces. They are, from north to south, the Corozal, Orange Walk, Belize, Cayo, Stann Creek, and Toledo Districts. Most visitors will spend the bulk of their time in the Belize District, which encompasses the international airport, Belize City, and such northern islands as Ambergris Caye and Caye Caulker; and the Cayo District, where the town of San Ignacio and most jungle lodges are located. Of growing interest to visitors are the southerly Stann Creek and Toledo Districts, noted for their nature reserves, Maya ruins, and pristine offshore waters. The northerly districts of Corozal and Orange Walk are the most agricultural areas of Belize and thus receive the fewest number of visitors.

TRAVEL STRATEGY
Although this is a small nation, getting from one place to another takes some time: Most roads are bad and the islands (called "cayes," pronounced "keys") can only be reached by small airplanes or boats. In order to get the most out of the country, you should plan to spend at least a week in Belize. Travel is time-consuming and sometimes rough.

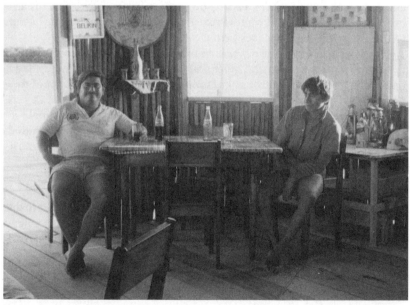

A lobster fisherman and his helper rest in a café at Bluefield Range.

Hurricane Mitch Spares Belize

For a couple of frightening days in late October 1998, Belizeans stared down one of the strongest Caribbean hurricanes of the twentieth century. With sustained winds of up to 180 miles per hour, Hurricane Mitch had the potential of causing unparalleled damage in low-lying areas. But the big storm moved south instead of west, unleashing most of its fury on Honduras and Nicaragua.

Although Belize City was evacuated, no lives were lost and damage was minor. Mainland Belize experienced heavy rain and strong winds with little destruction, while the islands saw some erosion and pier damage due to wind and water surge. Most tourist businesses went unscathed, and nearly all were operating normally within a week of the storm. Underwater damage was minimal: sea fans and larger corals were broken and there was discoloration of a few species. As the sands shifted, some beaches got smaller, some larger. The number of fish grew in both number and variety.

Only five hurricanes have hit Belize since 1900, the worst being Hattie in 1961. Thanks to modern technology, visitors and residents are now warned of storms well in advance of their arrival. For Belize, Mitch's greatest long-term impact may be in the expected flood of new immigrants from storm-ravaged Honduras and Nicaragua.

The two areas of Belize that are of greatest interest to travelers are the Cayo District, in the country's west-central interior, and the offshore islands that arise along the barrier reef, particularly Ambergris Caye and Caye Caulker. Many island visitors are content to spend all of their time on Ambergris Caye, taking an occasional day trip to a Maya ruin or snorkeling and diving site. Although you'll probably enjoy yourself, this kind of trip won't give you a realistic look at the country. We recommend that you roam a bit from Ambergris to visit neighboring islands, or even spend a few nights on a caye or atoll that's less developed. In order to experience the best that Belize has to offer, we also urge you to spend at least two or three days exploring the area around San Ignacio, two hours west of Belize City via the Western Highway. Here you'll find comfortable jungle lodges, well-maintained nature trails, magnificent Maya temples, cool mountain rivers, sacred limestone caves, and such unusual attractions as butterfly farms, rainforest medicine centers, and traditional Mennonite villages. Along the way you can take in the Belize Zoo, Community Baboon Sanctuary, and Crooked Tree Wildlife Sanctuary, or float on an inner tube through the underground grottos of the Caves Branch of the Sibun River.

If you have more time to spend in Belize, a journey south will reward you with fascinating destinations like the Cockscomb Basin jaguar reserve, Laughingbird Caye National Park, Garifuna villages, and Glover's Reef. The more adventurous traveler will want to take excursions into the rainforests and Maya villages of the remote Toledo District. Others may want to head up the jungle rivers and through the wetlands of the Orange Walk and Corozal Districts to the north.

On the other hand, if your inclinations lean decidedly toward water recreation or Maya archaeology, you may want to set up a Belize itinerary that concentrates exclusively on either offshore or interior travel, with a possible side trip to the ancient city of Tikal in neighboring Guatemala.

We recommend reading this book before you make any final decisions about your schedule.

BELIZE HISTORY

Maya Civilization

At the peak of the vast Maya empire, archaeologists estimate that 1 to 2 million Native Americans lived within the borders of Belize, with an equal number dwelling nearby in what is now northeastern Guatemala and southeastern Mexico. Thousands more Maya were scattered across parts of Honduras and El Salvador.

The earliest Maya are believed to have spread into the confines of present-day Belize from Guatemala and Mexico about 2000 B.C., after their ancestors had crossed the land bridge from Asia many centuries earlier. There is evidence that archaic tribes roamed the area as early as 7500 B.C., at a time when Central America's climate and habitat were somewhat less tropical, given over to grassy savannas and broadleaf woodlands.

The early, or pre-Classic, Maya period extends from 1000 B.C. to A.D. 300. The Maya civilization reached its height during the Classic era, from about A.D. 300 to 900. From around A.D. 1000 until the arrival of the Spanish 500 years later, the Maya were plunged into a precipitous decline (the post-Classic phase), and the underlying structure of their society fell apart.

Richard Mahler

The temple of Canaa towers 140 feet above the ancient Maya city of Caracol.

No one knows for certain why the civilization disintegrated or why many of its members migrated north into the northern Yucatán peninsula and left many—but not all—of their city-states abandoned. Perhaps it was a prolonged war or a loss of faith in the priestly royalty who ruled with absolute authority. It is also possible that a series of droughts, earthquakes, or other natural disasters contributed to the breakdown. Archaeologists are collecting data that may someday help us answer such questions.

What is now generally agreed upon is that the area currently known as Belize was for many years the very heart of the Maya empire. From A.D. 300 to 900, this was the center of their complex collection of city-states, linked by trails, rivers, and Caribbean trade routes. Recent excavations have shown that Caracol, the country's largest site, is even bigger than Tikal, long considered the most significant Maya restoration. Archaeologists now believe that Caracol defeated Tikal militarily as the neighboring cities competed for dominance during the Classic period. Many aspects of the ancient Maya civilization have disappeared from Belize (about 15 percent of the country's current population are directly descended from the Maya), but the major archaeological sites at Xunantunich, Caracol, Altun Ha, and Lamanai still reflect its impressive achievements.

What distinguishes the hundreds of Maya sites of Belize from those of neighboring countries is their relatively pristine character. For various reasons, Belize has left many of its ruins in much the same condition as they were found. Excavations and restorations are sporadic, only undertaken when funds and personnel become available—which isn't often.

5

In many ways, the ancient Maya were more advanced than their contemporaries in Greece, Italy, France, and England, reaching the zenith of their power during Europe's Dark Ages. These Native Americans were skilled astronomers and mathematicians, and accomplished farmers and engineers. They developed an elaborate religious system that incorporated many complex rituals and commemorated diverse natural phenomena. Their calendar system, for example, is precise within a matter of seconds in tracking phases of the moon, planets, and stars. Over the years, the Maya became expert artists and traders. Excavations in Belize have yielded seashells from the distant Pacific Coast, obsidian and gold from northern Mexico, pottery from South America's Andes mountains, and jade from the Central American highlands. There is even physical evidence suggesting that Maya trade routes extended as far as New Mexico.

Yet many dimensions of the Maya way of life are dimly understood, and experts can only speculate on what the Maya's daily routine was like. By the time the first Europeans came to the region in the early 1500s, some Maya still lived in a few of the ancient cities. Their intricate civilization had largely dissolved by this time and the conquering Spanish tried to destroy much of what remained. Contrary to popular belief, however, the Maya culture is still very much alive, particularly in rural areas of Belize, Guatemala, and the Mexican state of Chiapas. In Belize's southern Toledo District, Kekchí-speaking Maya still tell folktales that originated during the days of the Maya empire and perform ritual dances held sacred by their ancestors. In the Cayo District, near Caracol, Mopán- and Yucatec-speaking Maya have revived the ancient art of slate carving, gathering stones from riverbeds their ancestors mined centuries ago. Each subgroup also retains great knowledge of plants, farming, astronomy, and spirituality.

The European Presence

European knowledge of Belize began in 1502, when Christopher Columbus sailed along Central America's coast and named the Bay of Honduras, which begins at the southern end of Belize's barrier reef. Other Spanish navigators followed throughout the 16th century, but few were willing to make the tricky crossing of Belize's reef, and none saw fit to establish a permanent outpost. Other than a successful, plunderous raid on the Maya trading city of Santa Rita (now Corozal) in 1513, the initial Spanish presence was limited to a few minor explorations and some missionary work. Catholic churches were established at Lamanai and Tipú in the early 1500s, but the Spanish clerics were ejected around 1640.

Probably the first permanent settlement of foreigners in Belize began in the early 1600s when English-speaking Puritan traders, then based on the swampy Mosquito Coast of eastern Nicaragua, established outposts on strategic islands, including Tobacco Caye. The colonists ignored the

How Did Belize Get Its Name?

The camp set up by a Scottish sea captain, Peter Wallace, eventually became Belize City. Some say that the name "Belize" is derived from the Spanish pronunciation of "Wallace," which could sound something like the word. Others speculate that Belize comes from the Mayan words belix, *meaning "muddy water," or* belikin, *translated as "land that faces the sea." Perhaps it derives from the French* balise, *a reference to the beacons used to guide pirates back to port at night. Yet another theory is that the name comes from the old British verb* obelize, *which means to mark a map with an obelus, a sign that suggests a place is corrupt and undesirable. During its many years as a pirate haven, English mapmakers routinely obelized the camp founded by Peter Wallace.*

fact that Vicente Yanez Pinzon and Juan Díaz de Solis, among other explorers, had already claimed the area for Spain. Despite their own lack of interest in starting a Belizean colony, Spanish forces routed the Puritans from their trading posts in 1641.

Seemingly unknown to the Spaniards, a separate group of shipwrecked British sailors had started building their own tiny community on the coast some three years earlier. They were a motley crew, including many buccaneers who had learned of Belize through contact with the Puritan merchants. Gradually, over the next 150 years, more and more English settlers would move into the same area. They were later joined by a contingent of disbanded English sailors and soldiers who fought for the successful British liberation of Jamaica from Spain in 1655. Some of these early settlers were engaged in hardwood logging, others in piracy, and a precious few in farming. All would be forced to defend their primitive villages from sporadic attacks by the Maya and the Spanish.

With few inhabitants, disease-infested backwaters, and a dangerous offshore reef, Belize was an ideal hideout for the raiders of the Caribbean. By the late 1600s, the most infamous Scottish, French, and English pirates had established permanent bases in Belize, from which they

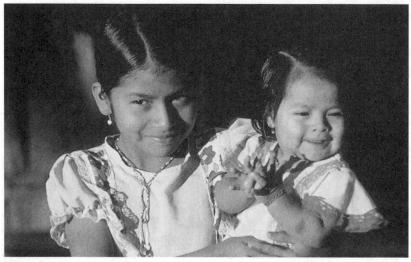

Maya girl with baby sister in San José Village

© Tony Rath

mercilessly attacked Spanish galleons carrying gold, silver, dyes, hard-woods, and other raw materials back to Europe.

Belize's first documented lumbering was undertaken by buccaneer Bart Sharp and his mates about 1660. The cutters were eager to remove logwood (a source of textile dyes) and mahogany (an excellent hardwood used to make fine furniture). Sharp and his cohorts called themselves "Baymen," after the Bay of Honduras to the south. Unable to eject the Baymen by force, Spain finally signed treaties with Britain, in 1763 and 1786, which secured government cooperation in the suppression of piracy and protection of lumber interests. The British would be allowed to remain as long as they kept to certain areas and left the treasure-laden galleons alone.

As they gradually turned more of their attention toward timber cutting, the white settlers began importing hundreds of African slaves from Jamaica and other British-controlled islands of the Caribbean. They relied on the strength of their charges to accomplish the difficult task of cutting huge logs and hauling them to ships for export. By the 1700s, lumber was a booming industry and the English were going far into the Belizean interior to selectively cut the largest trees they could find.

Slowly but surely, British influence in Belize grew during the early 1800s. When Spain dismantled its New World empire and granted independence to Mexico and Guatemala in 1821, Britain's Foreign Office loudly rejected those countries' immediate claims to Belize; for separate

Why Belizeans Speak English

For almost 200 years, the legal status of the region now known as Belize remained vague. At one point, English authorities even ceded control over the area to Spain, with the understanding that its woodcutting concessions could remain. Other agreements barred the Baymen from erecting fortifications, governing themselves, and establishing plantations. The stouthearted settlers, true to the lawless spirit of their forebears, generally ignored such treaties and set up their own laws. Eventually, with great reluctance, London sent official representatives to the Bay Settlement during the late 1780s.

This action infuriated the Spanish, who felt Britain was overstepping the bounds of its treaties. The showdown came in a 1798 skirmish off St. George's Caye, near Belize City, where a few hundred angry settlers and a British schooner drove off a powerful, battle-hardened wing of the Spanish Armada. September 10 is still celebrated as Belize's "National Day," with a separate holiday on September 21 to mark independence from England in 1981.

reasons, each considered the "province" of Belize to be part of its own rightful inheritance from Spain.

By 1826, the Baymen woodcutters had extended their timber harvesting to the Sarstoon River, the present southern boundary of Belize, and had become so prosperous that England could not help but take notice. At the same time, Guatemala remained adamant in its determination to annex the region and periodically waged war against the "trespassing" settlers. In 1859, fearing continued political instability would be bad for its now-sizable business in the region, Britain finally signed a treaty with Guatemala in which the latter confirmed the present-day boundaries of Belize in return for British financing for construction of a road from Guatemala's capital to Belize City. In 1991, Guatemala's newly elected president, Jorge Serrano, officially recognized Belize's independence in hopes of settling the long-running dispute, but there is still tension between the two countries.

Similarly, Mexico's claim to Belize was not easily settled. Throughout the 19th century, the Mexican government insisted that the northern half—and perhaps all—of Belize was an extension of its Yucatán holdings. Tensions escalated during the Caste War of 1847 to 1858, when thousands of Maya and mestizo (mixed-race) slaves in the Yucatán revolted against their masters and fled across the border in search of British protection. Mexican authorities decided not to pursue the renegades; thus, several thousand refugees became the nucleus for settlement in the northern districts of Belize, which remain largely Spanish-speaking. Mexico finally renounced any claim to Belize in an 1897 treaty with England.

The Colonial Period

In 1840, after establishing through various abolition-of-slavery acts that the Central American settlers were indeed its subjects, Great Britain declared Belize to be "the colony of British Honduras." But the declaration was in name only, and administration of the colony did not begin until 1862. It would be another nine years before British Honduras received formal recognition as a Crown colony, and it was not until the 1880s that the territory was administered separately from Jamaica.

With its formal establishment as a colony finally accomplished, development of Belize became more organized. Supervision was badly overdue, since a lack of diversification in industry and overdependence on imported goods had sent Belize into decline during the Victorian era. The concentration of land ownership made it difficult for entrepreneurs to start projects that might wean the colony from its motherland. By the late 19th century, a single London-based company (Belize Estate & Produce) owned more than a million acres of land, or one-fifth of the entire territory.

During this period, Belize went through a series of profound cultural changes, yielding a multiethnic society that remains remarkably cohesive. Many of the original English and Scottish settlers intermarried with freed slaves to form the Creole majority that still dominates the population. In the north, Mexican citizens crossed the border and began cultivating small farms. Many of their descendants now grow sugarcane, the country's most lucrative crop. To the south, Kekchí and Mopán Maya sought refuge from forced-labor plantations in Guatemala, and a small contingent of weary Confederate Civil War veterans arrived from the United States to found a plantation colony they called Toledo. From the Bay Islands off Honduras came a large number of Garifuna people. These

Richard Mahler

The face of this Benque Viejo boy reveals his Maya/Spanish heritage.

blacks of mixed African and Carib-Indian ancestry had been forcibly expelled from the West Indies in 1797.

Others immigrating to Belize in smaller numbers during the 1800s included Chinese sugarcane workers and Lebanese shopkeepers. Ethnic Sepoys were conscripted to the colony from India after an 1857 rebellion, and many West Indian plantation workers were recruited to do fieldwork by the end of the century. A handful of expatriate Europeans and North Americans also decided to make Belize their home.

Early attempts to diversify the economy met with mixed success. The lack of roads, high transportation costs, and a limited pool of skilled labor stymied developers, and many new crops fell victim to exotic diseases and poor soil conditions. Periodic hurricanes devastated the country, uprooting trees and flattening houses. Then, as today, Belizeans were unable to produce enough food to feed themselves and had to rely heavily on expensive imports.

Early Twentieth Century

By 1900, British Honduras had grown to have a population of 37,000. Yet the economy was moribund, wages were low, and discontent was endemic. A destructive 1931 hurricane compounded the colony's problems. By the late 1930s, Belize's deteriorating economic conditions prompted some residents to begin calling for independence. (Sensing this unrest, Guatemala renewed its claims to sovereignty and to payment from Britain for the promised road to Guatemala City that had never been built. Over the next

11

20 years, Guatemala became more adamant in its demands, and several forays across the frontier had to be repelled by the British.)

After World War II, many Belizeans returned to a land where living conditions were miserable, work opportunities were limited, and political power was concentrated in the hands of a wealthy and mostly white elite. Fearful colonial administrators responded to the growing unrest by passing restrictive laws and banning public marches. But in 1950, after a sharp devaluation of the local currency, Belizeans decided they'd had enough. The independence movement, led by George Price—an American-educated, cautiously liberal Creole divinity student—rapidly increased in size and influence. In 1954 voting rights were extended to all adults, and in 1955 a form of ministerial government was introduced. By 1961, London had agreed to begin the process of setting Belize free.

Meanwhile, the economy of the colony began to diversify. German-descended Mennonites began homesteading in the late 1950s and greatly improved the domestic food supply. The first tourists began arriving about the same time, most of them divers and fishermen attracted by the offshore marine life. The economic diversification was matched by political change, part of an international move toward self-governance.

Full internal, elected self-government was instituted in 1964, modeled after the Westminster parliamentary system. Britain remained in charge of foreign relations, defense, and internal security. A bicameral assembly (House and Senate) was established, and its members were popularly elected. (After George Price's People's United Party, the largest political party is the more conservative United Democratic Party, in office from 1985 to 1989, and again from 1993 to 1998.)

In 1973 the colony's name was officially changed from British Honduras to Belize and on September 21, 1981, Belizean independence was formally declared. With British troops on full alert and the border sealed, the Guatemalan invasion that some had seriously feared never took place, and in 1992 Guatemala finally acknowledged Belize's sovereignty. The region was judged secure enough for Britain to withdraw nearly all of its armed forces from Belize during 1994, although the former colony is still a protectorate and a member of the British Commonwealth.

While Belize has successfully thwarted foreign claimants since 1798, it is quietly experiencing a subtle transformation into a Spanish-speaking country. Large numbers of Guatemalans, Salvadorans, and Hondurans have crossed its borders since independence, many of them illegally. In fact, during the early 1990s mestizos (persons of mixed Spanish and indigenous descent) reportedly replaced Creoles as Belize's largest single ethnic group. The vast majority of these newcomers are unskilled peasant farmers, attracted by an abundance of available land and relatively high wages, as well as a tradition of peace and political stability. The latter is a

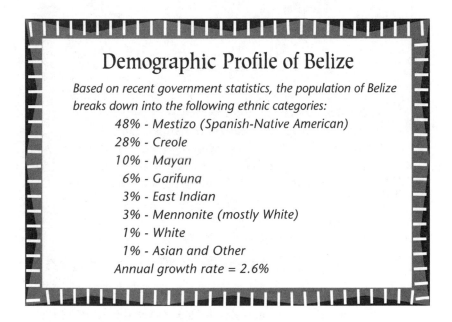

Demographic Profile of Belize

Based on recent government statistics, the population of Belize breaks down into the following ethnic categories:

48% - Mestizo (Spanish-Native American)
28% - Creole
10% - Mayan
6% - Garifuna
3% - East Indian
3% - Mennonite (mostly White)
1% - White
1% - Asian and Other
Annual growth rate = 2.6%

truly significant factor for people who have known only military dictatorships, political warfare, and genocidal terrorism.

Present and Future

Since 1994, when almost all British troops left, Belize has been on its own. Except for a token British force and a handful of U.S. Peace Corps volunteers, there's very little "official" foreign presence, and as a result politics has evolved in a distinctively partisan Belizean-style. With the colonials gone and the border dispute with Guatemala settled, politicians have turned their attention inward, and there is more than enough to occupy their attention.

Thousands of immigrants have streamed into Belize in recent years, many of them Spanish-speaking peasants who harvest plantation crops or tend to their own homesteads. For the first time, Belize is reevaluating its centuries-old practice of welcoming hardworking newcomers with open arms and free land. Meanwhile, the nation's fragile economy limps along, crippled by high taxes and import duties as well as the vagaries of international commodity prices. The conservative United Democratic Party, in office from 1993 to 1998, made little headway in curbing unemployment and reducing Belize's enormous national debt. The government changed again in August 1998, when the P.U.P. was returned to power in a national election. Prime Minister Said Musa immediately

Belizeans Abroad

Tens of thousands of Belizeans living in the United States and Canada remit millions of dollars to family members every year. Today, one-third as many Belizean citizens live outside the country as inside, with the largest concentrations in Los Angeles, New York, and Chicago, as well as Toronto and Vancouver. Because the average in-country Belizean earns less than $500 a month, the money that relatives send home keeps the nation afloat economically, providing the extra income needed to buy conveniences like refrigerators and TV sets.

launched a privatization campaign designed to return some major bureaucracies to the private sector. This initiative by Musa, an attorney of Palestinian-Belizean descent with many years of experience in dealing with the government, was welcomed by Belize's business community.

As this book went to press in the spring of 1999, the new prime minister was largely following the moderately liberal policies of the People's United Party. Musa and his party strongly attacked the unpopular 15 percent Value Added Tax imposed by the previous administration, which was replaced with a smaller sales and lower property and personal income taxes. In a belt-tightening measure, the government shut down the 61-year-old national broadcast service, Radio Belize, while allocating a bigger share of the budget for promotion of tourism. A more difficult issue facing Prime Minister Musa is violent crime, which rose sharply in 1998 with a series of high-profile robberies, car-jackings, kidnappings, and shootings, including the murders of a U.S. tourist near Placencia and a British aid worker near Dangriga. Observers blame such incidents largely on an influx of legal and illegal aliens, and the presistence of drug abuse and trafficking. Thankfully, most visitors to Belize are untouched by such incidents and the actual rate of crime is far lower than that of the country's neighbors.

The future of Belize may well depend on how its citizens and their leaders respond to the country's rapidly changing demographics—it is gradually becoming poorer and more mestizo—and to the uncertainties inherent in an economy that remains largely dependent on fluctuating agricultural markets and the fickle tourist industry. The critical political decisions made during the next several years will likely determine the path Belize will follow for decades to come.

ECONOMY

Compared to other Central American countries, Belize enjoys relative prosperity, adequate health services, improving sanitation, a good public school system, and little of the income disparity that divides its neighbors into feuding factions of rich and poor. Still, Belize is heavily dependent on foreign aid—both governmental and private—for its survival. Out of necessity, most oil, food, manufactured goods, and consumer products are imported, and often paid for through loans and grants provided by aid programs from the United States, Great Britain, and other European Economic Community members. As a result, about one-third of the national budget goes to servicing the country's huge national debt.

While the country's economic base is broadening, progress has been painfully slow. In candid moments, government officials admit that illicit transport and trafficking in marijuana, cocaine, and heroin has been a major contributor to the bottom line. Major narcotic busts occur regularly in Belize but seem to have little impact on the drug business.

Although timber is still an important Belizean export (most of it pine and cedar now, not hardwoods like mahogany), the major agricultural crops are sugarcane and citrus, cultivated in the north and south, respectively. Bananas and fish products (mainly shrimp, conch, and lobster) are also important exports, along with honey, maize, pineapples, beans, mangos, papayas, cocoa, and rice. Poultry and cattle are raised domestically, and light manufacturing (mostly clothing and furniture) now accounts for about 15 percent of the gross domestic product.

Observers consider the Belizean economy "fragile," since the country imports much more than it exports and remains vulnerable both to fluctuations in the price of plantation products and to trade preferences imposed by other countries. In an attempt to improve the situation, during the early 1990s Belize added powerful new incentives for investors, including duty-free export zones near the Guatemalan and Mexican borders. The possibility of an offshore banking industry similar to that of the Cayman Islands is also under discussion.

Tourism competes with agriculture as the biggest contributor to Belize's bottom line, thanks to steady interest among foreign visitors. The tourist business is fickle, however, and has been subject to boom and bust cycles here during the 1990s. In 1998, for example, country-wide hotel occupancy was in the 35 percent range: poor by industry standards. Nevertheless, the government of Belize and many in the hospitality business are openly and firmly committed to making natural history tourism a top priority for their country's future.

15

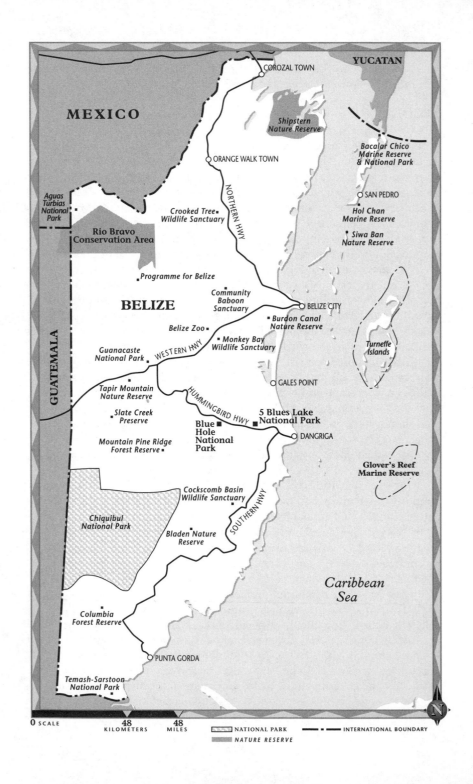

CONSERVATION AND RESPONSIBLE TOURISM

2

At one time or another, most of us entertain a tropical island fantasy. We dream about getting away from it all on an idyllic vacation in a remote, sunny paradise. We picture ourselves sprawled on a sandy beach under the shady fronds of a swaying coconut palm, sipping a rum punch, and staring hypnotically at a shimmering horizon. Or perhaps we see ourselves gliding through warm, turquoise water, sharing a dazzling marine environment with Technicolor coral, jaunty sea horses, and eye-catching parrot fish.

Maybe you've been lucky enough to take such a trip—only to return with the unsettled feeling that something vital was missing. Like eating a rich dessert full of empty calories, the experience was pleasing but not quite satisfying. Next time, I recommend an adventure in what we call "natural history tourism," which is exactly the sort of unusual vacation Belize has to offer. In the pages that follow, I'll take you to our favorite destinations in this plucky little country.

In many ways, Belize is far ahead of other less-developed nations in shaping tourism as an economic strategy that can preserve, rather than destroy, its priceless natural and cultural resources. Belize has won praise from international conservationists for the so-called sustainable development strategies it has implemented to protect its impressive treasures of nature and artifacts of Maya history, while at the same time making sure that its people benefit from the public lands set aside for environmental and other purposes. It has largely succeeded in this campaign despite constant monetary problems and growing pressure from agricultural and industrial interests. Many of Belize's government officials have looked around them to see the danger of following another path.

Large portions of neighboring Guatemala, Mexico, and Honduras are now completely deforested, with plantations, timber interests, and slash-and-burn subsistence farms quickly replacing the remaining tropical forests. In contrast, an estimated 65 percent of Belize's land area is still covered with forest, only some of which has been thinly and selectively logged in the past (compared, for example, to the barely 2 percent of intact forest remaining in nearby El Salvador, a bit smaller than Belize but with more than 30 times its population). More importantly, an impressively large proportion—about one-third—of Belize is under some form of officially protected designation.

PROTECTING NATURE'S TREASURES

Between 1990 and 1992, some 535,235 acres were put under permanent protection by Belize, including more than 200,000 acres of tropical forest in the Chiquibul region; 6,000 acres of mangrove wetlands in the Burdon Canal zone; and 97,000 acres of critical watershed in the Bladen Nature Reserve. During that same period, the Cockscomb Basin Wildlife Sanctuary (the world's only jaguar refuge) was expanded from 3,600 to 102,000 acres. Since then, Belize has added more parks and reserves, including designation of the entire 75-square-mile Glover's Reef atoll as a marine reserve and of the 23-square-mile Bacalar Chico area as a combination marine reserve and national park.

Belize has shown remarkable leadership in protecting tropical forests and marine resources, and many Belizeans deserve credit for these positive actions. Now the government is shifting its attention from establishment of parks and protected areas to long-term, on-the-ground area management. In order to accomplish this, the country's natural resources need to pay for themselves.

WHAT IS ECOTOURISM?

Nature-based tourism—often referred to as "ecotourism"—is strongly and officially encouraged in Belize. Politicians and bureaucrats are hopeful that Belize can learn from the mistakes of others, weighing the advantages of badly needed foreign income against the irreversible damage that unbounded traditional tourism and agriculture can inflict. But just as "it takes a village" to raise a child, it takes an entire country to carefully preserve and wisely manage natural resources. Hotels, tour operators, trade organizations, educators, individuals, and entrepreneurs throughout Belize have responded to the call for enlightened action.

"We in the private sector have a tremendous opportunity to do something for conservation in conjunction with government," Jim Bevis, past president of the Belize EcoTourism Association (BETA), told me in an interview. "I see private enterprise as the facilitator to get things done." (Later in this book you will read about some specific, laudable environmental-protection projects undertaken by Bevis and other members of the business community, including the establishment of a private 4,000-acre nature preserve.)

BETA was formed in 1993 by a few members of the Belize Tourism Industry Association as a conservation-oriented branch of that trade group. BETA's mission is to promote environmentally responsible tourism, to be sensitive to the impacts of tourism, to promote education for locals and visitors, and to promote such concerns as pollution prevention. While Jim Bevis was president of BETA, many tourism businesses teamed with private citizens, schools, private industry, and community groups to carry out a successful nationwide "Adopt a Roadway" anti-litter campaign, dubbed "Beta No Litta." Visitors may notice green BETA signs bearing the names of sponsors of this program posted along major roadways.

SAVING TROPICAL HABITATS

Environmentalists are well aware of what can—and often does—occur when travel in the tropics is promoted with little regard for natural resources: protective mangrove trees are stripped by builders from sandy

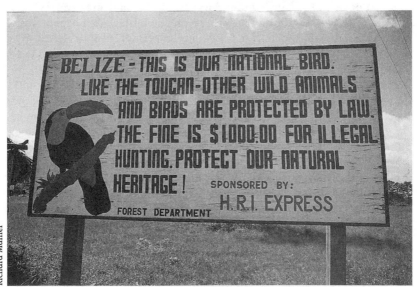

Conservation education is a popular theme on Belize billboards.

19

shorelines; fragile coral reefs are damaged by inquisitive but uninformed divers and snorkelers; commercial marine species, such as conch and lobster, are depleted to meet restaurant demands; indiscriminate poaching may decimate wildlife populations; and oblivious amateur cavers may degrade speleothems formed over thousands of years. Despite its own best efforts, Belize has not escaped this long list of injuries. Yet many individuals, in government, academia, and private industry, are making a determined effort to provide effective conservation education to each and every visitor.

Perhaps the part of the country facing the most intense development pressure is the marine environment, particularly the coral reef formations immediately surrounding the most-visited cayes, Ambergris and Caulker. Coral reefs are the marine equivalents of tropical rainforests.

"In most coral species, each individual polyp lays down a skeletal container of calcium carbonate that surrounds and protects its soft body," biologist Edward O. Wilson wrote in *The Diversity of Life*. "Coral colonies grow by the budding of individual polyps, with the skeletal cups being added one on another in a set geometric pattern particular to each species. The result is a lovely, bewildering array of skeletal forms that mass together to make the whole reef—a tangled field of horn corals, brain corals, staghorn corals, organ pipes, sea fans, and sea whips." Some formations are thousands of years old.

Belize's barrier reef suffers injury every time a boat anchor is randomly cast and hauled in or a diver bumps against a piece of living coral. When these centuries-old marine architects are touched, they often begin to turn black and die. Unfortunately, many collectors cannot seem to resist the urge to (illegally) collect sea fans, black coral, and even aquarium-bound fish. Commercial fishing throws the food chain out of balance when desired species are removed en masse. Important breeding and feeding grounds for lobster, conch, turtles, grouper, and waterfowl are destroyed by unrestricted fishing or when mangrove and sea grass beds are removed (often illegally) by developers. Over the long run, no one knows what the cumulative effect of all these changes will be.

PRIVATE SECTOR PARTICIPATION

A continuing trend in Belize, fortunately, is the active involvement of private citizens and tourism entrepreneurs in preserving and protecting their environment. On Caye Caulker, for example, tourist guide Lionel "Chocolate" Heredia has taught visitors and fellow boat operators how to proceed with caution and respect around Caribbean manatees, a shy and endangered species that is holding its own in Belize. Chocolate has taken the initiative of lobbying the government for designation of official manatee reserves and donates a percentage of his manatee-derived income to a

Steele Wotkyns

One of the greatest threats to Belize's remaining forests is the clearing and burning of land for citrus and sugarcane plantations.

nonprofit foundation that advocates on their behalf. He is one of many Belizeans who is willing to do something to keep his country the amazing natural wonderland that it is.

Meanwhile, in Belize's interior, habitat destruction in the form of deforestation and selective woodcutting continues to cause serious damage to pristine ecosystems. According to the government, hundreds of refugees and migrant workers are entering Belize each year from other Central American countries, mostly Guatemala and El Salvador. They are drawn by Belize's relaxed attitude toward homesteading, and they bring with them a strong tradition of slash-and-burn agriculture. Unfortunately, this milpa approach quickly drains nutrients from the shallow soil, and new trees must be cleared every few years to secure fresh farmland. Many refugees also hunt wild game in order to supplement their meager diets.

Equally significant, owners of large citrus, banana, pineapple, and sugarcane plantations are lobbying government ministries to change the status of several forest reserves to allow more large-scale agriculture. The citrus industry in particular has charged ahead in recent years, clearing vast tracts of pristine tropical forests. Meanwhile, poorly regulated logging and oil-drilling concessions have created significant devastation of the Belize environment in recent years.

ECONOMIC TRADE-OFFS

Belizeans pay the price for this kind of development in the fouling of their potable water by acidic, pesticide-laden runoff from citrus fields. The sugarcane industry has dumped nutrient-rich effluent into rivers and wetlands that had become important wildlife habitats and popular tourist attractions. The removal of natural vegetation is also a factor in local and regional climate changes, upsetting the cycles of rain and drought. In many areas, large-scale farmers are rapidly clearing forests to plant grain and other crops. Cattle ranchers are also eager to increase their territory.

A series of droughts in the 1990s has resulted in a series of devastating fires in the region, including those in Belize's Mountain Pine Ridge. Spring 1998 forest fires—many intentionally set by farmers to clear forests and fields—created massive clouds of smoke that obscured visibility as far north as Chicago. Health alerts were declared in many communities due to the pollution, which followed one of the longest regional droughts in memory. These dry spells are sometimes followed by unusually heavy rains, as occurred in Guatemala and the Mexican state of Chiapas in the summer of 1998.

Experts aren't sure of the exact cause of these cycles of extreme weather, although there's widespread agreement that destruction of the area's forest cover is a contributing factor. When the forest is cleared, local temperatures rise and less moisture is given off by vegetation, disrupting a centuries-old ecosystem.

In a nation that still cannot feed itself it is very tempting to give in to pressures for more agricultural exploitation. In many instances, however, the government of Belize, along with enlightened individuals and members of various tourism organizations, is operating under the premise that there are more gains to be realized through nature-based tourism than through nonsustainable agricultural and industrial development. Visitors won't pay to see cultivated orchards and fields or poorly planned housing projects, but they will keep coming back to explore tropical forests, jungle rivers, and coral reefs.

Yet, with the opportunities of tourism come fresh challenges. Such growth forces decisions about establishment of a better infrastructure of roads, communications, hotels, police protection, and food distribution. Many tour guides have expressed specific concern about the need for better tourist facilities (or at least *some* facilities) at the country's most frequently visited natural and archaeological destinations. Deterioration of cultural institutions and ancient Maya ruins is an ongoing problem. Meanwhile, promotion of tourism must be carried out in a way that benefits Belizeans and is not detrimental to the very sites that foreigners are being lured to visit.

*Immigrant homesteaders' huts are a common sight
along the Hummingbird Highway.*

CONSERVATION SOLUTIONS

As one of the world's most environmentally aware countries, Belize has already set a standard of behavior that speaks for itself in big and small ways. The Belize EcoTourism Association, for instance, has successfully implemented several projects that appear to have increased environmental awareness. Later on in this book you'll read about the Community Baboon Sanctuary, the Cockscomb Basin Wildlife Sanctuary, the Crooked Tree Wildlife Sanctuary, the Shipstern Nature Reserve, and the Río Bravo Conservation Area. These are just five of the many innovative examples of how the demands of conservation can be successfully balanced with the fundamental economic needs of local people.

An innovative project in the southern part of the country demonstrates such sensitivity in action. In the largely undeveloped Toledo District, Maya villagers have opened thatch-roof guest houses for travelers. Others have opened their simple homes to visitors who want a firsthand look at a subsistence farming culture that has persisted for centuries. You can read more about this in Chapter 9, Southern Belize.

Similar community-level approaches are proving to be key models for long-term protection of Belize's forests. The Friends of Five Blues, for example, was formed to manage the spectacular Five Blues Lake National

23

Ecofriendly Exports

Herbal remedies. Natural chewing gum. Coconut soap. Cashew candy. Palm nut jewelry. Dried jungle fruits. These are some of the new Belizean products now being exported by environmentally aware businesses in an effort to make the country's tropical forests pay their way (an alternative to cutting them down).

Besides earning a profit and preserving natural habitat, a top priority of Rainforest Rescue Ltd. is "making jobs for local, indigenous people," company spokesman Roger Taylor told Profiles *magazine in a 1996 interview. Rainforest Rescue pays those who live in or near the forest to gather materials in a way that doesn't unduly harm the ecosystem, thus providing an alternative to timber cutting, hunting, and slash-and-burn agriculture. Native nuts, berries, and fruits, for example, are collected, washed, and dried, then packed for sale as a "jungle trail mix." Similarly, the hard nut of the cohune palm is collected and carved to make buttons and earrings. Six percent of all revenue is donated to the*

Park, with its 200-foot-deep inland lake surrounded by some 4,200 acres of lush, broadleaf tropical forest, interwoven with an otherworldly labyrinth of limestone caves. The Friends of Five Blues' complementary goal is to ensure that the local community directs natural history tourism and that the people living nearby realize financial rewards from tourism-related enterprises. (See details in Chapter 7, Western Belize.)

WHAT THE FUTURE HOLDS

Belize has an admirable record of achievement in conservation, but there's no guarantee that environmental preservation will remain a top priority. Battles to protect the country's natural resources are constantly being waged.

For example, a coalition of Belizean environmental groups and animal rights activists have opposed development of a swim-with-the-dolphins theme park in the Cangrejo Caye area near San Pedro. The

Belize Audubon Society, which manages many of the country's national parks.

Rainforest Rescue is one of a growing number of ecofriendly exporters in Belize. Programme for Belize is involved in the sustainable harvesting of chicle to make chewing gum. The nonprofit PFB has been helping residents of four villages near its 229,000-acre forest conservation and management area learn how to tap chicle resin from sapodilla trees without harming them. The chicle is then sold to local entrepreneurs who package it and sell it as "100-percent natural" chewing gum.

"We're training them," Audrey Wallace, senior project coordinator of Programme for Belize (PFB) told Profiles, *"but we're not going to hold their hands for ten years."*

Thanks to investment laws that encourage the influx of foreign capital, Belize is able to successfully marry sustainable development with green exports, while keeping much of its undeveloped land under official protection.

enterprise was reportedly close to being launched in 1999 by a Mexican company, which developed a larger park in Cancún.

In June 1998, on the other hand, the governments of Belize, Guatemala, Mexico, and Honduras signed an agreement to expand protection of the 600-mile-long Caribbean barrier reef shared by all four countries. Besides environmental safeguards, the accord calls for judicious tourism development and restoration of natural fisheries in the area.

HOW YOU CAN HELP

Through the simple act of visiting Belize, you are helping the conservation initiatives described in this book. That's partly because a percentage of the exit tax you pay upon leaving the country goes directly into an environmental protection trust, but also because your visit is an implicit endorsement of Belize's decision to promote nature-oriented tourism.

If you would like to make a more direct contribution to conservation in Belize, I can recommend no better way than to make a financial contribution to one (or more) of the nonprofit organizations in Belize that is battling on the front lines of environmental protection. You can be assured that your money will be put to excellent use by any of the following organizations.

Belize Audubon Society, 12 N. Fort St., Belize City; 2-34988, base@btl.net, www.belizeaudubon.org. Manages national parks and nature reserves throughout Belize; conducts public education campaign designed to heighten environmental awareness; sponsors surveys of birds and other wildlife.

Belize Tropical Forest Studies/Slate Creek Reserve, Box 208, Belmopan; 92-3310, tfs@bcsl.com.bz. Supports scientific research in tropical forests of Belize; manages large tract of land along Slate Creek watershed; provides public education and programs that support sustainable development.

Belize Zoo, Box 1787, Belize City; 8-13004, www.belizenet.com/belizezoo. Operates the country's only zoo; internationally known for its humanitarian conditions and strong emphasis on public education.

International Tropical Studies Foundation, c/o Papiliorama, Case Postal 31, CH 2074 Marin/Neuchâtel, Switzerland; (032) 753-4350, itcf@papiliorama.ch, www.papiliorama.ch. Manages Shipstern Nature Reserve in northeast Belize, one of the largest and most ecologically diverse private reserves in the country; supports public education and sustainable development programs; sponsors scientific research.

Ix Chel Tropical Research Foundation, Ix Chel Farm, San Ignacio; 9-23870. Supports ongoing research into medicinal uses of native plants found in Belize; gathers and preserves knowledge of traditional healers throughout the country; sponsors public education programs relating to conservation and healing use of plants.

Programme for Belize, 2 S. Park St., Belize City; 2-71248, pfbel@btl.net. Manages one of the largest intact stands of tropical forest in Belize; operates Chan Chich eco-lodge; conducts ongoing research into sustainable development of Belize's natural resources.

Swallow Caye Reserve Project, Box 986, Belize City. Working to establish a marine reserve to protect manatees at Swallow Caye.

Toledo Institute for Development and Environment, Box 150, Punta Gorda; pgwil@btl.net. Working to establish Port Honduras Marine Reserve and to write a management plan for Paynes Creek National Park.

HOW TO TRAVEL RESPONSIBLY

Even if you make no direct contact with any environmental groups, it is important to know that simply visiting the destinations described in this book makes you a part of ongoing efforts to save a precious part of our planet. By financially supporting and/or volunteering with the groups or communities of your choice, you empower them to keep working to protect the natural heritage of Belize (and the world).

If you use the services of a so-called "ecotourism" hotel, guide service, or travel operator, we urge you to take a careful look at their practices. Do they hire local guides and book guests into locally owned hotels? Are they actively involved in training, conservation, or supporting local communities or field research in Belize? Are they a member of the Belize EcoTourism Association and do they subscribe to BETA's code of ethics? Do they display the toucan emblem of Belize's environmentally responsible tourism operators? I suggest you ask such questions before booking your trip.

In the meantime, while you are in Belize, I hope you'll keep in mind the following guidelines to responsible travel, which are published by BETA.

Steele Wotkyns

Mussel Creek is one of the country's most pristine (and least protected) wetland ecosystems.

The upper Macal River is one of the most popular whitewater streams in Belize.

Richard Mahler

1. **Stay on the Trail**: Don't trample delicate vegetation.

2. **Plants**: Do not remove or disturb them.

3. **Marine**: Do not stand on, touch, or kick sand on coral reef systems. Sand raised by fins can suffocate coral or lower its disease resistance. Enjoy the view without using your hands.

4. **Wildlife**: Maintain a minimum distance of 30 feet from wildlife; stay on the periphery of animal assemblages; never surround an animal or group of animals or come between parents and their young; never follow or harass birds or animals for the sake of a photograph; keep decibel levels low; listen to the sound of the jungle; be unobtrusive when viewing wildlife.

5. **Sustainability**: Local guides, landowners, and conservation representatives should tell you their plans to ensure the sustainable use of wildlife habitats as you participate together in implementing these plans.

6. **Waste Disposal**: All trash must be contained and carried back to a designated landfill; no littering is tolerated.

Reef Conservation

Coral reefs throughout the world are facing enormous threats from a variety of sources. Here are a few of the nonprofit groups that are working to preserve them. If you want to become involved, each of them could use your help.

CORAL (Coral Reef Alliance), (510) 848-0110, www.coral.org
Coral Forest, (415) 788-REEF, www.blacktop.com/coralforest
Cousteau Society, (757) 523-9335, www.cousteau.org
Ocean Futures, (714) 456-0790, www.oceanfutures.org
Project AWARE Foundation, (714) 540-0251,
  www.projectaware.org
ReefKeeper International, (305) 358-4600, reefkeeper.org

7. **Wilderness**: Trips to wilderness areas must be led by experienced, well-trained, responsible naturalists and guides.

8. **Souvenirs**: Do not buy any sea turtle products, or any other products from wild animals, even if they are incorporated in artwork.

Here is an item of my own that I would like to add to this roster:

9. **Participate**: Become a positive contributor to Belize's experiment in developing a new, responsible tourism ethic. You help such a country's conservation projects succeed by joining, by financing, by visiting, or by volunteering to participate in them. Your presence is itself a vote of confidence in the difficult decisions government and business leaders must make.

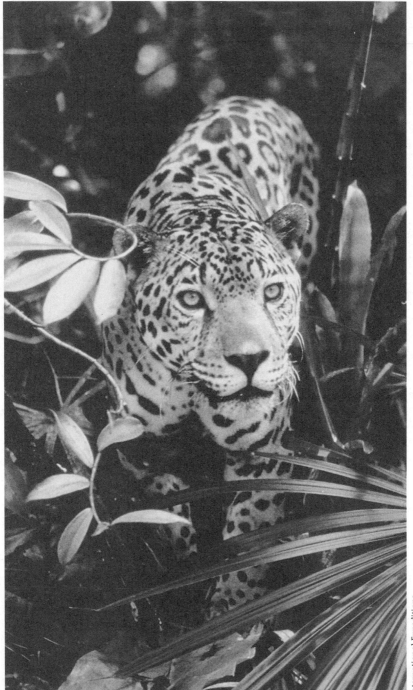

Jaguars inhabit Belize's many forests.

FLORA AND FAUNA OF BELIZE

3

Thanks in part to its diverse topography, soil characteristics, and weather patterns, Belize is blessed with several of the world's richest habitats. No fewer than 4,000 different species of native flowering plants are found within its borders, along with about 700 species of trees and several hundred species of other plants.

Scientists are only now beginning to perform an exhaustive inventory of Belize's plants. The task is daunting: More than 60 percent of the country is under some kind of forest cover, and almost half of Belize's primary forest is still standing. (Happily, a major part of this forest enjoys some degree of government protection.)

In the animal kingdom, the numbers are even more staggering. Literally thousands of varieties of insects are native to the five major ecosystems of Belize, along with hundreds of types of mammals, reptiles, amphibians, and fish. Some of the rare or endangered species found here in relatively abundant numbers are the tapir, howler monkey, anteater, ocellated turkey, king vulture, Morelet's crocodile, sea turtle, manatee, and jaguar, the hemisphere's largest cat. *Checklist of the Birds of Belize*, a pamphlet published by the Carnegie Museum of Natural History, lists over 540 species that have been sighted here, including more than 200 migratory birds from North America who winter in the tropics. In many parts of the inland forest, it is not unusual to see as many as 120 different birds over a period of as few as four days. And of the world's more than 90,000 butterfly species, a very large percentage are found here.

Part of this species diversity is a result of Belize's relatively small population and the pristine quality of its wilderness. Another reason is the variation in habitat zones. The basic ecological regions include: northern hardwood, southern hardwood, mountain pine ridge, coastal savanna and pine ridge, and mangroves and beaches. Within these categories, distinctions can be drawn based on rainfall amounts (varying widely from north to south), altitude (from sea level to nearly 4,000 feet), and soil types (from very poor to very fertile).

Scientists are still finding plants and animals in Belize which are completely new to science or previously unrecorded in Belize. One expedition into the Maya Mountains, for example, sighted a bird in the latter category dubbed the scaly-throated foliage gleaner. Several new species of amphibians and flowering plants have been found during the 1990s.

Rather than attempt an exhaustive discussion of Belizean ecosystems and their native inhabitants in this limited space, I will simply provide thumbnail sketches of some of Belize's most intriguing flora and fauna. Many of these have one or more colorful names used by locals. Among my favorites is an unusually prickly jungle palm tree known as the "give-and-take palm" or "poke no dah boy."

BIRDS

KEEL-BILLED TOUCAN

You'll see this brilliantly colored creature, designated the national bird of Belize, on signs and symbols throughout the country. (The toucan is probably better known in the United States as "the Fruit Loops® bird" because of its association with the ad campaign of a popular breakfast cereal.) The keel-billed toucan is fairly common in Belize and prefers to live in tall trees, particularly those that bear nuts or fruit. The bird tends to swoop low as it flies, owing to the weight of its canoe-shaped bill. The toucan's stubby wings seem undersized for such a big load. The red-tipped beak is apple green with a triangle of orange on top and a streak of powder blue below. The toucan has green around its eyes, yellow on its collar, red under its tail, and its legs and feet are bright blue.

Belize's most famous keel-billed toucan, "Rambo," lives at the Belize Zoo. He'll introduce you to the distinctive toucan call, a froggy *creek-creek* that is usually made during a flapping, soaring glide from one big tree to the next.

JABIRU STORK

The jabiru is the largest flying bird in the Western Hemisphere, standing up to 5 feet tall and with a wingspan reaching up to 10 feet or more. It is also one of the rarest birds in Central America. Besides its size, the jabiru can be identified by its massive, slightly turned-up black bill, its all-white wings and body feathers, and its bare black head, which has a wide, inflatable crimson band at the base of the neck. It feeds on fish, snails, frogs, and snakes.

In Belize, where the jabiru is fully protected, a population of about 30 storks nests during winter months along swamp edges and roadside pools, as well as in wet savannas and lowland pine ridges. Considered "rare" in Belize and "imperiled" in other parts of its range, Belize's jabirus return from Mexico around November to make their nests, usually at the tops of tall, secluded trees. Breeding continues until early April, when the birds begin migrating back to Mexico for the summer. Crooked Tree Wildlife Sanctuary is a favorite breeding ground of this enormous bird, and its nests are carefully protected. The jabiru is most commonly seen in Belize from December through March.

PARROTS

Seven species of parrots, one species of parakeet, and one species of macaw make Belize their home. Parrots have few enemies in the jungle except for larger predators, who tend to eliminate the weakest or most vulnerable birds. A far bigger threat is posed by humans, who continue to destroy the parrots' forest habitat, capture it for commercial purposes, or even kill it for food.

International Expeditions

Keel-billed toucan

The capture of young parrots usually does considerable damage to the environment, since nesting trees are often cut down in the hope that chicks will somehow survive the fall. The species captured in greatest numbers here is the yellow-headed parrot, prized in North America as a fluent and easily trained "talker." Other vocal members of the same family are the Aztec (or olive-throated) parakeet and mealy (or blue-crowned) parrot. The latter mates for life and almost always flies in a two-by-two formation with its partner. These species are quite social and like to live near others of their kind.

The common names of parrots are inspired by easily identifiable head markings ("lore" refers to the area between eyes and beak, "crown" is the top of the head, and "front" is the forehead, while "hood" and "head" are self-explanatory). The less gregarious parrots found in Belize are the brown-hooded, red-lored, yellow-lored, yellow-headed, white-fronted, and white-crowned. Only sharp-eyed birders are usually able to tell the latter two species apart.

Like many tropical animals (and people), parrots usually nap during the heat of the day and are most often seen during later afternoon and early morning feeding periods. The birds roost in groups overnight.

SCARLET MACAW

One of the rarest birds in Belize is the scarlet macaw, the third-largest of the world's 16 surviving macaw species. It is one of eight such species in danger of extinction throughout much of its range, which extends from subtropical Mexico south to Bolivia.

A macaw sighting is an unforgettable experience. Mature birds, locally referred to as parrots or guacamallos, are over 2 feet tall and adorned with brilliant plumage, particularly bright red wing feathers speckled with dabs of yellow, orange, and blue.

The greatest threat to this magnificent bird is the destruction of its forest habitat, nest-robbing for the wild bird trade, and killing for meat and feathers. The first systematic study of scarlet macaws in Belize was carried out by the Center for the Study of Tropical Birds. It concluded that the bird has a relatively confined range in the dense central forests of the country, extending from the Maya Mountains divide north to the Mountain Pine Ridge. A few individuals and small flocks have been seen in other areas from time to time. In recent years, however, no more than 30 birds have ever been seen at any given time or location.

"It is certain that the status of the scarlet macaw in Belize is precarious," concluded the final report of the Center. "Not only are there the persistent threats of habitat destruction . . . logging operations, plant collectors, etc., but the threat of wild birds being caught for the pet trade continues," despite the latter's illegality. There's at least some good news to counter this pessimistic outlook, however. In 1997 it was reported that scarlet macaws had begun to reinhabit the Cockscomb Basin, after disappearing for many years. The absence of hunting and logging in this wildlife sanctuary has apparently restored food trees favored by the birds and removed the threats once posed by humans.

BLUE-CROWNED MOTMOT
This beautiful and relatively large bird is sometimes called "Good Cook," because its deep-throated, *hoot-hoot* call (usually heard at dawn or dusk) sounds like those two words. It is also distinguished by its indigo head feathers and long tail. The latter acquires an oddly pointed shape through removal of central feathers by preening and wear. While the blue-crowned motmot is fairly common, its cousin, the keel-billed motmot, is one of the rarest birds in Central America, and only a few sightings have been documented. The bird is believed to be extinct in Mexico. There have been only two known sightings in Guatemala, and until mid-summer of 1994, the keel-billed motmot had not been seen in Belize for more than eight years. A recent sighting was made at the Tapir Mountain Nature Reserve, and there may be other individuals in remote protected areas.

MAMMALS

JAGUAR
The jaguar was among the most revered animals of the ancient Maya, and even today this jungle cat commands great respect among Belizeans, who often refer to it as tiger, or *el tigre*. Up to 6 feet long and weighing as much as 250 pounds, its likeness turns up on modern T-shirts as well as eroded Maya ornaments. Originally found from the southwestern United States to Argentina, the jaguar (largest cat in the Western Hemisphere) has become extinct or endangered throughout its range. In Mesoamerica only a few hundred jaguar are believed to remain. In Belize, however, the animal is still seen in many areas, even within a 30-minute drive of Belize City. This nocturnal predator feeds primarily on peccary, paca, fish, or deer, along with an occasional bird, lizard, or turtle.

Contrary to local belief, jaguars will not attack humans unless provoked and usually do not kill livestock unless their habitat has been destroyed and their natural prey replaced by cattle. The respected *Neotropical Rainforest Mammals* field guide recommends that humans never try to run from a jaguar, since fleeing may give it cause to chase. Human encroachment continues to limit the cats' territory, and hunters, operating illegally, occasionally kill perfectly healthy animals in Belize for their hides.

Jaguars are very territorial, ranging over vast areas of forest and savanna. The male, a solitary creature who partners with one female at a time, marks the boundaries of his kingdom with tree scratches and ground scrapings. The other four native cats of Belize are the puma, ocelot, margay, and jaguarundi.

BAIRD'S TAPIR

Called a "mountain cow" by locals, this largely nocturnal species is the national animal of Belize. Although it can grow as big as a small cow, the tapir is more closely related to the horse and hippopotamus. Still fairly plentiful here, the Baird's tapir has almost disappeared from the rest of its native Central America and Mexico, earning it a place on the endangered species list. It spends almost 90 percent of its waking hours feeding on fruits, browse, and grasses. Despite the fact that tapirs have thick hides and a disagreeable flavor, their ranks have been thinned by native hunters, many of whom mistakenly believe these docile vegetarians will attack and kill their domestic animals.

The tapir is adaptable to almost any Belizean environment, but today it is most plentiful in mountain forests where there is water nearby. Although it can weigh up to 650 pounds, the Baird's tapir is surprisingly agile and has splayed feet for navigating mud holes. The herbivore's long, flexible upper lip and strong molars are well-suited for foraging and swallowing twigs, nuts, and other tough plant tissues. The tapir has excellent senses of smell and hearing, although its eyesight is weak. The shy beasts are usually solitary and tend to avoid confrontation by steering clear of other large animals. Perhaps the best-known Baird's tapir is named April and lives in the Belize Zoo, where she has become both a favorite of visiting schoolchildren and a kind of national mascot. April was joined by a mate named Scotty several years ago and is now a proud mother.

DOLPHINS

Atlantic bottle-nosed dolphins are common off the coast of Belize, and research is now being done on these marine mammals at Blackbird Caye on the Turneffe atoll. Thanks to the media exploits of Flipper, the bottlenose is the most well-known dolphin species in the world. Individuals may be gray or whitish in color and can grow up to 10 feet long. These very social animals can often be seen riding the bow wave of powerboats. They breathe air and give birth to live young, which they subsequently nurse.

The complexity of the social interactions among dolphins, scientists believe, may help explain the evolution of their large brains. The creatures emit a variety of complex buzzing, whistling, and clicking sounds that bounce off objects like sonar echoes and enable dolphins to "see" long distances under water. This process is called *echolocation*. The sound beams can apparently even penetrate living tissue, which seems to allow male dolphins to "see" when a female is approaching fertility.

Dolphins travel widely and have been observed along the Belize coast in almost every marine environment, including lagoons and jungle rivers. They sometimes show up off the coast of San Pedro, Caye Caulker, Hopkins, and Placencia, where they can easily be seen from the shore.

© Tony Rath

Bottle-nosed dolphins off Long Coco Caye

REPTILES

HICKATEE

The Central American river turtle is making one of its last stands along the waterways of Belize. Locally referred to as the hickatee, it can be found only here and in the most isolated parts of southern Mexico and northern Guatemala. Prized as a food source, this turtle spends almost its entire life in the water, except when it lays its eggs in rotting vegetation along the riverbanks, where the eggs incubate themselves. The hickatee is brown or olive drab on its back, with a cream-colored underbelly. Large males weigh as much as 50 pounds.

Unfortunately, the animal seeks out fish and aquatic plants by night, then sleeps or floats much of the day, making it an easy target for human hunters.

SEA TURTLES

Three of the world's eight species of sea turtles are known to nest in Belize: the green, loggerhead, and hawksbill. Although the situation is changing, many are still killed by local residents for their flesh, eggs, and shells.

Increasingly, turtles are being kept from their traditional nesting areas by fences, buildings, people, pets, bright lights, and loud noises. For these reasons, all three species found in Belize have been declared endangered. Visitors are urged to respect the nesting season (June 1 to August 31), refrain from buying turtle meat or products, and avoid littering the sea with plastic bags in which turtles can easily (and fatally) become entangled.

No one knows how the female loggerhead turtle, called *lagra* in Belize, finds her way back to nesting beaches as many as 50 years after leaving that same stretch of sand to spend her life in the sea. Yet that is exactly what happens when this large turtle (up to 300 pounds) returns to Belize to lay up to 100 leathery eggs at a time. After a two-month incubation, tiny babies emerge from the shells and make a mad dash for the water. Most are caught en route by birds, crabs, lizards, and humans. Less than 5 percent typically survive to reproduce.

The green turtle is an even larger species, measuring up to 4 feet in length and weighing up to 600 pounds. Because its greenish meat and tender eggs are considered delicacies, this turtle has been hunted extensively. It also sometimes gets caught in shrimp nets while surfacing from the sea grass beds where it feeds.

One of the smaller sea turtles is the hawksbill, which gets its name from its sharp, hooked beak. The animal's top shell is covered with multicolored scales that have long been popular for use in combs, eyeglass frames, hair clips, and jewelry. The hawksbill is often killed before it reaches maturity, which has had a devastating effect on the species' ability to reproduce.

Remarkably, sea turtles have been on Earth for about 150 million years (outliving dinosaurs) yet little is known about their lives in the wild. We do know that they can stay underwater for several hours, returning to

How to Help Turtles Survive

All eight known species of sea turtle are considered endangered. Each of us can make a difference in their long-term survival by refusing to buy any product made from turtle shells; by refusing to eat turtle eggs, soup, or any other turtle dish; by encouraging projects that preserve nesting beaches as nature reserves; and by not disturbing or scaring turtles, particularly during their June through August mating season. In Belize there are several nesting beaches that can benefit from your volunteer and financial support.

the surface to breathe for only a few minutes before diving again. Due to unrestricted hunting and other human-related threats in much of the world (including Belize), there are probably half as many sea turtles today as in the 1970s.

BASILISKS AND IGUANAS

Once you've seen a basilisk in action, you'll know why Belizeans have labeled it "the Jesus Christ lizard." The prehistoric-looking animal moves with such great speed—often on its hind legs—through its riverside habitat that it seems to be able to skim right across the surface of a creek or river without sinking, disappearing into foliage on the opposite bank. Researchers have determined that the reptile actually forms a bubble of air beneath its feet that prevents it from sinking; extra flaps of skin across the toes of its enlarged rear feet make this water-walking trick possible.

While these omnivorous reptiles appear fierce—like a miniature *Tyrannosaurus rex*—they prefer to munch on leaves, flowers, and fruit in their favorite trees (often a giant ficus), in addition to the occasional insect or bird. They can be distinguished by their ridged backs, ranging in color from yellow-brown to muted gray, and (among males) reddish throat sacs. Local people love to eat the raw eggs of the basilisk, and the creatures are becoming scarce in areas where pesticides are used. Predatory birds are another enemy. The dominant males are quite territorial and can be seen perched on high tree limbs, surveying their domains along inland waterways.

Two iguanid species also live in Belize: the green iguana, also called the "bush-chicken," and the smaller black or land iguana, locally called a "wish-willy." These creatures spend most of the day sunbathing on high branches and are very territorial, responding to trespassers with repeated patterns of head-bobbing. Iguanas (and their eggs) are easy prey for hungry villagers, as well as for birds, snakes, and coati. Wish-willies are commonly encountered on the offshore cayes of Belize, where they frequent vegetation near beaches and mangrove forests. Because so many iguanas are killed each year by Belizeans for food, several groups are now raising them in captivity and releasing them in the wild to restore depleted populations.

FER-DE-LANCE

Variously known as the yellow-jaw tommygoff, *barba amarilla*, and *tres minutos*, the fer-de-lance is a nocturnal pit viper related to the water moccasin and tropical rattlesnake. Because of its fast-acting venom, it is considered to be among the world's deadliest snakes. There are many reliable reports in Belize of individuals who have died soon after stumbling on the animal in the bush. However, unless it's provoked or you are very unlucky, the viper will generally avoid you and stick to birds, rats, and other small mammals.

The fer-de-lance is at home in any part of Belize, including cities, and can be vicious if it does decide to attack. Adults can reach 8 feet in length, enabling them to strike from a coiled position. Their two retractable fangs are the largest of any snake in proportion to size. Keen awareness of smell and temperature enables the fer-de-lance to accurately pinpoint warm bodies in the dark, when it is most likely to be active. It is easily identified by its arrow-shaped head, diamond-patterned back, and thick-set body. If you are bitten, seek medical help at once. The best prevention is wearing boots, since most fer-de-lance bites are in the feet and ankles.

If you hear a rattle as you approach an unfamiliar snake, it is probably not a fer-de-lance but a tropical rattlesnake (or *cascabel*), the only rattlesnake species in Belize. It is the most poisonous of all rattlers and can grow up to 7 feet in length.

FISH

Hundreds of species of fish and other marine animals are found in the diverse offshore ecosystems of Belize: estuaries, lagoons, sea grass beds, mangrove thickets, coral reefs, and deep-sea channels. A colorful, magical world opens up in these seldom-seen environments. In order to more easily identify name creatures, ask your hotel manager, guide, or outfitter for laminated identification cards that can be taken under water. Many coastal or reef resorts also have nature reference libraries that allow you to learn more about Belize's marine life as well as the plants and animals found in the country's interior.

Squirrel-fish are among the most numerous of fishes in the dimly lit recesses of the coral reef and their distinctive large eyes provide exceptional visual acuity in the dark. Nocturnal feeders, these fish sometimes leave their daytime shelters to forage for small crustaceans.

The four-eyed butterfly fish, another common reef species, is so named for the false eyespots on either side of its tail. These markings are designed to confuse predators.

Among the coral you will also frequently see the queen angelfish, easy to identify with its brilliant yellow, blue, and violet colors. Crawling and feeding on coral branches are such sea snails as the flamingo tongue, identified by its black-bordered, leopard-like spots. The scarlet-colored fire sponge is another interesting reef resident; it is harmful to touch but has yielded eight antibiotics for the biomedical industry.

© Tony Rath

Diver with a school of spade fish at Carrie Bow Caye

TREES

PALMS

The cohune palm, widespread throughout Belize, is one of the forest community's most useful members. Its fronds are used as thatch in roofs, and a valuable oil can be extracted from its fruit. Husks from the tree's palm nuts make excellent fuel, and the nut meat is pounded into a flour. The nuts are very hard and can be carved into clothing buttons and even jewelry. The cohune was highly regarded by the ancient Maya, who considered it a symbol of fertility. Because of the palm's many practical uses, it is almost always spared when forests are cut down for subsistence agriculture.

Dominant in low-lying marshes and along riverbanks are palmetto palms, which can grow to great heights and provide fronds used in traditional house construction.

Coconut palms are not native to the region but were introduced on the cayes and coastal strip in the late 18th and early 19th centuries as a commercial crop. A few coconuts are still harvested for their oil, meat, and husks (an excellent fuel for making charcoal), but the industry has pretty much died out in Belize. Many of the existing palms are now dying from a disease known as "lethal yellowing."

41

Steele Wotkyns

Belize guide standing before a mahogany, the country's national tree and symbol.

MANGROVES

Almost the entire coastline of Belize, including the fringes of its many cayes, are covered by dense stands of black, white, and red mangrove, with the latter species dominating. Different types of mangroves are adapted to varying degrees of salinity, and you will notice them changing as you go away from sources of saltwater. While 90 percent of the world's original mangrove forests have been destroyed, Belize can boast that 90 percent of its mangrove habitat remains intact.

The ancient Maya made extensive use of the mangrove wetlands, as evidenced by the use of crocodile and manatee images in their artwork. Mangroves as tall as 100 feet or more can be seen along some waterways, such as the Toledo District's Temash River within the Temash/Sarstoon National Park. A more accessible protected area in which to visit mangroves is the Burdon Canal Nature Reserve, just west of Belize City, and the Drowned Cayes to the city's east.

Although these tangled saltwater thickets have traditionally been despised by settlers, who often cleared them as quickly as possible, they protect shorelines from erosion during storms and provide an irreplaceable nursery for small fish, turtles, and crustaceans. Snorkeling near mangrove roots often is more rewarding, in terms of marine life, than swimming in open water or near coral reefs. Above the waterline, visitors can see egrets, herons, ibises, roseate spoonbills, pelicans, frigate birds, raptors, and boobies amid the tangled roots and branches. Coatimundis, crocodiles, tapirs, jaguars, raccoons, and boa constrictors are also found in these wetland areas.

MAHOGANY

The national tree of Belize has never been very common and, after centuries of logging, it is even more rare. Its beautiful dark wood has long been prized for use in fine furniture and cabinetry. This tropical hardwood tree—more properly referred to as the Honduran or bigleaf mahogany—is what attracted some of the first European settlers to Belize, and it is displayed prominently on the country's coat of arms. It has a reddish-brown bark and can grow to over 100 feet tall (although this takes at least 70 years). A mature mahogany will be supported at its base by great buttresses that spread up to 20 feet across the forest floor. Look for its pear-shaped seed pods and small whitish flowers.

Very little mahogany is exported from Belize these days, although some entrepreneurs are cultivating the trees commercially. Several have been planted in front of the visitors center at Guanacaste National Park, near Belmopan. Another good place to see a mahogany is in the Río Bravo Conservation and Management Area, northwest of Belmopan, where tropical forest ecologist Nick Brokaw supervises research on harvesting methods that allow the tree to replace itself. Brokaw's methods, controversial among some environmentalists, include removing other trees that compete with the native mahogany for sunlight, a practice that attempts to duplicate the natural thinning process ordinarily carried out by hurricanes.

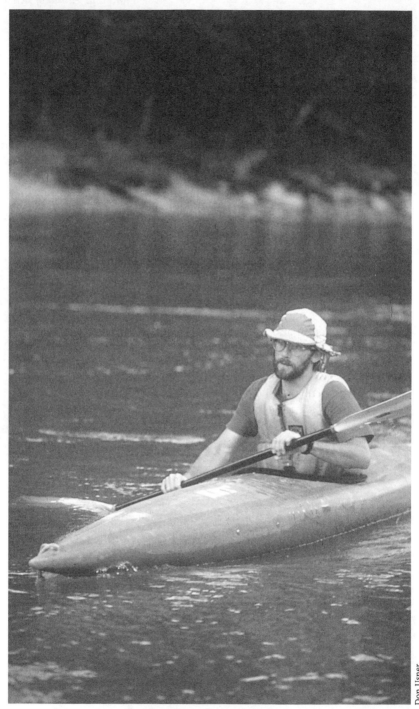

A kayaker takes on a jungle river.

SPECIAL INTERESTS AND ACTIVITIES

4

For enthusiasts of diving, snorkeling, fishing, birding, hiking, sailing, natural history, archaeology, or simply taking it easy, a trip to Belize presents almost unlimited opportunities. For the most part, Belize *is* the outdoors. Those expecting lively nightclubs, gourmet restaurants, and sophisticated shopping will probably be disappointed by what they find. The mind-boggling variety and seemingly endless cycles of nature are the main event here, although the human domains of the ancient Maya and modern Belizeans are definitely worth seeing.

Although Belize is best known for water-based sports, the range of activities is continually expanding, with an emphasis on outdoor pursuits that take full advantage of the country's tremendous natural resources, such as hiking, birding, caving, and mountain biking.

For specific details on experienced guides and professional services catering to these specialized interests, please review the outfitter names, addresses, and phone numbers listed at the end of each section. In these special interest listings, note that some businesses offer a service in more than one category. All seven-digit and 800 numbers are in the United States or Canada and all six-digit numbers are in Belize, unless otherwise indicated. Prices here, as throughout this book, are in U.S. dollars.

DIVING AND SNORKELING
In 1989, *Skin Diver* magazine described Belize as "one of the western Caribbean's premier dive destinations," praising its unspoiled tropical

waters, diversity of marine life, and easy access. Today, many of the publication's readers might argue that Belize has since become the most highly regarded diving spot in all the Caribbean, and certainly one of the top five scuba and snorkel destinations in the Western Hemisphere.

With so many coastal waterways to choose from—along with literally thousands of little-known reefs, sand bores, islands, and marine formations—there is something here for every interest and level of ability. Belize's offshore waters are consistently calm, warm, shallow enough to make long dives pleasurable, and amazingly clear—up to 150 feet visibility is common in outlying waters. Closer to shore, visibilities usually range from 50 to 150 feet. Trade winds bring easterly breezes.

Water temperatures range from about 74 degrees Fahrenheit in winter to 84 degrees Fahrenheit in summer. A bodysuit is adequate much of the year, and you never need more than a warm-water wetsuit for thermal insulation. Your body temperature is 98.6 degrees Fahrenheit, however, and low-grade hypothermia can set in if you stay in the water long enough without a break or some kind of protection. A 3-mm short or full wetsuit is recommended for repetitive diving.

In order to fully experience the best of what Belize has to offer—such as viewing deep-water gorgonia, black-coral forests, and the most exotic tropical fish—underwater explorers have three basic options. First, they may head for one of the more remote island hotels or resorts. Good choices include one of the several tourist operations on the Turneffe Islands, Glover's Reef, Lighthouse Reef, Spanish Lookout, Ambergris, or South Water Caye. Second, they may sign on with one of the several live-aboard dive boats shuttling among Belize's many uninhabited islands and isolated reef structures. And third, they may charter a boat, individually or as part of a larger group, so as to have maximum flexibility in destination and schedule. Any of these choices can be easily accomplished with the help of a local travel agent, dive shop, or large hotel.

Obviously, trade-offs are inherent in each selection. The less-accessible lodges are relatively expensive and usually require a minimum stay of six nights. Live-aboard dive boats are also somewhat costly, with fixed schedules and routes that generally exclude the Belize interior. The expenses involved in chartering a private boat can also add up quickly, and the trip may be limited by the abilities of craft and crew.

At the end of this section you'll find a comprehensive list of specialists involved in the three types of diving vacations just described. For further details, I suggest you contact these sources directly for advice on the most appropriate option. Keep in mind that many dive resorts also cater to anglers, so it is feasible to combine both pleasures in a single Belizean vaca-

Klaus Eiberle

Scuba diving amid brain coral off the barrier reef

tion. Examples include Blue Marlin Lodge, Ramon's Village, Blackbird Caye Resort, Turneffe Flats, Ranguana Reef Lodge, Lighthouse Reef Resort, and Manta Reef Resort. Such operators usually have special rates for nondiving and nonfishing travelers as well as off-season visitors.

Diving for All Levels of Experience

For those with little or no open-water experience, diving around Ambergris Caye, Caye Caulker, Placencia, South Water Caye, and the Hol Chan Marine Reserve will likely provide more than enough variation in underwater scenery and marine life. These areas are usually calm and well-patrolled, with a relative abundance of marine life.

Although there is much to see close to Ambergris and Caulker, the experienced diver or snorkeler will probably want to go even farther afield, exploring areas of the barrier reef that have not suffered as much habitat damage at the hands of commercial fishermen and tourists. Many small species of fish, crustacean, sponge, fan, and coral inhabit the more well-traveled areas, but such larger and more timid creatures as turtles and grouper are notably absent. Among the walls, spur-and-groove canyons, and reef systems of more distant destinations you'll see eagle rays, barracuda, jewfish, groupers, turnicates, sponges, and several species of shark. Schools of amberjacks and sergeant majors are common. Overall, it's not unusual to count 50 or 60 fish species on a single dive, along with dozens of species of hard and soft coral, sea whips, anemones, urchins, fans, sponges, and gorgonia.

Major Snorkel Sites

Ambergris Caye
Hol Chan Cut (marine
reserve)
Shark/Ray Alley
Mata Rocks Cut
Mexico Rocks

Glover's Reef (atoll)
Emerald Forest Reef
Baking Swash Reef
Long Caye Wall

Southern Barrier Reef
Goff's Caye
Laughingbird Caye
Queen Cayes
South Water Caye Cut

Turneffe Islands (atoll)
Blue Creek
Hollywood

Lighthouse Reef (atoll)
Blue Hole
Half Moon Caye Flats
Sand Bore Caye

Major Dive Sites

Ambergris Caye
Sandbar
Pillar Coral
Cypress
Tackle Box Canyons
Tres Cocos
Basil Jones Canyons
Hol Chan
Mata Rocks Cut
Mexico Rocks

Glover's Reef
Emerald Forest Reef
Split Reefs
Baking Swash Reef
Southwest Caye Wall
Middle Caye Reefs
Long Caye Wall
Shark Point
Grouper Flats

Lighthouse Reef
Hat Caye Drop-off
Tres Cocos
Long Caye Ridge
Quebrada
Eagle Ray Wall
Blue Hole
West Point

Turneffe Islands
Blue Creek
Triple Anchors
Hollywood
Permit Paradise
Wreck of Sayonara
The Elbow
Myrtle's Point
Leftie's Ledge
Black Beauty
Majestic Point
Front Porch

If you're headed for the three atolls beyond the barrier reef you'll see even more variety of marine flora and fauna. Fortunately the circular structure of the atolls makes it possible to find refuge on a leeward side or amid interior patch reefs when winds and seas kick up.

What to Bring

Be sure to bring your scuba certification card; reputable operators will not accommodate your scuba requests without it. While you can rent any necessary gear in Belize, it's always better to bring your own masks, wet suits, and other items that you've been fitted for and are used to. Some resorts only supply weights and tanks in their packages; ask what's provided before you leave home. TACA airlines is especially good about stowing diving equipment.

Where to Arrange a Dive Trip

Most of the major hotels, especially those on Ambergris Caye, offer one or more dive activities, plus whatever related equipment may be required. The Fiesta Hotel and Belize Dive Connection in Belize City, Belize Yacht Club and Ramon's Village on Ambergris Caye, Maya Landings on Moho Caye, Rum Point Inn in Placencia, Turneffe Island Lodge on Caye Bokel, St. George's Lodge on St. George's Caye, and Blue Marlin Lodge on South Water Caye are also good places to inquire about diving trips and other water-related sports. Also recommended are Kitty's Place in Placencia, Jaguar Reef in Hopkins, and International Zoological Expeditions on South Water Caye.

Telephone and Internet services to the Belize mainland and the developed areas of Ambergris Caye and Caye Caulker are good, and you can contact dive resorts directly from the United States and Canada. Some of the outlying islands can be reached only by cellular telephone or VHF marine-band radio. As in the United States, Channels 16 and 68 are the standard hailing frequencies. Live-aboard boats and charter craft also stand by on Channel 78. Many resorts now have e-mail addresses and Web sites, often at [name of resort].btl.net.

Where to Arrange a Snorkel Trip

Although most dive boats and diving resorts happily accommodate snorkelers and can easily supply any necessary equipment, it may be both easier and cheaper to arrange personalized day trips and hire your own boat operator. This is most easily done at hotels that have their own marinas, such as the Ft. George, Bellevue, Fiesta, Victoria House, and Sea Breeze (Ambergris Caye). Local fishers and guides are often willing to drop off

Diving the Blue Hole

One of the most famous and popular dive spots in Belize is the Blue Hole (not to be confused with an inland and very different Blue Hole that's the focus of a national park). Located about 3 hours from Ambergris Caye at Lighthouse Reef, this Blue Hole is an enormous limestone sinkhole, some 412 feet deep and 300 feet wide, and surrounded by a shallow coral crust. This monstrous depression—and the flooded caverns that extend from its sides—was the subject of a Jacques Cousteau documentary some years ago and reportedly remained one of Cousteau's favorite dive spots. The walls are vertical for the first 125 feet, then widen into stalactite-adorned passages. This is a fairly challenging dive because of its depth, but the rewards are a chance to see some of the larger sea creatures that sometimes cruise the Blue Hole's cobalt blue waters.

Day trips to the Blue Hole can be arranged through, among others, Out Island Divers, Blue Hole Dive Shop, and Fantasea Watersports on Ambergris Caye, or from the nearby Lighthouse Reef Resort on Northern Two Caye.

snorkelers and swimmers in good locations, then pick them up a few hours later. Small sandy cayes—notably Congrejo, Goff's, Laughingbird, Rosario, Montego, English, and Rendezvous—are especially recommended. Even on the more active islands of Ambergris, Caulker, and St. George's, plenty of nearby reef—away from populated areas and traffic lanes—offers an astonishing array of marine life.

The 45-foot catamaran *Stingray*, based in Belize City, is recommended by experienced snorkelers. Contact owner/operators Michael and Donna Hill through the Fiesta Hotel. Another snorkel-only boat is operated by Ecosummer Expeditions.

Where to Learn to Dive

Some of the better places to receive scuba instruction are Coral Beach Dive Club and Amigos del Mar in Ambergris Caye; Second Nature Divers on Tobacco Caye; Frenchie's Dive Service and Belize Diving Service on Caye

Richard Mahler

A Belizean guide hands out snorkeling equipment off South Water Caye.

Caulker; Manta Reef on Glover's Reef; and Hugh Parkey's Belize Dive Connection in Belize City. We have also heard excellent reports about the Living Reef Dive Center on South Water Caye and Glover's Reef. It usually takes at least four days to complete a PADI or NAUI open-water certification course, with prices ranging from $300 to $400 per person. Less extensive courses are available, with prices starting at about $125.

Specialty Diving

Night diving and cave diving are popular in Belize, and the major dive specialists can provide necessary guides and maps, along with lights and other gear. Night dives at Hol Chan are a treat, often including glimpses of black-tip shark, lemon shark, squid, eels, and octopus.

You also may want to explore the marine caverns here, some of the largest in the world. Frenchie's and Belize Diving Services on Caye Caulker; Bottom Time Dive Shop, Amigos del Mar, and Reef Divers Limited on Ambergris Caye; Turneffe Lodge on Caye Bokel; and Kitty's Place or the Rum Point Inn in Placencia are all highly recommended.

Live-Aboard Dive Boats

From Caye Caulker, an outfit called Sea-Ing Is Belizing offers excursions that last up to eight days and include the outer atolls and reef

51

Diving and Snorkeling Safety

Once in Belize, divers and snorkelers should not enter the water before identifying its possible hazards. Besides ever-fragile, living coral polyps, which should not be touched or stepped on for reasons of ecology as well as health, there are the usual urchins, anemones, jellyfish, and stingrays to look out for. Fire worms (also called bristle worms) and certain types of sponges can cause a burning sensation if brushed against, and the aptly named scorpion fish will sting if stepped on. The sinister-looking barracuda and nurse shark cruise Belize's reefs by the hundreds, but will not attack unless deliberately provoked or drawn by the scent of fresh food or blood (i.e., from spearfishing). Definitely don't pull the nurse shark's tail. Dolphins, also, generally prefer not to be touched, especially on certain sensitive spots. In general, it is best not to feed fish underwater. Every species is hungry, and some, such as the moray eel, have teeth sharp enough to remove a finger or two. A good pair of booties, fins, or Patagonia Reef Walkers will help reduce the risk of foot injuries. As a rule, it's not a good idea to dive or snorkel alone, or to dive or snorkel after drinking alcohol (some outfitters demand this).

Snorkelers must remember that the sun is beating down on them despite the fact that they're in the water. Those without a

structures. Your live-aboard vessel is a 28-foot sailboat. Nearby Ambergris Caye boasts a number of well-equipped, diesel-powered dive boats, as does Placencia. Popular live-aboards based in Belize City include the 36-passenger *Rembrandt van Rijn*, and the 14- to 18-passenger *Belize Aggressor III* (and *II*). All of these vessels are equipped with diving platforms, tank racks, freshwater rinses, and other services.

tan will want to apply (and reapply!) waterproof sunblock and perhaps wear a T-shirt or wetsuit top. Check the location of your boat and companions frequently, and if you're traveling with your own kayak make sure you are tied off to dead coral or tie a lead rope to your wrist.

Medical experts recommend that beginning or infrequent divers over age 35 get a physical exam before diving, preferably from a physician who is familiar with the sport. Among older divers, one out of every four fatalities involves cardiovascular problems. Other conditions that should preclude diving, at any age, are severe asthma, seizure disorders, insulin-dependent diabetes, and any disease that could result in a loss of consciousness.

Divers should always be aware of the risks of decompression sickness, or "the bends," caused by entrapment of nitrogen bubbles in the bloodstream. It is treatable by oxygen therapy or by spending time in a decompression chamber, but decompression chamber treatments typically run $400 an hour, and only one unit is available in Belize (on Ambergris Caye, 26-2425, funded by a tax on tank refills). Because aircraft cabins are pressurized to the equivalent of about 8,000 feet, it is strongly recommended that scuba divers not fly for at least 12 hours, preferably 24 hours, after a dive.

Photo Processing

For underwater color photo processing, try Wade Bevier at Placencia's Rum Point Inn (which also operates the 42-foot, 12-passenger *Auriga* custom dive cruiser). James Beveridge on Caye Caulker and Joe Miller on Ambergris Caye also provide processing and underwater camera rental. Miller also sells photographic prints of marine life at his excellent San Pedro gallery.

Equipment and Boat Rental

Rental of a full complement of scuba gear generally starts at about $45 for a single-tank day, with an additional $75 and up for two tanks worth of diving around the barrier reef. Dive trips to Lighthouse Reef and other popular atoll dive sites start at about $200 per day per person. For day trips to Lighthouse, Ambergris-based Out Island Divers has been particularly recommended by experienced divers.

Overnight trips on snorkel-only boats start at about $125 per person, with charters about $20 higher, based on a two-person minimum. Day trips start at around $40, less for a half-day trip.

It's a good idea to thoroughly examine any rental equipment before heading offshore. You should also ask around before hiring a diving instructor since the level of expertise varies considerably. And do not let anyone try to rent you a surfboard in Belize: Except during hurricanes, surf is nonexistent.

Advance Reading

Before departure, I also recommend that serious water-sports enthusiasts check one or more of the specialty magazines and guidebooks that profile Belize on a regular basis. These are often available at large dive shops, sporting goods stores, or newsstands. There are several good guidebooks specializing in underwater sports off the coast of Belize, among them *Diving Belize*, by Ned Middleton, AquaQuest Publishing, and the *Diving and Snorkeling Guide to Belize*, by Franz O. Meyer, Lonely Planet Publications, 1998.

Diving and Snorkeling Outfitters

Adventures in Watersports, Ambergris Caye; 26-3706; advwtrspts @btl.net. Complete dive center.

Amigos del Mar Dive Shop, Box 53, San Pedro, Ambergris Caye; 26-2706, fax 26-2648, (800) 346-6116, amigosdive@btl.net. Complete dive shop. Recommended.

Belize Dive Center, San Pedro, Ambergris Caye; 26-2797 U.S., (800) 938-0860, bzedivectr@btl.net. Dive packages, instruction; located at Belize Yacht Club.

Belize Dive Connection, Box 1818, Belize City; 2-34526 or (888) 223-5403, fortst@btl.net. Dive packages and PADI instruction, marine ecology tours. Recommended.

Belize Diving Service, Caye Caulker; 22-2217 or marine VHF Channel 68. Complete dive shop, rental and instruction. Recommended.

Blackline Marine Service, Box 332, Mile 2 Northern Highway, Belize City; 2-44155, fax 2-31975, marine VHF Channel 70. Complete dive shop, hull and engine repairs, fishing/diving and sight-seeing charters, marina with fuel, water, and ice.

Blue Hole Dive Center, San Pedro, Ambergris Caye; 26-2982, bluehole@ btl.net. All dive services.

Blue Marlin Lodge, South Water Caye, P.O. Box 21, Dangriga; 5-22296, fax 5-22296. Full-service diving and fishing resort.

Bottom Time Dive Shop, San Pedro, Ambergris Caye; 26-2348, fax 26-2821. Dive shop, scuba instruction, night diving, sailing charters, equipment rental; located in Sun Breeze Hotel.

Caribbean Charter Services, Mile 5 Northern Highway, Belize City; 2-45814. Offering boat charters, car rental, diving and fishing tours.

Chocolate's, Caye Caulker; 2-22151, chocolat@btl.net. Reef and manatee tours, fishing trips. Recommended.

Coral Beach Hotel and Dive Club, San Pedro, Ambergris Caye; 2-62013, fax 2-62864, forman@btl.net. Packages for snorkelers, divers, anglers, beachcombers.

Discovery Divers, 126 Freetown Rd., Belize City; 26-3484, 26-2881, discovery@btl.net. Complete dive center.

Dive Connection, Box 1818, Belize City; 23-2890, fax 27-8808, fortst@btl.net. Dive instruction and diving trips, based at 4 Fort St. Guesthouse. Recommended.

Fantasea Scuba School & Watersports, Ambergris Caye; 26-2576, fantasea@btl.net. Dive instruction and diving trips. Based at Victoria House Hotel.

Frenchie's Diving Services, Caye Caulker; 22-2111 or 22-2234. Fishing and diving guides, PADI instruction.

Gaz Cooper's Dive Belize, Sun Breeze Hotel, Ambergris Caye; 26-3202, fax (954) 351-9740, gaz@btl.net.

Harrison Cadle, Caye Caulker; 22-2263. Guided snorkeling and manatee trips. Recommended.

Hustler Tours, Ambergris Caye; 26-2279, fax 26-3468, hustler@btl.net. Full-service dive shop.

Lighthouse Reef Resort, Northern Two Caye, Lighthouse Reef, Box 26, Belize City; 2-31205, lighthouse@btl.net. Complete fishing and diving services.

The Living Reef Diving Center, 8 Magoon St., Dangriga; 5-22214, (800) 548-5843, tread@btl.net. Low-cost dive packages off Long Caye (Glovers Reef); packages also offered from South Water Caye. Recommended.

Manta Resort, Glover's Reef, Box 215, 3 Eyre St., Belize City; 2-31895 or (800) 342-0053, marine VHF Channel 70. Dive and fishing resort on 12-acre island.

Maya Landings, Box 459, Belize City; 25-2002, fax 025-2298. Complete dive shop and diving resort on Moho Caye.

Out Island Divers, Box 7, San Pedro, Ambergris Caye; 2-62151, (800) BLUE-HOLE. Dive boat specialists.

Paradise Dive Shop, 26-2797, paradive@btl.net.

Pisces Dive Service, Mike and Beverly McCarty, Placencia; 6-23183. Certified NAUI and NASDS scuba instruction, also offers photography services.

Placencia Dive Shop, Ran Villanueva, Placencia; 6-22027, pds@btl.net. Complete dive shop, transportation to reef and atolls; also bicycle rentals, river trips, kayaking. Recommended.

Ramon's Dive Shop, Ramon's Village, San Pedro, Ambergris Caye; 26-2071, fax (601) 649-1996, ramons@btl.net. Complete dive shop. Recommended.

Reef Divers Ltd., San Pedro, Ambergris Caye; 2-63134, fax 26-2943, reefdivers@btl.net. Complete dive shop.

Ricardo's Adventure Tours, Caye Caulker; 2-22087. River trips, island hopping, fishing, diving, snorkeling.

Robert Blease, Caye Caulker; 22-2154. Guided snorkeling, manatee trips.

Sea & Explore, 1809 Carol Sue Ave., Suite E, Gretna, LA 70056; (800) 345-9786, fax (504) 366-9986. Diving and fishing trips; represents several live-aboard dive boats.

Sea Masters Company, Ltd., Ambergris Caye, Box 59, Belize City; 26-2173, fax 26-2028. Fishing and diving services.

Second Nature Divers, Dangriga; 5-37038 or 2-72109, divers@btl.net. PADI "Discover Scuba" and open-water courses off Columbus and Tobacco Cayes, special trips to Shark's Cave/the Black Hole. Accommodations with Island Camps, Tobacco Caye.

Slickrock Adventures, Box 1400, Moab, UT 85632,(800) 390-5715, slickrock@slickrock.com. Kayak/diving combinations. Based on Long Caye, Glover's Reef. Recommended.

Travel Belize Ltd., 637-B S. Broadway, Boulder, CO 80303; (800) 626-3483. Dive packages, tours, air connections.

Turneffe Flats, Blackbird Caye, Turneffe Islands; 2-45634 or (605) 578-1304, fax (605) 578-7540. Sportfishing and diving specialists.

Turneffe Islands Lodge, Caye Bokel, Turneffe Islands, Box 480, Belize City; (800) 338-8149, fax 3-0276. Dive and fishing specialists.

Dive Boat Services
Belize Aggressor III, based at Ft. George Pier, Belize City, and Drawer K, Morgan City, LA 70381; (800) 348-2628, divboat@aol.com.120-foot dive boats, 18 passengers.

Coral Bay and Offshore Express, Coral Beach Dive Shop, San Pedro, Ambergris Caye; 26-2013 or (800) 433-7262 or (305) 563-1711. Sixty-two-foot dive boat, the *Offshore Express*.

Hotel Fiesta, Barracks Road, Belize City; (800) 228-9898. Berth for various dive boats.

La Strega, Box 673, Belize City; 2-3108 or (800) 433-DIVE. Eighty-five-foot dive boat.

M.V. Manta IV, Box 13, San Pedro, Ambergris Caye; 2-62371 or (800) 473-1956, fax 2-62028. Overnight dive trips to Turneffe and Lighthouse atolls; interior tours.

M.Y. Gallic, 2-31351 or (800) 468-0123. Fifty-two-foot dive boat, specializing in Glover's and Lighthouse Reefs.

Out Island Divers, Box 7, San Pedro, Ambergris Caye; 2-62151 or (800) BLUE-HOLE. Operators of *Reef Roamer I, Reef Roamer II,* and *Reef Roamer III.*

Wave Dancer, based at Ft. George Pier, Belize City, and Peter Hughes Diving, 6851 Yumuri St., Suite 10, Coral Gables, FL 33146; (800) 932-6237, dancer@peterhughes.com. One-hundred-twenty-foot dive boat, 20 passengers.

SPORTFISHING

All the joys of the ocean are found in the waters of Belize. Great fishing—spin, fly, or troll—can be enjoyed year-round, and the abundance of species guarantees excellent sport. Some anglers insist that it is virtually impossible to go fishing in Belize and not catch something. A distinct advantage here for non-Spanish-speaking fishermen (and women) is that virtually all guides and boatmen speak English. The estuaries and mouths of jungle rivers of Belize are best known for their tarpon, black snapper, jack-revalle, cubera, and snook; lagoons and coral flats for their bonefish, permit, triggerfish, and barracuda; reef formations for their king mackerel, kingfish, jackfish, grouper, barracuda, and snapper; and the deeper waters off the outer reefs and atolls for amberjack, sailfish, shark, wahoo, pompano, blackfin tuna, yellowfin tuna, bonito, dolphinfish, mahi-mahi, and marlin.

Species availability varies considerably, depending on the depth and clarity of water, proximity to reefs and rivers, and time of year.

Where to Fish

If fishing is the primary purpose of your trip, you'll want to spend little or no time in Belize City. There is no beach here and the waters are foul.

Luckily, with some advance planning, you can easily transfer to a better base of operations on the day you arrive. Many fishing lodges have airport pickup service and often arrange overnight accommodations in Belize City, departing the next morning on chartered boats. Scheduled domestic airline service is also easily arranged from Belize City to Ambergris Caye and Caye Caulker, as well as the outlying coastal towns of Placencia, Dangriga, Corozal, and Punta Gorda, all located near rich fishing sites. The only other island with an operating airstrip is privately owned Northern Two Caye, at Lighthouse

Fishing boats

Dan Donar/Lighthawk

Reef. There are a few seaplanes in Belize, but they are expensive to charter and seem to get little use.

Fishing the Interior

Because of the unique conditions and high quality of the country's offshore waters, freshwater fishing in the interior receives scant attention from visitors. Conditions are excellent in many streams, however; you should inquire locally about when and where to go. Take a spinning rod up a jungle river and you're liable to hook a tarpon, snook, jack, or snapper. River fish are easiest to snag when the water is clear and low, from February through May. Some of the better inland waterways for fishing are the Sittee, Monkey, Belize, and New Rivers.

Coral Flat Fishing

Many saltwater fly-fishers come to Belize to stalk the elusive bonefish, an almost transparent fish known for its feisty spirit and crafty ways. As the name implies, the creature is too bony to make a decent meal. Although the bonefish is relatively small—averaging 2 to 6 pounds—ounce for ounce it is considered the toughest fighter in the sea. This predator is often found in knee-deep, crystal-clear coral flats, particularly from September through January, where it attacks smaller fish with lightning speed. The bonefish is taken on both fly and lure. Fishing resorts that specialize in guided bonefish excursions include Turneffe Flats, Turneffe Island Lodge, Maya Landings,

Belize River Lodge, Ranguana Lodge, and Wippari Caye Lodge. The shallow, grassy, hard-sand coral flats of the Turneffe Islands are a particularly fine habitat for bonefish—bring your waders!

The same marine habitats also teem with permit, especially on coral flats at incoming tides. Many fishing lodges claim Belize is the "permit capital of the world," with specimens weighing in at 30 or more pounds. The largest concentrations of this wily species are in the southern coastal waters of Belize. For those determined to snag a permit, we recommend the outfitters listed above for bonefishing, along with the Blue Marlin Lodge on South Water Caye and Pow Cabral in Placencia. The coastal lagoons and coral flats of southern Belize are especially good places to find permit, often at the end of an incoming tide. Permit fishing is best from August through October and again from March through June.

Reef Fishing

Tarpon, barracuda, and cubera snapper are equally plentiful near Belizean reefs. Forty-pound or larger tarpon are fairly common here, sometimes in the same coral flats where you'll find permit and bonefish. Although they are not considered good eating, a large tarpon can easily take 90 minutes to subdue with a 10-weight fly rod. Tarpon can be fished year-round, but are most plentiful from October through mid-December and again in June and July.

Good-size snook are reported all winter, both in rivers and estuaries. These species can be found around reefs, flats, and mangrove cayes the rest of the year. The aggressive barracuda are notorious for breaking leaders in the water or, once landed, snapping at fishers' feet. Mutton snapper, ladyfish, and crevalle jack also frequent the coral flats, along with the occasional grouper and red snapper. Fishing outfitters specializing in snook and tarpon include Maya Landings on Moho Caye, Blackline Marine Service in Belize City, and El Pescador on Ambergris Caye. Trolling and bottom fishing along the reef can yield grouper, king mackerel, jack, cobia, kingfish, snapper, wahoo, bonito, and tuna, depending on the season and water depth.

Deep-Water Fishing

The much deeper, ocean side of the barrier reef often serves up king and Spanish mackerel, grouper, snapper (several varieties), bonito, blackfin tuna, and wahoo, along with sailfish and marlin. You will also encounter many shark, porpoise, and dolphin. The warmest months often offer the best chance to hook grouper, mutton snapper, tarpon, sailfish, and mangrove snapper. Deep-sea fishing is not particularly popular in Belize, although spring and fall are good times to catch marlin and sailfish.

Lobster Fishing

Lobster season is March 15 to July 14, but most of these spiny crustaceans (lacking the large claws of the cold-water species off the Maine coast) are taken by local fishers, who also commercially harvest conch, shrimp, snapper, and other species. You won't see many Maine-size lobster here due to many past years of over-harvesting.

Saltwater Fly-Fishing

Saltwater flyfishing is best in the southern part of Belize, where the presence of divers, snorkelers, and Belizean fishers has been felt the least. Anything south of Dangriga is likely to be especially promising. It's not unusual to go for days at a time without seeing another rod or line.

How to Arrange a Fishing Trip

Many resorts, boat operators, lodges, and guides serve the needs of sportfishers (see the end of this section for a complete list of names and addresses). Almost any hotel near the water can easily provide you with a fishing guide, a boat, and tackle—for rent by the hour, day, or week. Flies, as well as extra tackle items, are available for sale to guests who need them, although it's better to bring your own favorite tackle. Many dive shops, dive resorts, and dive boats also welcome fishing enthusiasts. Fishing instruction is widely available and no licenses are required.

Hiring a Fishing Guide or Outfitter

Because of their years of experience, many private fishing boat operators are also excellent guides. Some resorts hire skilled locals whose only job is to help you find and catch the fish of your choice. With hundreds of varieties to choose from, simply making a selection may be a daunting task. Native Belizean "consultants" are sometimes included in the price of package tours, especially the week-long excursions to outer islands.

The services of such guides can also be engaged for about $200 a day, including boat, tackle, and fuel. Week-long fishing packages begin at around $1,200 for six days of actual fishing. These Belize-born experts are considered some of the best fly-fishers in the world.

Local guides, such as Charles Leslie of Placencia's Kingfisher Belize Adventures, specialize in fly-fishing guiding, spin fishing, and offshore fishing. Other recommended guides include Richard Young Jr. of Belize City; Casey Eiley, Eddie Leslie, Pow Cabral, and Kevin Madera of Placencia; Raul Young and Porfilio "Piggy" Guzman of Caye Caulker; and the Cabral family on Wippari Caye (10 miles east of Placencia). On Calabash Caye in the Turneffe Islands, David Young has an excellent

61

reputation as a fishing guide. In Sittee River, try the Lillpat Sittee River Resort.

The investment in a good "consultant" is worth it: During guided visits to nearly virgin Belizean waters, anglers regularly complete a "grand slam" by landing at least one tarpon, snook, bonefish, and permit within a 24-hour period.

On Ambergris Caye, the El Pescador Lodge is recommended as a well-equipped base of operations for saltwater anglers. The resort, which has its own sportfishing boats, guides, and marina, was built by a German-American couple with the help of local Mennonite carpenters. Another good place for fishing information is Rubie's Hotel in downtown San Pedro.

The flats between here and the Belizean mainland are renowned for their tarpon (called silver kings locally), recorded at up to about 100 pounds. I've also heard consistently positive reports about the Blue Marlin Lodge on South Water Caye, Pegasus Boat Service on Caye Caulker, and Ranguana Lodge in Placencia and Ranguana Caye. Another good choice is Angler Adventures, a Connecticut-based outfitter that represents a number of Belize fishing lodges and specializes in all-inclusive fishing packages.

One final word of caution about operators promoting offshore "fishing trips." Some are merely snorkeling trips where the guide fishes for you, then grills and serves his catch as a "shore lunch." When hiring a guide, make it clear that you want to fish.

What to Bring or Rent

Some fishing equipment can be rented from local hotels and outfitters in Belize, but the selection is rather limited (though improving). Live bait, for example, is sometimes hard to come by. Fortunately, you can usually make do with frozen shrimp or wriggling fingerlings plucked from the sea.

Indispensable for Inner Channel fishing (in the relatively shallow waters between the barrier reef and the mainland) are a good 9-foot fly rod, a sturdy reel, and an 8-weight floating saltwater tapered fly line. Experienced fishers often bring along one each of a light and medium spinning or fly rod, along with a heavier fly, spinning, or bait-casting rod and a deep-running lure.

Major resorts that specialize in sportfishing, such as El Pescador, the Paradise Hotel, or Victoria House on Ambergris Caye, can make exact recommendations on tackle, line strength, lures, rods, and reels, depending on what the angler is after and the time of the year. In general, equipment will vary considerably for the following conditions: coral flats,

mainland shoreline, mangrove lagoons, river-mouth casting, and deep-water jigging or trolling.

What to Do with Your Catch

Although foreigners can take up to 20 pounds of freshly caught fish when they leave Belize, the more common practice is to measure the creature and throw it back for the next customer. An alternative is to share the fish with your guide, boatman, and fellow fisherfolk as a supper entrée. Some fishing lodges require catch-and-release for ecological reasons.

Advance Reading

Those with a serious interest in fishing (and boating) are well served by Freya Rauscher and Julius M. Wilensky's 288-page *Cruising Guide to Belize and Mexico's Caribbean Coast* (Westcott Cove, 1991).

Sportfishing Outfitters

Angler Adventures, Box 872, Old Lyme, CT 06371; (800) 628-8605 or (203) 434-9624, fax (203) 434-8605. Represents many fishing lodges in Belize, specialist in all-inclusive fishing packages.

Belize River Lodge, Box 459, Belize City; (888) 275-4843, worldfishn@ worldnet.att.net. 58-foot live-aboard fishing boat.

Blue Runner Guiding, Kenny Villanueva, Placencia Village; 6-23153 or 6-23130. Heavy and light tackle or trolling sportfishing trips; snorkeling; reef, river, and coast.

Coral Beach Hotel & Dive Shop, Box 16, San Pedro, Ambergris Caye; 26-20139, forman@btl.net. Fishing trips.

El Pescadoro, Ambergris Caye; 26-2398, (800) 245-1950. All fishing services.

Francis "Billy" Leslie, Ambergris Caye; 26-2128. Fishing guide.

Kingfisher Belize Adventures, Stanley Winborne and Charles Leslie, Placencia; 6-23104 or (800) 403-9995, fax (919) 676-9910. Bar, flycast/spincast, inshore, offshore. Recommended.

Lillpat River Fishing, Sam Dawson, Hopkins; (805) 963-2501, lillpat@ aol.com. Bonefishing specialists.

Manatee Lodge, Gales Point, Box 170, Belmopan; 8-23321, fax 8-23334. Sportfishing specialists.

Melanie Paz, Ambergris Caye; 26-2437. Fishing guide.

Melvin Bandillo Jr., Caye Caulker; 22-2111. Fishing guide.

Nolan Jackson, Tobacco Caye, Box 10, Dangriga. Fishing guide.

Pegasus Boat Services, Caye Caulker; 22-2223. Guides and charters.

Pow Cabral Flyfishing, Placencia; 22-2234 or (800) 333-5691. Sport- and fly-fishing. Recommended.

Raul Young, Caye Caulker; 22-2133. Fishing guide.

Richard Young Jr., Belize City; 2-74385. Light tackle fishing guide specializing in tarpon, snook, and bonefish on flats or rivers. Recommended.

Roberto Bradley Jr., Ambergris Caye; 26-2116. Fishing guide.

Romel Gomez/Luz Guerrero, Ambergris Caye; 26-2034. Fishing guides.

Roque Badillo's Fishing Tours, Caye Caulker; 22-2014. Fishing guides. Recommended.

Wippari Caye Guiding, Wippari Caye; 6-23130. Cabral family fly-fishing guides specializing in bonefish, permit, and tarpon; lodging.

CRUISE SHIPS AND SAILBOAT EXCURSIONS

Belize does not show up on many cruise ship itineraries. There are several good reasons for this, including the lack of deep-water anchorages, limited onshore infrastructure (i.e. duty-free shopping malls), and the fact that the Belize government has taken a go-slow approach to cruise ship tourism, fearing that their presence could have a negative impact on the country's fragile marine ecosystem. Many in the domestic tourism industry are also fearful that cruise ships could drain precious dollars away from local enterprises.

Nonetheless, there are a handful of operators who offer specialized cruises along the barrier reef. Temptress Voyages, (800) 336-8423, for example, schedules cruises in Belize that feature nature and hiking activities for children (4 through 17) when the 65-passenger *Temptress* ship is in port. Adults will have their own adventures both on and off-shore, including snorkeling trips and excursions to Maya ruins. The MV *Sea Breeze*, a ship on the Premier Cruise Line out of Port Ever-glades, Florida, stops weekly in Belize, continuing on to Santo Tomás, Guatemala. Other cruise ship operators that occasionally make stops in Belize include American-Canadian Caribbean Lines, (800) 556-7450, and OdessAmerica, (800) 221-3254.

Ecosummer Expeditions ($1,250 and up, meals included) has a live-aboard sailing vessel that makes snorkeling, kayaking, and natural history trips along the cayes and east to Lighthouse Reef. Ecosummer's 48-foot Belizean sandlighter *Excellence* departs Belize City about once each week from January through April, stopping at Lighthouse Reef, Glover's Reef, Placencia, and the barrier reef. A guide familiar with the region and its natural history is onboard; special discounts are available for children and families. The offshore cruises are combined with extensions inland to Crooked Tree, Bermudian Landing, and the Cayo district that involve horseback riding, tubing, birding, and inter-pretive hiking.

Wilderness Travel ($1,100 and up, meals included) operates the *Rembrandt van Rijn*, a three-masted gaff topsail schooner as a sail/dive alternative in Belize. This elegant craft was built as a Dutch "herring lug-ger" in the early 1900s and was completely upgraded in 1993. It makes year-round, week-long trips from Belize City with intermediate- to advanced-ability dive stops off the Turneffe Islands, Lighthouse Reef, Glover's Reef, and Laughingbird Caye. Besides divemasters and a full onboard dive shop, the *Rembrandt van Rijn* carries water skis, Zodiacs, and a windsurfer.

Cruise Ships that Visit Belize

Ecosummer Expeditions & Tours, 1516 Duranleau St., Vancouver, BC V6H 3S4, Canada; (604) 669-7741, fax (604) 669-3244, U.S. (800) 465-8884, trips@ecosummer.com. Sea kayaking, river running, caving, Mayan ruins, exploratory trekking, horseback riding, nature tours.

Wilderness Travel/Oceanwide Sail Expeditions, 801 Allston Way, Berkeley, CA 94710; (800) 453-7245, oceanwh@infohwy.com or (510) 548-0420, info@wildernesstravel.com. Seven-day, live-aboard sail/dive tours on the *Rembrandt van Rijn*; the 184-foot boat holds 32 passengers.

RIVER TRIPS, KAYAKING, AND SAILING

White-Water Adventures

Although Belize is a relatively small and low-lying country, it gets plenty of rainfall and boasts 20 major river systems, plus innumerable perennial streams. These sources supply the nation's domestic water needs and the demands of local agriculture, but they are also a potential source of outdoor adventure.

Some rivers in the upland areas (especially of the Cayo District) have navigable whitewater, but it is best to check with tour operators for expert advice on where and when to go. The Mopán and the Macal, along with their tributaries, are your best bet. The upper Macal River was dammed in the early 1990s for a hydroelectric project and its flow is now carefully controlled, which makes whitewater floats possible downstream as far as Chaa Creek—even farther during wet months.

Slickrock Adventures offers a kayak or paddleboat day trip (with mountain bike and cave-float extensions) through Class III and IV rapids on the upper Macal that floats from the hydroelectric dam to Black Rock or Chaa Creek, past tall limestone canyons and thick jungle. Flows must be 90-cfs to make this trip, however, and discharge rates vary. Among local operators in San Ignacio, I recommend Remo Montgomery of Float Belize (he also owns the Sandcastle Restaurant), and in nearby Cristo Rey, Victor or Jeronie Tut of Crystal Paradise Resort. Slickrock added the Manatee River and Footprint Cave Creek to its float itinerary in 1998.

Raft, Canoe, and Kayak Adventures

Rafts and canoes have always been common modes of transportation on Belizean waterways, and such vessels can be rented through most major hotels and travel agencies. The cottage resorts of the Cayo District, for example, often supply inner tubes, canoes, and occasional kayaks to their guests or even casual visitors. The area's Macal, Mopán, and Belize Rivers are particularly well suited to these craft during the drier months, beginning in about January, or you may try Monkey, Sittee, Moho, and Temash Rivers farther south. Small boats can be rented for as little as one-half hour or as long as two weeks. Some operators arrange trips by raft, kayak, or canoe all the way from the Guatemalan border to Belize City.

This sort of journey is an excellent way to observe birds, plants, animals, and people along the riverbanks. Such travel is problematic during the rainy season, for obvious reasons. Lowland river trips by canoe (or kayak) can be arranged at Banana Bank Lodge, Chaa Creek Cottages, duPlooy's, Caesar's Place/Black Rock, Warrie Head Ranch, Jaguar Reef

Resort, Paradise Inn, and Jungle Drift Lodge, among others. In the Cayo District, outfitters renting canoes include Float Belize, Toni's Canoes, and Windy Hill Cottage Tours. Also recommended are U.S.-based Ceiba Adventures and Slickrock Adventures.

Powerboat Adventures

Popular destinations by guided powerboat include the offshore islands, Crooked Tree Wildlife Sanctuary, Community Baboon Sanctuary, and the Maya ruins of Cerros, Lamanai, and Xunantunich (see other chapters for complete coverage). A trip up the New River from Orange Walk to Lamanai is a must for birders, and the New River Lagoon is arguably the loveliest body of freshwater in the country. Boat trips are also recommended to the Northern and Southern Lagoons, Gales Point, Placencia, Sittee River, Monkey River Town, and the Temash River.

Sea Kayaks, Sailboats, Waterskiing, and Windsurfing

Sea kayaking and windsurfing are rapidly increasing in popularity along the coast of Belize. The calm and relatively shallow waters of the Inner Channel (between the barrier reef and the mainland) are ideal locations for enjoying these activities, and the islands' larger resorts can arrange equipment rental and instruction. Some of these hotels also rent small sailboats on a daily or weekly basis. Areas favored by sea kayakers include the waters of Chetumal Bay, Ambergris Caye, Caye Caulker, the Hol Chan Channel, and offshore atolls. Experienced kayakers can also follow the entire length of the barrier reef, camping along the way on such small islands as Bluefield Range, Spanish Lookout, Colson Caye, Half Moon Caye, and Northeast Caye. Wind-surfers report the best conditions are on the leeward sides of the cayes, especially in the shallow waters west and east of Ambergris Caye and Caye Caulker.

Windsurfers, Sunfish, and Hobie Cats are available for rent at some of the hotels on Ambergris Caye and Caye Caulker, as well as in Placencia and Hopkins. More sailing equipment is being added at outlying resorts, so be sure to inquire in advance if this is a pastime of interest. Some of the larger resorts now offer complimentary windsurfing, Sunfish sailing, and pier fishing in their vacation packages. Even small guest houses often have dories and canoes available for use by visitors. Be aware that currents and winds on the reef can be tricky, especially in the afternoon.

Waterskiing and windsurfing are particularly popular off Ambergris Caye. Check with Amigo Travel for suggestions. The SunBreeze Hotel, Ramon's Village, and Journey's End Caribbean Club on Ambergris all rent equipment, as do the larger hotels on Caye Caulker.

Richard Mahler

Windsurfer off Caye Caulker

From December to August, Slickrock Adventures offers sea-kayaking trips (including windsurfing and kayak surfing) in the waters off Glover's Reef and Ecosummer Expeditions runs kayaking trips around Lighthouse Reef. Canada-based Island Expeditions offers sea-kayak excursions offshore from Dangriga as far as Glover's Reef, and into the interior via the Monkey and Manatee Rivers. The company has extensions to Tikal, Caracol, the Toledo District, and other inland destinations. Monkey River Expeditions has guided kayak trips around Placencia and up the Monkey River. Laughingbird Adventures runs sea-kayaking expeditions from Placencia as far as Honduras. Kayaking equipment is also available in Placencia and on Ranguana Caye from the Ranguana Reef Lodge through their association with Reef-Link Kayaking, a recommended outfitter, particularly for the serious kayaker. On Ambergris Caye, rent kayaks by the hour or day from Travel & Tour Belize, or from the larger hotels. Expect to pay $30 per day for single-seat kayaks, $60 for doubles.

Advance Reading

The best book by far on the region's kayaking is the very detailed *Belize by Kayak*, self-published by Kirk Barrett. To buy a copy, call him at (515) 279-6699, or write to 3806 Cottage Grove, Des Moines, IA 50311.

Those with their own sail or powerboats are well served by Capt. Freya Rauscher's *Cruising Guide to Belize and Mexico's Caribbean Coast* (Wescott Cove Press), which features 119 charts (including a foldout cruising chart for offshore Belize) as well as diagrams, maps, and sailing itineraries.

River Trips, Kayaking, and Sailing Outfitters

Adios Charters, Placencia; 6-23154. 36-foot trimaran for day charters to area cayes for snorkeling.

Amigo Travel, Ambergris Caye; 26-2180, amigotravl@btl.net. Travel agency recommended for outdoor recreation.

Baboon River Canoe Rentals, Burrell Boom, Belize; 28-2101. Boat trips on Belize River and Mussel Creek.

Belize Land and Sea Tours (BLAST), 58 King St., Belize City; tel/fax 2-73897. Wide range of services, including bus excursions, two-man submarine, 34-foot cabin cruiser, and customized tours.

Caye Caulker Sailboats, The Reef Hotel, Caye Caulker; 22-2196. Sailboat rentals.

Ceiba Adventures, Box 2274, Flagstaff, AZ; (520) 527-0171, fax 527-8127, ceiba@primenet.com. Kayaking, whitewater, ruins. Recommended.

Fanta-Sea Charters, Box 768, Belize City; 2-33033, fax 2-3712, or (303) 226-1193. Day and overnight snorkel trips on 45-foot catamaran *Stingray*, based in Belize City at Fiesta Hotel marina. Recommended.

Heritage Navigation, Paradise Hotel Dock, San Pedro, Ambergris Caye; 26-2394. Recommended island and reef cruises on 66-foot sailboat.

Hinterland Tours, 3 Eve St., San Ignacio; 92-2475. River, ruin, and jungle trips.

Island Expeditions, 368-916 West Broadway, Vancouver, BC V5Z 1K7, Canada; (800) 667-1630 or (604) 452-3212, fax (604) 452-3433, island@whistler.net. Sea kayaking, snorkeling, fishing, windsurfing, river floating, camping, photography, birding, caving, archaeology, ecology, Garifuna drumming and culture, diving. Specializing in nature adventures; 4 to 21 days long. A supporter of Belize environmental organizations. Recommended.

Journeys of Discovery, 1516 Duranleau St., Vancouver, BC V6H 354 Canada; (800) 688-8605, Canada (800) 465-8884. Sea-kayaking and rain-forest expeditions.

Monkey River Expeditions, 1731 44th Ave., S.W., Suite 100, Seattle, WA 98116; (206) 660-7777, fax (206) 938-0978, mre@halcyon.com. Monkey River tour by sea kayak; visits to Mayan ruins and caves.

Pegasus Boat Charter, Box 743; 2-31138. Boat charter for reef, river, and caye trips.

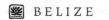

Reef-Link Kayaking, Ranguana Lodge and Reef Resort, Placencia and Ranguana Caye; 6-22027 or (515) 279-6699. Sea kayak rentals and tours; manages bungalows and campground for kayakers on Ranguana Caye. Recommended.

Sailing Fantasy, Ramon's Resort, San Pedro, Ambergris Caye; 2-62439. Catamaran trips and rental, operators of *El Tigre.*

Slickrock Adventures, Box 1400, Moab, UT 84532; (800) 390-5715 or fax (435) 259-6996, slickrock@slickrock.com. Sea kayaking, windsurfing, snorkeling, mountain biking, white-water rafting; week-long trips to Glover's Reef. Recommended.

Sunrise Boat Tours and Charters, Caye Caulker; 2-22195. Trips to cayes near and far, including weekly excursion to Half Moon Caye.

Timeless Tours, 2304 Massachusetts Ave., Cambridge, MA 02140; 27-2119, or (800) 370-0142. Seven to 12-day sailing/camping excursions with 38-foot schooner based in Punta Gorda.

Toni Canoes, 22 Burns Ave., San Ignacio; 92-2267. Offers river and canoe trips.

Travel & Tour Belize, Ambergris Caye; 26-2137. Full-service travel agency in San Pedro.

BIRDING, CAMPING, AND NATURE EXCURSIONS

Largely because of its small population and lack of industry (including a limited amount of agriculture), Belize is blessed with hundreds of square miles of virtually undisturbed animal habitat. Birders in particular, have the opportunity to see hundreds of species in a wide variety of ecosystems. Many of these creatures are still thriving in Belize after becoming locally extinct or endangered in neighboring countries. It's not uncommon to observe 50 or more bird species during a single walk, out of the more than 500 species of residents and migrants that have been recorded here.

Birding

A growing number of hotels and tour companies in Belize are catering to the special needs and interests of birders, and a few (notably Chan Chich near Gallon Jug, Caribbean Villas in San Pedro, and Chau Hiix near Crooked Tree) are targeting birders specifically. You'll find nature trails, recorded species lists, and viewing platforms at many locations throughout the country, particularly among the Cayo District lodges.

Birding tours of Belize are offered by several U.S.-based outfitters, including Victor Emanuel Tours, Massachusetts Audubon Society, and Field Guides. In Belize City, the Belize Audubon Society (originally a chapter of the South Florida Audubon Society) is a terrific resource for birders and can provide several books and bird lists tailored to Belize. I particularly like Dennis Rogers' *La Ruta Maya: A Guide to the Best Birding Locations in the Yucatán, Belize, Guatemala, Honduras, and El Salvador* (Site Guides, 1994). Other recommended guides for the area include Roger Tory Peterson's *Field Guide to Mexican Birds*; *A Guide to the Birds of Mexico and Northern Central America* (Steve N.G. Howell and Sophie Webb); and *A Field Guide to the Birds of Mexico* (Ernest P. Edwards).

The first annual Belize Bird-Fest was held October 2–8, 1998, under sponsorship of the Belize Audubon Society. Northward migration peaks in early October and rare transients can be spotted along with resident birds. Itineraries take birders to reef, wetland, savannah, and forest habitats. The Bird-Fest is organized in cooperation with local hotels, guides, and outfitters, at all-inclusive rates starting at about $1,100 (double-occupancy, excluding airfare). Contact Belize Audubon at 235-004, base@btl.net, www.belizeaudubon.org.

Camping

Camping throughout Belize is restricted by government regulation. Unless otherwise posted or granted, prior permission must be obtained from private owners before camping on deeded land or, on government land, by writing the Ministry of Natural Resources, Attention: Permanent Secretary, Belmopan, Belize, C.A.; 8-22630. Camping is still something of a novelty in Belize, although a growing number of tourism operators cater to campers, and camping is now permitted at many national parks and archaeological sites, with prior permission. Personal items on any camping trip in Belize should include a flashlight, insect repellent, rain gear, sun protection, first aid kit, and waterproof shoes or boots. A set of warm clothes is a good idea, too, since it can get chilly at night.

Throughout this book I've mentioned campsites (and camping fees) wherever I've encountered them. If you're interested in roughing it, you'll have the greatest odds of success at the government protected areas, such as Cockscomb Basin Wildlife Sanctuary, Mountain Pine Ridge Forest Reserve, Monkey Bay National Park, and Chiquibul National Park. Off-shore, inexpensive camping is offered at Glover's Atoll Resort.

Nature Tours

More wildlife tours are coming into their own and many hotels can arrange excursions to suit your particular interest. Many lodges main-tain extensive, well-interpreted nature trails and at least one, Chan Chich, publishes an extensive guidebook to the region's natural habitats (*Exploring the Rainforest*). Another resort, the Hidden Valley Inn, has established a carefully mapped trail network that would take days to navigate. The national parks, sanctuaries, and nature reserves of Belize are all well served by local guides and, in many cases, knowledgeable resident caretakers.

For more than a dozen years, Colorado-based Natural Habitat Adventures, (800) 543-8917, (303) 449-3711, has taken travelers to remote areas of Belize for up-close encounters with wildlife. The company's Belize Explorer trips also highlight the country's rich cultural history. The 10-day trips are limited to 10 travelers and cost about $2,700 each. Destinations include Crooked Tree Lagoon, Lamanai, Hopkins, Gallows Point, Cayo, Cockscomb, and the barrier reef.

The Central American Institute of Prehistoric and Traditional Cultures (CAIPTC), offers a field school and seminar program that includes natural healing and alternative medicine instruction based on medicinal plants found in the forests of Belize. Additional courses are presented on tropical resources and wildlife ecology, with a focus on the relationship between traditional Maya and Garifuna cultures and their environment. CAIPTC maintains a Web site at http://world.std.com. Also recommended: rainforest tours by International Expeditions and Maya Mountain Lodge.

Recommended Belize companies offering guided nature hikes include Pelican Beach Resort, Jaguar Reef Lodge, Jungle River Tours, Melmish Mayan Ecotours, Mountain Equestrian Trails/The Divide Ltd., Chaa Creek Inland Expeditions, Placencia Tours, and Native Guide Systems.

Birding, Camping, and Nature Trek Outfitters

Above The Clouds Trekking, Box 398, Worchester, MA 01062; (800) 233-4499. Nature treks.

Backroads, 801 Cedar St., Berkeley, CA 94710; (800) 462-2848, fax (510) 527-1444. Walking, cycling, and hiking trips, overnights in lodges.

Belize Expeditions, Mile 61, Western Highway, Cayo; 9-23452. Provides natural history guiding services as a Belizean arm of International Expeditions.

Belize Lodge & Excursions, Punta Gorda; 2-70843. Nature and adventure travel outfitter serving the Toledo District. U.S. contact via International Expeditions (see below).

Chaa Creek Inland Expeditions, Box 53, San Ignacio; 9-22037, fax 9-22501, chaacreek@btl.net. Guided expeditions to Mayan ruins, Mountain Pine Ridge, Vaca Plateau, Macal River, Tikal; horseback riding, nature trails, canoeing, trained mules for extended jungle trips.

Crystal Paradise Resort, Cristo Rey Village; 92-2772 or (800) 552-3419, evas@btl.net. Nature treks, birding, horseback riding, Maya ruin tours, cave and river trips. Recommended.

The Divide Ltd., Nord Farm, Mile 63, Western Highway, Central Farm, Cayo; 8-22149, fax 8-23235. Natural history tours, rafting, horseback trips, caving, waterfalls, Mayan ruins, wilderness camping.

Eco Adventures, 632 Emerson St., Palo Alto, CA 94301; (415) 321-1113. Customized nature-oriented itineraries for independent travelers.

Environmental Journeys/Earth Island Institute, 300 Broadway, Suite 28, San Francisco, CA 94133-3312; (510) 655-4526, fax (510) 547-2881. Dolphin research, snorkeling, diving on the barrier reef through Oceanic Society Expeditions.

Field Guides, Box 160723, Austin, TX 78716; (800) 728-4953 or (512) 327-4953. Birding tours.

Forum Travel International, 91 Gregory Lane #21, Pleasant Hill, CA 94523; (510) 671-2900, fax (510) 671-2993, www.forumtravel.com. Adventure and natural history travel throughout Belize, Guatemala, and other Latin American countries.

Great Trips, P.O. Box 1320, Detroit Lakes, MN 56501; (800) 552-3419 or (218) 847-4441, fax (218) 847-4442, belizejq@Tekstar .com. Interior, reef, and sportfishing trips; wide range of destinations including nature reserves, Mayan ruins, and tropical forests.

Holbrook Travel, 3540 NW 13th St., Gainesville, FL 32609; (800) 451-

7111, fax (352) 371-3710. Specialist in educational, natural history, and cultural travel. Small guided tours and custom itineraries.

International Expeditions, One Environs Park, Helena, AL 35080; (800) 633-4734 or (205) 428-1700, fax (205) 428-1714, nature@ietravel.com. Archaeological, birding, barrier reef, and natural history tours; family trips; ecology workshops; rain forest pharmacology workshops; extensions to Tikal; co-sponsor of Crooked Tree Cashew Festival. Recommended.

International Zoological Expeditions, 210 Washington St., Sherborn, MA 01770; (800) 548-5843 or (508) 655-1461, fax (508) 655-4445. Marine and rain forest ecology seminars and excursions in Toledo District and on barrier reef and Glover's Reef. Recommended.

Journeys, 3516 NE 155th, Suite B-2, Seattle, WA 98155; (800) 345-4453. Conservation-oriented tours.

Manomet Bird Observatory, Box 1770, Manomet, MA 02345; (508) 224-6521. Birding tours.

Mark Smith Nature Tours/Full Circle Tours, 2421 Quimy NW, Portland, OR 97210; (503) 223-7716. Natural history/birding specialist.

Massachusetts Audubon Society, 208 South Great Rd., Lincoln, MA 01773; (800) 289-9504. Birding and natural history tours.

Maya Mountain Lodge, Box 46, San Ignacio; 9-22164, fax 92-2029; jungle@mayamountain.com. Excursions to Caracol, Cockscomb Basin Wildlife Sanctuary, and barrier reef; specialists in educational seminars and family-oriented nature travel.

Mountain/Sobek Travel, 6420 Fairmount Ave., El Cerrito, CA 94530; (510) 527-8100. Conservation-oriented expeditions.

Oceanic Society Expeditions, Ft. Mason Center, Bldg. E, San Francisco, CA 94123; (800) 326-7491, fax (415) 474-3395. Dolphin research trips to Blackbird Caye, with extensions to Half Moon Caye, Tikal, and interior Belize; manatee and turtle research trips to Gales Point; bird and howler monkey research trips to Lamanai; tropical marine biology workshops for teachers. Recommended.

Remarkable Journeys, Box 31855, Houston, TX 77231-1855; (800) 856-1993, fax (713) 728-8334, cooltrips@ remjourneys.com. Natural history–oriented interior, reef, and sailing trips with Tikal option, also adventure trips to Mexico and Honduras; yoga retreats in Belize. Recommended.

School for Field Studies, 16 Broadway, Beverly, MA 01952; (508) 927-7777, fax (508) 927-5127. Offers month-long tropical ecology course on Sittee River, with trips to Cockscomb Basin and Wee Wee Caye.

Tread Lightly, One Titus Road, Washington Depot, CT 06794; (800) 627-8227. Rainforest ecology, conservation; contributes to local environmental projects.

University Research Expeditions Program, University of California at Berkeley, Berkeley, CA 94720; (510) 642-6586. Research in environmental studies, archaeology, humanities, paleontology.

Victor Emanuel Nature Tours, Box 33008, Austin, TX 78764; (800) 328-8368 or (512) 328-5221. Birding and other nature-oriented tours.

Voyagers International, Box 915, Ithaca, NY 14851; (607) 257-3091. Natural history, ornithology, photography.

Wilderness Travel, 1102 Ninth St., Berkeley, CA 94710; (800) 368-2794, info@wilderness.com. "Rainforest to reef," 10 day tours.

Winter Escapes, Daniel Weedon, P.O. Box 429, Erickson, MB R0J 0P0, Canada; (204) 636-2968, fax (204) 636-2202. Birding, nature tours.

BICYCLING

A growing number of tour operators, resorts, and lodges are now catering to the needs of bicycle enthusiasts, and an infrastructure is gradually developing. Four of the best are Bike Belize in Belize City, Chaa Creek Cottages and in Pine Ridge Lodge in the Cayo District, and Jungle Reef Lodge in Hopkins. Several lodges, including a couple in the Cayo, now have bicycles available for free or low-cost use by their guests.

The biggest problem bikers will encounter in Belize is the limited network of roads in the country and an even smaller number of trails suitable for bicycle transportation. Belizean roads are notoriously bad, characterized by potholes, mud bogs, sharp rocks, and sand traps. Even the best thoroughfares, such as the Western Highway from Belize City to Benque Viejo, typically have narrow traffic lanes, few service stations, and virtually no shoulders. The quality of bicycles available for rental is also highly variable; avid cyclists should bring their own bicycles for the best experience. Expect to pay $15 to $25 per day for bike rental.

Where to Ride

Currently the most accessible and rewarding area of Belize for bicyclists is the Cayo District, especially the Mountain Pine Ridge forest reserve. Mountain biking is increasingly popular, and a few lodges now have bikes to rent. Try Chaa Creek Cottages near San Ignacio, Pine Ridge Lodge on the Chiquibul Road, or Pacz Hotel in San Ignacio. In the U.S., try Backroads (800-462-2848). Most of the region's many attractions are easily reached from any of the Cayo's lodges or campgrounds, and there are a number of destinations worth visiting. The main routes are well-maintained dirt roads, and they are relatively uncrowded. This area's primary advantages are slightly cooler temperatures and lower humidity than the coast, with relatively few biting insects. Watch for rain, however, as these mostly dirt roads become mud in a hurry.

Side trips from either the Cayo or Belize District include the Belize Zoo, Guanacaste National Park, Community Baboon Sanctuary, Blue Hole National Park, St. Herman's Cave, Five Blues Lake National Park, Crooked Tree Wildlife Sanctuary, Gales Point Manatee Sanctuary, and the Maya ruins of Altun Ha. Because Belize is a narrow country (about 70 miles wide), an ambitious cyclist can make it from Belize City to Guatemala in a single day. A good midpoint is Monkey Bay Wildlife Sanctuary, which welcomes cyclists and provides food, drink, and lodging. Another one-day excursion is from Dangriga to the Cockscomb Basin Wildlife Sanctuary, with interesting rest stops at Hopkins and Maya Center.

Bicycling Hazards

Due to the rainy climate and lush vegetation, trails are often difficult to negotiate, even for those on foot. Bicyclists should be aware that unstable, slick, and mucky surfaces and narrow passageways are the norm off-road, not the exception. Trails are frequently blocked by fallen trees and branches, including those of many plants whose burrs, thorns, and nettles can lead to painful rashes and puncture wounds. Some very common varieties, such as the aptly named "give-and-take" palm and "sticky" bamboo, cause cuts that can easily become infected.

A different set of obstacles confronts bikers setting out on the crowded streets of Belize City and other big towns. Roads are sometimes very narrow and congested, crammed with jostling people, cars, trucks, and other bicycles. In addition, your bike may be much coveted by an impoverished Belizean, so make sure it is secured when unattended. Better yet, bring it indoors whenever possible.

On the cayes, the hard-packed sandy lanes that pass for modest thoroughfares are fine for wide-tired bicycles, but watch those potholes! Ambergris Caye has the most navigable trails, and both Amigo Travel and Travel & Tour Belize in San Pedro (among others) rent bikes for a reasonable fee. The proprietors can direct visitors to scenic areas north and south of the town. On Caye Caulker, the Island Sun Guest House rents bicycles. For those who want to peddle around Corozal, a flat and pretty area, try Stephan Moerman's rental agency at 37 First Avenue.

Bringing Your Bicycle

Customs officials at the international airport and land border crossings are now accustomed to seeing tourists bring bicycles into Belize, but it is a good idea to carry proof of ownership or have your passport stamped with the bike specifically listed by serial number. This is a precaution against having to pay import duty on the item, since authorities may assume the bicycle will be sold in Belize, where they are very expensive. In traveling to the cayes, remember that domestic airplanes are small, propeller-driven craft that may be unable to accommodate large bicycles unless they are disassembled. Most passenger boats and buses, however, can easily store such cargo.

Bicycling Outfitters

Amigo Travel, San Pedro, Ambergris Caye; 26-2180, amigotrav@ btl.net. Scooter and bicycle rental, sailing, other services.

Bike Belize, 104 New Road, Belize City; 2-33855. Moped, minibike, scooter, and bicycle rental; camping, guided tours throughout Belize.

Pacz Hotel, 2 Far West St., San Ignacio; tel./fax 92-2110, pacz.btl.net. Rents mountain bikes suitable for on-road/around-town use.

Pine Ridge Lodge, Box 2079, Belize City; 9-23310, (800) 316-0706, pop.mindspring.com. Mountain bikes for Cayo touring.

HORSEBACK RIDING

One of the best ways to see Belize is from the back of a horse. This is especially true in jungle areas where the terrain is often muddy and steep.

In these situations a sure-footed horse can get you more places—faster—than you're likely to go on your own two legs.

Cayo District horseback riding specialists include Mountain Equestrian Trails, Windy Hill Cottages, Chaa Creek, Parrot's Perch, Ek'Tun, Banana Bank Ranch, and duPlooy's. Easy Rider offers guided trips along the Macal River and through the Mountain Pine Ridge (half and full-day trips available). Our favorite among these is Mountain Equestrian Trails, 8 miles south of the Western Highway on the Mountain Pine Ridge Road. MET's owners, run good, well-trained horses on more than 60 miles of back-country trails, many of them former logging roads. You can ride to remote Maya ruins, caves, waterfalls, and nature reserves—overnight if you'd like.

There are a few outfitters and private individuals who rent horses on Ambergris Caye and in other districts: inquire locally at hotels and travel agencies to contact those currently involved.

Horseback Riding Outfitters

Banana Bank Lodge, Box 48, Belmopan; 81-2020, bbl@btl.net. Terrific riding on a 4000-acre ranch.

Easy Rider, Box 70, San Ignacio; 9-23310. Guided horseback tours, free pick-up and return.

Guacamallo Treks, 1-49117 or c/o S& L Travel, Box 700, Belize City; 2-77593, fax 2-77594. Horseback trips throughout the Cayo, affiliated with Maya Ranch.

Mountain Equestrian Trails, Central Farm P.O., Cayo; 9-23310, fax 8-23505, met@bcsl.com.bz. Horseback riding on 60 miles of trails, also caving and nature tours.

Pacz Hotel, (see listing on previous page). Horseback tours of Cayo.

CAVING

Thanks to its porous limestone topography and moist climate, Belize is an ideal place for the formation of caves. Hundreds of cave systems have been discovered and explored here, and new passages are being discovered every year. Experts believe that one of these underground networks, called the Chiquibul, may be the most extensive in Central America and that, when fully surveyed, it could rank as one of the longest caverns in the world.

Caving Hazards

Caving is a sport with considerable risks, and you're advised to check with knowledgeable locals before attempting any cave adventure. For experienced cavers, Belize can be a dream come true. Underlying most of the country are the kinds of limestone platforms and uplifts that almost guarantee the formation of extensive cavern networks. Unlike the western rim of the Americas, Belize has almost no volcanic activity.

Because of their isolation, some Belizean caves have not been fully explored. It is likely that many entrances have not even been discovered.

According to Logan McNatt, a former Department of Archaeology employee who spent many years exploring Belizean caves, most of these sites should remain closed to the general public. "There are three main problems," McNatt told me. "First, most of the caves are important archaeological sites that have not yet been evaluated or protected. Second, many cave systems of Belize are subject to sudden, unexpected flooding that can make them very dangerous. Finally, few maps of the inner passageways exist."

Cave Archaeology

Many Belize caves show clear evidence of ceremonial usage by the ancient Maya, who considered such places to be sacred passages to the underworld and the domain of the gods. Ceremonial fire pits with ancient ash and charcoal, utility and ceremonial pottery, obsidian knife blades, jade beads, and other artifacts are often found in dusty yet pristine condition.

For those with a keen interest in archaeology and a tour that includes the Caves Branch area, I recommend Far Horizons Archaeological & Discovery Trips, (800) 552-4575 or (505) 822-9100. In the past Far Horizons has offered a package trip called "The Ceremonial Underworld of Belize"—using a Caves Branch Jungle Lodge guide—that brings participants face-to-face with remnants of Maya pitch pine torches, an ancient altar table used in blood-letting and rain-making rites, and an intact human skeleton. The itinerary also includes parts of St. Herman's Cave, Che Chem Ha Cave, Xunantunich, and the possibility of a Tikal extension.

Where to Go

The easiest caves to visit are Che Chem Ha, Río Frío, St. Herman's, Caves Branch, and Barton Creek in the Cayo District; Little Quartz Ridge Blue Creek in the Toledo District; and Blue Hole (a collapsed underwater cave) at Lighthouse Reef. Exploration of any of these—with the exception of Río Frío and St. Herman's—should not be undertaken without an experienced and responsible guide.

In recent years "float trips," on the inflated inner tubes of truck tires, have become popular. The best of the lot is the Caves Branch tour offered by Ian Anderson's Adventure Company through his Caves Branch Jungle Lodge, which explores a sacred Maya cave along the Caves Branch of the Sibun River. The Jaguar Paw Jungle Resort offers similar floats on a separate set of Caves Branch passages. In the Cayo, Mountain Equestrian Trails arranges float trips through Barton Creek Cave. For a high-quality guided tour of an awesome archaeological prize, visit the Che Chem Ha Cave, near the Guatemala border. Owner William Morales and members of his family do the guiding. Fees for each of these trips varies, but you should expect to pay $20 and up. Bring your own flashlight or dive lights if you have them. Slickrock Expeditions also offers excursions to Caves Branch and Footprint Creek caves and Island Expeditions has trips with caving components.

Caving Outfitters

Crystal Paradise Resort, Cristo Rey Village, Cayo District; 9-22823, (800) 552-3419, evas@btl.net. Jeronie Tut, whose family owns and operates this fine lodge on the Macal River, offers tours of nearby caves.

David's Adventure Tours, c/o Martha's Kitchen, San Ignacio; 92-3647. Tours of Barton Creek Cave by one of the area's most experienced cavers.

Hotel Pacz, 2 Far West St., San Ignacio; 92-2110, pacz@btl.net. Co-owner Pete Zugrzycki offers some of the best guided cave tours in Belize, with lots of details about their Mayan use. Recommended.

Ian Anderson's Adventure Tours, Box 356, Belmopan; tel/fax 8-22800, caves@pobox.com. Expeditions by inner tube through cave river systems, jungle expeditions, and dry-land cave trips. Also offers horseback riding, jungle treks, and birding.

Jaguar Paw Jungle Resort, Box 1832, Belize City; 8-3023, (800) 33-JUNGLE, cyoung@btl.net. Cy and Donna Young offer walks through dry caves as well as inner-tube floats on the Caves Branch of the Sibun River. Their lodge is about 45 miles west of Belize City.

Pine Ridge Lodge, Box 2079, Belize City; 9-23310, (800) 316-0706, prlodge@pop.mindspring.com. Manager Richard Roth can arrange guided tours of caves throughout the Cayo District.

Slickrock Adventures, Box 1400, Moab, UT 84532; (800) 390-5715, slickrock@slickrock.com. Dry and tubing cave trips throughout Belize. Recommended.

Tessa Fairweather, 24 Santa María, Belmopan; 8-22412, 8-23234. Specializing in caving, nature tours, and Maya archaeology.

William Morales, c/o Eva's, 22 Burns Ave., San Ignacio; 9-22267 or 9-32109, evas@btl.net. Tours of family-owned Che Chem Ha Cave, an underground Maya ceremonial site in pristine condition. Recommended.

River-tubers enter a cave near Jaguar Paw Jungle Resort.

© Tony Rath

ARCHAEOLOGY TRIPS

There are a handful of outfitters catering specifically to those with an interest in Maya archaeology. My favorite is Far Horizons Expeditions, which is closely involved with on-site archaeologists and offers tours that are usually led by professional archaeologists. Another interesting option is an archaeo-astronomy tour offered by Pennsylvania's Steppingstone Environmental Education Tours, and the focus on shamanism, rainforest medicine, and natural healing (among many other topics) presented in the field schools and seminars of the Central American Institute of Prehistoric and Traditional Cultures (based in Florida and Belize). Various universities in the United States also arrange fieldwork expeditions that "amateurs" can join as short-term volunteers. For an update on who's doing what in Belizean archaeology, contact the government's Department of Archaeology in Belmopan at 8-22106, or the Archaeological Fieldwork Opportunities Bulletin at (800) 228-0810.

Archaeology Outfitters
Central American Institute of Prehistoric and Traditional Cultures, 777 E. Atlantic Ave., Suite Z-376, Delray Beach, FL 33483; (561) 279-2262, fax 279-0518, hacmol@world.std.com. Field school and seminar programs in shamanism, ethnobotany, tropical ecology, and other subjects related to Maya and Garifuna cultures.

Earthwatch, 680 Mt. Auburn St., Watertown, MA 02272; (800) 776-0188, www.earthwatch.org. Work-study archaeological tours.

Far Horizons Archaeological and Discovery Trips, P.O. Box 91900, Albuquerque, NM 87199-1900; (800) 552-4575 or (505) 822-9100, journey@farhorizon.com, www.farhorizon.com. "Cultural discovery" trips to Maya villages and ruins, led by archaeologists trained in Belize; Far Horizons also can arrange canoeing, horseback riding, fishing, snorkeling, caving, wildlife observation, and boat trips. Highly recommended.

Institute of Mayan Antiquities, 6828 Wofford Drive, Dallas, TX 75227; (214) 381-2311. Remote-sensing research trips to Maya ruins.

Maya Research Program, St. Mary's University, Box 15376, San Antonio, TX 78212; (512) 826-1672. Fieldwork at Blue Creek site in Orange Walk District; contact Thomas H. Guderjan.

Steppingstone Environmental Education Tours, P.O. Box 373, Narberth, PA 19072; (800) 874-8784, fax (610) 649-3428. Vacation and educational tours for school groups, nature and archaeology enthusiasts, and birders. Botanical artists workshops. Supports conservation.

University of Pennsylvania Museum of Archaeology and Anthropology, 33rd & Spruce Sts., Philadelphia, PA 19104; (215) 898-9202. Tours of Maya ruins led by archaeologists and anthropologists active in the field.

University Research Expeditions Program, University of California at Berkeley, Berkeley, CA 94720; (510) 642-6586, fax (510) 642-6791. Research expeditions in archaeology, including Río Hondo sites; develops cooperative projects with scientists from developing nations.

Vincent Gillett, Department of Archaeology, Belmopan; 8-22106. Archaeology tours.

Wildland Adventures, 3516 NE 155th St., Seattle, WA 98155; (800) 345-4453. Tours specializing in Maya archaeology, cultural diversity, tropical nature, and the barrier reef; hires local guides and contributes to conservation and community projects through the Earth Preservation Fund.

VOLUNTEER OPPORTUNITIES

There are many ways you can do volunteer work in Belize, whether it's sifting through Maya ruins, counting howler monkeys, or observing dolphin behavior. These opportunities are often offered by specialized outfitters based in the United States and Canada. Other excellent resources include the specialized magazines and newsletters catering to specific interest groups. *Archaeology* magazine, for instance, publishes an ongoing roster of volunteer fieldwork opportunities in its "Travel Guide" section. Some organizations distribute catalogues that describe their trips in detail. The catalogue of *Oceanic Society Expeditions*, for example, lists volunteer research trips involving dolphins, manatees, howler monkeys, and sea turtles.

For those with an interest in ancient Maya ruins, the nonprofit Programme for Belize (2 S. Park St., Belize City, 2-71248; pfbel@btl.net) offers tours that include direct involvement in the excavation of La Milpa, a ceremonial site in northwestern Belize. A similar project, developed with the Lamanai Outpost Lodge, offers a chance to help archaeologists.

Even though you're volunteering your time and labor, you'll likely pay for your own trip, including airfare, food, and lodging, although you may get discount rates. Because the Belize government is essentially broke and its business community is small, we encourage you to consider these travel options, which can be very rewarding.

Volunteer Opportunities

Earthwatch, 680 Mt. Auburn Ave., Watertown, Massachusetts; (800) 776-0188, www.earthwatch.org. Volunteers drive research in sea grass ecology and other marine habitats.

Global Citizens Network, St. Paul, MN; (800) 644-9292. Past projects include renovating schools and installing water systems in Maya villages. **Institute for Central American Development Studies**, P.O. Box 025216, Department 826, Miami, FL 33102-5216. Internships dealing with social justice, agriculture, and immigration.

Oceanic Society Expeditions, Ft. Mason Center, Bldg. E, San Francisco, CA 94123; (800) 326-7491. Volunteer fieldwork involving monkeys, dolphins, sea turtles, and manatees.

BELIZE CITY

5

Characterizing Belize City as the nation's hub is an understatement. For many, this community of about 70,000 residents *is* Belize. Located on the Caribbean Sea at the mouth of Haulover Creek (a name given to the last few miles of the Belize River), this port town is the country's largest urban center. Belize City supports a growing tourism infrastructure, as well as other services, industries, and retail businesses. Despite the relative hustle and bustle, it still manages to retain a decidedly laid-back atmosphere. This may be the busiest place in Belize, but don't expect anything to get done in a hurry.

Sadly, the reputation of Belize City has gone from bad to worse in recent years, fueled by well-publicized accounts of street crime, drug trafficking, and panhandling. There seems to be no end to the number of horror stories visitors tell about their unfortunate adventures in this ramshackle, slightly seedy community. It's my opinion that Belize City is not as dangerous as many people make it out to be, although reasonable precautions should be taken when going from one place to another, especially on foot. An upgrading of security here is ongoing.

I have found that here, as elsewhere in the country, 99 percent of Belizeans are helpful, courteous, and genuinely happy to welcome visitors. In my view, Belize City's smiling residents and relaxed pace are among its greatest attractions. From hotel employees to restaurant workers, bank tellers to conservation leaders, almost everyone is eager to share information and exchange pleasantries. This laid-back, tolerant attitude is perhaps a tribute to Belize City's colorful history and multicultural traditions.

HISTORY

The first full-time residents of what is now Belize City are believed to have been the ancient Maya, who maintained a busy fishing camp on nearby Moho Caye (now a private diving resort) for several centuries. Bones and other artifacts excavated at this site suggest there was abundant marine life, including large numbers of turtles and manatees. In the late 1600s, after the area had been mostly abandoned by the Maya, pirates from Scotland, England, and France began to spend time during the annual rainy season at the mouth of the Belize River. Over the years, these buccaneers and their African slaves harvested tropical hardwoods in the interior and used the broad, slow-moving waterway to float the precious timber to oceangoing vessels anchored offshore.

By the 18th century, the settlement of Belize Town had been solidly established by members of what the British referred to as their Bay Settlement (named after the nearby Bay of Honduras). Historians say the city is built on a foundation of loose coral, logwood chips, and rum bottles. Whatever its exact composition, this pile of debris seems to be sinking, as much of the urban area is now barely above sea level. Despite this swampy environment, the climate is fairly pleasant, owing to near-constant trade winds and an aggressive, ongoing government campaign against mosquito larvae.

Several violent hurricanes and accompanying surges have battered

A British Caribbean–style guest house in the Ft. George district of Belize City

Belize City over the years. These storms occur primarily in autumn, as evidenced by Hurricane Hattie's destructive visit on October 31, 1961, which took hundreds of lives and nearly leveled the town. This was the prime motivation for Belizeans to move their capital some 45 miles inland to Belmopan, even though most residents have chosen to take their chances by staying in Belize City. (Only about 6,000 people reside permanently in Belmopan and a large percentage of government workers commute every day.) In spite of Mother Nature's unpredictable and sometimes destructive forces, Belize City remains home to about one-third of the country's population.

GETTING AROUND BELIZE CITY

Walking alone in certain areas—ask at your hotel or travel agency for a detailed description of trouble spots—is not recommended because a small but aggressive contingent of Belizeans is persistent in demanding money or selling drugs. At night, a single person on foot may encounter even more significant trouble; the dangers of being attacked and robbed are very real here. Taxis within Belize City's limits are inexpensive and readily available. I advise you to use them, and to avoid carrying unnecessary valuables on your person.

Although Belize City does have a local bus system, I hesitate to recommend it because routes are confusing and not well posted. Watch for the radio-equipped Tourism Police (identified by special uniforms and caps), who patrol heavily-touristed areas on foot and are trained to answer visitors' questions as well as to keep the peace.

Taxis

Within Belize City itself, taxis—any vehicles with green license plates—are generally the best way to travel, unless you have your own car or have arranged transportation in advance. In 1999, standard fare was about $2.50 for most in-city destinations. A taxi can be hired for $15 an hour for out-of-town trips. Remember, tipping of taxi drivers is not customary in Belize.

From the Airport

From **Phillip Goldson International Airport**, the 15-minute taxi ride into Belize City cost $15 in 1999. Rates are fixed by an informal cab-drivers' union—which squeezed out a hotel shuttle service a few years ago—so it does no good to bargain or shop around.

Visitor Information

The main office of the **Belize Tourist Board** is at 83 N. Front Street, 2-77213. Go up two flights and the friendly staff will answer your questions and give you informative brochures about the country. Guidebooks, maps, T-shirts, and other items are on sale. (Like most businesses, the Tourist Board is closed from noon to 1 p.m.) Also try the Belize Tourism Industry Association at 99 Albert Street (2-75717).

SHOPPING

Romac's Supermarket, at 27 Albert Street, and **Brodie's,** directly across the street at the corner of Albert and Regent, come in handy for all those provisions you need for exploring the barrier reef or tropical forest. Brodie's has a pharmacy, a produce section, and an exceptionally good selection of Belizean books and magazines. You can stock up on even cheaper fruits and vegetables at the public market, in the **New Custom's House** about three blocks north on Regent Street.

Among the best places to buy Belizean souvenirs are the **National Handicrafts Centre**, at 3 Fort Street in the old TACA warehouse, 2-33636, and **Go Tees & Graphics**, 23 Regent Street, 2-74082. The **Belize Audubon Society,** 12 N. Front Street, 2-34987, sells T-shirts, hats, nature books, and other gift items. Belize isn't particularly known for its arts and crafts, but some carvings, baskets, and weavings are good buys. I urge you to avoid buying products made of endangered wildlife, such as turtles, black coral, big cats, or crocodiles.

TRAVEL AGENCIES

Belize City is an ideal place to finalize travel arrangements and pick up lots of insider tips on things to do. I recommend, particularly for the ecology-minded visitor, **Jal's Travel,** 148 N. Front Street, 2-45407, and **Tubroos Tree Adventures**, 146 Barracks Road, 2-33398. **Belize Land Air Sea Tours**, 27 Dean Street, 2-73897, provides daily Belize City tours as well as customized, nature-oriented excursions.

For day trips to the howler monkey sanctuary, Altun Ha, and other northern destinations, I particularly recommend tour guide **Winston Seawell,** 2-31979, manager of the **G & W Holiday** travel agency, 2-52461 at the International Airport and 14-8756 on his mobile phone. Expect to pay $50 and up for such day trips. Make sure your guide is knowledgeable before you leave.

THINGS TO SEE AND DO

Several landmarks have withstood the various hurricanes and can be seen during even a brief walking or taxi tour of Belize City. Another good way to see the city is via guided tour buses.

At the gateway to Belize Harbor is **Fort George Lighthouse**, dominating a finger of land that was originally the easternmost point on what once was **Fort George Island**. The channel separating the island and mainland was filled in during the 1920s, long after Fort George had fulfilled its function as an army base. Views of nearby cayes covered in mangroves now await visitors to the site, and brown pelicans often fish in small groups near the shore.

Next to the lighthouse is a small park and the **Baron Bliss Memorial**, a tribute to the "Fourth Baron Bliss of the former Kingdom of Portugal," Henry Edward Ernest Victor Bliss. An Englishman by birth, this eccentric adventurer sailed to Belize in 1926 and fell in love with its soothing climate, unspoiled waters, and palm-studded islands. As a result of food poisoning Bliss suffered in Trinidad, the baron was too ill to come ashore.

Belize schoolgirls find that their books make effective sun shades.

He spent several months aboard his yacht, the *Sea King*, fishing in the harbor as he tried to recover his health. Bliss was impressed by the kindness and respect fellow sportfishermen and colonial officials showed him. Before Bliss died aboard his boat, he specified in his will that a trust fund of almost $2 million be established for the sole benefit of Belizeans.

The interest generated from the Bliss Fund has been used to help build clinics, water systems, and libraries. The baron stipulated that a portion of the trust funds be used to stage an annual yacht regatta in Belizean waters. This is the focal event of the national holiday on March 9, which honors his contributions.

In the heart of Belize City, at the corner of Front and Queen Streets, is a wooden colonial-style building that houses the main post office. Here in the **Paslow Building** you may purchase the colorful Belizean stamps, among the most beautiful in the world. They depict brocket deer, storks, marine life, tapir, jaguar, macaws, and many other native animals. Postage rates are one of the few bargains in Belize. A special sales counter for stamp collectors is on the Queen Street side of the post office. Upstairs, some of the best maps of Belize (divided into north and south sections) are available from a government office for about $10 each.

Facing the main post office is the **Swing Bridge**, reportedly the only such manually-operated bridge still in service. It was constructed in Liverpool, England, and has been cranked open for Haulover Creek's high-masted boat traffic since 1923. At about 6 a.m. and 5:30 p.m.,

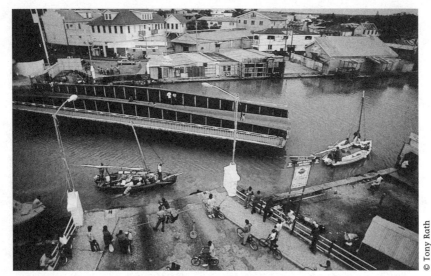

© Tony Rath

The Swing Bridge over Haulover Creek

police officers stop pedestrians and vehicles on either side of the bridge while men insert long poles into a capstan and gradually open a passageway that allows tall-masted vessels to pass upriver or out to sea. The swing mechanism was upgraded in 1998 but still depends on musclepower.

Next to the bridge, in the renovated historic fire station, is the **Maritime Museum and Boat Terminal**, with scheduled water taxi service to Caye Caulker and Ambergris Caye. Several gift shops and cafés are under the roof of this large building, along with restrooms and a pay telephone. The terminal opens at 7 a.m. and closes at 6 p.m. The museum, which describes Belize's maritime history and marine ecology, is open from 8 a.m. to 4 p.m. daily (admission $2).

South of the Swing Bridge, facing Battlefield Park on Regent Street, is the imposing **Supreme Court Building**. Built in 1923 in classic British Colonial–style (complete with dome-topped clock tower), it stands on the site of the original settlement courthouse built in 1818. The courthouse has been rebuilt twice: It was demolished in 1878 and destroyed again in a 1918 fire that took the life of then-governor William Hart Bennett. For a slice-of-life experience, step into a courtroom and watch the Belizean justice system in action.

Near the courthouse on Bliss Promenade (also called the Southern Foreshore) is the **Baron Bliss Institute**, which, with its modern-looking circular second floor, seems out of place amid the Victorian gingerbread of Belize City's oldest neighborhood. The institute displays (poorly) some ancient Maya artifacts from Caracol and other Belizean archaeological sites. It also houses a modest public library, auditorium, and art gallery, as well as the **National Arts Council**. Slide shows and lectures on science, history, conservation, and culture are held here. If you go, take a taxi; this has become a tough neighborhood in recent years.

Headquartered on the south side of the Swing Bridge, near the busy intersection of Regent and Albert Streets, is Belize City's main public market, housed in a modern three-story building called the **New Customs House**. Another public market operates in an old warehouse on North Front Street, a few blocks west of the Fort George Lighthouse.

At the south end of Regent Street is a venerable mansion called **Government House**, a historic British Colonial landmark that is now a museum (open weekdays 8:30 a.m. to noon and 1 p.m. to 4:30 p.m., admisson $2.50.). In this former residence of the colony's governors, you'll see archival records and artifacts in addition to well-curated exhibits documenting the history of British Honduras. Take a few minutes to stroll the beautiful grounds and imagine the grand receptions once held here. There's even a tiny swimming pool—the first ever in Belize!

Across the street is **St. John's Anglican Cathedral**, the first Protestant church in Central America and one of the oldest buildings in Belize. Built in 1812 by slaves using bricks brought over as ballast in the hulls of ships from Europe, the church was the site of three coronation ceremonies for Indian "kings" of the Mosquito Coast, held between 1816 and 1845. These self-styled kings were members of an indigenous ruling class that once presided over the native tribes that lived along what is now the Caribbean coast of Honduras and Nicaragua. Inside the church are dozens of plaques commemorating prominent Anglican colonists, and you're welcome to wander around. Admission is free.

Belize City nightlife is pretty much restricted to dancing at hotels (Fiesta and Bellvue), karaoke (Radisson and Biltmore), and bar-hopping.

BUS SERVICE TO OTHER PARTS OF BELIZE

There are several bus stations in Belize City, each corresponding to the several competing companies that serve outlying areas. Because these terminals are in questionable neighborhoods, we recommend taking a taxi rather than walking to them. Buses to most large towns depart hourly throughout the morning, less often in the afternoon and evening. One-way bus fares average about $1.50 for each hour of travel. Smaller bus companies serving specific villages depart from other locations (inquire locally for details).
• **Batty**—for points north and west, 15 Mosul St., 2-72025, fax 2-78991
• **Dawson Buses**—Bermudias Landing, Barracks Road (no phone)

- **James**—for points south, Pound Yard Bridge
- **Jex Brothers**—to Crooked Tree, Magazine Road (no phone)
- **Novelo's**—for points west, 19 W. Collet Canal, 2-71160 or 2-7732
- **Venus**—for points north, Magazine Road, 2-73354
- **Z-Line** —for points south, Magazine Road, 2-73937

CAR RENTAL

For those who want to rent a car for their visit, I recommend **Crystal** at 1.5 Mile Northern Highway, 2-31600 or 2-30921. The American owner offers a wide variety of slightly used cars, vans, and even motor homes at reasonable prices (all major credit cards accepted). A good four-wheel-drive specialist is **Safari**, International Airport and 73 Eve Street which rents only well-maintained Isuzu Troopers: 2-35395, (800) 447-2931, safari@btl.ne.

Other vehicles are available at the offices of **Avis,** at both airports, 2-52385; **Budget**, Mile 5 Northern Highway, 2-32435, jmagroup@btl.net; **National**, 126 Freetown Road; and **Hertz** (Radisson Ft. George), 2-35395, and at the international airport, 2-31586. Inquire about road conditions before you select your car; some destinations require four-wheel-drive.

Rates for car rentals are surprisingly high, starting at about $65 a day, plus $15 per day for insurance. Comprehensive insurance is not generally available in Belize and, unless stated otherwise, the person renting the car may be held responsible for any and all damage, including flat tires. The best insurance terms are offered by Budget. Gasoline prices are about double what you'd pay in the United States or Canada. There are few gas stations, so fill up while you can.

GETTING TO THE ISLANDS FROM BELIZE CITY

The Marine Transportation Terminal on N. Front Street (immediately east of the Swing Bridge) coordinates water taxi service to Caye Caulker and Ambergris Caye. An 11:50 a.m. express boat takes passengers to Chetumal, Mexico, where bus connections are easily made to Cancún and Mérida.

Allow about 45 minutes for the trip to Caulker ($7.50 one-way, $12.50 round-trip), 75 minutes to Ambergris ($15 one-way, $25 round-trip), and roughly 2 hours to Chetumal (prices start at $30, one-way). Note that round-trip fares to the islands are for *same day* return only. Departure times and rates are posted inside the terminal, which has food vendors, gift shops, and a maritime museum. In 1999 there were five daily water taxi departures for Caulker but only one (at 9 a.m.) for San Pedro.

There is a scheduled daily departure for Ambergris Caye by the *Andrea* from the Bellevue pier, in front of the Bellevue Hotel on Marine

Parade. Prices are similar to those charged at the Marine Transportation Terminal. You can bargain among independent boat operators moored along Haulover Creek for trips to other islands, or at the Texaco station terminal, off 73 N. Front Street.

WHERE TO STAY IN BELIZE CITY

Bellevue Hotel, 5 Southern Foreshore; $60; 2-77051, fax 2-73253, fins@btl.net. On the waterfront, with modern rooms and a lively upstairs bar decorated like an old ocean liner. Boat service to Ambergris Caye and Caye Caulker. Good restaurant.

Best Western Biltmore Plaza, Mile 3, Northern Highway; $100 and up; 2-32302 and (800) 528-1234. A luxury hotel near the airport, with a consistently bad reputation.

Chateau Caribbean Hotel, 6 Marine Parade; $85; 2-30800, chateauc@btl.net. Comfortably upscale, with an ocean view and sea breeze (if you ask for a waterfront room). The restaurant and bar, which also feature a Caribbean view, are fairly good. The Chateau has been a consistent supporter of natural history tourism in Belize.

Colton House, 9 Cork St.; $60; 2-44666, fax 2-30451, coltonhse@ btl.com. A five-room, 1928 colonial-style wooden house with high ceilings and paddle fans. The spacious "garden room" apartment ($60) is equipped with TV, fridge, coffeemaker, and air-conditioning. The Belizeans who run the place are happy to answer any and all questions about what to see and do hereabouts. This is my favorite guest house in the breeze-cooled Ft. George neighborhood.

Fiesta Inn & Marina, Newtown Barracks Road; $100 and up; 2-32670 or (800) 343-7821, fiestainbz@btl.net. Belize City's biggest hotel, boasting all the goodies one would expect with a high-rise price tag. Several decent restaurants lie within; try the Calypso.

Fort Street Guest House, 4 Fort St.; $65, breakfast included; 2-30116 or (800) 240-FORT, fax 2-78808, fortst@btl.net. This classy B&B occupies six rooms above a co-owned first-rate restaurant and gift shop. A long-time favorite of conservationists (although the shared bath may give some folks pause). American owners Hugh and Teresa Parkey are experts on things to do in Belize, and Hugh runs a full-service dive shop.

Hotel Mopán, 55 Regent St.; $35; 2-77351, hotelmopan@btl.net. A clean but rather shabby establishment with a modest restaurant and bar.

The Mopán is run by Jean and Tom Shaw, longtime environmentalists who can answer questions about any of Belize's "natural destinations." Some shared baths.

North Front Street Guest House, 124 N. Front St., 2-77595. An old favorite among budget travelers, with eight simple rooms that share a bath. Not the best neighborhood, but close to the water taxi terminal. Practically across the street is another good budget hotel: the **Mira Río**, at 59 N. Front St., 2-44970. Note: the downstairs bar can get noisy.

Radisson Ft. George Hotel, 2 Marine Parade; $120 and up; (800) 333-3333 or 2-77400, rdfgh@btl.net. This modern, upmarket hotel has a well-stocked gift shop, very good restaurant (especially breakfast), swimming pool, and bar. You can rent Avis cars here, and the hotel maintains a full-service marina across the street. It also owns the **Great House**, 2-77400, across the street, which offers similar rooms and amenities.

Seaside Guest House, 3 Prince St.; $5 dorm, $14 private; 2-78339, friends@btl.net. Basic but clean and secure lodging for those on a budget. Shared bath; Quaker run. Breakfast available.

WHERE TO EAT IN BELIZE CITY

Dit's, 50 King St. The best pastries and Creole cowfoot soup in town.

El Centro Hotel, 4 Bishop St. Excellent, reasonably priced pizza and authentic Creole cuisine. Air-conditioned.

Fort Street Restaurant, 4 Fort St. One of the best places to eat in Belize City, serving excellent and imaginatively prepared dishes (albeit at a borderline-exorbitant price).

G G's Café and Patio, 2B King St. A pleasant courtyard atmosphere, efficient service, and good food; try the Creole-style grilled chicken.

Macy's Café, 18 Bishop St. Serves Belize's inexpensive and ubiquitous main dish of rice 'n' beans, with extras ranging from stewed chicken to freshly squeezed lemonade. Actor Harrison Ford ate here during the filming of Mosquito Coast some years back and proclaimed Macy's his favorite restaurant anywhere. But not even a movie star's presence affects the casual atmosphere, friendly staff, and humble furnishings. Do the natural world a favor, though, and resist the temptation to order wild game, which appears occasionally on the menu here and at a number of other Belizean restaurants.

Mango's, near the Fiesta Hotel at 164 Newtown Barracks Rd. Very good steak and seafood dinners.

The Marlin, 11 Regent St., West. Very good Belizean cuisine.

New Chon Saan Palace, 184 N. Front St. Some of the biggest portions of the best Chinese food in town. Air-conditioned.

Pizza House, 11 King St. Excellent pizza!

IN CASE OF EMERGENCY
The most modern medical facility in Belize, Karl Heusner Memorial Hospital, is on Princess Margaret Drive (23-1548). Private physicians can be visited at Belize Medical Associates, 5791 St. Thomas Street (2-30303). Well-stocked pharmacies include Brodie's Department Store (Albert and Regent Streets), Central Drug Store (1 Market Square), and Community Drug Store (Albert St.). For emergency calls to the police, dial 911; for fire and ambulance call 90.

INTERNET SERVICES
The staffers of many Belize City hotels will share use of their e-mail accounts with guests as a courtesy for a small fee. E-mail services are also available at BTL (the government-owned telephone company) on Church Street and at Angelus Press at 10 Queen Street. (2-35777).

MEXICO

CHETUMAL
Bahia de Chetumal
COROZAL
YUCATAN PENINSULA
Banco Chinchorro
XCALAC

ORANGE WALK TOWN

NORTHERN HIGHWAY
OLD NORTHERN HIGHWAY

Ambergris Caye

SAN PEDRO

Caye Caulker
Caye Chapel
Long Caye

Moho Caye
St. George's Caye
Drowned Cayes
Crawl Caye
Northern Two Caye

BELIZE CITY

Spanish Lookout Caye

Turneffe Islands

Lighthouse Reef

Goff's Caye
English Caye
Blackbird Caye

HIGHWAY
COASTAL HIGHWAY

WESTERN
BELMOPAN

Middle Long Caye
Bluefield Range
Alligator Caye
Half Moon Caye
Long Caye

GALES POINT
Caye Bokel

HUMMINGBIRD HIGHWAY

Southern Long Caye

Caribbean Sea

DANGRIGA
Tobacco Caye
South Water Caye

HOPKINS

BELIZE

SOUTHERN HIGHWAY

Carrie Bow Caye
Glovers Reef
Northeast Caye
Wee Wee Caye
Long Caye
Southwest Caye
Middle Caye

Gladden Caye
Wippari Caye

BIG CREEK
PLACENCIA
Laughingbird Caye

MONKEY RIVER TOWN

Ranguana Caye

Wild Cane Caye

Snake Cayes

Sapodilla Cayes
Hunting Caye
Nicholas Caye

PUNTA GORDA

B a r r i e r   R e e f

0 SCALE   39 KILOMETERS   39 MILES   INTERNATIONAL BOUNDARY

N

THE CAYES AND THE ATOLLS

6

The main—and often the only—attraction of interest to many first-time visitors to Belize is the country's barrier reef, a spectacular coral-based formation that runs almost the entire 185-mile length of the east coast and swings from within 10 to 40 miles of the mainland. In sheer size, this magnificent natural wonder is surpassed only by Australia's Great Barrier Reef and a couple of others in the South Pacific. It is by far the largest barrier reef in the Western Hemisphere.

One of the richest ecosystems on the planet, Belize's reef is punctuated by scores of beautiful tiny cayes (pronounced "keys"), sand bores, patch reefs, canyons, and various underwater structures that are home to 220 species of fish and untold hundreds of varieties of invertebrates—all thriving in relatively clear, unpolluted, 78- to 86-degree water.

So exquisite is this habitat that the United Nations has named the reef as a World Heritage Site, arguing that its deterioration or disappearance would result in "a harmful impoverishment of the heritage of all nations of the world." One writer has equated the experience of snorkeling here to "sipping a fine glass of wine and soaking in a Jacuzzi at the same time, the water teeming with a mirage of color."

Belize finds itself engaged in a delicate balancing act. It vigorously promotes tourism, diving, snorkeling, and fishing on its barrier reef, while at the same time struggles to protect this exceedingly fragile environment from harmful human influence. Certain commercial species, such as lobster, conch, and shrimp, are already severely depleted, and some irreversible damage has been done to the reef by careless fishermen and visitors. It's important to realize that the reef is a living entity, dependent for its very existence on the health of living coral polyps and other reef-building organisms. Coral Forest (www.blacktop.com/coralforest) is a nonprofit group that posts "action alerts" about activities around the world that endanger reefs and provides guidelines for writing effective protest letters. The Nature Conservancy is a partner in Reef Check, www.ust.hk/~webrc/reef, which monitors reef ecology in Belize and elsewhere. If you see someone damaging a reef, contact either organization—and local officials—at once.

The government is involved in an aggressive public education and environmental protection campaign to preserve and protect its marine resources. Among other things, this involves shifting some foreign visitors away from high-impact areas—namely the Ambergris-Caulker-Chapel Caye corridor—toward lesser-known destinations that can more easily absorb the impact of newcomers. Impending development on Ambergris Caye prompted the government to declare the northern two-thirds of the island off-limits to further exploitation, but not before one last major project broke ground.

Despite this trend, there are still dozens of islands along the southern half of the reef that are completely uninhabited and have much to offer visitors, including first-rate scuba diving, snorkeling, sailing, kayaking, windsurfing, and fishing. Also overlooked in most discussions of Belize's coastal waters are the several atolls, banks, and offshore reefs that exist beyond the barrier strip. As a whole, Belize has an estimated 350 miles of coral reef line and 280 square miles of island land mass. About 25 cayes have lodging.

The atolls and southernmost cayes are not as accessible and have more limited accommodations than the northern barrier reef islands, but they do offer some very unusual and rewarding experiences. For serious anglers and divers, these sites provide the chance to fish and dive in little-disturbed natural environments that teem with marine life.

Since many outer destinations are an easy day trip from the hotels on Ambergris Caye and Caye Caulker, it is arguably more efficient to use those islands (or Belize City) as a base for exploring such remote offshore locations as Lighthouse Reef and the Turneffe Islands (or Glover's Reef from Dangriga). Although there are places to stay and eat on these atolls, cost and access may be a problem for travelers with tight budgets or time constraints. Those fortunate enough to have their own kayaks and sail or powerboats will be pleased to know that the barrier reef provides innumerable safe anchorages and some of the finest paddling and sailing conditions anywhere.

THE BARRIER REEF AND CAYES

Most of the 200-odd cayes of Belize lie in relatively shallow water along the barrier reef itself. The long, narrow stretch of water between the reef and the mainland—known as the Inner Channel—is also dotted with small islands, as are some of the country's inland lagoons.

The word *caye* is testimony to the varied history of the islands. It is a corruption of the Spanish cayo, translated as "small island." Early Spanish explorers were the first Europeans to set foot on the barrier chain, and they apparently stopped regularly to obtain fresh water and repair their ships. The Spaniards no doubt encountered the Maya, who established many fishing and trading outposts here over a period of centuries.

English, French, and Scottish pirates, along with Puritan traders, were next to arrive. They found the cayes ideally suited for their respective sea-based livelihoods, and old coins, bottles, and tools are sometimes still found on the sandy beaches, along with Maya pottery and other artifacts. Europeans also settled here as fishermen, whalers, and plantation owners. They were joined in the late 1800s by a wave of Mexican immigrants eager to escape the brutal Yucatán Caste Wars.

AMBERGRIS CAYE

Getting There: From Belize City, 15 minutes by plane or 1¼ hours by boat.

Main Activities: Diving, snorkeling, fishing, windsurfing, kayaking, birding, sailing.

Visitor Information: Ambergris Caye's Web site, www.ambergriscaye .com, provides access to home pages of hotels, dive shops, restaurants, and other tourist-related businesses. The Belize Tourist Board and Belize Tourism Industry Association's Belize Visitor & Tours, on Pescador Drive, north of the airstrip; 26-2728, fax 26-2402.

The largest and best known of the cayes, Ambergris is part of a wide limestone peninsula dangling south from the Yucatán coast of the Mexican state of Quintana Roo.

Most Ambergris residents are of Mexican ancestry and speak Spanish among themselves. Early in Belize's history, its northern neighbor even laid claim to the island. Ambergris Caye has about the same land area as the Caribbean island of Barbados, although much of Ambergis is uninhabitable mangrove swamp.

The island's name is a holdover from colonial days and refers to a waxy substance found in sperm whale intestines that was once used in making perfume. Some say that ambergris washed up here regularly

Richard Mahler

Downtown San Pedro along Front Street

during the colony's early history, but marine biologists are skeptical. They maintain that whales have never been common in this part of the Caribbean and argue that sightings of ambergris have always been very rare.

Most visitors reach the island by taking a boat or airplane across lower Chetumal Bay from Belize City, 35 miles to the southwest. Locals refer to passenger boats as "skiffs" and their smaller canoe-like vessels as "dories." The crossing takes about 1¼ hours by skiff and less than 15 minutes by plane.

Fishing was once the caye's principal industry, but within the last 20 years tourism has taken over. Many fishers now use their boats exclusively to cater to visitor needs: snorkeling, sportfishing, diving, and manatee watching. **San Pedro**, the island's only town, offers a wide choice of hotels, restaurants, bars, gift shops, outfitters, and travel agencies to suit every recreational interest and pocketbook, although food and services are relatively expensive here.

While San Pedro in some ways seems to be suffering under the strain of rapid growth, Ambergris Caye still has much to offer. People are friendly, accommodations are comfortable, and there's plenty to do. Resorts on the outskirts of San Pedro are noticeably more expensive, but tend to be more tranquil and luxurious than hotels in town. Hikers and bicyclists will find that much of the island is covered with a high broadleaf forest interspersed with freshwater sinks that attract lots of wildlife, including an abundance of birds.

Birders can spot warblers, egrets, herons, pelicans, and frigate birds. **Bird Caye**, located on the bay (leeward) side of Ambergris, shelters rookeries for 30 species, including the reddish egret, greater egret, and cormorant. Spoonbills, avocets, and ducks also congregate here. Turtles nest on certain yet-undeveloped beaches, and even large cats prowl through the mangroves. Thousands of shells litter the beaches. (The coral reef is less than a mile offshore.)

Ambergris has the largest single concentration of tourist services in Belize yet still manages to retain a laid-back atmosphere. The streets are sandy and belong to slow-paced strollers. Vehicles (mostly electric golf carts) are few and far between. The water is iridescent blue and immediately accessible. A cooling trade wind sweeps in from the northeast much of the time, keeping insect pests at bay. A variety of food and drink is available, and some of the country's best cooks are happy to prepare fresh seafood exactly the way you like it.

The vast majority of San Pedro's 2,000 residents are good-humored and tolerant, their lifestyle casual and simple. The tin-roofed, colorfully painted wooden houses are cheerfully dilapidated, giving the distinct impression that you can relax all day if that's your choice.

For all these reasons, Ambergris Caye makes a fine base for excursions to nearby attractions and the more distant islands. Experienced guides are easy to find and some of the best outfitters for fishing, snorkeling, windsurfing, sailing, kayaking, and diving are based here. There are massive coral canyons full of caves and tunnels near San Pedro, and snorkelers report aquarium-like conditions. Within the confines of the reef itself, the **Mata Rocks** and **Mexico Rocks** area on the windward side are highly recommended. (See Chapter 4 for other snorkel and dive spots.) Conditions are ideal here and among the island's 13 lagoons for sailing, windsurfing, and kayaking.

Travel Tips

A few words of caution are in order. Some of the more than 700 hotel rooms on Ambergris Caye are very basic by American or European standards. Furnishings and other physical amenities are usually minimal, so what you're paying for often is location and service, not luxury. For most visitors this is no problem, because they spend so much time outdoors. The more elegant resorts are located north and south of the village; many of these have freshwater swimming pools, satellite TV, and hot tubs. Don't expect broad beaches, however: Ambergris Caye isn't made that way.

San Pedro has only a half-dozen streets, and staying in town puts you close to the action—or noise, depending on your point of view. If you stay outside the town, transportation to and from San Pedro is usually provided by your hotel. Bicycles, golf carts, and motor scooters are available for rent or you can simply walk or take a taxi. The northern part of the island is accessible by bicycle or car via a hand-pulled "Huck Finn" ferry that runs until 6 p.m. daily (5 p.m. Sundays). The fare starts at 50¢ for pedestrians.

In general, the more sociable visitors will be happier in San Pedro, while those in search of a more rustic, inexpensive setting would do well to investigate on Caye Caulker and other islands.

Diving

If you wish to scuba dive during your visit, there are many half-day, all-day, and overnight excursions available. It pays to ask around for suggestions, since some operators are definitely better than others. I've heard the most positive comments about the **Amigos del Mar** dive shop, 26-2706, amigosdive@btl.net, based on one of the in-town piers; **Blue Hole Dive Centre**, bluehole@btl.net, 26-2982, which operates *Blue Hole Express*; and **Coral Beach Dive Shop**, 26-2013, which offers half-day, full-day, and night-dive trips. Also try **Fantasea Watersports & Scuba School**, 26-2576, fantasea@btl.net, a full-service dive shop at the Victoria House pier. One-tank dives are about $20 and two-tank dives around $50, including tanks, belts, and weights.

If you're learning to become a NAUI or PADI certified diver, expect to pay $350 or more for a four-day course. Other recommended diving outfitters include **El Pescador** (26-2975), **Amigos del Mar** (26-2706), **Ramon's Village** (26-2071), **and Hustler Tours** (26-2279, hustler@btl.net). The latter can arrange a daytrip (about $150 per person) to the Blue Hole via a fast boat. **Tortuga Tours** has one of the largest dive boats on the caye (at 49 feet) but trips are cancelled if not enough divers sign up. You'll pay about $45 for a two-tank daytrip.

Snorkeling

For snorkeling, **Ramon Badillo** (26-2804) is well-liked for his glass-bottom boat tours and gentle way with first-time snorkelers. **"Lil Alfonse" Graniel** (26-2584) and **Tulu Villanueva** also have good reputations. **David Nuñez**, 26-2314, and **Amigos del Mar**, 26-2706, are recommended for both snorkeling and fishing trips. Expect to pay about $15 per person for a half-day of snorkeling, $35 for a full day (ask if the fare includes the Hol Chan entrance fee). Most snorkel and dive trips leave at about 8:30 a.m. and again at 1:30 p.m. Besides **Hol Chan**, the best snorkeling locations are **Punta Azul**, **Mexico Rocks**, **Mata Rocks**, **Coral Gardens**, and **Los Cocos**.

We recommend day-long, three-stop snorkel trips on Roberto Smith's beautifully restored island trader *Winnie Estelle* (26-2394), which include a stopover on Caye Caulker. The trip happens three times a week and costs about $45, including lunch. The catamaran *Me Too* has a similar snorkel-sail package trip to Caulker for around $40.

Fishing

Fishing is still a way of life for many San Pedranos, and there are dozens of guides to choose from. You should inquire locally for current recommendations, but I've heard good comments about **Pete Graniel, Luz Guerrero** (26-2705), and **Severro Guerrero** (26-2517). **"Lil Alfonse"**

A villa-style resort on the south end of Ambergris Caye

Graniel, 26-2584, and **Tacio Badillo** are particularly recommended. Tacio also arranges windsurfing and sailing adventures, and his brother Geraldo specializes in moonlight sailboat rides. Prices start at around $20 per person. **El Pescador** (26-2975) specializes in fishing packages, with an emphasis on tarpon, permit, and bonefish. Guided fishing trips run from about $100 for a half-day to $175 for a full day ($125 for night fishing). Deep-sea rates are higher, from $250 to $350 per day. Lunches are sometimes extra.

Other Things to See and Do in Ambergris Caye
Besides the usual water sports, volleyball, and birding, Ambergris tour options include a turtle-nesting beach on the northeast corner of the island, offshore bird rookeries, and several unrestored but difficult-to-reach ancient Maya sites. Visitors can fill their days with outdoor recreational activities and their nights with wining, dining, and dancing.

I also recommend spending at least part of one day simply walking around town, seeing how San Pedranos live, work, and play. There's a pleasant path along the beach south of San Pedro, which takes you past several luxury resorts and an octagonal building that is the home of **Barry Bowen,** Belize's most successful entrepreneur and the owner of Belikin beer (that's why his house is painted "Belikin green"). Next to Bowen's house is a private school that he built for his children and other island residents on San Pedro's last empty stretch of beachfront.

On beaches like these, you can step outside at night and see a glittering array of constellations, including (in winter) the majestic Southern Cross. You can warm up at one of the bars along the waterfront. Bicycles rent for about $10 a day; golf carts for around $60 a day.

Inland Day Trips

A number of local travel agencies arrange day trips up jungle rivers to the Altun Ha and Lamanai Maya ruins on the mainland, as well as the Community Baboon (Howler Monkey) Sanctuary. Expect to pay $60 to $125 per person for these outings. My favorite guides for these trips are **Daniel Nuñez** and **Carlos Alejos**. Day trips are easily arranged to Tikal (and other Maya sites) from San Pedro. Inquire among the local airlines for scheduled flights to Flores/Santa Elena (the Tikal airport), which cost about $250 round-trip, including a guided tour of the ruins.

Nightlife

Drinking and dancing pretty well sums up San Pedro's nightlife, and there are plenty of watering holes to choose from. Among the more popular bars are the **Purple Parrot** (on Barrier Reef Dr.), **Big Daddy's Bar** (Ambergris St. at the water), and the **Tackle Box**). The latter is famous for its Wednesday night "chicken drop," wherein contestants bet on where our feathered friend will drop its load. For dancing, try the aforementioned or **Tarzan's Nite Club** (Barrier Reef at Ambergris) and the **Genesis Bar** at the SunBreeze Hotel. **Big Daddy's** is the spot for karaoke on Thursday and Friday nights, and movies are shown at **World Fantasy** on Barrier Reef Drive. If that's not enough, there's always cable TV and/or communing with your loved one(s).

Shopping and Services

San Pedro services include a bank, several pharmacies, a post office, a BTL (phone company) office, and a public library. One source of general information is the well-written weekly newspaper, the *San Pedro Sun*, sanpdrosun@btl.net. The best book about the island is *The Field Guide to Ambergris Caye*, locally published by co-authors R.L. Wood, S.T. Reid, and A.M. Reid. Its chapters are packed with information on the history, biology, archaeology, and geology of the caye.

There are plenty of souvenir shops in San Pedro, offering everything from T-shirts to wood carvings. Black coral jewelry is sometimes offered. Locals can get permits to collect this rare coral by free-diving, but I discourage its purchase on environmental grounds.

Visitors recommend both **Amigo Travel,** 26-2180, amigotrav@btl.net, and **Travel & Tour Belize** in San Pedro, 26-2137, fax 26-2185, for arranging excursions throughout Belize and for information on Ambergris Caye, including how to arrange long-term house or condo rentals. Amigo also rents scooters and bicycles. CyberCoffee has Internet access at Island Plaza.

The **Ambergris Caye Museum** on Barrier Reef Drive ($2.50) opened in1998, displaying a small collection of local artifacts.

At least one local entrepreneur, **Island Equestrian Trails,** offers horseback riding, and sailing can be arranged through **Islands & Reef Cruise** at the Paradise Hotel pier. You can rent golf carts for about $5 an hour and bicycles for around $1.50 an hour. Inquire at **Ramon's Wheel Rental** (26-2790), at the airport. Underwater cameras and video recorders are also widely available for hire, as are windsurfers and Hobie-cat sailboats. Several supermarkets sell groceries and liquor, but prices are high. Internet and e-mail access is provided by some hotels and by the Tropic Access cybercafé on Barrier Reef Drive.

Festivals
Annual events include the San Pedro Carnival (the week before Lent), Festival of St. Peter, June 26–29 (which includes the blessing of the fishing fleet), and the Air & Sea Show, a community-wide July or August celebration of San Pedro's diverse cultures and traditions.

Getting There
Tropic and Maya Island Airlines have as many as nine daily flights each to Ambergris from Belize City'sairports. The flight from Belize City lasts about 15 minutes and costs about $45 each way. Maya Island Air flies daily to Caulker for about $25 one-way (7 minutes).

Connecting flights are easily arranged to other Belize cities, Mexico, and Tikal. If you're coming from the Yucatán, it's an easy hop from Corozal to San Pedro, and Tropic has five flights daily ($30 one-way). In 1999 there was talk of direct flights between San Pedro and Mexico; these may have started by the time of your visit. Ambergris Caye can also be reached by private or chartered aircraft. San Pedro's airport is within walking distance of town and taxis await every flight. A taxi union rotates drivers at pick-up points and there's little fare-gouging; expect to pay $2.50 for most destinations.

Boats regularly ply the channel between Ambergris and the mainland, departing from several locations in Belize City. The main Belize City departure point is the Front Street Marine Terminal, east of the Swing Bridge. The trip takes about 1 hour and 15 minutes each way and cost about $12 (one-way) in 1999.

Manatee Watching

Many guides take visitors in search of the West Indian manatee, an endangered marine mammal that's holding its own in Belize. This huge, placid animal—sometimes called a sea cow—looks like a cross between a walrus, elephant, and whale. Please don't try to swim with manatees: They are timid creatures and the presence of humans in the water disrupts their natural eating and breeding patterns. The Belize government has issued guidelines about how close you can get to a manatee, how you should act around juveniles, and when your boat's speed should be reduced to avoid propeller damage. Motors should be cut entirely in the vicinity of manatees and a pole used to get around. Because of their shyness, you'll be lucky to see a manatee for longer than a fleeting instant,

The *Andrea II* (about $13 one way) leaves Belize City's Bellevue dock (5 Southern Foreshore) weekdays at 4 p.m. and Saturday at 1 p.m., returning at 7 a.m. from the Texaco dock next to the Conch Shell Hotel.

Other boats making the Belize City-San Pedro shuttle are the *Triple J*, *Thunderbolt*, and *The Hustler*. Each leaves Ambergris around 7 a.m., returning from Belize City's Swing Bridge area at about 4 p.m. You'll pay about $12 for a one-way ticket.

A 25-passenger ferry, the *Island Express*, offers nine round-trips daily (8:15 a.m. to 11:30 p.m.) between the Sun Breeze Hotel dock and northern Ambergris Caye, stopping at Tres Cocos, Essene Way, and Journey's End. Fare is $4 one-way; it takes about 20 minutes to get to the northernmost stop.

Private boats can also be chartered, or you can hop a ride from Belize City with a supply or fishing vessel (try the customs wharf on North Front Street near the Fort George lighthouse).

Once on Ambergris, there are regular boats to Caye Caulker, plus charters to virtually any scrap of reef or atoll you care to visit. Most boats leave for Caulker at about 7 a.m. and charge about $7 for the 20-minute trip. You can also look around the public docks for a boat marked "CC" and ask if you can pay for a lift to Caye Caulker.

although sometimes a dozen or more will hang around and stare at the humans.

Costs for manatee watching trips, which usually include snorkeling, vary from about $30 to $65 per person. On these and other excursions you may see Atlantic bottlenose dolphins, which are fairly common in Belize waters and will sometimes let humans swim with them—permissible if one doesn't get too close.

If you want to help preserve and protect the manatees for future generations, write a support letter or make a donation to the Swallow Caye Reserve Project of Belize, P.O. Box 986, Belize City, which has been fighting to establish a government-sanctioned marine reserve on their behalf in the area of Drowned and Swallow Cayes. E-mail to chocolate@btl.net.

Where to Stay on Ambergris Caye

Barrier Reef Hotel, in town; $80; 26-2075, fax 26-2719, barriereef@ btl.net. Long-lived institution with Caribbean ambiance.

Belize Yacht Club, next door to Ramon's, on the beach; $150; 26-2777 or (800) 688-1767, bychotel@btl.net. Upscale restaurant, bar, and meeting facilities were added in 1996. Dive shop has the largest boat on the caye.

Captain Morgan's, 3.5 miles north of San Pedro; $140 and up; (800) 447-2931 or 26-2567, information@captainmorgans.com. Freshwater pool, restaurant, bar, 21 beachfront casitas, excursion options. Meal plans are also available.

Caribbean Villas, south of town, on the beach; $175 and up; 26-2715, fax 26-3399, c-v-hotel@btl.net. Operated by San Pedro's only dentist, American expatriate Wil Lala, and his wife, Susan. Condo-style accommodations and "barefoot luxury." All rooms have full kitchens and are steps away from a well-groomed beach. Amenities include two outdoor hot tubs, a five-level "people perch" for bird (and sunset) watching, and an offshore swimming hole. The couple give free golf-cart tours of San Pedro to every arriving guest and are full of expert advice on what to see and do. Tours and day trips are booked easily from here. Recommended.

Changes in Latitudes, on the southern edge of San Pedro; $80; 26-2986, latitudes@btl.net. A clean, friendly, Canadian-owned bed-and-breakfast. Recommended. Lower off-season rates.

Coconut's Caribbean, about 5 minutes from San Pedro; $85; 26-3500, fax 26-3501, coconuts@btl.net. With refrigerator and bicycles for guests at no charge. All 12 rooms are air-conditioned and some have a TV. Recommended.

Corona del Mar All Suites Hotel, in San Pedro; $75–150; 26-2005, corona@btl.net. Kitchen-equipped suites that sleep up to six. Private whart and marina, includes breakfast.

Hideaway Sports Lodge, southern edge of town; $45 and up; 26-2141, fax 26-2269, hideaway@btl.net. Canadian-owned with 17 large rooms, a pool, and the friendly Crazy Canuck Restaurant; meal plan available.

Hotel del Río, in town; rates start at $24 (with shared bath), with the fanciest rooms going for $85 a night (air-conditioned cabaña); 26-2286, jewel@globalreach.net. My favorite budget place.

Journey's End, at the northern tip of the island; $90 and up; 26-2054, fax 26-2397, (800) 460-5665, journeysend@neosoft.com. A luxury resort with tennis, drive shop, restaurant, and pool. Free transport from San Pedro.

Laidy's Apartments, $85; 26-2682. A four-unit, north-side place specifically designed for long-term visitors.

Paradise Villas Condominiums, next to Paradise Hotel; $120 and up; 26-3077, (800) 626-3483, cayeman@btl.net. All hotel amenities plus full kitchens and living rooms; easily accommodating two couples per condo. Rates vary, depending on season

Ramon's Village, south side; $140 and up; 26-2071 or (800) 624-4215, ramons@c-gate.net or ramons@btl.net. One of the island's biggest resort hotels—and with a consistently positive reputation—with the highly regarded Parrot's bar and a Cajun-style restaurant. The hotel is immediately south of town and is particularly popular with families, catering to virtually every need and whim. There's a fully equipped dive and snorkel shop on-site.

Rocks Inn, on the north end of San Pedro; $95; 26-2326, (800) 331-2458, fax 26-2358, rocks@btl.net. Kitchens and air-conditioning. A good value for groups. Staff here can set up dive or snorkel trips.

San Pedro Holiday, in town; $93; 26-2014, fax 26-2295, holiday@ btl.net. The island's first hotel, owned by San Pedro native Celi McCorkle. Close to the action, all rooms with air conditioning.

SunBreeze Resort, within walking distance of the airport; $100; 26-2191, fax 26-2251, sunbreeze@btl.net. Well-appointed poolside rooms, 100-foot pier.

Victoria House, a 10-minute bike ride or courtesy shuttle drive south of San Pedro, on the beach; $110; 26-2067 or (800) 247-5159, victoria @btl.net. Good bar, restaurant, pool, and full-service dive shop. New villas in 1998, some have kitchens and air-conditioning. Fishing and snorkeling tours.

Where to Eat on Ambergris Caye

Big Daddy's, seafront, south end of town. Where else can you get "lobster peanut butter"? Terrific barbeque.

Capricorn, a romantic spot north of "the river" (a narrow waterway dividing Ambergris Caye) and just south of Capt. Morgan's Retreat. The food is superb (try the stone crab claws), and there are three cabañas and rooms for rent if you decide to spend the night (rooms $75 and up, 26-2809, capricorn@btl.com). Because the ferry stops at 6 p.m., one can arrange a moonlight boat ride from San Pedro—I recommend Skipper George's *Rum Punch II*. Moderate to expensive.

Drive-up Daiquiri, in downtown San Pedro. Don't miss this place, where you can order a daiquiri or piña colada without leaving your golf cart. (San Pedro's post office has drive-up P.O. boxes, too!)

Duke's Place, south end, across from Ramon's. Try the Mayan eggs and shrimp fajitas. Good steaks, too. Moderate prices.

El Patio, on Coconut Drive. Try the tropical chicken. Expensive.

To Eat or Not to Eat?

The environmentally aware traveler may want to think twice before ordering lobster, shrimp, shark, or conch in Belize. While most restaurants are conscientious about not serving such species out of season (or buying undersized specimens), these creatures have been severely depleted in local waters due to strong demand here and in neighboring Mexico. Many lobsters are also exported to chain restaurants in the U.S. and Europe. No one knows when—or if—offshore Belize will recover from past overfishing, although there are many hopeful signs that the situation is improving. It's up to you to decide what to eat, but you might ask where the items came from (a growing number of fish and shellfish in Belize are now raised on aquatic farms) and whether they are "in season."

Jade Garden, half-mile south of the airstrip. A long-time Chinese cuisine favorite with a large menu. Moderate.

La Margarita, south of town on Coconut Drive. Texas-style Mexican food and sunset views, plus 40-ounce margaritas. Expensive.

Mary Ellen's Little Italy, Barrier Reef Drive in the Spindrift Hotel. San Pedro's best Italian food. Moderate to expensive.

Mickey's, on Tarpon Street. Best burritos on the caye, especially the Wednesday special. Moderate.

Patty's Fruit Stand, on Middle Street. The best tropical fruits and veggies in the village. Inexpensive.

Rasta Pasta, upstairs at the SunBreeze. Particularly recommended for those on a budget (try the homemade ginger beer and wine, which go well with Albert and Maralyn's inventive seafood and veggie dishes). Live music, too, and big breakfasts. Moderate.

Sweet Basil's, a fancy deli just south of Capricorn. Delicious lunches; stocks imported cheeses, patés, wines, and picnic supplies. Expensive.

Other Options
The Reef, Lily's, or **Celi's,** all in town, are all known for well-prepared fish and Belizean cuisine. Many San Pedro restaurants have barbecue or buffet specials once or twice a week that are an excellent value, and the weekly **Lion's Club Barbecue** (a fundraiser for its Ambergris Caye clinic) is not to be missed. Also recommended is the Sunday beach barbeque at **Charlene's.** At **Elvi's,** kids love the "chicken fingers." Note that most restaurants stop serving at 9 p.m. and service is often slow.

HOL CHAN MARINE RESERVE
Location: Less than 5 miles southeast of San Pedro, along the barrier reef.
Size: About 5 square miles.
Hours: Dawn to dusk.
Visitor Information: The Hol Chan Visitor Center in San Pedro, Caribena Street; 26-2420. Open daily from 9 a.m. to 5 p.m. Well stocked with brochures and information about the underwater flora and fauna.

About 4 miles southeast of San Pedro, off the tip of Ambergris Caye, is a natural break in the barrier reef called **Hol Chan,** Mayan for "little channel." The cut is around 30 feet deep, has been protected since 1987 as a national marine reserve, and has become a major spawning ground that is strengthening underwater plant and animal populations.

Hol Chan's Ecological Zones
The reserve is divided into three distinct ecological zones, marked on the water's surface by anchored buoys. **Zone A** is the reef channel itself, where swimmers should be mindful of strong tidal currents while diving or snorkeling. **Zone B** encompasses broad beds of sea grasses as well as the Boca Ciega. The sea and turtle grass serve as an important feeding and breeding ground; visitors will see hundreds of tiny fish here. **Zone C** encompasses several mangrove cayes, a source of important nutrients and a critical habitat for the youngest sea creatures, who subsequently migrate into the sea grass beds and finally the outer waters. Above the surface, the mangrove islands provide a nesting area for several large bird species such as herons, egrets, pelicans, rails, frigate birds, and ospreys. The mangrove ecosystem is also home to sponges, anemones, sea urchins, crabs, jellyfish, mollusks, sea squirts, and young lobsters.

    Hol Chan Marine Reserve was the first park of its kind in Central America, and donations are welcome. Your contribution will encourage Belize and neighboring countries to expand such worthy ventures.

School of blue-striped grunts at Hol Chan Marine Reserve

© Tony Rath

Exploring Hol Chan

As you explore Hol Chan, remember that all flora and fauna are protected. Feeding the fish is discouraged, since it upsets the balance of nature, promotes dependence on humans, and can lead to some potentially dangerous encounters with certain sharp-toothed animals.

The Belize Audubon Society advises visitors to any coral habitat in the country that collecting these tiny organisms is prohibited, and that overturning or disturbing any live coral will eventually kill them. Always be very careful when stepping or dropping anchor on the ocean floor, and try to avoid touching live coral at all costs. Even a vigorous kick by a swimmer can stir up enough sand to clog their orifices. Contact with fire (also called red) coral can be especially painful. Here, as in other areas with busy marine traffic, be careful of speeding powerboats that may be unable to see you bobbing in the water: an encounter can be deadly.

Radio-equipped patrol boats regularly visit the area, on the lookout for anyone in trouble—or anyone who is at odds with the law. Mooring buoys should always be used when available.

Shark/Ray Alley

The newest addition to Hol Chan is an area known as Shark/Ray Alley, where visitors often see good-sized sharks, barracudas, and rays. They've been drawn to this area for years because anglers traditionally clean their fish here. Today guides throw scraps (chum) into the water to keep them coming. They'll encourage you to scratch a nurse shark's belly and use an eagle ray for a hat. Biologists discourage this sort of thing and there is some danger—animals in a feeding frenzy are unpredictable—but Belize authorities seem oblivious. Meanwhile, the show is pretty amazing. Remember that, for the most part, reef sharks are no more interested in humans than in the surrounding sand and coral: just don't act like an injured fish.

Belize Tourist Board

Snorkeling

Snorkelers will find that Hol Chan is unusually rich in marine life, including hundreds of fish species and a variety of living corals

Diver above coral and sea fans

(including elkhorn, starlet, brain, and sheet). You may also come across colorful sea fans, sponges, sea whips, gorgonians, crabs, rays, and eels. (Don't get too close to the nearsighted green moray eel, which can chomp off a finger in an eye-blink.) Humans share the clear waters here with everything from nervous squirrelfish to curious grey angels, from jaunty sea horses to parading parrot fish. Large schools of yellowtail snapper, horse-eye jacks, and blue-striped grunts cruise by, along with spotted eagle rays and purple cleaner shrimp.

The sides of the channel, lined with both living and dead coral, are interrupted from time to time by small limestone caves and sinkholes, including the spectacular **Boca Ciega**, a collapsed cave with underwater freshwater springs that teem with tropical fish. Swimming inside the Boca Ciega should be explored only by experienced divers. Advance permission must be obtained from Hol Chan headquarters.

If you have small children who wish to snorkel, it's wise to hire an experienced guide who can help keep an eye on them in the water. They—and their parents—should wear water-repelling sunscreen and consider wearing T-shirts to avoid burning. If you've just arrived in Belize—without a tan—it's prudent not to snorkel any more than an hour on the first day.

Diving

Divers can take advantage of Hol Chan's relatively shallow depth and stay down for an hour or more, drifting among the lovely spotted drum, hatfish, damsel, and butterfly fish. If a diver remains stationary, the shy hermit crab may make an appearance. Night diving can also be very rewarding, providing a rare chance to glimpse flaming scallops, octopus, spider crabs, lobsters, and other nocturnal species. Eerie bioluminescent ostracods (tiny shrimp-like creatures) shimmer like tiny fireflies atop the water's surface, becoming especially noticeable in the wake of passing boats.

Getting There

Because of its close proximity to San Pedro, Hol Chan can easily be visited for a half-day (or even an hour) by booking a boat through a hotel, or simply showing up on any of the east-side piers in San Pedro. Dive and snorkel boats usually head out about 9 a.m. and again at 2 p.m. each day, returning about 3 hours after departure. Expect to pay at least $15 and up for a round-trip, with two snorkel or dive stops. Several glass-bottom touring craft follow a similar schedule. Guards on powerboats collect the reserve's $2.50 entrance fee and monitor anchoring activities.

BACALAR CHICO NATIONAL PARK AND MARINE RESERVE

Location: At the northern tip of Ambergris Caye, 20 miles from San Pedro.
Size: About 20 square miles.
Hours: Dawn to dusk.
Visitor Information: Inquire at the Hol Chan Marine Reserve office in San Pedro for the latest information about Bacalar Chico.

One of Belize's newest protected areas, the 28,000-acre Bacalar Chico comprises the northernmost part of Ambergris Caye and its surrounding waters. Until a few years ago much of this area was private land slated for development as a golf course and luxury resort.

The name refers to the narrow channel that separates the island from mainland Mexico. This canal was supposedly excavated by ancient Maya around A.D. 500 so that their trade boats would have a shortcut into Chetumal Bay. The park's ranger station and visitor center are, in fact, at the badly eroded **San Juan** archaeological site, under excavation by a Texas university. Another ancient Maya trading camp in the area, **Chac Balam**, is being studied by a Canadian team, and five other sites have been located within the park.

Birders will find much to see on a boat trip to Bacalar Chico, since more than 200 species have been identified in the area. Less visible are the mammals recorded here, including ocelots, deer, raccoons, peccaries, and

The Marine Maya

Beyond the border of the reserve, at the swampy southern extremity of Ambergris Caye, is the Marco Gonzalez archaeological site. This small and badly eroded Maya ruin, named after the young boy who found it, was once part of a large trade network linking inland Indians with settlements along the Mexican and Central American coast. Trade items originating as far away as present-day Peru and New Mexico made their way along this route.

Occupied between 200 B.C. and A.D. 1500, Marco Gonzalez has been excavated since 1986 by Canadian archaeologists, who confirm that some structures are built entirely from conch shells. The location is not well marked and is best approached with the help of a knowledgeable guide. Bring mosquito repellent!

boa constrictors. Evidence of pumas and jaguars has even been reported. Green sea turtles and loggerhead sometimes come ashore near **Rocky Point**, where the barrier reef actually touches the shoreline. (Except for a few other cayes and Manatee Bar beach on the mainland, this is the only known turtle-nesting site in Belize.) The offshore marine habitat was once known as a breeding area for Queen conch (now in decline due to overfishing) as well as a seasonal spawning bank for Nassau and yellowfin groupers. Rangers can advise about closed fishing areas.

The best birding is in mangrove lagoons along the coast, and in the high-ridge (littoral) forest that runs parallel to the beach along the east side of Ambergris Caye. Bring binoculars!

Offshore buoys and anchor sites have been installed by Bacalar Chico's management, which allows camping on the park's limited dry land. Be sure to bring whatever water, food, and supplies you'll need. The best snorkel sites are off the caye's northeast shoreline.

Outfitters
The tourism infrastructure of Bacalar Chico is still being developed, but most San Pedro guides will take you there if asked. Expect to pay a bit

more, $30 and up, than you would for a Hol Chan trip because of the cost of fuel. Another option is to stay at one of the north-island lodges and start your excursion from there. Bacalar Chico has a $2.50 admission charge. The mainland communities of **Sarteneja** and **Corozal** are also involved in Bacalar Chico's development, and boat operators there can whisk you across Chetumal Bay for a reasonable fee.

CAYE CAULKER

Location: About 11 miles south of San Pedro and 21 miles northeast of Belize City, just west of the barrier reef.

Visitor Information: No formal tourist information center, but good sources of information are the various gift shop and hotel operators. Best all-around visitor resource: Dolphin Bay Travel Agency, middle of town on Front Street; 22-2214, dolphinbay@btl.net. They can arrange lodging, day trips, and airplane tickets, and can change money when the Atlantic Bank is closed.

Lying directly south of Ambergris, Caye Caulker (sometimes spelled Corker) is a popular destination among many visitors who want an experience more akin to the laid-back San Pedro town of the 1970s, before the latter was "discovered." Your dollar still goes a long way here.

Caulker is "less" of many things San Pedro has become: less expensive, less crowded, and less noisy. However, it also has fewer hotels, restaurants, and services than its northern neighbor. The beach isn't raked and manicured here as it is on Ambergris Caye, and you'll share the street with lots of flea-bitten dogs (and the occasional great blue heron). It's okay on Caulker to live in a rotting shack or a rusty camper shell—and even the best hotel in town couldn't compete with Motel 6. Some visitors absorb the "action" of Ambergris for a while and then slow the pace down on funky Caye Caulker.

The island was dubbed *Hicaco* by the Spanish, their name for the many coco-plum palms found here. Over the years, the English pirates who settled here apparently began pronouncing it "Corker," and, with their British accents, the word finally evolved into "Caulker." The British are mostly gone now, replaced by Mexican immigrants in the 19th century. Unlike their Ambergris neighbors, the mestizos of Caulker largely have given up Spanish and now speak Creole English.

The caye is fairly small, and the inhabited portion covers a few sandy blocks. There are only two main north/south streets: Front (east, along the beach) and Back (west). Like Ambergris, a good portion of Caulker is bug-infested mangrove swamp, and the northern half of the island has only a handful of residents. Visitors walk everywhere, since nothing is far away, and vehicles are almost nonexistent. A golf cart is the only airport taxi.

About 900 people live on Caye Caulker year-round, and, within a few days' time, it seems a traveler has waved to or chatted with them all. This friendliness, coupled with comparatively modest prices and a full range of services, has enticed many first-timers to extend their stay on Caulker. A few foreigners—budget-minded regulars on the "gringo trail"—have stayed for years and intermarried with the locals.

An airport opened in 1991 and the island's tempo has speeded up somewhat, but by keeping a measure of control over Caulker's pace of progress, residents have been able to remain owners and operators of most of the rustic guest houses, home-style restaurants, and simple shops that cater to visitors. Don't expect a lot of action on Caye Caulker; there isn't any. Most visitors schedule snorkeling or sightseeing day trips, then mosey out in the evening to shop, eat, and drink. The island offers many of the same attractions as Ambergris, including snorkeling, diving, sailing, windsurfing, kayaking, sunbathing, hiking, and fishing.

Travel Tips

Among the few persistent annoyances on Caye Caulker are sand flies and mosquitoes, which can make hikes very uncomfortable in calm or rainy weather. Since most buildings are on tall stilts, these biting insects are less of a nuisance indoors. Make sure your room has a fan or air-conditioning.

Vagrants and street hustlers have been a problem in the past, but a recent crackdown has brought things under control. There's a highly visible police station in the center of Caulker that's put the word out that drug abuse won't be tolerated. If you find yourself being hassled, my best advice is to ignore and avoid the offenders, then report any subsequent trouble to the police and/or your hotel owner.

Fishing, Snorkeling, and Manatee Watching

Caulker natives have long been known as fishing experts (lobster, conch, snapper) and skilled boatmen, so you are sure to find top-notch guides here for virtually any water-related activity.

San Pedro native **Lionel "Chocolate" Heredia,** 22-2151, likes to take visitors to a manatee-watching area en route to superb snorkeling, fishing, and island camping sites. As many as 12 manatees at a time gather above what appears to be an underwater spring or collapsed cave (a location Chocolate doesn't wish to publicize for environmental reasons). The Belize government is in the process of extending official protection to manatee feeding areas and guides are already subject to a $250 fine if they violate rules designed to protect this shy beast. Remember, don't get into the water with the manatees!

Other recommended snorkeling guides include **Raul Young,** 22-2133, **Robert Blease,** 22-2154, and **Harrison Cadle,** 22-2263, in particular.

On Caye Caulker, piers are known as "bridges."

Harrison makes excursions almost daily to Hol Chan and Goff's Caye. The going rate for all-day snorkling was about $35 in 1999, or $30 without a "shore lunch" of fresh fish and picnic items. Most trips depart with a minimum of five passengers (and a maximum of 12). Also recommended is **Rogue's** (22-2014) and **Charles Young**, 22-2128.

Vega's Inn, on the beach, 22-2142, arranges snorkeling or fishing trips. It also rents snorkeling gear and small (Sunfish) sailboats. **Driftwood Snorkel & Dive Connection** (22-2011) guides excellent snorkel, dive, and manatee-watching tours ($15 and up).

For fishing trips, we recommend **Porfilio "Piggy" Guzman** (especially for bonefish, 22-2152) and **Raul Young** (22-2133), available through **Tom's Hotel**; the owner is his brother. If neither is available try **Rocky Badillo** (22-2214) or **Roly Rosado** (22-2058). **Frenchie's Services** and **Pegasus Boat Service** also provide fish-finding expertise. **Ricardo's Adventure Tours** (22-2087), will organize river trips, island hopping, fishing, snorkeling, and even beach barbeques. You name it, and Ricardo Aloala will try to arrange it. Fishing excursions start at about $45 per day and dive trips slightly more, depending on equipment needed.

Diving
One of the better dive shops is **Frenchie's**, 22-2234, on the north end of the island (Frenchie's brother Abel runs the Caye Caulker School of

Scuba). Also recommended is **Belize Diving Services**, 22-2143, bzdiveserv@btl.net, next to the soccer field on Back Street. NAUI and PADI classes are available; try **Caye Caulker School of Scuba** (22-2292), next to Edith's. You can arrange for Ambergris Caye dive operators to pick you up on Caulker for their offshore trips. Expect to pay about $45 for a two-tank local dive (add $10 if you need to rent equipment), and $130 for an off-the-reef dive to such destinations as the Blue Hole. Typical marine life seen on a barrier reef dive off Caulker might include spotted eagle rays, nurse sharks, lobsters, and moray eels. The barrier reef about a mile east of Caye Caulker and Hol Chan Marine Reserve is an easy day trip. Other popular dive (and snorkel) locations include **North Cut, Swash, Sponge Avenue, George's Cut**, and **Mackerel Hole**. Diving is not recommended in the dangerous underwater cave network off the island's west side.

Swimming

The best swimming (the offshore water is otherwise very shallow) is in a 100-foot channel called **The Split**, which bisects the island at the north end of the village. It was formed in 1961 by powerful Hurricane Hattie, the same storm that leveled Belize City. The water here is clear and relatively clean, but beware of currents and near-constant boat traffic. There's no beach, but the wooden dock and tiki bar are comfortable places to hang out.

Hiking and Birding

Its idyllic tropical scenery makes Caulker a nice place to hike. A sandy path to the southeast part of the island brings visitors to a quieter, less developed side of Caulker (punctuated by the roar of an aircraft taking off or landing at Caulker's airstrip). On this path you're treated to fine views of the Caribbean through the mangrove, and you may glimpse iguanas, ospreys, or perhaps a roseate spoonbill. Migrant birds are biannual visitors, most prevalent from early November through mid-December and again in March and April.

Other Things to See and Do in Caye Caulker

Windsurfers, kayaks, and Hobie-cat sailboats can be rented from several outfits on Caye Caulker; inquire locally or watch for signs. Expect to pay about $15 for half-day use, or rent by the hour. Try **Daisy's Hotel** for kayaks, 22-2150.

One recommended nighttime diversion is the slide show and lecture given at **Seeing Is Belizing**, 22-2189, tourism@cayecaulker.org.bz, a Front Street bookstore and gift shop operated by Dorothy Beveridge and her photographer husband, James, an expert on the area's natural history and ecology. For about $2.50 you can see Beveridge's excellent photos of Belizean flora and fauna, with accompanying expert commentary. Typical topics include "the birds of Caye Caulker" and "the Belize rainforest." The slides are for sale at about $1.50 each.

Ellen McRae's **Galeria Hicaco**, 2-22178, on Front Street is a must-see attraction: a combination gift shop and natural history museum. Married to a Belizean, Ellen is a well-informed expatriate marine biologist who has lived here for many years. She conducts highly recommended ecology-oriented tours of the island ($6 and up) and barrier reef through her company, **Cari Search**.

Daytrips and charters aboard the *Sunrise* are available from skipper **Jim Novelo**, who knows where the manatees and dolphins hang out. Excursions as far as Glover's Reef and Half Moon Caye can be arranged. Call 22-2195 or inquire at Island Designs, operated by Jim's wife Cindy. Sailing trips to the Turneffe Islands are also offered by **Tom Young Sr.** (22-2102) aboard his sailing sloop *Valentina*.

Each May a three-day **Coconut Festival** is held on Caulker that commemorates the introduction of coconut plantations on the island in the 19th century. Besides the crowning of a Coconut King and Queen, there are tree climbing, husking, tossing, chipping, and grating contests, along with a coconut food fair and tours of the local processing plant.

Nightlife

Most restaurants close by 9 p.m. and bars a few hours later. Nightlife on the island consists of dancing, drinking, and hanging out at the Rastafarian-style **I & I** reggae club (where they have swings and hammocks instead of chairs!) or **Oceanside** (open 'til 4 a.m. on weekends). And, of course, there's always television. (Yes, even Caye Caulker has satellite dishes.)

Getting There

Members of the Caye Caulker Water Taxi Association (CCWTA), 22-2992, will whisk you between Belize City, Caye Caulker, and Ambergris Caye at regularly scheduled times (at least five each day). In 1999 the fare was about $7.50 for the one-way ($12.50 round-trip), 45-minute trip between Caulker and Belize City; $6 to or from San Pedro. Advance purchase at the CCWTA office (near the main dock) or Belize City Marine Terminal (next to the Swing Bridge) is recommended because boats sometimes fill up and a second craft is not always available. In 1999, water taxis left the main dock in Caulker in the morning at 6:45, 8:00, and 10:00, as well as 3:00 in the afternoon. Belize City departures were at 9 a.m., 11 a.m., 1 p.m., 3 p.m. and 5 p.m. Boats to Ambergris leave at 10 a.m. ($750) and return at 3 p.m.

Maya Island Air and Tropic airlines make a total of 15 or more daily,

13-minute flights to Caye Caulker from Belize City's municipal airport. Some travelers fly to Ambergris Caye and later make the remaining short hop (7 minutes) to Caulker by water or air. Expect to pay about $20 for the one-way trip by air to or from Caulker, slightly more to or from Belize City.

Where to Stay on Caye Caulker

If you plan to be on Caye Caulker for a while, it pays to shop around for accommodations. Some of the guest houses and "cabins" are dirty and run-down. One option is to find something acceptable for the first night, then look for something better the next day. (Be advised that hotel owners here aren't usually up before 8 or 9 a.m.) The least friendly accommodations on the island are the dilapidated **Ignacio's Cabins**, surrounded by ominous signs that threaten all trespassers.

The Anchorage, a bit south of town on the beach; $40; 22-2304 or 24-5937, tourism@cayecaukler.org.bz. Half-price in summer. Decent lodging in a pleasant location.

Barbara's Guest House, on the northern edge of the village; $15; 22-2025. Basic, friendly. Excellent fish, veggie, and chicken burritos. Caters to single women traveling alone.

Castaways, south of the village; $16; 22-2294. Restaurant and bar. Shared bath.

Chocolate's Guest House, north end of Front Street; $60; 22-2151, chocolate@btl.net. The Guest Room is a large, lovely roof-top annex to the home of Belizean boatman, "Chocolate" Heredia and his American wife, Annie Seashore. Amenities include a huge mahogany bed, fresh Guatemalan coffee, and a mini-refrigerator. A breezy balcony overlooks the human parade. Advance reservations are advised.

Heredia's House Rental, on Front Street; 22-2132. Houses typically rent for between $200 and $450 a month. Houses can be rented for stays of two days or more.

Iguana Reef Inn, next to Belize Diving Service on the "back" (west) side of the island; $75; iguanareef@btl.net. No ocean view, but owner Mario Guizar is a Belizean architect who has created a nice facility.

Island Sun Guest House, on the north end near The Split; $25; 22-2215. Clean, friendly, low-cost accommodations include a café that offers the best fruit and yogurt in town—and packed lunches for day trips.

Mara's Hotel, north end next to Island Sun Guesthouse; 22-2156. Four rooms ($30) with private baths and cable TV. Very nice, very clean.

Rainbow Hotel, Front Street in the middle of town; $28; 22-2123. Basic rooms with TVs and fans but not much atmosphere.

Sea Beezzz, on the beach at the south end; $40; 22-2176. A laid-back hangout with a popular restaurant and bar. Closed May–November.

Seaview Hotel, on the water at the southern edge of the village; 22-2205. Built in 1996, at $30 (and up), a good value, with attractive rooms and nice furnishings. Now under the ownership of budget hotel veteran Fred Prost.

Shirley's Guest House, on the far south side of the village, set back from its own beach; $30; 22-2145, shirley@btl.net. Attractive and quiet.

Tom's Hotel, on Back Street; $25; 22-2102. A cement-block place, popular with budget travelers. Cabins also available.

Tropical Paradise, on Front Street, next to the graveyard; $50; 22-2124 or 22-2063. Offering hot water, fans, TV, and a choice of 10 main building rooms or five beachfront cabañas. This large hotel is rather run-down and some guests have complained about fumigation odors, yet its restaurant is one of the best on Caulker.

Other Options

Camping on Caulker is available from **Vega's Inn**, $6 a night, 22-2142, tourism@cayecaulker.org.btl, which also rents rooms. Camping is prohibited on the island's beaches.

Where to Eat on Caye Caulker

It should be noted that, like everything else on Caye Caulker, restaurant service is on the slow side. Remember that you're on vacation; what's the hurry? Prices are relatively expensive.

Glenda's, on Back Street near the soccer field. Prepares Caulker's best Belizean food, specializing in Creole-style breakfast and lunch. Try the fresh orange juice and cinnamon rolls.

Little Kitchen, on Front Street. Inexpensive, delicious meals praised by locals and visitors alike.

The Sand Box, next to the water taxi pier. Provides a volleyball court for its patrons to use while their food is being cooked. This is also one of the best restaurants (and bars) on the island, though somewhat overpriced. Vegetarian and fish dishes a specialty.

Sea Beezzz, on the beach. Tasty margaritas and Margaritaville ambiance. Great breakfasts.

Syd's, near Glenda's on Back Street. Slightly fancier than Glenda's; a good choice for fresh fish. Very slow service.

Tropical Paradise, at the hotel of the same name. The food is good and the place even has tablecloths! Try the fish with curry.

Other Services

Some of Caulker's eateries are simply open-air kitchens operated by local women outside their homes. Children sometimes hawk home-baked coconut bread. A friendly woman named Cordelia sells delicious fish, chicken, and veggie burritos at **Barbara's Guest House. The Pizza Guy**—Damiano Clemente—sells homemade pizza from his bicycle.

You can stock up on supplies at **Chan's,** on Back Street; **Jan's Deli,** on Front Street; and other small groceries. The **Princess del Mar** tortilla factory is on Back Street across from Marin's Restaurant. You can sometimes buy the fruit picked from large breadfruit and citrus trees near the center of the village.

As elsewhere in Belize, e-mail services are available to guests at an increasing number of hotels, usually for a small fee (if that). On-line access (rates start at $1) is available on Front Street at **Island Girl Productions** (22-2309), which publishes Caye Caulker's *Village Voice* weekly newspaper. Open from 9 a.m. to noon and 4 p.m. to 7 p.m.

SIWA-BAN NATURE PRESERVE

Location: *The northern tip of Caye Caulker, beyond The Split, about a mile or two from the village.*
Size: *150 acres.*
Hours: *Any time.*
Visitor Information: *Contact marine biologist (and former Californian) Ellen McRae at Galería Hicaco in the village, 2-22178, sbf@btl.net, or write the Siwa-Ban Foundation, 143 Anderson Street, San Francisco, CA 94110.*

A small yet important reserve being established at the north end of Caye Caulker, Siwa-Ban (the local name for the island's endemic—and increasingly rare—black catbird), is dedicated to protecting critical mangrove habitat, littoral forest, sea grass beds, and offshore coral reef. The reserve, formed in cooperation with the Belize Coastal Zone Management Unit, is an important habitat and food source for birds, fish, and reptiles, including crocodiles.

Local conservationists—with support from their U.S. counterparts—established Siwa-Ban in the mid-1990s and access is by private boat. Well over 100 species of birds have been confirmed in the area, including many winter migrants who thrive on the fruits and berries found in the island's dense forest.

Siwa-Ban is not to be confused with a tiny "mini-reserve" next to the Caye Caulker airport that advertises itself as a conservation project of the Belize Tourism Industry Association. A posted sign calls for $1 admission, but usually there is no one there to collect it. Besides an overgrown nature trail and locked meetinghouse, there is not much to see.

Getting There/Outfitters
A guided boat tour can be arranged among any of the outfitters in the village for about $20. If you wish, they will deposit you at the reserve and return to pick you up at a designated time. There is also a kayak and windsurfer available for rent ($15 and up) at **Galería Hicaco**, the park's current headquarters. Pack mosquito repellent for any visit!

A co-sponsor of the reserve, the **American Littoral Society** (908-291-0055), offers nature-oriented tours of the area that include time spent at Siwa-Ban and Caye Caulker. Group tours, in April and May, cost about $1,400 (excluding airfare).

CAYE CHAPEL AND LONG CAYE
Location: 15 miles northeast of Belize City.
Size: 1 mile by 3 miles.
Visitor Information: Belize Tourist Board, (800) 624-0686.

Heading southeast from Caye Caulker, the next island in the barrier reef chain is Chapel, distinguished by its long sandy beaches and large groves of coconut palms. Because is rises about 10 feet above sea level (higher than most cayes in Belize), the island has been spared much of the hurricane damage its neighbors have suffered. Chapel is easily visible across the horizon from Caulker and lies about 15 miles northeast of Belize City.

As this book went to press, the status of Caye Chapel was unclear. Although it is blessed with magnificent scenery, a long airstrip, and a fine lodge/restaurant complex, the island remains off-limits to uninvited guests. The island's previous owner, the Pyramid Island Resort, closed several years ago and it is not known when (or if) accommodations for travelers will become available. The new American owner has built a nine-hole golf course on Chapel's south end and added sea walls on the north and back sides. Environmentalists are displeased, fearing fertilizer runoff will damage the offshore coral ecosystem. There are rumors that an upscale resort will soon open or that a residential development or retirement center will be built here. In the meantime, tourists are discouraged from setting foot on Caye Chapel. If and when the situation changes, expect to pay about $20 for the short airplane flight or $10 for the boat ride from Belize City.

Part of Caye Chapel's claim to fame is its use as a resting place for the Spanish Armada after the decisive 1798 battle that effectively ended Spain's claim on Belize. Some of the fleet's soldiers were buried here, along with English colonials who came later to fish and grow coconuts. Mayan artifacts point to human occupation at least a thousand years ago.

In past years a small lodge has operated on Long Caye, south of Chapel, but it was closed at last report. The University of North Carolina has reportedly been in discussion to buy Long (also called Northern Long Caye) and turn it into a marine study center. Inquire locally about the propriety of diving, fishing, snorkeling, sailing, and windsurfing in the vicinity of Long Caye and Caye Chapel.

ST. GEORGE'S CAYE
Location: About 9 miles northeast of Belize City.
Size: Less than 1 square mile.
Visitor Information: Belize Tourist Board, (800) 624-0686.

During Belize's early years as a haven for British pirates and traders, its largest settlement was on St. George's Caye. It served as the Bay Settlement's informal capital for more than a century, starting in the mid-1600s. Manatees and turtles were slaughtered here by the thousands, their smoked meat later sold to the crews of oceangoing vessels; thus the island's old name: Kitchen Caye.

This small island is best known as the focal point of a great sea battle between a ragged band of Baymen, a single British schooner, and seasoned Spanish naval forces (in 32 warships). Despite the overwhelming odds against them, the Belizeans prevailed. Thus, the anniversary of the day Spain was defeated, September 10, 1798, is a national holiday (St. George's Caye Day). On the island's southern tip is a small cemetery where some of the early soldiers and settlers were buried. Tropical storms have washed away most of the grave markers (along with dozens of houses and much of the island), but old coins, bottles, and other artifacts are still occasionally found.

There are a number of piers (called "bridges") on St. George's where day-trippers can tie up for an hour or so. A footpath runs the length of the island and the snorkeling offshore is excellent (there's even an underwater cave that you can swim through). St. George's Caye is home to a few lobster fishermen and has several retreats that belong to wealthy Belizeans. Old maps will show nearby Sergeant's Caye, a once-inhabited island that was reduced by Hurricane Hattie to little more than a three-palm sandbar—a great place for a picnic and a day of snorkeling.

Getting There
There is no regular public transportation to St. George's Caye (transportation is prearranged for guests), but private boats can be hired for the 20-minute crossing from Belize City ($10). En route, visitors will pass a number of uninhabited mangrove cayes that have little or no dry land, including Mapp's, Swallow, and Riders Cayes. Keep the binoculars handy, since this dense foliage harbors plenty of birds, and manatees often cruise nearby. The trip to St. George's Caye provides a good chance to observe the wooden, sail-driven cargo ships, known locally as "island traders" or "sand lighters," which ply the waters from Mexico to Honduras.

Where to Stay and Eat in St. George's Caye
St. George's Lodge, highly regarded but questionably expensive at $140, meals included; 2-12121 or (800) 678-6871; and co-owned **Island Cottages**, 2-44190. St. George's Lodge and the Island Cottages cater almost exclusively to avid scuba divers (certification available), although fishing enthusiasts and snorkelers are welcome. The two-part resort is supplied with energy by windmills and solar collectors. Some of the ten cabañas are built on stilts right over the waters, others are on the island's sandy soil. The food served here (family style) is first-rate. Bring your own liquor if you wish to drink. Unlike many diving lodges, the atmosphere is very relaxed. You may be tempted to curl up in a hammock all day and do nothing but watch the diving pelicans.

The Cottage Colony, at the opposite (northern) end of the island. A cluster of five charming bungalows called The Cottage Colony was out of business and seeking a new operator in 1999. This upmarket resort may have reopened by the time of your visit. Inquire at the Bellevue Hotel, 2-77051, in Belize City, its most recent owner.

MOHO AND DROWNED CAYES
Location: One-half mile off the coast, opposite St. John's College on north side of Belize City.
Size: These cayes are each less than an acre in size.
Visitor Information: Belize Tourist Board, (800) 624-0686

Moho Caye is a very small island with a big past. It's the site of an ancient Maya fishing camp where thousands of pounds of old manatee bones have been found. The mammals were apparently butchered in great numbers here, and the meat then prepared for transport to other Maya communities. Fortunately, manatees can still be found in these waters, especially around the Drowned Cays, east of Moho. While they hold almost no dry land, these swampy mangrove cayes provide excellent anchorage during storms and are an important manatee habitat. Local outfitters can arrange excursions to the area.

Whiskered manatee noses also can be seen popping up in breathing holes near the Municipal Airport, where the Belize River enters the sea.

During colonial times, Moho was used as a quarantine area for those suffering from smallpox and other contagious diseases. A small graveyard marks the final resting place of many victims. The privately owned caye is now home to a yachting and diving resort, **Maya Landings**, 2-45798, mayalandings@btl.net, which offers week-long dive/sail trips as far as Lighthouse Reef's Blue Hole and Guatemala's Río Dulce.

CENTRAL BARRIER REEF CAYES
Location: 7–10 miles southeast of Belize City
Size: These tiny cayes vary in size.
Visitor Information: Belize Tourist Board, (800) 624-0686

Each of these tiny cayes retains the kind of charm visitors typically associate with exotic tropical islets. They are only a few acres in size, consisting of little more than a mound of sandy beach and a dozen or so coconut palms. Even native Belizeans like to visit for an afternoon or weekend of snorkeling, diving, fishing, and picnicking. No regularly scheduled transportation serves them, but day trips can easily be arranged through larger hotels, local guides, and travel agencies.

As you approach the islands from Belize City or points farther north, you may pass flat-bottom sugar barges taking their loads out to oceangoing cargo ships that cannot anchor any closer because of the shallow water. Within the Inner Channel depths range up to 150 feet; they quickly plunge to 2,000 feet or more beyond the barrier reef.

Gallow's Point Caye, about 7 miles southeast of Belize City, derives its name from the (now gone) hangman's gallows used here many years ago for the execution of convicted criminals. Today the island is home to **The Wave: Gallows Point Resort** ($100 and up, meals included, 2-73054) a six-room fishing and diving facility (in a large house) that offers a variety of services, including yacht anchorages at its **Weir Dow Marina**. Transportation is arranged from Belize City, and the resort also provides day trips and weekend excursions from the mainland.

The Life of a Lobsterman

Staying with Ricardo Castillo offers visitors the unusual opportunity of observing traditional Belizean lobster fishing first-hand. Ricardo is a lifelong fisher and free diver, originally from the boat-building village of Sarteneja. He will take you along as he checks traps over a meandering route above sea grass beds. Lobsters are still plentiful enough in these waters that they can be enticed into bait-free traps—such as wooden cages equipped with trapdoors and anchored with stones—that rely entirely on the animal's natural inclination to seek refuge during the day in dark places. Ricardo is a by-the-book member of Belize's large fishing cooperative and immediately throws back any undersized lobster, along with the occasional crab or fish that wanders into his traps. Later, you will dine on fresh lobster cooked to perfection. Boats hail Castillo via marine-band radio from as far away as Guatemala to make dinner reservations in the tiny restaurant.

English Caye, a few miles south of the swampy Gallows Point Reef, has been an important navigational aid for hundreds of years. It marks the entrance of the deep English Caye Channel that large commercial ships follow into the Belize City harbor. The tiny island is dominated by a brick lighthouse, where oceangoing ships stop to pick up one of the two pilots who navigate them through the Inner Channel. The lighthouse keeper has a small home where overnight stays can be arranged with special permission. Day-trippers are welcome to stop and visit the historic lighthouse at any time.

Goff's and **Rendezvous Cayes** are mere specks of palm-shaded sand off the major shipping lanes that make excellent stopovers for snorkeling (especially by beginners), fishing, swimming, and diving. Both islands are perched right on the edge of the barrier reef, which allows visitors to swim in either deep or shallow water. Overnight camping and anchorage is allowed, but please be careful about damaging the ecosystem.

Local fishers frequently visit Goff's and Rendezvous Cayes in their

Richard Mahler

*Lobsterman and fisherman Ricardo Castillo throws
undersized lobsters from his trap.*

shallow-draft dories, mostly to find lobster and conch that will be sold to restaurants in Belize City and San Pedro. Not far from Goff's Caye is an area where manatees can almost always be found. Consult local guides for details.

Spanish Lookout Caye is 10 miles southeast of Belize City and 2 miles west of the main barrier reef. Once used by British pirates to spy on Spanish galleons, it now holds a 10-unit, bungalow-style lodge, **Spanish Bay Resort**, $100 and up, meals included; 2-77288 or (800) 359-0747, sbrturton@btl.net, with over-the-water lodging and an accompanying restaurant, bar, dive shop, and experienced fishing guides. Dive packages (with instruction) can be arranged. I recommend this Belizean-owned facility, which caters to nature lovers, fishing enthusiasts, divers, and snorkelers. It is well positioned for those who wish to patrol the outer reef or atolls, and you can arrange to be dropped off on a remote island for a day on your own. A powerful dive barge—complete with compressors and other necessary paraphernalia—can take visitors to uncharted waters. The atmosphere is casual and friendly.

Oceanic Society Expeditions, (800) 326-7491, uses Spanish Bay as its headquarters for manatee research trips to nearby cayes as well as a

NAUI specialty course in research diving certification (dive sites are less than 30 minutes from the lodge). Bottlenose dolphin and coral reef monitoring are other Oceanic Society projects here that visitors can participate in. Transportation is provided from Belize City (20 minutes away) for guests.

MONTEGO AND HICKS CAYES
Location: *10 miles southeast of Belize City*
Size: *Less than an acre each.*
Visitor Information: *(415) 452-0418*

Tiny Montego Caye, 10 miles southeast of Belize City, houses the lobster camp of Luis Rosado and his wife, Wendy Berkelman. They provide rustic accommodations and meals to those with a sense of adventure as well as an active interest in local marine life. Wendy, a graduate of the University of California, is particularly interested in teaching children and educational groups about the marvels of the barrier reef ecosystem, which thrives just beyond her home. You'll sleep in simple clapboard buildings or a tent. Camping is also available on nearby Hicks Caye, which is equally small (and uninhabited). For information, contact Luis or Wendy at (415) 452-0418, Montego_Caye@geocities.com, or www. geocities/com/TheTropics/ Cabana/2927. Prices vary.

BLUEFIELD RANGE, ALLIGATOR CAYE, AND MIDDLE LONG CAYE
Location: *Approximately 20 miles southeast of Belize City.*
Size: *Each of these cayes comprise less than an acre of dry land.*
Visitor Information: *Belize Tourist Board, (800) 624-0686.*

Along Belize's barrier reef, the word "range" refers to the marshy clusters of mangroves that seem to be half land and half water. At least part of every caye seems to fit this description; therefore, I do not mention here the scores of islands on which it is virtually impossible to set foot. (The Belize government has imposed a ban on the purchase of unoccupied islands in the hope that many, if not most, can someday be included in an offshore national park system.)

Bluefield Range is unusual in that it supports several habitats. A couple of its mangrove cayes are permanently soggy, while the largest has a thin strip of high ground that accommodates **Ricardo Castillo's Beach Huts**, 2-31609 or 2-44970. Ricardo and his family have built (very rustic) guest cabañas and a restaurant on their tiny island. Several tent sites on a pleasant stretch of sand are also available at about $5 per person per day (this is a favorite stopping point for southbound sea kayakers). Cabañas are about $100 a night, including meals. The owner will pick you up in Belize City. Manatees and crocodiles are sometimes seen offshore.

Excursions from Bluefield Range

Bluefield Range is a good base for excursions to other nearby cayes and reefs, plus the many fine diving and fishing sites hereabouts. Ricardo Castillo serves as an experienced guide to little-known underwater limestone caves, coral canyons, and unoccupied cayes. Snorkelers and nature buffs can easily arrange trips to remote islands where exotic birds and other creatures make their homes.

Recommended nearby destinations include **Columbus Caye,** which has an underwater sinkhole more than 140 feet deep where large jewfish and sharks are often sighted, and **Caye Glory**, a submerged coral formation off Southern Long Caye, which is an important breeding ground for grouper and other fish. Snorkelers and divers in this area will see black coral and, occasionally, sea turtles.

Saltwater crocodiles and waterfowl are plentiful on **Middle Long Caye** (also called Alligator Caye), a few miles north of Bluefield Range. This large, swampy island has been the site of a small lodge in the past (inquire locally about its present status), and for many years local fishermen have used Middle Long's tiny beaches as campgrounds.

Richard Mahler

Rendezvous Caye is one of dozens of uninhabited islands along the barrier reef.

How to Help Study the Reef

From an Island Camps base on Tobacco Caye, various squirrelfish species have had some very dedicated scientists and volunteers following them around Tobacco Reef for the past seven years. (The squirrelfish is a reddish, largely nocturnal fish with a prominent, spiny dorsal fin and large, squirrel-like eyes.) In 1997, Dr. Susan Hammen-Winn of the University of Rhode Island was completing the fieldwork on an intensive squirrelfish study with the help of Earthwatch volunteers working in two-week rotations. This study focused on habitat mapping, a squirrelfish census, and recording fish behaviors of these sometimes elusive species that feed on small crustaceans. Scientists attach small glowing lights to individual squirrelfish and rotating teams of volunteers help record their movements throughout the night for a foraging segment of this study.

*Other teams from the nonprofit **Earthwatch** organization,*

TOBACCO CAYE

Location*: 12 miles southeast of Dangriga, on the barrier reef.*
Size*: About 5 acres.*
Visitor Information*: Belize Tourist Board, (800) 624-0686.*

Farther south from Belize City, east of the town of Dangriga, several little-known cayes offer attractions and services to visitors eager to explore the reef in relative solitude.

The islands of the Tobacco Range have been heavily used over the centuries for fishing camps, trading centers, and coconut plantations. In fact, Puritans set up a post here more than 350 years ago from which goods (including tobacco) were exchanged with visiting mariners.

On 5-acre Tobacco Caye, the largest island in the complex, travelers can choose from several modest accommodations. Local fishermen and their spouses operate most of the friendly rustic resorts and restaurants here as a supplement to their income during months when sea creatures are breeding or when the weather is too foul to venture out in boats.

(800) 776-0188, www.earthwatch.org., *are needed to partici-pate in what scientists hope will be ongoing research on the ecology of nearby sea grass beds and other marine habitats. This study is uncovering new information about habitats around Tobacco Caye, building an important long-term data-base that will enable scientists to assess damage and changes in the reef community over time. According to the late Dr. Howard Winn, who pioneered the Tobacco Caye project, "the reef's biodiversity and wealth of complex interactions provide a unique and outstanding laboratory for studying the theoretical aspects of community ecology, the mechanisms of evolution and speciation, and the relative benefits of various social behaviors. Such information will benefit Belize in efforts to man-age coastal zone planning, establish parks, and address fishery problems."*

Snorkeling and Diving at Tobacco Caye

Excellent snorkeling begins as soon as you enter the water on the wind-ward (reef side) of Tobacco Caye. Snorkelers can either swim around the southern end of the caye to explore the reef near the **Reef End Lodge** or wade across a shallow lagoon from in front of **Ocean's Edge Lodge** to a break in the reef. (I strongly recommend wearing Reefwalkers or old ten-nis shoes that you don't mind sacrificing to saltwater.) If larger waves are breaking, either wait for calmer water (when the water visibility is better anyway) or swim around the reef from the south end.

Offshore are pristine "forests" of many-branched elkhorn coral along-side common sea fans interspersed with brain and scores of other coral species. Among countless other reef dwellers, you may see the bluehead, a very colorful fish with a blue head, white stripe, and emerald-green tail; the hogfish, with its distinctive flattened face; and several species of color-ful parrotfish, munching away at the coral.

PADI instructors Martin Spragg and Jeanette Melvin of **Second Nature Divers,** 5-37038 or 2-72109, divers@btl.net, offer a half-day

"**Discover Scuba**" diving course, a four-day PADI open-water certification, a dive shop, and excellent diving at nearby Columbus and Tobacco Reefs. **Island Camps** has a partnership with Second Nature for the lodge's guests. Trips for experienced divers can be made 8 miles north to **Shark's Cave**—also called **The Black Hole**, where underwater enthusiasts will occasionally see a reef shark—as well as to Glover's Reef and Turneffe atoll.

Getting There/Outfitters

Contact Raymond Stephen at **Ocean's Edge Lodge**, 14-9633, to arrange a boat transfer to Tobacco Caye from Dangriga, or ask Jim at Dangriga's **New River Café**, 5-39908, about transportation to Tobacco. **Shipmate's Restaurant** is also a good place to make arrangements. Several reputable boatmen depart regularly from the **Stann Creek River** dock near the New River Café; expect to pay at least $15 one-way for the hour-long crossing.

If you want to visit the caye directly from Belize City, contact Mark Bradley at **Island Camps**, 2-72109 or 14-7160, who makes a weekly run (usually Fridays) to the **Fiesta Hotel Marina** (formerly Ramada Royal Reef) in Belize City, charging about $20 per passenger. Be prepared for a sometimes rough ride and, if necessary, take Dramamine in advance or use sea-bands around your wrists to help ward off seasickness.

Where to Stay and Eat in Tobacco Caye

Gaviota Coral Reef Resort, in the center of the caye; $25–55, with meals; 14-9763 or 5-22085. Bert and Marie Swasey offer home-cooked meals and a comfortable bed in a relaxing, quiet setting.

Island Camps, north end of the island; $50–65, with meals; 2-72109 or 5-23433. Mark Bradley at Island Camps offers private, well-spaced cabañas, a fine restaurant, and bar. All electrical systems on Bradley's compound are solar operated.

Ocean's Edge Lodge, $60, with meals; 14-9633. Operated by friendly, helpful Raymond and Brenda Lee Stephen. Comfortable accommodations with private bath and hot water, a restaurant with great family-style Belizean meals, and a pleasant bar. Ocean's Edge also arranges saltwater fly-fishing or casting trips as well as half- or full-day sailing trips. The lodge arranges airport pickup on request.

Reef End Lodge, $70, with meals; 5-22419. The name speaks for itself; lodge, restaurant, and bar are at far south end of caye next to a shallow lagoon—an easy swim to the reef.

SOUTH WATER CAYE

Location: About 14 miles southeast of Dangriga.
Size: About 14 acres.
Visitor Information: Belize Tourist Board, (800) 624-0686

A wide range of services are available on South Water Caye, a picturesque palm-covered island a few miles south of Tobacco Range. An unusual aspect of this privately owned caye is the fact that it is located directly atop the barrier reef, next to one of the deepest channels through that reef. As a result, South Water enjoys some of the best and most easily accessible snorkeling and diving in Belize. The island is clean and quiet, home to many birds, including ospreys, royal terns, green herons, pelicans, and kingfishers.

There's talk about turning the offshore area into a national marine reserv, and the government of Belize may have taken this action by the time you visit.

Outfitters

At a 2.5-acre, solar-powered facility on South Water, marine ecology workshops are offered to the general public by **International Zoological Expeditions (IZE)** ($80 and up, 508-655-1461, ize2belize@aol.com, www.ize2belize.com). With more than 25 years experience in Belize, this Massachusetts-based outfitter is known for the quality of its instruction and accommodations (all meals included). Day trips are made to nearby cayes and reef formations to study birds and marine life.

A full-service, affordable dive operation, the **Living Reef Dive Centre**, 5-22214, tread@btl.net, is affiliated with IZE and has all necessary dive and snorkeling gear available for rent, plus PADI-certified scuba instructors and a marine lab. Day trips can be arranged for divers interested in exploring dive sites off Hunting Caye, Glover's Reef, and other locations. Living Reef's divemasters and instructors are also trained in marine biology and focus on education in marine ecology including fish identification, coral identification, reef ecology, and study of mangrove systems for both certified and novice divers alike. Living Reef—which also operates from Long Caye at Glover's Reef—has many options for divers including a half-day "Discover Scuba" resort-type course to get beginners the basic training they need to begin diving as soon as possible, while also providing a great foundation for those participants who want to go ahead with full PADI certification. Dive sites are 5 to 20 minutes away.

IZE's guests stay in a 15-bed "marine lodge" dorm or at **Leslie Cottages & Cabañas** (contact information is same as IZE), a comfortable five-unit complex operated by members of an extended Belizean family. Snorkeling and fishing trips can easily be arranged here. Cottage guests

© Tony Rath

Cottage at South Water Caye

have free use of kayaks, a Sunfish sailboat, and a windsurfer. IZE maintains separate research stations on Long Caye (Glover's Reef) and at Blue Creek in the Toledo District rainforest. Some IZE workshops can be taken for college credit.

Getting There

Guests of the lodges on South Water will be given transport to the island as part of their package; others can arrange to hire a private boat from Dangriga for $20 and up one-way. Allow about 45 minutes to an hour for the crossing.

Where to Stay and Eat in South Water Caye

Blue Marlin Lodge, at the north end of South Water; $120 and up, including meals, four-night package minimum; (800) 798-1558 or 5-22243, marlin@btl.net. Fourteen double rooms and six bungalows, plus a restaurant, bar, volleyball pit, billiard table, and complete dive and fishing shops. Boats, guides, and a divemaster are also available for the eager anglers and scuba enthusiasts. Game fish found near South Water Caye include tarpon, snook, grouper, bonefish, permit, marlin, sailfish, tuna, and wahoo. Blue Marlin is a PADI dive-training facility praised for the quality of its instruction. A seven-night dive package starts at about $1,400.

Dangriga's Pelican Beach Resort, at the south end of South Water Caye; $60 and up; 5-22044, pelicanbeach@btl.net. Maintains two sets of accommodations, both made environment-friendly through the use of solar power, composting toilets, and rainwater collection. On the grounds of a renovated Catholic convent are two cottages (the Heron's Hideaway), a three-bedroom house (the Osprey's Nest), and a five-room main building (the Pelican's Pouch). The second set of rooms is at Pelican's University, a five-bedroom building near the center of the island that caters to student and educational groups. There are kitchen facilities for guest use, and the hotel will send over a resident cook to prepare meals on request (for a fee). Dive packages can be arranged with the island's dive shops, and fabulous snorkeling is as near as the water.

CARRIE BOW, MAN-O'-WAR, AND WEE WEE CAYES
Location: *See text below.*
Size: *Wee Wee Caye is 7 acres in size; Carrie Bow and Man-o'-War each are less than 1 acre.*
Visitor Information: *Belize Tourist Board, (800) 624-0686.*

Carrie Bow Caye is only about an acre in size—it was twice as big before the mangroves were chopped down and several devastating storms struck. The Smithsonian Institution leases it from Dangriga's Bowman family, which also owns part of South Water Caye. Scientists from all over the world come to Carrie Bow to study the hundreds of species of underwater plants and animals, including mangrove and other important flora and fauna. As many as five scientists at a time are working on the island, whose waters provide some of the Caribbean's best snorkeling. Over the years, these experts have set up a baseline of valuable data that are being used to track the impact of agriculture, fishing, storm systems, pollution, and other influences on the fragile coral reef ecosystem.

Visitors are welcome at the research center by prior appointment, which can be arranged (along with transportation) through Tony Rath or Therese Bowman Rath at their **Pelican Beach Resort** in Dangriga. Overnight accommodations in the house and dormitory are limited to Smithsonian personnel. The underwater marine area surrounding Carrie Bow teems with many varieties of multicolored fish, sponges, and coral and is easily accessible from the island's concrete pier. Again, beware of strong currents through the reef cut.

The Smithsonian, active in the area since 1977, also conducts research on **Twin Cayes**, several miles northwest of Carrie Bow. Studies on this island, which is not permanently occupied, concentrate on the mangrove ecosystem flora and fauna. In one curious (and unsuccessful) experiment, scientists attempted to rebuild nearby **Curlew Caye** by planting mangrove at the site of the island, which became submerged some years ago by a series of hurricanes.

Man-O'-War Caye, a few miles to the northwest, is an important rookery for several species of large water birds, including the magnificent frigate bird (also called the man-o'-war bird). If you pass by during mating season, you'll see the male puffing out his immense red throat balloon. Boobies and terns can also be seen on this mangrove-dominated island. Man-O'-War Caye is federally protected, and you should not attempt to land here. A short distance west is a former pirate hang-out called **Coco Plum Caye**, a crescent-shaped island with a fine beach and secluded picnicking spot.

A small, privately operated marine research station is based on **Wee Wee Caye**, about 8 miles farther south, run by Paul and Mary Shave of

Possum Point Biological Research Station (52-2888) on the Sittee River. Overnight accommodations at Wee Wee Caye are limited and should be arranged well in advance. The name, by the way, derives from the local name for leaf-cutter ants: wee wees.

THE SOUTHERNMOST CAYES
Location: Remote locales; see text for details.
Size: Varies.
Visitor Information: Belize Tourist Board, (800) 624-0686.

As visitors head farther south in Belizean waters, the barrier reef gradually swings away from the mainland. These cayes are remote and, for the most part, uninhabited. Aside from fishing shanties, rustic cabins, and sandy campgrounds, there are only a few overnight accommodations. This situation is changing; inquire locally about any new lodges that have opened since this book's publication.

In large measure because they are so inaccessible, these islands and the marine life surrounding them are probably similar to what they were centuries ago, when the Maya paddled among them in dugout canoes.

Birders can expect to log dozens of species here, including many varieties of tern, gull, pelican, booby, heron, and egret. Grackles, vireos, hummingbirds, cuckoos, and pigeons also breed on the cayes. During the winter, many migratory birds visit these cayes on their way to and from North and Central America.

Some of the cayes also shelter a surprising number of land-based animals—lizards, frogs, crabs, snakes, and even large mammals, including opossums, raccoons, pacas, and armadillos. Apparently some of these creatures were swept out to sea on log rafts and washed up on beaches, then managed to sustain themselves and procreate.

Several of the southern cayes, including **Laughingbird**, **Bugle**, **Colson**, and **Lark**, are popular destinations for day trips out of Placencia, where the services of boats and guides are easily arranged. Other than group excursions out of Placencia, Punta Gorda, and Dangriga, the best way to visit these pristine areas is by chartered boat.

Wippari Caye
Divers, snorkelers, and fishing enthusiasts eager for a taste of Creole life in a seldom-visited part of the reef are encouraged to visit Wippari Caye (sometimes spelled Whiprey), where friendly George and Hortense Cabral operate the six-cabin **Wippari Caye Lodge**, $25 and up, 6-23130, which provides excellent meals and first-class guide service. George is a former Placencia storekeeper who moved his family to Wippari—the local word for eagle ray—about 15 years ago. They've planted trees, established an exten-

sive garden, and discovered one of the country's best bonefish flats on the perimeter of their tiny island, located about 9 miles east of Placencia. Two of the couple's sons—Pow and Breeze—are among the best fishing guides in Belize. Contact the Cabrals by VHF radio, or through either the **Rum Point Inn** or **Kitty's Place** in Placencia. (see Chapter 9, Southern Belize).

French Louis Caye

For those who really want to get away from it all, this miniscule island (less than an acre in size) may be the place. Rustic accommodations ($50, including all meals), transportation, and snorkeling/diving/kayaking gear are provided by **Kitty's Place**, (6-23227, kittys@btl.net), a beachside resort about 7 miles west in Placencia. There's not much to do on the island itself beyond sleeping, eating, and lounging in a hammock. Although not visited by the author, other travelers have described the island's caretaker as "surly," though an excellent cook.

Little Water Caye

On Little Water Caye, about 12 miles southeast of Placencia, is the small, exclusive **Little Water Caye Resort** ($100 and up, 2-31237 or 6-22267). The lodge reopened in 1995 under new ownership (after being shot down in its first incarnation as a nudist colony). It offers full scuba services, snorkeling, fishing, sailing, and a full-service restaurant.

Ranguana Caye

Rustic but comfortable bungalow accommodations are available on Ranguana Caye, about 20 miles southeast of Placencia, at **Eddie Leslie's Ranguana Reef Resort** ($50). Visitors are reminded to bring their own food, and bathrooms are shared. Fishing and diving trips are a specialty here, but you'll need to bring your own equipment. Ranguana is one of the few places in Belize where sea kayaks can be rented, from **Reef-Link Kayaking**, (515) 279-6699. Paddling conditions are excellent, and camping is also available for a modest fee.

Other Southern Cayes

Lodges on nearby **Nicholas Caye** and **Lime Caye** have been in the planning stages for several years; check locally on their status, facilities, and access to these privately-owned islands. **Mosquito, Hatchet**, and **Pompion Cayes** are also privately owned.

Island-hoppers heading south will find a campground on **Rendezvous Caye**, directly east of Placencia (not to be confused with the island of the same name near Bluefield Range) and nearby **Colson Caye**. Overnight visits are now discouraged at **Laughingbird Caye**, a national park, in order to encourage the return of the nesting gulls for which the island is named.

Excellent snorkeling is reported at nearby Abigal Caye.

By the time you reach the **Toledo District**, the barrier reef is nearly out of sight across the eastern horizon. Because the archipelago is a considerable distance from the mainland, travelers should expect to stay overnight and pay a hefty price for the trip. A campground, a picnic area, and sparsely furnished cabins are available for general use on **Hunting Caye**; a diving/fishing lodge there is under development. The same caye also hosts a small outpost of the Belize Defense Forces, charged with interdicting smugglers and other lawbreakers.

Laughingbird Caye

SAPODILLA CAYES

The waters of the Sapodilla island complex, southeast of Placencia, remain almost completely unexplored by anyone except local fishers and Guatemalan vacationers. The coral walls that plunge steeply into the ocean's depths offer spectacular viewing opportunities for experienced divers and snorkelers. The islands have secluded, shaded beaches that make idyllic camping and picnicking spots. British scientists began a long-term ecological study of the Sapodilla Cayes in 1992. An effort is underway to create a marine reserve here that would assure long-term protection.

SNAKE CAYES

From Punta Gorda, excursions can also be arranged to the Snake Cayes, small islands hugging the coastline a few miles northeast of town. Many of these are swampy mangrove ranges, but a few have enough high ground to support significant numbers of coconut palms, wild figs, buttonwoods, and other native trees. These cayes are not a part of the barrier reef system, but instead lie on their own coral reefs emerging from a limestone ledge that extends several miles into the Caribbean Sea. One small island near the mainland, **Wild Cane Caye**, is the site of an important ancient Maya ceremonial center that is now being excavated. The area's sportfishing is excellent (especially around river mouths), and several hotels and guest houses in Punta Gorda make a good base of operations. The town is also a jumping-off point for trips to Guatemala and, from there, Honduras and the Bay Islands. In recent years, several resorts specializing in sportfishing and diving have operated north and south of Punta Gorda, around Punta Negra and Punta Ycacos. Contact **Kingfisher Sports** in Placencia or **Nature's Way Guest House** in Punta Gorda for details. (See Chapter 9, Southern Belize.)

THE ATOLLS

An atoll is a ring-shaped coral island and associated reef that fringe an enclosed, relatively shallow lagoon. While such formations are common in the South Pacific and some other tropical oceans of the world, only four of any size exist in the Caribbean. Three of the four atolls are located off the barrier reef of Belize (the other is near Trinidad). Because of their isolation from the mainland, atolls are often home to species of flora and fauna rarely seen anywhere else. Their waters tend to be exceptionally clear, calm, and unpolluted, which makes them ideal for diving, fishing, snorkeling, windsurfing, sailing, and kayaking.

The islands themselves are frequently used as breeding sites by birds and other animals that prefer undisturbed habitats for raising their young. Belize has moved swiftly to preserve the relatively pristine quality of its offshore atolls. For example, day trips can be made to **Lighthouse Reef** for birding, diving, and snorkeling. At Lighthouse you may encounter Pita, a very friendly female dolphin who often plays in the bow waves and wakes of passing boats. A trip to one or more of these destinations takes extra effort (and money), but the rewards are unmatched.

TURNEFFE ISLANDS
Location: About 25 miles east of Belize City.
Size: The archipelago measures a maximum of 30 miles long and 10 miles wide, covering a surface area of 205 square miles.
Visitor Information: The Belize Tourist Board, (800) 624-0686, and the Belize Tourism Industry Association, (800) 585-5081.

The Turneffe Islands comprise the largest of the country's three atolls and is also the atoll nearest the mainland, separated from the barrier reef by a 6- to 10-mile channel that plunges to a depth of 1,000 feet or more. Like its companion atolls, Glover's Reef and Lighthouse Reef, Turneffe has been given a deceptive name. Instead of "islands," the archipelago is actually a cluster of about 35 tiny coral islets and swampy mangrove ranges (also known as "wet cayes") encircling a shallow lagoon punctuated by seaward channels.

Most of the cayes at Turneffe are covered with thick forests of red and black mangrove that form a rich and vital breeding ground for conch, lobster, and fish, as well as waterbirds. Close inspection reveals many of the islands on the west (leeward) side to be little more than dense masses of mangroves clutching at shallow sandbeds. On the east (or windward) side a few acres of land rise high enough to support human habitation, and several of these sites (easily identified by coconut palm clusters) are occupied by either sportfishing/diving lodges or the informal "fish camps" of Belizeans. Openings between the mangrove thickets are called "bogues," and they connect the shallow interior lagoons with the open Caribbean.

During the Classic and Late Classic Maya periods, fishers and traders established small outposts here as well as at Glover's Reef. Later, pirates set up camps on the Turneffe Islands (bringing Maya slaves with them) and preyed on passing Spanish trade ships. In the early 20th century the Turneffes were well-known for their sponges and coconuts, largely wiped out by diseases and hurricanes in recent decades. Only a few lobster and coconut collectors, along with a handful of resort operators, now call the islands home.

Things to See and Do
The snorkeling and diving here are excellent. The water is more crystalline here than on reefs closer to the mainland, where some turbidity is caused by the muddy runoff from mountain-draining rivers. Visibility in the warm water (74- to 84-degrees Fahrenheit) is often more than 150 feet in any direction.

The waters around the Turneffe atoll, especially the wadeable coral-debris "flats," are teeming with permit, barracuda, and bonefish. Tarpon are plentiful from March through June around Turneffe's channels and inlets. Larger, deeper-water species include mackerel, bonito, marlin, blackfin tuna, grouper, sailfish, and wahoo. Billfish are most common here from January through April.

Divers and snorkelers are especially fond of the atoll's steep drop-offs and tall coral heads adorned with colorful tube sponges, fan coral, sea fans, and gorgonians among the natural crags and occasional shipwrecks. Black coral and sponges are especially evident in the inland waters of **Vincent's Lagoon. Black Beauty** is a favored dive spot where black coral covers a small reef. **Mauger Caye**, at the atoll's north end, is another popular location among divers, who find a wide variety of sharks there. The island is identified by its lighthouse, in place since 1821.

On the east side of the atoll, **Soldier's Caye** is a sanctuary for nesting roseate terns and white crowned pigeons, both rare in Belize. Animals native to the Turneffe archipelago include boa constrictors, raccoons, lizards, and land crabs.

Research at the Turneffe Islands

A Texas A&M University research station at **Blackbird Caye** has been studying the behavior of Atlantic bottled-nosed dolphins, which frequent nearby lagoons. This is said to be the first such research undertaken in a diverse environment where mangrove islands, coral reefs, and sea grass beds form a delicately balanced ecosystem.

On **Calabash Caye**, immediately south of Blackbird, **Coral Caye Conservation** and the **Planetary Coral Reef Foundation (PCRF)** have a research station where coral reef ecology is being studied. Visitors must have permission to visit. Calabash and the other islands south to the tip of Turneffe have been declared a national marine reserve by the Belize government. An important part of the scientific analysis is comparing reef response to Blackbird's tourism and Calabash's restricted visitation.

Two areas in the Turneffe Islands group have been recommended by the Belize Center for Environmental Studies for establishment as government reserves. **Vincent's Lagoon** (also known as **Northern Lagoon**) is a breeding ground for the Morelet's crocodile and Caribbean manatee, both endangered. **Soldier's Caye**, mentioned above, is the nesting site of several important bird species. Increased human activity could have a negative effect on both areas.

Getting There/Outfitters

There is no regular public transportation to the Turneffe Islands. The vast majority of visitors arrive as part of sportfishing or diving packages offered by the handful of resorts based on the islands (transportation from Belize City is prearranged by private skiff). Because it is close to the mainland in comparison to the other two atolls, Turneffe can be reached fairly easily through arrangements with local charter or live-aboard boat operators, either as a final destination or a stopping point en route to Lighthouse Reef and/or Glover's Reef. Expect to pay at least $85 per person for the 1½- to 2-hour trip from Belize City.

Where to Stay and Eat in Turneffe

Blackbird Caye Resort, on Blackbird Caye; $125 and up, meals included; (888) 271-3483, 2-32767, dive@blackbirdresort.com. Occupying a magnificent stretch of east-facing beach on 4,000-acre Blackbird Caye (named for the great-tailed grackles found here in abundance), this bungalow-style lodge caters to fishing and diving enthusiasts. Amenities include a full-service restaurant/bar, electricity, hot water, fishing guides, and dive shop. The close proximity of seldom-visited reefs, marine walls, and tidal flats provide excellent diving, snorkeling, and fishing opportunities. Many dolphins and sea birds also frequent the area. The resort was up for sale as this book went to press, thus prices, services, and facilities may have changed by the time you read this.

Turneffe Flats Lodge, midway up the atoll's east side on the northeast tip of Blackbird Caye; $130 and up, one-week minimum; 2-2046 or (800) 815-1304, fax (605) 578-7540, flats@blackhillscom or tflats@btl.net. Built on the site of an old fishing camp that dates back to the Maya era, the piles of weathered conch shells here are several feet high. The American-owned lodge can accommodate 12 guests among several bungalows. Beach camping is allowed by advance reservation. The facility specializes in saltwater fly-fishing, although divers, birders, and snorkelers are welcome. Bonefish, permit, and tarpon are the most sought-after species here, and all are found in abundance. Guides, boats, equipment, transportation, and meals are provided.

Turneffe Island Lodge, on 12-acre Caye Bokel at the southern tip of the atoll; $140 and up; 21-2011 or (800) 874-0118, info@turneffelodge.com. Twelve rooms, plus a dining hall and bar. Several boats are outfitted for diving and fishing. The lodge caters to experienced divers, who explore such popular nearby underwater destinations as the Elbow, Myrtle's Turtle, and the shipwreck *Sayonara*. Wall diving off the reef is a favorite pastime here. The resort's 38-foot dive boat can take visitors to remote locations for up to three dives a day. Saltwater fly-fishers are pleased to learn that bonefish, tarpon, and permit are found in large numbers near here. The lodge limits anglers to six per week. Also offers snorkeling, sailing, kayaking, and windsurfing.

LIGHTHOUSE REEF
Location: About 50 miles east of Belize City.
Size: 28 miles long; 2 to 6 miles wide.
Visitor Information: Belize Tourist Board, (800) 624-0686.

The center of this largely uninhabited offshore atoll is almost completely surrounded by coral formations, which form a solid ridge on its east side. Its six islands are widely separated and form a near-perfect semicircle. Lighthouse is best known to most visitors as a diver's paradise (there are more than 40 popular dive sites) and as the home of **Half Moon Caye Natural Monument**.

Vegetation on the cayes is rich and varied, thanks in part to the natural fertilizer provided by thousands of birds and reptiles. Ficus (fig) trees, ziricote, gumbo-limbo, sea grape, spider lily, and coconut palm are all abundant here.

Half Moon Caye Natural Monument

Established as Belize's first protected area in 1981, Half Moon Caye Natural Monument comprises 10,000 acres of the atoll and more than 15 square miles of surrounding waters. The monument shelters a large nesting colony of rare red-footed boobies, an estimated 77 migratory bird species, and the magnificent frigate bird (an arch-enemy of the booby with up to an 8-foot wingspan). The 4,000-member booby colony is one of only two in the Caribbean (the other is on Tobago Island off Venezuela), and the nesting area can be observed from a special 15-foot viewing platform at the end of a half-mile trail. Along the way you may see male frigate birds in their mating display, which involves puffing their crimson throat pouches into giant balloons.

The slow-witted boobies are so named because they showed no fear of early sailors, who killed them easily and indiscriminately for food. Red-footed boobies are usually dull brown (with red feet), but most of the Half Moon Caye birds have white feathers accentuated by pale gold heads and long blue-gray beaks.

The Belize Audubon Society, caretaker of the sanctuary, has counted over 100 bird species on tiny Half Moon, among them the black-chinned hummingbird, white-crowned pigeon, and mangrove warbler. Several species of reptiles also live here, and both hawksbill and loggerhead turtles lay their eggs on the caye's beaches, where you may also encounter the largest species of land crab in Belize.

Hiking

Hiking is allowed on Half Moon Caye with consent of the resident warden, who can provide maps and information on sanitation facilities. Overnight camping has been suspended by Belize Audubon because of over-visitation. A historic lighthouse, first built in 1820 and now sun-powered, provides good views of the atoll and bird colonies. As you walk you'll probably see many iguanas scurrying about. German U-boats refueled here during World War II, but no physical evidence of their visits remains.

Diving, Snorkeling, and Marine Life

The underwater area immediately surrounding Half Moon Caye is protected and is full of marine life—more than 220 species of reef fish have been identified. Conch, which has almost disappeared from local waters, is gradually being reintroduced. The underwater park surrounding Half Moon is easily accessible from a broad sandy beach and pier. Swimmers, divers, snorkelers, and kayakers are all welcome, provided they stay in designated areas and observe conservation rules.

Some distance north of Half Moon is **Sandbore Caye**, which has an old lighthouse as well as excellent diving and snorkeling areas. Despite the presence of such stations, many ships have gone down in these waters. The Spanish trade ship *Juan Batista* sank about a mile offshore in 1822 and is said to have carried a cargo of still-unrecovered gold and silver bullion.

At popular dive sites in the area depths plunge dramatically from 30 feet to several thousand feet within a short distance. The range of marine life includes some deep-water species that seldom enter Belize's shallower reef areas. Also look for enormous sponges, grouper, hogfish, and snapper.

BLUE HOLE NATURAL MONUMENT

Location: About 50 miles east of Belize City.
Visitor Information: *The Belize Tourist Board (800) 624-0686, and the Belize Tourism Industry Association, (800) 585-5081.*

Eight miles north of Half Moon Caye and roughly in the middle of Lighthouse Reef is the popular Blue Hole, an almost perfectly circular limestone sinkhole that is more than 300 feet across and 412 feet deep. Created by the collapse of an underwater cavern some 12,000 years ago, the Blue Hole was the subject of a 1977 documentary by underwater explorer Jacques Cousteau, who concluded that a network of caves and crevices extends far beneath the entire reef. The presence of stalagmites and stalactites supports the conclusion that offshore Belize was dry land

Belize Tourist Board

The Blue Hole is a collapsed underwater cave at Lighthouse Reef.

during the last age, which ended about 11,000 years ago. In 1996 a 1,023-acre parcel that includes the Blue Hole was protected by the Belize government as a natural monument.

Sport divers (limited to a depth of 130 feet) can admire the Blue Hole's outstanding stalagmite and stalactite formations, while swimming in crystal-clear water that appears to be a peculiar shade of deep blue when seen from the surface. The Hole is a habitat for shrimp and jewfish, but you should not expect to see much besides an occasional shark or tuna if you dive here. Surrounding waters are only about 20 feet deep and big fish have trouble making their way to the

Blue Hole. Most outfitters limit drivers to only 10 minutes or less at the 130-foot depth.

Outfitters
Ecosummer Expeditions, (604) 669-7741, fax (604) 669-3244, trips@ecosummer.com. Ecosummer, of Vancouver, BC, has offered week-long sea kayaking expeditions to Lighthouse Reef, including the Blue Hole, since 1982. Participants anchor at Half Moon Caye and spend their days exploring the area. Instruction, equipment, meals, and transportation from Belize City are provided. Ecosummer also arranges one-week sailing trips to Lighthouse Reef from San Pedro aboard the 48-foot traditional Belizean lighter *Excellence*. Guests are taken to the best snorkeling and fishing spots, including the Turneffe and Glover's atolls. Meals and accommodations are provided, and trip extensions to the Belize interior can be arranged. See the Ambergris Caye listing in this chapter for day-trip outfitters.

Getting There
Day trips to Half Moon Caye and the Blue Hole start at about $125 per person ($175 for divers) for groups of several individuals (the atoll is 3 to 4 hours from Belize City and about 2 or 3 hours from San Pedro). Some live-aboard dive boats based in Belize City, Ambergris Caye, and elsewhere make trips to Lighthouse, as well as the two other atolls. Call **Out Island Divers**, 26-2151, in San Pedro for information on its dive trips to Lighthouse. (Out Island also maintains a tent camp on Long Caye.) Expect to pay a minimum of $160 per day for live-aboard boats and ask around before making a commitment—some visitors have complained about poor conditions on some of the boats.

Because of its remote location, boat excursions to the atoll by individuals or couples are fairly costly; it is wise to make the trip with other passengers to reduce the per-person expenses. Boats are allowed to dock only at the pier on the leeward side of Half Moon Caye, and deep-draught vessels may anchor only in designated areas. Charter flights can be made to the Northern Two Caye strip with permission of the Lighthouse Reef Resort.

Where to Stay and Eat Near the Blue Hole
Lighthouse Reef Resort, on 16-acre Northern Two Caye (sometimes called Northern Caye), provides the atoll's only lodging; $200 and up, one-week minimum; 2-31205 or (800) 423-3114, fax (941) 439-2118, reservations@scubabelize.com or lighthouse@btl.net. A 20-unit full-service diving facility, with private paved airstrip for shuttling guests to and from Belize City. The lodge specializes in diving and fishing, seven-night packages start at about $1,350, with all meals, guides, and other

services included. Registrants may use kayaks and windsurfers free of charge. Non-guests must bring their own food, drink, and fuel. Advance permission is required to land on the airstrip. The flying time is 45 minutes to Belize City, via Tropic Air charter.

GLOVER'S REEF ATOLL

Location: About 20 miles east of the barrier reef, 30 miles from the mainland, and roughly 50 miles southeast of Belize City.
Size: The atoll encompasses roughly 100 square miles.
Visitor Information: The Belize Tourism Board (800) 624-0686, and the Belize Tourist Industry Association, (800) 585-5881.

Glover's is a splendid offshore atoll, the most remote island group in the country. Rising from an ocean depth of over 2,000 feet, Glover's consists of a well-defined, oval-shaped coral formation (19 miles long and 7 miles wide) that surrounds more than 700 patch reefs inside a 100-square-mile crystalline lagoon. A special area on the northeast side of Glover's Reef— closed seasonally by the Belize Fisheries Department—is an important breeding ground for grouper and snapper. Surrounding walls begin at about 30 feet and drop suddenly to well over 2,000 feet. Because of its unusual diversity, *Skin Diver* magazine has proclaimed this reef one of the three best dive/snorkel sites in the world.

The atoll is named after 17th-century pirate John Glover, who used the remote islands as the base for his raids against Spanish galleons heading in and out of the Bay of Honduras. One of his ancestors lived on **Northeast Caye** well into the 20th century and several alleged pirate graves can be seen on that island. The ancient Maya had camps here long before Glover, however, and centuries-old artifacts still turn up.

During the early 1970s, a visiting team of international scientists pronounced Glover's the biologically richest atoll in the Caribbean Basin. It is one of the region's only nesting sites for the white-capped noddy, least tern, and marine turtles. In 1993 the entire Glover's Reef atoll was declared a marine reserve by the Belize government. All six of the atoll's islands except Northeast Caye are zoned as conservation areas and one, **Middle Caye**, is a designated wilderness. Seasonal closures and strictly enforced conservation and fishing restrictions allow the reserve to maintain its biological integrity for future generations and for species to recuperate.

In 1991, Middle Caye was purchased from its private owner by the Wildlife Conservation Society (formerly the New York Zoological Society), which now manages the 15-acre island. Middle Caye has been called the keystone to the long-term preservation of Glover's Reef, in that scientists and Belize Department of Fisheries employees can now use Middle as their base for monitoring activities around the atoll. In

1997 the Belize Department of Fisheries had a manager and ranger stationed on the island. Marine ecologists study the area's rich flora and fauna, while government enforcement officers work to protect the remote area from such human disturbances as overfishing, garbage dumping, and careless diving. There is concern that unrestricted human activity in this fragile ecosystem could degrade what remains one of the world's most pristine marine environments.

Researchers have been studying a variety of fish species here, as well as conch and lobster. Recent results suggest that Glover's Reef remains an important breeding ground for marine creatures that have been overharvested in other parts of Belize.

A visit to Middle Caye is by permission only, although those staying on nearby islands are routinely welcomed for guided tours. The island has a small freshwater lagoon and a surprising variety of animals and plants. Facilities include a small museum, a wet lab, and a marine research aquarium. The research center is a model of self-sufficiency: producing its electricity from the sun and wind, obtaining water from a reverse-osmosis desalinization plant, and disposing of its human waste in composting toilets.

Two commercial lodges operate year-round on Glover's Reef atoll and for part of each year a sea-kayaking outfitter (**Slickrock Adventures**) operates on Long Caye, which is also used by an adventure travel company (**International Zoological Expeditions**).

Sea Kayaking
Sea kayaking off Glover's Reef is exceptional, and the atoll works well for both experienced and novice paddlers. Outfitters provide expert guides for boat-handling instruction and safety briefings. Kayaks are used to visit other islands as well as for snorkeling adventures to patch reefs and the outer reef.

Snorkeling and Diving
The snorkeling here is truly world-class. The perimeter of the atoll is lined with awesome elkhorn coral forests that are filled with dozens of fish species. A deeper sandy zone is home to bigger fish, and visitors finally reach a "wall" that eventually drops off some 2,600 feet to the ocean floor about a mile east of Glover's. The diversity of sea creatures within these environments is staggering.

Outfitters
International Zoological Expeditions, 5-22119 or (800) 548-5843, travel@ize2belize.com or jrosado@btl.net. Arranges visits to Long Caye, which the outfitter now owns. IZE maintains services here primarily as an

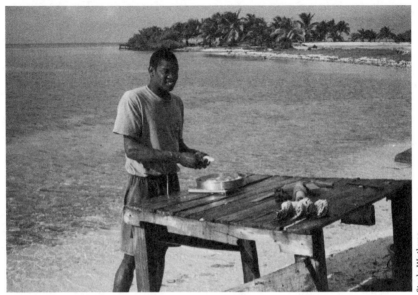

Steele Wotkyns

A Belizean tour guide prepares a "shore lunch" for kayakers at Glover's Reef.

annex for participants in its marine ecology seminars, based on South Water Caye. I recommend visitors try IZE's affordable, well-maintained camping facilities on Long Caye's south end. In 1998, IZE added a new main lodge with a kitchen/dining room and a few cabañas. Similar to IZE's arrangement with the **Living Reef Dive Center** on South Water Caye, Living Reef and IZE are cooperating to stress marine conservation principles and marine ecology education for student groups and other visiting divers on Long Caye. Living Reef's knowledgeable Long Caye manager is **Tony Read**, 5-22214, tread@btl.net. See the previous section about South Water Caye for a description of his company's services.

The northern portion of Long Caye is used by **Slickrock Adventures**, (800) 390-5715, slickrock@slickrock.com, www.slickrock.com, which offers recommended 6- and 10-day package trips featuring kayaking, windsurfing (short and long boards), snorkeling, fishing, and diving. Guests spend part of each day paddling among the islands, observing underwater flora and fauna in remote parts of the atoll. Instruction, most equipment, meals, and rustic accommodations (as well as tent sites) are provided, along with transportation by boat to and from Belize City or Dangriga. Visitors bring their own snorkeling masks, fishing gear, and fins. Slickrock offers trip extensions to the Belize interior as well as Honduras. Diving instruction, certification courses, and a variety of world-class, open-water dives can be arranged through the above-mentioned Living Reef Dive Center.

Slickrock's unobtrusive facilities on the island include passive-solar showers, composting toilets, rainwater collection systems, volleyball court, sun deck, dining pavillion, and a special nesting platform for a resident osprey family.

Glover's Atoll Resort (5-12016, glovers@btl.net) offers kayaking, windsurfing, fly-fishing, snorkeling, and diving, as well as camping and birding. Instruction and certification is available. Based on 9-acre Northeast Caye, the resort provides weekly transportation to and from the island by boat via Sittee River Village.

Manta Reef Resort (800 326-1724, info@mantaresort.com) is oriented primarily to experienced divers and fishers who come on week-long packages. A full complement of boats, guides, and equipment are provided, along with meals and lodging.

Getting There

Glover's Atoll Resort, Manta Reef Resort, International Zoological Expeditions, and **Slickrock Adventures** each provide transportation to and from the atoll as part of their packages, which usually last from one to two weeks. Because of the distance from the mainland, expect to pay a minimum of $150 for a charter boat to Glover's Reef, probably departing from Dangriga, Placencia, or Big Creek. An alternative is to sign onto one of the several live-aboard dive boats that regularly anchor off the atoll. **Glover's Atoll Resort** guests are picked up every Sunday morning at the dorm-style Glover's Guest House ($5–$8), on the Sittee River south of Dangriga, for the 5- to 6-hour voyage to Northeast Caye. The boat returns the following Saturday afternoon, and both trips are included in the price of lodging. The resort prefers advance reservations and reduces rates for second-week stays. (Closed September–November.)

Where to Stay and Eat on Glover's Reef

Manta Reef Resort, on privately owned Southwest Caye on the archipelago's southern tip; $140 and up (meals included); 23-1895 or (800) 326-1724, fax (310) 937-6473, info@mantaresort.com. Caters to serious divers and fishers (one-week minimum) eager to explore the underwater world or to hook bonefish, permit, and barracuda, which are abundant on the atoll's coral flats. Conditions are also excellent for tarpon, snapper, grouper, marlin, jack, tuna, bonito, wahoo, sailfish, and other billfish (plus the huge manta rays that give the resort its name). Manta provides lodging on the 12-acre island in thatched-roof cabañas and transportation

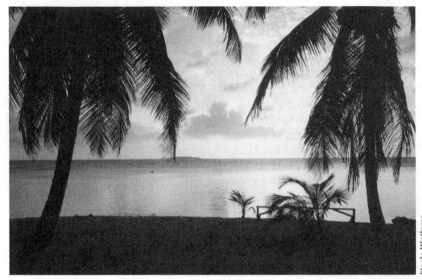

Sunset is a quiet time on Glover's Reef.

Steele Wotkyns

for divers in small V-hull boats. Forested with coconut palms, like each of this atoll's islands, Southwest Caye is bisected by a hurricane-created cut and dominated at its southernmost end by a government-operated lighthouse. Transportation to Manta Reef Resort is by boat (included in the price) from Belize City.

Glover's Atoll Resort, on Northeast Caye; $100/week cabin, $80/week camping, meals not included; 1-48351 or 5-12016, glovers@btl.net, www.belizemall.com. This rustic camping/cabaña facility specializes in diving, kayaking, windsurfing, snorkeling, and fishing trips for individuals and small groups. Attractions on 12-acre Northeast Caye include an old and massive gumbo-limbo tree, which shelters the alleged graves of pirates who lived here over two centuries ago. Turtles nest on the island's beaches and ospreys are common. Canoes, powerboats, tents, guides, air compressors, and water recreation gear are usually available, but remember that there is no electricity, refrigeration, or indoor plumbing: conditions are primitive. Meals (expensive) can sometimes be purchased at the resort's headquarters, but visitors are strongly encouraged to provide their own food (cooking gear, fishing line, and water are provided for a fee, as is camping equipment). Transportation arranged by boat each Sunday morning from Glover's Guest House in Sittee River Village.

FAVORITE DIVE AND SNORKEL LOCATIONS ON THE ATOLLS

Marine life is so varied and abundant in the offshore waters of Glover's Reef that virtually any location is bound to please the eye. Since Caribbean swells are fairly relentless along the north end of the atoll, most divers prefer the southern sections of the reef, particularly the walls and grooves around each of the cayes. Recommended dive sites include Octopus Alley, Dolphin Dance, Turtle Tavern, Manta Reef, Grouper Flats, Shark Point, and Emerald Forest Reef. Snorkelers gravitate toward the windward (east) slopes of the cayes as well as the many patch reefs inside the atoll.

There is plenty of underwater flora and fauna at Lighthouse Reef Atoll, and some divers rank this location among the best in the world. Particularly noteworthy is the spectacular array of sponges, coral growths, invertebrates, and multi-colored reef fish. Many dive boats cruise the atoll, anchoring at such favored locations as Half Moon Caye Wall, Silver Cayes, Tres Cocos, West Point (stepped reef walls), Southwest Cut, and Nurse Shark Lodge (off Long Caye). Snorkelers will find plenty to see in the waters around Half Moon, Northern Two, and Long Cayes.

WESTERN BELIZE

7

CAYO DISTRICT

Until the late 1980s, few visitors ventured west of the Belize Zoo unless they were heading across the Guatemalan border to the ancient city of Tikal. The conventional wisdom was that, except for the capital of Belmopan and the Maya ruins of Xunantunich, there was not much to see in the country's interior. We have talked to some travelers whose only memory along the Western Highway is of the roadside Belize City cemetery and an unsightly municipal garbage dump, since closed down.

Fortunately, the interior's infrastructure has improved to the point where many rewarding destinations can (and should) be added to any visitor's itinerary. Besides the country's most extensive Maya ruins and a growing number of comfortable lodges, Belize's interior offers the best opportunity to encounter the marvelous flora and fauna of a relatively undisturbed subtropical forest. Although some of the nation's newest nature sanctuaries and wilderness preserves offer virtually no access to the casual visitor, others provide an "up close and personal" experience you are not likely to forget. In addition, there are caves, rivers, horse paths, waterfalls, foot trails, mountain bike tracks, butterfly farms, museums, whitewater rapids, campsites, and flora and fauna galore, just waiting to be discovered—in some cases quite literally, since much of the interior remains virtually untouched by humans.

Cayo (Spanish for "small island") is the second-largest district in Belize. The district begins about 35 miles south and west of Belize City and encompasses roughly 1,500 square miles, including much of the

Canoeing on the Macal River of the Cayo District

Macal River watershed and Maya Mountains. In 1999, the population in Cayo was estimated to be about 46,000.

The capital city of **Belmopan** lies at the district's eastern border and its western edge is the Guatemalan frontier. In between, besides thick forests and wild rivers, visitors find some of the nation's richest farmland, at times so carefully manicured by Mennonites that it looks more like rural Pennsylvania than Central America. Besides cattle, poultry, and pigs, Cayo farmers raise corn, sorghum, beans, fruit, and various vegetables for both domestic consumption and export. Significant amounts of pine, rosewood, Santa María, cedar, and mahogany are harvested by timber interests.

San Ignacio, on the Macal River, is the hub of commerce and tourism for western Belize. Other Cayo District towns include **Santa Elena**, San Ignacio's sister city across the suspension bridge, and **Benque Viejo**, which practically straddles the border. Both of the latter communities are largely Spanish-speaking, and you are likely to encounter marimbas, fiestas, and colorful social customs centered around Catholic holidays and the rituals of baptism, confirmation, and marriage. Many inhabitants are descended from Maya and Guatemalan immigrants who crossed the border into Belize to escape political persecution and economic exploitation.

SAN IGNACIO AND VICINITY

SAN IGNACIO

Location: *Roughly 22 miles west of Belmopan and 9 miles east of the Guatemala border, 72 miles west of Belize City.*

Population: *About 8,000 (1999 estimate).*

Visitor Information: *Local travel agencies; the Belize Tourism Industry Association, 2-75717, or their Cayo representative, Windy Hill's Robert Hales, 92-2017; the Belize Tourist Board, 2-77213 or (800) 624-0686. The tourists' social hub is Eva's Restaurant (see "Where to Eat in San Ignacio").*

San Ignacio is the largest town in the Cayo District, and its many services make this a fine place to have a meal, mail a postcard, arrange a tour, fill the gas tank, fix a flat tire, exchange currency, and load up on supplies. There are many pleasant hotels in San Ignacio, although most visitors prefer to find accommodations in the surrounding countryside.

The town is laid out on a series of bluffs alongside the Macal River, at an elevation high enough to be noticeably cooler and less humid than the coastal plain. The people are friendly and happy-go-lucky, pointing with pride at their Hawkesworth Bridge, a scaled-down version of the Brooklyn Bridge, erected in the late 1940s and still the only suspension span in Belize.

Things to See and Do

Locals will steer you to the partially restored Maya ruin of **Cahal Pech**, just past Main Street at the crest of a hill, and **Arts & Crafts of Central America**, a well-stocked souvenir and bookstore at 1 Wyatt Street.

Day trips throughout Cayo and to Tikal can be arranged through **Yute Expeditions**, 92-2979, fax 92-2076, run by reputable tour operator Sergio Paiz. Also recommended is **Collego Tours** (92-2483) and **David's Tours** (at Hannah's Restaurant).

About 6 miles west of San Ignacio, near the Xunantunich site and along the Mopán River, is a stretch of surging white-water rapids that some travelers enjoy running in canoes, kayaks, rubber rafts, or inner tubes. There are fine swimming holes in the area and birding is excellent. Several area operators arrange excursions down the Mopán and other nearby rivers. Check with Remo Montgomery at the **Sandcastle Bar & Grill** in San Ignacio for suggestions.

International Archaeological Tours specializes in local Maya sites and can arrange guided trips into Guatemala and Mexico. Principal guide Ramon Silva (iatours@btl.net) is an expert birder, very knowledgable about Maya culture, and an active member of the Belize Audubon Society.

Getting There

San Ignacio and western Belize are easily reached by private or rental car by way of the Western Highway, or by the same route via the low-cost Batty, Novelo, Piache, and Shaw bus lines. Check locally for schedules and fares (about $4 between Belize City and San Ignacio), or check the updated information posted on the Internet at www.belizenet.com.

A twice-daily shuttle ($25 one-way, 92-2267) runs between San Ignacio and Belize City's domestic and international airports, where it meets all TACA, American, and Continental flights. Passengers are dropped off about 2 hours before departing international flights. The pick-up point in San Ignacio is in front of Eva's Restaurant on Burns Ave. "On request" stops and pick-ups are made along the Western Highway.

The drive between Belize City and San Ignacio takes about 2 hours (slightly longer by bus or shuttle). Most resorts can arrange transportation to and from the Belize City airports for a fee of between $75 and $125.

You can hire taxis for for day trips and local sightseeing. Look for them in san Ignacio on the west side of the Macal River suspension bridge, at Market Plaza in Belmopan.

There is no scheduled air service to the Cayo District, although charters will fly to air-strips at Gallon Jug, Central Farm (near San Ignacio), and Blancaneaux Lodge.

Where to Stay in San Ignacio and Santa Elena

Cahal Pech Village, near the ruins; $40 and up; 92-3203. Excellent value. Friendly, helpful staff and good restaurant. Some rooms with air-conditioning and TV.

Clarissa Falls Resort, at Mile 5.5 on the Western Highway, west of San Ignacio; $40; 9-23196. Rustic cottages without electricity or private baths. Camping and meals available. You can arrange inner-tube floats, horseback rides, and visits to nearby Maya ruins. Restaurant on site.

Cosmos Camping, 15 Branch Mouth Rd., San Ignacio; 9-22116. Lovely. lush grounds along the Macal River. Campsites are $3 per person, cabañas $8 double-occupancy. You can also rent a hammock space for a small fee. Walk to town takes about 20 minutes.

El Chiclero, near Cahal Pech ruins, west side of San Ignacio; $20; 9-24119. Meals available. You can watch sapodilla sap being "cooked" into a chewing-gum base and see a replica of a traditional of a *chiclero* (sapodilla-tapper) camp.

Martha's Guesthouse and Kitchen, 2 blocks from bus terminal; $25;

92-2132. Downtown location with clean rooms and great food (try the pizza). Eco-tours of Cayo and Guatemala arranged by friendly, knowledgable staffers.

Mida's Resort, on Branch Mouth Road, near downtown; $50; 92-3845 or 92-3172. Thatch-roofed cabins rented by local family who arrange canoeing, sight-seeing, and nature treks, as well as inexpensive camping. A full complement of meals available. Campsites: $7.

Pacz Hotel, 2 Far West St., San Ignacio; $20; tel./fax 92-2110, canoeing, horseback riding, pacz@btl.net. Clean, basic, inexpensive rooms. Airport shuttle, mountain bike rentals, canoeing, horseback rides, and local sightseeing (including day trips to caves).

Piache Hotel, 22 Buena Vista St.; $25; 92-2032, piache.hot@btl.net. A dozen comfortable rooms and outdoor bar. The owner, Godsman Ellis, offers tours of the cayes and Tikal.

San Ignacio Hotel, 18 Buena Vista St.; $50; 92-2034, sanighot@btl.net. Fine restaurant, spacious rooms, satellite TV, basketball court, and the best swimming pool in town. A nature trail and iguana hatchery are added attractions. Recommended.

Snooty Fox Guest House, 64 George Price Ave., Santa Elena; $25; 9-22150. Several types of rooms to choose from, some with private bath and cable TV. There's a bar with a pool table and canoes for hire.

Where to Eat in San Ignacio and Santa Elena
Eva's Restaurant, 22 Burns; 92-2267, evas@btl.net, www.webspanner .com. American-style hamburgers, Belizean rice 'n' beans, plus several veggie dishes. A convivial meeting place, with cold beer and CNN, too. Run by English expatriate Bob Jones and his Belizean wife, Nestora. Open 7 a.m. to 11 p.m. daily, 'til midnight Friday through Saturday. Eva's is the unofficial nerve center of the district, its walls adorned with local travel literature and its tables crowded with bonafide Cayo characters. Bob Jones is a walking encyclopedia of what to see and do here, and will cheerfully dispense suggestions suited to any budget and interest. E-mail and Internet access ($8 an hour), plus souvenirs.

Maya Café, on Burns Avenue. The best coffee, pastries, and reading material in town. The owners provide information on mountain bike and canoe rentals. Also recommended is the nearby Yesteryear Café.

Mystic Moon Country Kitchen, 5 Mossiah St. A friendly, moderately priced restaurant specializing in Italian and vegetarian dishes, along with fresh fruit, shakes, and coffee. A couple of former New York City artists run the place.

Palpito's Upstairs, on Mission St. Good meals, friendly service, and budget prices. Top choices: Mexican dishes and tropical cocktails.

Sandcastle Bar & Grill, next to the bus stop. Some of the best food and drink in town (plus open-air blues, jazz, and reggae music). Try the delicious algae drink!

Serendib, 27 Burns Avenue. This Sri Lankan is justifiably revered for its spicy curry. Prices are moderate and the service is friendly.

RESORTS NEAR SAN IGNACIO

Tucked into the folds of the lush green hills are more than a dozen "cottage" resorts ranging from rustic to elegant, each catering to the visitor who wants to get away from urban distractions in a wooden bungalow, stilt-supported tree house, or palm-thatched cabaña. Some of these charming retreats are located on working farms or ranches, while others are luxury lodges exclusively dedicated to a kind of gracious, low-key, tropical tourism that brings to mind images of the African veldt or Costa Rican jungle.

Each set of accommodations is slightly different in style and character, with its own specialization. Some focus on horseback riding or canoeing; others cater to forest trekkers and birders. Still others can arrange mountain biking tours, white-water rafting, kayaking, strenuous camping trips in the unexplored wilderness, or investigations of little-known caverns. All, however, supply meals and other basic amenities to their guests, and most can set up tours of the nearby Maya ruins at Xunantunich, Caracol, Cahal Pech, and Tikal. A few even have reciprocal agreements with resorts on the coast or cayes that allow visitors to package a "surf and turf" holiday. Rates and accommodations vary widely, from budget dorms to comfortable tent-camping to five-star villas, depending on such variables as location, meals, services, and transportation costs.

Most Cayo resort operators take individual preferences into account, making breakfast at 5 a.m. for birders, for example, or eliminating the meal entirely for late-risers who wish to sleep in. If you want to be chauffeured, they will pick you up at the Belize City airport or San Ignacio bus stop, for example. If you have private transportation, operators will be happy to give you detailed instructions and maps to whatever destination pleases you. The least expensive rooms in Cayo are generally found within the town limits of San Ignacio, although there are a growing number of budget and moderately priced options in the countryside. All of the luxury resorts are in rural areas of the Cayo. Taxi rides from San Ignacio start at about $15.

Black Rock Jungle River Lodge, $65, meals included; 92-2341, fax 92-3449, blackrock@btl.net. A short distance upriver from Ek' Tun, this 250-acre bungalow compound along the Macal offers simple accommodations, but the lodge is surrounded by thick forests and towering limestone cliffs. You can make arrangements through the co-owned Caesar's Place, between Belmopan and San Ignacio on the Western Highway.

Chaa Creek Cottages/Macal River Camp, 7 miles upstream from San Ignacio; offering Maya-style cabañas $135, including meals, and safari-style camping on a bluff above the Macal River for $90, including meals; 92-2037, fax 92-2501, chaacreek@btl.net. Established in 1981 by British expatriate Mick Fleming and his American wife, Lucy. Tents boast comfortable cots and open-hearth cooking, while the spacious cottages have thatched palapa roofs and mahogany furniture. Visitors are serenaded by exotic birds every morning. Nature-oriented tour operators regularly bring their clients here because of the resort's high standards, diversity of activities, and commitment to environmental education. The adjacent **Butterfly House**

Typical cabaña bungalow of the Cayo District

161

($115) is a perfect getaway for vacationing couples, with a kitchen and solar electricity. Make arrangements here for one of the smoothest day trips available to Tikal, as well as to many Cayo sites, including the little-known Chumpiate Maya Cave. Highly recommended. Fine bar and restaurant.

Crystal Paradise Resort, 4 miles upriver from San Ignacio; $75 and up (rates include breakfast and dinner); 92-2772 or (800) 552-3419, evas@btl.net. This 100-acre farm, operated by a Maya-Creole family, offers birding (binoculars provided), horseback riding, and boat trips. Manager Jeronie Tut and his staff go out of their way to please guests and know the Cayo as only lifelong residents can. Extensive natural history library and impressive historic artifacts. The homegrown coffee and Teresa Tut's Creole cooking are delicious. Free pickup by boat or van from San Ignacio. More unusual activities include stargazing (with a powerful telescope), nighttime horseback rides, Maya ruin tours, guided exploration of nearby caves, and trips to Laguna Aguacate (a jungle lake near a Mennonite settlement). Birding and hiking here are excellent.

duPlooy's Resort, just up the river from Chaa Creek; $95 and up; 92-3101, fax 92-3301, or (803) 722-1513, duplooys@pobox.com Developed by an American-Zimbabwean couple, this lodge is also an active member of the Belize EcoTourism Association. Known for its lush tropical garden and orchid nursery. Besides the usual day trips and meals, duPlooy's offers bungalow, guest house, and family-style accommodations. About 4 miles west of the Western Highway. Package rates include sightseeing.

Ek'Tun, Macal River about 12 miles southwest of San Ignacio; $160; 93-2536 or (303) 442-6150, fax 93-2446, ektun@btl.net. American expatriates Ken and Phyllis Dart have created a lovely and luxurious two-cottage retreat on their 200 acres of pristine jungle. It is worth the extra effort (four-wheel-drive Land Rover and boat) to get to this compound, built on the grounds of an ancient Maya village. The Darts love to pamper their guests with personal, customized service, ranging from gourmet meals (extra charge) to canoe trips down the Macal and guided tours of unexcavated ruins. Committed environmentalists, the Darts are growing mahogany, teak, and other valued trees that have become scarce through exploitation. Check out the Ek' Tun Web site at http://www.ektunbelize.com.

Maya Mountain Lodge & Tours, a half-mile mile south of Santa Elena on the Cristo Rey Road; $40 room, $80 cottage; 92-2164, fax 92-2029, jungle@mayamountain.com, www.mayamountain.com. Emphasizes cultural tourism; encompasses a forest preserve and Mayan ruin on the slopes of Maya Mountain. Owners Bart (a prime mover in the Belize EcoTourism

Association) and Suzi Mickler have helped develop a ceramic handicrafts industry using local artisans, teachers, and materials. Besides sightseeing trips, Maya Mountain offers guided horseback trips, canoe rides, birding walks, archaeological tours (destinations include Che Chem Ha Cave and Tikal), and nature treks. The facility maintains an educational field station and reference library for cultural, archaeological, and wildlife studies. One of the few Belize lodges that actively *encourages* families to visit, providing a growing number of activities for parents and their children. Family or group experiences include sharing Belizean folklore and rainforest stories, demonstrating Maya handicrafts, cooking local and international foods, and providing a unique culture exchange through overnight "home visits" (booked in advance) with participating families in the immediate area and other parts of Belize.

Special summer workshops are available for interest groups, including artists, families interested in ecology or multiculturalism, and teachers studying tropical ecology or Maya culture. Accommodations range from comfortable cottages to a bunkhouse for budget student groups. Free e-mail service for guests. A pool was added in 1998.

Mountain Equestrian Trails, Mile 8 on the Chiquibul Road (turn off at Georgeville) and one mile north of the Mountain Pine Ridge boundary; 92-3310 or (800) 838-3918, met@pobox.com. Stay at the safari-style tent camp ($50) or in beautiful bungalows ($100 and up); all meals available. A 150-acre, 20-horse ranch adjacent to the private Slate Creek Nature Preserve, MET offers several options for an authentic horseback riding experience (tailored for equestrians of all abilities, including novices). Also available are vehicle-based tours of Xunantunich, Pacbitun, San Antonio, the Mountain Pine Ridge, Caracol, and El Pilar. Adventurous travelers can choose from 4- or 5-day Chiclero Trails Base Camp adventures or MET's 6-day Wildlife Encounter/Kayak Expedition. Well-informed local guides lead visitors on horseback to remote caves, waterfalls, the Mountain Pine Ridge, and a large sinkhole called **The Vega**. Resident guide **Francisco Rash**, the apprentice of a Maya bush doctor, shares information during scheduled presentations on Maya culture and points out medicinal plants during his nature tours. **Jan Meerman**—one of the most experienced conservation scientists in Central America—conducts ecology and conservation workshops.

Nabintunich, west along the Mopán River near Xunantunich; $40, meals available; 93-2096. This 400-acre working ranch has 11 stone cabins and lots of horses. Bridle trails extend through miles of dense bush.

Parrot Nest, on a bend in the Belize River near the Maya/mestizo village of Bullet Tree Falls; $20 with shared bath; 9-37008, parrot@btl.net. Features low-key adventure and fine food (for a fee). Up to eight visitors at a time are accommodated in rustic, stilt-supported, thatch-roof tree houses. Swimming and birding are excellent, and the owners can arrange all sorts of sightseeing and adventure tours. $5 to $8 taxi ride from San Ignacio (7 miles away). Recommended.

Tropical Wings Nature Center and Trek Stop, near Xunantunich on the Western Highway in San José Succotz; 93-2265, susa@btl.net. A budget ($10 per person) resort with a "youth hostel" atmosphere (i.e., communal kitchen and living room) and small butterfly house/nature museum. Friendly owners and fellow travelers. Rents bikes ($7.50) and tents with campsites ($6.50), as well as kayaks and inner tubes.

Windy Hill Resort, a few miles west of San Ignacio on the Western Highway; $70; 92-2017, fax 92-3080, (800) 946-3995, windyhill@ btl.net. A cattle ranch with luxurious private cottages. Arranges local tours, including daily departures to Tikal for $75 per person (a good value, although meals are expensive). Fine food, satellite TV, and a swimming pool.

Tha above roster is far from complete. Other lodges in the Cayo countryside include **Log Cab-Inns**, **Riverside Resort**, and **Woodlands Resort**. Check at Eva's in San Ignacio or log on belizenet.com for contact information.

IX CHEL TROPICAL RESEARCH CENTER AND RAINFOREST MEDICINE TRAIL

Location: *About 7 miles southwest of San Ignacio, at the end of Chaa Creek Road.*
Hours: *Daily 8 a.m. to 12 noon and 1 p.m. to 5 p.m.*
Fees: *A self-guided tour of the mile-long Rainforest Medicine Trail is $5.75 per person. A guided tour and lecture by an Ix Chel staffer is $17.25, if arranged in advance.*
Visitor Information: *Ix Chel Tropical Research Center, 9-23870.*

Ix Chel Tropical Research Center is a pioneering medicinal research facility specializing in the healing properties of plants. It is nestled on a hill above the Macal River and is surrounded by thick second-growth subtropical vegetation. A maze of pathways snakes through this foliage, and among these is the remarkable Rainforest Medicine Trail.
    The Rainforest Medicine Trail winds through a living display of arboreal and herbal remedies making it an essential component to Ix

Chel's success. Signs describe the plants, many bearing unusually descriptive names. The tres puntas plant—distinguished by its large three-pointed leaves and also known as "jackass bitters"—is used to treat and prevent such ailments as salmonella, intestinal parasites, and skin infections. A few steps farther is skunk root, effective in treating pain and ulcers, and wild grapevine, filled with an antiseptic used to wash newborn infants. Nearby grows the fiddlewood tree; its bark in an herbal bath kills the parasite known to cause a painful condition called leishmaniasis. Also present is the wild yam, a popular Belizean household remedy for urinary tract ailments and arthritis pain.

One section of the trail, **Granny's Garden**, displays about 50 useful common plants from various parts of the world. These include amaranth, basil, rue, marigold, lemon grass, and hibiscus. All are marked and correspond to descriptions found on laminated sheets used in a self-guided tour.

Yet another Ix Chel endeavor is the cultivation and marketing of plants for production of herbal formulae used in cosmetics. Besides its own production of these items, the Ix Chel team is helping local farmers rejuvenate their degraded lands by cultivating medicinal cash crops that can be an effective alternative to slash-and-burn agriculture. The program thus provides a new, health-oriented alternative to traditional practices that deplete soils (in return for short-term subsistence crops) while destroying thousands of valuable native plants and their habitat.

Ix Chel sells many herbal elixirs and potions—with names like Belly Be Good and Female Tonic—as well as fresh allspice berries (used in cooking and for the relief of fever, toothache, and stomach ache). Prices for such items start at around $10. Some of these products are also available in gift shops and groceries in other parts of the country; look for the Rainforest Remedies label, which is also marketed in the U.S. by Lotus Light. A percentage of sales goes to traditional healers and educational programs in Belize. Owners Rosita Arvigo and Greg Shropshire welcome donations to support their work, either sent directly to Ix Chel or the Traditional Healers' Foundation, General Delivery, San Ignacio, Belize.

Ix Chel's Rosita Arvigo

A dedicated herbalist and botanical field practitioner from Chicago, Rosita Arvigo is in a race against time. She and her family, staff, and volunteers are scouring the Central American forests in search of tropical plants that may help win the war against a number of deadly diseases. With her husband, Greg Shropshire, Arvigo works at the place where the timeless wisdom of venerable native healers intersects with the theories of Western medicine.

"Much of what I have learned was from Don Elijio Panti," she explains, referring to the Maya healer who began—albeit reluctantly at first—sharing his secrets (beginning at age 86) with Arvigo. Over 106 years old when he passed away in 1996, Panti's legacy survives in a new generation of healers through the Belize Association of Traditional Healers (referred to locally as BATH).

Arvigo has accomplished one important goal: to preserve the encyclopedic herbal lore that Panti memorized during his lifetime. Major progress has also been made in determining the healing properties of hundreds of native plants that may never have been ingested by humans and thus have unknown biochemical effects.

The work under way at Ix Chel and elsewhere in Belize by members of BATH is spurred by the knowledge that the world's forests have already yielded such medicines as quinine (an antimalarial), vinblastine (used to treat Hodgkin's disease), and taxol (a treatment for ovarian cancer). Many so-called miracle drugs are plant-derived compounds from tropical forests. Examples include tubocurarine (curare), used in operating rooms to relax muscles and prevent spasm, and pilocarpine, used for the treatment of glaucoma.

Arvigo and Shropshire regularly conduct medicinal plant seminars at nearby Chaa Creek Cottages, and the couple sell a variety of materials directly to the public at their gift shop. Since 1993, Ix hel has collaborated with BATH in the protection of a tract of forest in western Belize for the

Rosita Arvigo displays dried leaves of the tres puntos plant.

166

specific purpose of growing and harvesting medicinal plants. The resulting 6,000-acre medicinal plant reserve, **Terra Nova**, is now managed by the Belize Enterprise for Sustainable Technology and is not currently accessible to tourists. One of the innovative projects at Terra Nova recruits and trains Belizean youths to help rescue young native medicinal plants that are in areas scheduled for development.

Getting There

Follow the Western Highway west of San Ignacio and exit left (south) on the Chaa Creek Road. About 4 miles from the Western Highway, the road splits, with a right fork heading toward duPlooy's Resort and the other to Chaa Creek Cottages. Immediately before reaching the lodge, a well-marked left fork leads down a steep hill to Ix Chel.

CHAA CREEK NATURAL HISTORY CENTRE AND BUTTERFLY FARM

Location: About 7 miles from San Ignacio, on the Macal River.
Size: 330 acres.
Hours: 9 a.m. to 5 p.m. daily.
Fees: $6 covers admission to both Butterfly Farm and Natural History Centre.
Visitor Information: 92-2037, fax 92-2051, or chaacreek@btl.net.

About 7 miles southwest of San Ignacio is a compound near the confluence of the Macal River and one of its small tributaries, Chaa Creek. What started many years ago as a small farm and lodge has been transformed by Mick Fleming, an expatriate of Britain, and his American wife, Lucy, into a haven for nature lovers.

Blue Morpho Butterfly Breeding Centre

A short nature trail leads up the hill from Chaa Creek's office to the Blue Morpho Butterfly Breeding Centre, open to the public for a $6 fee. Here your guide points out the four distinct changes the brilliant neon-blue morpho undergoes during metamorphosis from a pale green egg to a striking, indigo-colored butterfly. The guide explains the butterfly's eating habits as it progresses through the caterpillar stage. If your timing is right, you'll witness the miracle of a blue morpho's emergence from its strange brown pupa. The center releases into the wild about 45 percent of the some 200 butterflies it breeds each day; the rest are exported to help keep this educational enterprise operating.

Natural History Centre

As part of the same admission, visitors may explore Chaa Creek's exceptional Natural History Centre, situated near the blue morpho flight cage.

The Howler Monkey Reintroduction Program

In the last couple of years, a black howler monkey reintroduction program has operated in conjunction with the villages of Cristo Rey, Scotland Halfmoon, and Monkey River Town. Sponsored by Chaa Creek and the Foundation for Wildlife Conservation with involvement by the Yerkes Regional Primate Center, a successful first stage of the program was completed with the release of eight black howlers (captured at the Community Baboon Sanctuary in north-central Belize) at Chaa Creek's Macal River Camp. The program is designed to help ensure the long-term survival of these monkeys in Belize and to promote reforestation of the lower Macal River—enhancing a key portion of a wildlife corridor that stretches over 60 miles across the Maya Mountain divide. After monitoring the movements of the original group—reported to be doing well as this edition went to press—the plan was to capture another 8 to 12 individuals from the Monkey River area in southern Belize and release them along the Macal.

This is probably the most comprehensive such facility in Belize. Its research room includes a rarely found archive of scientific studies carried out over the years in Belize, as well as a complete collection of books and field guides to help you answer those nagging questions about an exotic animal or plant you may have seen.

Designed to stimulate awareness and understanding of the local environment for both Belizeans and visitors, the Centre features a **Cayo Room**, introducing visitors to the biological and archaeological diversity of the immediate area. There is an exhibit on birds and mammals, including a display about bats (featuring the amazing fishing bat of Belize). High on one wall is a time-line of the Maya civilization along with a special exhibit on local archaeology. You'll also find a butterfly exhibit, reptiles and amphibians display, gift shop, and yet another research room containing topographic maps, books, and a variety of color slides.

SLATE CREEK RESERVE

Location: *About 15 miles southeast of San Ignacio, in the foothills of the*
Mountain Pine Ridge.
Size: *Around 4,000 acres.*
Visitor Information: *Mountain Equestrian Trails, 92-3310, or write c/o*
Central Farm Post Office.

More than a dozen local landowners are responsible for the creation and
management of the hilly, heavily forested Slate Creek Reserve, a one-hour
drive south of San Ignacio via the Georgeville-Mountain Pine Ridge
Road. These individuals, working with Spanish-speaking immigrants in
the area, are striving to preserve this impressive natural resource while
providing local farmers with an economic alternative to slash-and-burn
agriculture, including handicraft production and nature-oriented tourism.
As this book went to press, however, access to the reserve was limited.

The great variety of trails that wind through Slate Creek Preserve's
unique biological corridor (connecting the Mountain Pine Ridge and its
limestone karst foothills east to the Tapir Mountain Nature Reserve)
make this an ideal place for visitors to encounter flora and fauna on foot
as well as on horseback. The birding, in particular, is excellent. In all,
more than 240 bird species have been identified here.

BARTON CREEK CAVE

This small but interesting cave is accessible only by water and only via a
prearranged 4- to 5-hour tour. For your trouble you'll see a sacred Maya
burial chamber, where a few of the ancient Maya were laid to rest alongside large pottery vessels. A natural bridge used by early visitors is
adorned with a carefully placed skull. Because this is a registered archaeological site, nothing may be touched or removed. Tours are by canoe
along the slow-moving river that flows through the cave then exits into
Upper Barton Creek. Nearby is a village of the same name, inhabited by
traditional Mennonites (please do not photograph them without their permission). The cave itself has miles of passages and rooms with ceilings
reported to be as much as 300 feet high. Expect to pay about $30 for a
guided tour, arranged through nearby **Mountain Equestrian Trails**,
Maya Mountain Lodge, or **Pook's Hill Lodge**, among others. A local
specialist is Dave's Adventure Tours (92-3647).

THE MOUNTAIN PINE RIDGE

Location: *About 10 miles southeast of San Ignacio, extending for about 20*
miles south toward the Maya Mountains.
Size: *Nearly 300 square miles.*
Hours: *24 hours, 7 days a week.*

Other Slate Creek Area Attractions

*I recommend that visitors stop in directly across the Chiquibul Road from MET to meet Jan Meerman and Tineke Boomsma, who can provide a tour of their national passionflower (Passiflora) collection and **Green Hills Butterfly House**. As part of their nonprofit organization, Belize Tropical Forest Studies, the couple has opened a biodiversity research facility with low-cost lodging for research groups, a 1,000-square-foot butterfly flight area, and a butterfly rearing facility. Green Hills is usually open during regular morning-to-afternoon hours from Christmas through Easter. Contact them at P.O. Box 208, Belmopan, 92-3310 or tfs@pobox.com.*

*Another good option for visitors to the Slate Creek Preserve area is the moderately priced **Huru Kaan Lodge**, 92-2755, at mile 8.5 on the Chiquibul Road. Like his neighbors at MET and Papillon, Huru Kaan proprietor Ben Butenschoen is a Slate Creek Preserve member. His resort is located in part of a 1,600-acre, family-owned valley protected by the family since 1972. Huru Kaan offers rainforest treks, mountain-stream swimming, and inexpensive half- and full-day jungle safaris, to name a few outdoor adventures. Accommodations in Huru Kaan's thatch-roofed pavilions are by reservation only.*

*Also try **Cool Shade Resort**, 92-3089, cool-shade@btl.net, a working farm on Georgeville Road.*

Fees: *There is no entrance fee to the reserve.*
Visitor Information: *Inquire at local travel agencies and lodges, or the Belize Tourist Board, (800) 624-0686.*

A peculiar sight for many travelers is their first glimpse of stately pine forests carpeting the steep hillsides of the Cayo District's subtropical Maya Mountains. After winding through moist broadleaf jungle en route to this highland ecosystem, you are suddenly confronted with a landscape straight out of red-dirt Georgia. As far as the eye can see, tall, skinny pine trees reach to the deep blue sky. The sandy terrain is covered with rust-colored pine needles interspersed by tiger bush ferns, a sparse grass called dumbcane, and delicate wildflowers. In some areas, clusters of oaks, miconias, and other hardwoods grip the thin topsoil. Gymnosperms, cycads, and palms crowd the boggy banks of surface streams.

The Mountain Pine Ridge—in Belize, the term "ridge" refers to a forest type and not a geographic formation—is an unusual natural phenomenon covering nearly 300 square miles.

The ancient Maya chose not to settle here, apparently concluding that seasonal droughts and shallow soils made the area unsuitable for farming. They did, however, extensively use the many caves along its limestone perimeter. Unpaved but well-maintained logging roads and nature trails cross the forest reserve, and the terrain is especially suited for hiking, mountain biking, and horseback riding. Birds and butterflies are as vivid as they are numerous. Travelers will spy many unusual varieties of colorful bromeliads, orchids, and other air plants among the boulders and branches.

Along the edges of the pine ridge are waterfalls, white-water rivers, and sharp escarpments that offer sweeping views. The almost total lack of human habitation means that much of this wilderness is virgin, although hurricanes and selective logging have occurred in some areas.

A few San Ignacio-area operators rent mountain bikes that can be used to tour the dirt roads and trails of the Mountain Pine Ridge (see Special Interests chapter for details). This can be a great way to see the area for experienced bikers who don't mind getting hot and sweaty in the near-constant warm and humid climate.

Primitive camping is allowed in certain areas with permission from the Department of Forestry (check with officials at the main entrance or at the Douglas DeSilva forest station). Rustic cabins can also sometimes be rented by the forest station for a modest fee.

*Mountain biker on
Mountain Pine Ridge*

Hidden Valley Falls

Hidden Valley Falls, also known as Thousand-Foot Falls, is one of the Mountain Pine Ridge's primary attractions. This is believed to be the tallest waterfall in Central America, plunging almost ¼ mile over a granite precipice into a deep jungle canyon. The distance is so great that the bottom of the waterfall becomes lost in mist and green foliage.

To see the falls, follow Baldy Beacon Road east of the forest reserve's main entrance for about 5 miles. Then proceed as directed by the well-marked signs for a couple of miles to an overlook area. This is a good place to take photographs, savor a picnic, and observe bird life. The king vulture and rare orange-breasted falcon are sometimes seen riding the thermal air currents here—the latter bird nests near the waterfall. On a clear day, the capital buildings of Belmopan shimmer on the horizon.

Across from the caretaker's cabin is the **Hidden Valley Institute for Environmental Studies**, a private research facility. Bungalows accommodate visiting naturalists and there is a small natural history museum. Immediately below the institute is a rugged 4-mile trail to the base of the waterfall. The trail is not well maintained and should not be attempted without a guide. A round-trip hike may take all day.

Guests of the nearby Hidden Valley Lodge have access to three other waterfalls: **King Vulture**, **Tiger Creek**, and **Butterfly**. Inquire at the resort about permission to visit them on your own.

Río On Pools

About 10 miles southwest of the Hidden Valley Falls overlook, the forest reserve's main road crosses the Río On, a cascading upland tributary of the Macal River. As it makes its way down from the Mountain Pine Ridge, the Río On swirls and splashes through a maze of granite boulders. The warm pools formed by these enormous rocks are as much as 15 feet deep and make delightful swimming holes, especially after a long day of hiking, biking, or horseback riding. The smooth stones make natural water slides, and many visitors like to stretch out and sunbathe on them in the tropical sun. There are outhouses (doubling as changing rooms) and picnic tables nearby, plus a freshwater tap. The parking lot accommodates a growing number of visitors, which may swell to several dozen on weekends and holidays, when Belizeans like to picnic here.

Río Frío Cave and Nature Trail

Not much farther south, a few miles past the forest reserve headquarters in the village of Douglas DeSilva, visitors descend into subtropical vegetation and one of Belize's best-known cave districts. Look for a sign indicating the start of the Río Frío Nature Trail, which makes its way through dense forest to the largest and most spectacular cave in the group. (Río Frío Cave can also be easily reached by driving a mile or so down the same road to a picnic area outside the cavern's entrance.)

Richard Mahler

*The Río On is a popular swimmers' destination
in the Mountain Pine Ridge.*

The nature trail takes about 45 minutes to negotiate and displays a
wide variety of trees, each carefully labeled. There are even naturally occurring rubber, mahogany, and sapodilla trees (the latter is the source of chicle,
a natural chewing gum base). Birds and other wildlife are abundant.

The Río Frío Cave extends about 300 yards through a limestone
mountain. Centuries ago the tunnel was used as a ceremonial center by
the ancient Maya, but all artifacts have long since been removed or
washed away. There are enormous arched entryways at either end of the
cave, which narrows midway to a height and width of about 40 feet.

Because the Río Frío cuts a broad channel through the passage, the
cave is sometimes difficult to traverse during rainy months. Even in the
dry season, visitors will probably find it necessary to get at least their feet
wet. The interior of the cave is musty and cool but not entirely dark.
Enough daylight filters through from either end to make flashlights
unnecessary. Footholds can be slippery, however, and some rock climbing
is required.

The other caves in the region— including the **Domingo Ruíz**, **Blancaneaux**, **Skeleton Head**, and **Chiquibul** caves—should not be visited
without an experienced, knowledgeable guide. Information can be obtained

173

Río Frío cave interior

through hotels, travel agencies, or conservation organizations. Recommended local guides include Richard Shaw at **Pine Ridge Lodge**, and Mr. Bol, at **Bol's Guiding Service**, near the forest reserve's main gate.

Douglas DeSilva Village and Beyond

The headquarters for the Mountain Pine Ridge Forest Reserve is in a large wooden building in the settlement of Douglas DeSilva (renamed from Augustine in 1990 after a politician's grandfather). Only about 100 people—all forestry employees—live here, and the place has the look and feel of a run-down summer camp. Many of the houses are in disrepair and others are being used to store pine seeds for reforestation projects. Worth visiting are the self-guided nature trail on the headquarters grounds and the small store (the only source of supplies for many miles around). Thatch-shaded picnic tables are available, but there is no restaurant or gas station. Inquire at the headquarters about camping and overnight rental of government-owned guest houses.

If you are continuing on to the Maya ruin at Caracol (see Chapter 10, Archaeological Sites) you may want to check with the Forestry Department officer on duty in Douglas DeSilva. Access to Caracol is not granted when the road is judged to be in such poor condition that travel will be hazardous (both to visitors and the road surface itself). The Caracol road is sometimes closed to all but the toughest four-wheel-drive vehicles. Expect to pay about $150 for a one-day Caracol trip through local lodges. When the surface is dry, it takes about 45 minutes to reach Caracol from here. Heading in the other direction, Georgeville and San Ignacio on the Western Highway are 90 minutes and 2 hours away, respectively. It may be possible by the time you read this to pay your $5 Caracol entry fee at the forestry office here.

San Antonio Village

The more westerly of the two routes leading into the Mountain Pine Ridge—the Cristo Rey Road—passes through the small and mostly Yucatec/Mopán Maya farming village of San Antonio. (Note that there is another San Antonio, populated by Kekchí-speaking Maya, in the Toledo District near Punta Gorda.)

The Cayo's San Antonio village is situated in a lush valley where terraced fields of beans and corn have been carved out of the leafy forest. Agriculture has persisted here for thousands of years. Recently, a few small shops, restaurants, and museums have been opened in an attempt to diversify the local economy. Among the several attractions that are worth visiting in the San Antonio area is the Pacbitun archaeological site (described in Chapter 10, Archaeological Sites).

San Antonio Museums

Immediately north of the village on the main road to Cristo Rey and Santa Elena is **Tanah Maya Art**—a combination crafts shop, herbal medicine pharmacy, and Maya shrine. At least one of the five García sisters is always on hand, making and selling black-slate carvings that depict Maya-related masks, gods, and historic figures. Be advised that the museum has a steep $5 admission charge and that the García sisters are aggressive salespersons. A "medicine trail" and rustic lodge were added in 1998, along with a Web site at www.awrem.com.

Another family of local artisans, the Magañas, also operates an art gallery, "Maya culture preservation outpost," and gift shop. Javier, José, and Carmelita produce and sell wood and stone carvings that incorporate traditional themes. Glyphs from the Maya calendar are also hand-painted by family members on the same type of cloth supposedly used by ancient royalty. Their **Itzamna' Gallery & Gift Shop** is a few miles north of San Antonio on the Cristo Rey Road at a small Maya ruin called **Sac'Tunich**.

Getting There

The easiest way to see the Mountain Pine Ridge is by either renting your own car or by signing up for a minivan tour through a hotel or travel agency. This can be done easily through one of the lodges within the forest reserve or those located in the rest of the Cayo District. During the dry season, several vehicles a day explore the area, and overnight camping and equestrian trips can be arranged. There is no public transportation into the Mountain Pine Ridge except for taxis. Drivers of private vehicles are advised that the region's dirt roads are sometimes a challenge during rainy periods—four-wheel-drive is advised.

Where to Stay in the Mountain Pine Ridge

Blancaneaux Lodge, about an hour south of San Ignacio on Five Sisters Falls Road; $150; 92-3878, fax 92-3919, blodge@btl.net. Owned by movie director Francis Ford Coppola, set in a lush, 50-acre, pine-forested area crisscrossed by white-water rivers and nature trails. For those who can afford it, accommodations and meals are first-rate. Tours are arranged to destinations throughout the area (including nearby caves and the spectacular Five Sisters Falls). Guests arrive either via Blancaneaux's private airstrip—visitors can arrange to be flown in by the staff pilot—or 16 miles of dirt road from San Ignacio. Coppola has supervised the construction and furnishing of beautifully appointed Maya-style, thatch-roof cabañas and two-bedroom villas, set in garden-like surroundings beneath tall pines. Each room overlooks the Privassión River, where a large pool (suitable for swimming) is used to generate electricity through a hydroelectric turbine. Coppola imported a wood-burning oven from Rome to make pizza at Blancaneaux, and his dining room—open to the general public—also features wines from his own Napa Valley winery, as well as the Coppola family's imaginative pasta and seafood recipes. Produce and coffee is grown in an organic garden adjacent to the lodge. (Don't expect to meet Coppola; he spends only a few weeks here each year.) This remains one of the most beautiful resorts in Belize, upgraded extensively in 1998.

Five Sisters Lodge, perched on a high ledge above a beautiful series of cascades on the Privassión River, about 2 miles off Mountain Pine Ridge Road; $95; 92-2985, fivesislo@btl.net. Day-trippers are welcome to make their way down a steep stairway to the base of the falls, where the resort has an outdoor bar. There are cabaña-style rooms as well as a restaurant—with a fine overview of the Five Sisters Waterfall. Swimmimg, horseback riding, mountain biking, stargazing, hiking, and nature tours available.

Hidden Valley Inn, a few miles off Mountain Pine Ridge Road on the Cooma Cairn Road, which continues to **Thousand-Foot Falls** (also on the Inn's property); $180, includes meals; (800) 334-7942 or 8-23320, fax 8-23334. Maintained by the Georgia timber-cutting family that owns

18,000 acres of the adjacent pine forest and jungle, visitors can either stay in comfortable cottages or camp under the stars and pine boughs. Easy-to-follow trails lead to Central America's highest waterfall, several caves, and a small lake. A large section of the property constitutes the **Hidden Valley Reserve**, where biologists have found a new toad species and a rare nesting pair of orange-breasted falcons. Tours—including river rafting and photo safaris—are arranged to **Caracol**, the **Chiquibul** subtropical forest, **Tikal**, and other area attractions. Hidden Valley's bungalows are plush, complete with fireplaces and bathtubs (both hard to find in Belize).

Pine Ridge Lodge, about a mile from Blancaneaux on Mountain Pine Ridge Road; $85 and up, includes breakfast; 92-3310, prlodge@pop .mindspring.com, www.pineridgelodge.com. Friendly and comfortable, offers caving, hiking, river trips, birding, mountain biking, and both equestrian and archaeological explorations. This recommended, bungalow-style hotel also operates a small restaurant that serves excellent meals. Pains have been taken to make this lodge environment-friendly, and there are many trails to follow through the nearby pine forest and jungle, where you'll see orchids, possibly deer, and maybe even a jaguar. A nice feature is the "hammock room," a screened-in shelter where you can curl up with a glass of fresh, cold limeade and read a book or take a snooze. Ask about off-season (summer) rates. Both restaurant and bar are open to the public, although reservations are sometimes required.

Where to Eat in the Mountain Pine Ridge
There are no restaurants in the Mountain Pine Ridge except for those that are part of the few lodges in the area (see above). Most of these are open to the public.

THE UPPER MACAL REGION AND CHE CHEM HA CAVE
The mountainous stretches of the Macal River extend into a remote and seldom-seen area that drains the Vaca Plateau watershed and much of Chiquibul National Park. Access has improved in recent years through grading of new roads used in the construction of a Taiwanese-funded dam and hydroelectric plant, which flooded part of the upper Macal basin above the confluence of the Mollejon River in 1995.

Floating the Upper Macal
White-water raft and kayak trips are available from several operators on the scenic upper reaches of the Macal River gorge. One-day trips usually begin below the hydroelectric dam (accessible by Negroman Falls Road) and end either near the **Black Rock Jungle Lodge** (blackrock@btl.net)

or **Chaa Creek Cottages** (chaacreek@btl.net). The Class III and IV float takes you through a remote tropical forest dominated by limestone walls that tower as high as 1,500 feet above the river. Several easy portages are required during this 7-mile run. The area abounds in wildlife and the steep-sided canyon is covered with broad-leaf tropical forest.

Recommended is **Slickrock Adventures**, 2-34129 or (800) 390-5715, slickrock@slickrock.com. It originates its day trips at 7:30 a.m. from the San Ignacio bus depot and returns about 6 p.m. Expect to pay about $100 for a one-day white-water trip, which includes transport from San Ignacio, guide fees, equipment, and lunch. Guests of Chaa Creek Cottages (which books its visitors on Slickrock trips and is an occasional pull-out point) can be dropped off there on their return. You can make a two-day itinerary by combining with Slickrock's Class I "river of caves" float on the Caves Branch of the Sibun River.

Another rivertrip outfitter in the area is **Juan Marcos Parras** (c/o Maya Island Air, 26-2012, Ambergris Caye), a Guatemalan who was raised in Arkansas. Parras also provides guided tours of Tikal and other destinations in the Cayo and Petén.

Che Chem Ha Cave

The privately owned Che Chem Ha Cave (sometimes called Vaca Cave), located near Vaca Falls, a scenic and rocky plunge on the Macal River, is an extensive, important Maya ceremonial site, discovered in the early 1990s by farmer William Morales. It contains many pristine ancient artifacts, including over 60 ancient pottery vessels, paintings, incense burners, and a circle of special carved stones where animals were sacrificed and prayers spoken to underworld gods. These items have been left undisturbed for at least 1,000 years, and iron grates now protect them from looters and vandals. The interior of these caves is dark, wet, and slippery. Visitors should wear grip-tread shoes and bring a flashlight or diving light. Some climbing is involved but the effort is well worth it.

The **Morales and Pleitez families** (both Mopán Maya) provide rustic, bungalow-style accommodations and meals as well as guided tours of Che Chem Ha, which means "poison vine water." The family compound may be reached by local VHF radio (try Bob Jones at Eva's Restaurant, 9-2267, in San Ignacio) or through Maya Mountain Lodge, Ek'Tun, or Chaa Creek Cottages, all of which arrange tours. Visitors are asked not to enter Che Chem Ha Cave without a family member. This is not only for safety, but also to protect the integrity of the cave's fragile artifacts, which have been left exactly where they were placed many centuries ago.

The guided visit lasts roughly 90 minutes and costs about $15, with a minimum of three people on each tour. If you arrive in the late morning and place your order, the nearby restaurant will have lunch ready when you finish your cave tour and make the 30-minute hike back to the compound. Lunch costs about $6 and overnight lodging around $80 (double occupancy in bunks, including all meals).

From the Che Chem Lodge you can hike to the Macal River's spectacular **Vaca Falls** in about an hour, then trek onward to the previously described **Ek'Tun resort**, located a few miles downstream from the waterfall. Ek'Tun and Che Chem Ha Lodge have a reciprocal agreement for those who wish to overnight in both places. Horses can be obtained at either location for rides into the jungle. Trails lead from here as far as San Antonio and Caracol.

Getting There
Note that the road to Che Chem Ha can be treacherous when wet; it's not unusual for cars to get stuck in the last 100 yards of steep road, just below the Morales residence. The turnoff to Che Chem Ha is 6 miles south on the Negroman Falls Road from Benque Viejo, about 7 miles west of San Ignacio. Watch for the signs.

CHIQUIBUL NATIONAL PARK
Rather than loop through the Mountain Pine Ridge in only a day or two, some travelers continue south beyond the Río Frío Cave into some of the wildest areas of Belize. Only a handful of people live full-time in this area, mostly chicle tappers, Guatemalan immigrants, poachers, and looters. In 1991 the government of Belize established more than 200,000 acres of this former forest reserve as a national park, now accessible by crude road.

Inside Chiquibul National Park is the enormous Maya ruin of **Caracol,** currently under excavation (see Chapter 10, Archaeological Sites) and located about 30 miles southwest of Douglas DeSilva. Caracol is protected under a separate designation because of its archaeological significance. Chiquibul's broad tableland consists of hundreds of square miles of intact forest, the last stronghold of many wildlife and plant species that are rarely seen elsewhere in Central America and southern Mexico, such as the keel-billed motmot.

The national park also protects the **Chiquibul cave system,** about 8 miles south of Caracol, with more than 20 miles of explored passages and no end in sight. No systematic scientific exploration occurred until the late 1970s. Since then, in some of the caves, researchers have found ancient fossilized insects and crustaceans that have been extinct for centuries. The complex which cannot be entered without government permission, has yielded several previously unknown animal species, Maya artifacts, and one of the world's largest underground chambers. One cave, Cebeda, is thought to be the longest in Belize.

Is Chocolate the Love Drug?

Montezuma apparently thought so. The Aztec ruler reportedly drank up to 50 cups of hot chocolate each day and made sure he downed the brew before entering his harem. Having been introduced to the jungle-grown cacao bean (chocolate's source) by the Maya, who treated it like money, the Aztecs seduced Spanish conqueror Hernán Cortés with their delicious chocolate beverage. He liked it so much that he brought the sweet liquid to Madrid in 1528, where it became a favorite drink of royalty. By the 1700s, chocolate was the favored drink of the wealthy throughout Europe and it became available to the masses (in solid form for the first time) following the 1828 invention of the chocolate press. By 1875 the Swiss developed milk chocolate, now the preferred form of cocoa butter consumption around the world.

Travel in this area is now limited to horseback and high-clearance, four-wheel-drive vehicles. Overnight and day trips can be arranged to Maya ruins, caves, waterfalls, jungle rivers, and chiclero camps, as well as **Puente Natural**, a high-arch cave similar to Río Frío, through which a small river flows. Recommended for such rugged adventures is **Mountain Equestrian Trails** or **Chaa Creek Expeditions**. Because of the rough terrain and the absence of freshwater streams during the dry season, overland trips to the area are recommended only for travelers who are healthy and adventurous.

BELMOPAN AND VICINITY

BELMOPAN
Location: *About 45 miles west of Belize City via the Western Highway.*
Population: *Roughly 6,000 (1999 estimate).*
Visitor Information: *Belize Tourist Board, (800) 624-0686; Belize Tourism Industry Association, 2-75717; and local hotels or travel agencies.*

The capital city of Belize, on the eastern edge of the Cayo District, has yet to find its way onto the itinerary of most foreign visitors. This is not surprising, considering the community's meager attractions. Looking more like a second-rate college campus than a national seat of government, Belmopan's concrete and stucco buildings are spread over a wide expanse of weedy lawns and empty lots. The main complex is clustered around a central plaza that features a lively open-air market, several unremarkable restaurants, and a noisy bus depot.

The architecture and layout are designed to evoke a Maya ambiance. The name Belmopan combines the "Bel" of Belize with the name of one of the country's indigenous tribes, the Mopán Maya. Despite warnings that another big hurricane could level Belize City, as *Hattie* did in 1961, few have heeded the call to relocate to Belmopan.

One of the few attractions for travelers in Belmopan is the **National Assembly**, where you can sometimes watch politicians debate legislation. In the past it has also been possible to visit the **Department of Archaeology's walk-in vault**, which contains some fine Maya artifacts, but the government now tightly restricts access. Catering to tourists apparently became too onerous for the department's limited staff, who welcome donations to the Association for Belizean Archaeology (which supports establishment of a permanent museum).

Permission from the Department of Archaeology (82-2106) is required to visit certain remote Maya ruins. Serious students of the culture may wish to schedule a conversation with the Archaeology Commissioner.

The Belize government has long promised a national museum in Belmopan to house the Archaeology Vault collection and many other historic and cultural artifacts. Projected to cost at least $3.5 million, the facility hadn't gone past the drawing-board stage.

Services
Services in Belmopan include two banks, a post office, and several embassies. Free overnight parking is available to recreational vehicles at **The Oasis**, near Guanacaste National Park, which also has an inexpensive restaurant, restrooms, and a water tap.

Getting There
The road (Western Highway) between Belize City and Belmopan is the best in the country and one can make the drive in under an hour; the turnoff to Belmopan is opposite Guanacaste National Park. Although Belmopan has a small airstrip, there is no scheduled commercial air service. Several bus companies (Batty's, Z-Line, James) run buses daily to Belmopan from Belize City, Dangriga, and San Ignacio (about $2 one-way from each). Buses run about once every hour between these

communities from 8 a.m. to 5 p.m., less often on weekends and holidays. Because there are no significant tourist attactions in Belmopan, there are no outfitters or tour companies specifically serving the community. Airport transfers to local lodges cost about $45 per person, one way.

Where to Stay and Eat in Belmopan

Belmopan's restaurants are characterized by overpriced, undistinguished meals and slow service. The International Café and all Chinese restaurants here are best avoided.

Bull Frog Inn, 22 Halfmoon Ave.; rundown and overpriced at $75; 8-22111. Bar and traffic can be very noisy until the wee hours of the morning. Adequate restaurant on the premises with a pleasant outdoor terrace. Air-conditioning and TV.

Caladium, north end of the public market. Standard fare (in small portions), close to the bus terminal. Beef dishes are the best.

El Rey Inn, 23 Moho St.; $25; 8-23438. Recommended budget hotel (and café) located in a relatively quiet residential area. Spacious, clean rooms with private baths.

Yoli's Lounge, Constitution Drive. The best place in town for Belizean, Mexican, Italian, and American cuisine. A popular bar, too.

BELMOPAN AREA JUNGLE LODGES

In recent years the Belmopan area has become a kind of "mini-Cayo," offering travelers a growing number of worthy jungle lodge options. These have the advantage of being closer to the international airport and cayes, which can be an important consideration for those on a tight schedule. Other advantages include ready access to the region's many caves and several national parks.

Banana Bank Lodge, on the Belize River about 4 miles west of Belmopan (follow the signs at Mile 47); $80 and up, includes breakfast; 81-2020, fax 81-2026, bbl@btl.net, www.belizenet.com/banana.html. Former Montana cowboy John Carr and his artist wife Carolyn operate this 4,000-acre ranch with five guest cabañas and four rooms in the ranch house (all meals available). About half of the Carr's property is undisturbed subtropical forest, with nearly 200 species of birds identified as well as many varieties of mammals, reptiles, and amphibians. The focus here is on horseback riding, and the Carrs have two dozen mounts to choose from. You can take a guided tour of their old-growth jungle,

Horseback riding in the Cayo District

Richard Mahler

stopping occasionally at small Maya ruins. River fishing and canoeing (both on the Belize River), in addition to stargazing (with an 8-inch Meade telescope) are offered. Unusual extras include Carolyn's fine oil paintings of Belize wildlife and the couple's private zoo, which includes monkeys, kinkajous, peccaries, and a jaguar. There is also a gift shop and natural history museum. New trails and a birding "observatory" were added by the Carrs in 1997, as well as numerous day trips.

Cæsar's Place, Mile 60, Western Highway; 9-22341. Lodge ($40), bar, and restaurant, with an adjoining gift shop. Camping ($5) and RV hook-ups available. Transfers can be made here to co-owned Black Rock Jungle Resort, located on the upper Macal River southwest of San Ignacio.

The Grove Resort, Mile 65.5, Western Highway; (800) 735-7273, 9-22421, email@groveresort.com. Upscale ($120 and up) resort on 50 acres, offering swimming pool, volleyball, tennis, horseshoes, nature trails, aromatherapy, massage, and fitness center. Meals and spa services available.

Jaguar Paw Jungle Resort, at Franks Eddy, several miles east of Belmopan (at Mile 37) and accessible by a 7-mile private road; $155 with

Traditional thatch-roof cabañas at Pook's Hill

Steele Wotkyns

breakfast; (800) 335-8645 or 8-13024. On 215 acres along the Sibun River, a full-service luxury resort offering meals, air-conditioning, swimming pool, satellite TV, hiking (on 8 miles of nature trails), and innertube rides through flooded caves ($60 per person). Each room is decorated in a different international motif. The owners will provide transportation from Belize City. One drawback: noise from the 24-hour generator. Also, daytrip charges are extra. Travelers have given this lodge mixed reviews.

Pook's Hill Lodge, on 300 acres near Roaring Creek, a few miles west of Belmopan; $105 and up, includes breakfast; 8-12017, fax 8-23361, pookshill@btl.net. Well-appointed facilities situated in a small Maya plaza, includes eight screened cabañas with private bath (hot showers) and an elegant, diverse-menu bar/restaurant. Horseback riding through a variety of habitats via 4 miles of well-maintained trails (superb for hiking, too). Swimming in a private Roaring Creek pool, refreshing inner tube floats down the same stream. Pook's Hill Lodge is raising (and reintroducing into the wild) green iguanas. Off-season rates May–November. Recommended.

Warrie Head Lodge, 137-acre ranch at Mile 56 on the Western Highway, about 15 miles west of Belmopan; $60 and up; 2-77257, fax 2-75213. Caters primarily to groups, but will accommodate independent travelers. Besides a restaurant, this former colonial logging camp offers horseback riding, nature treks, birding, canoeing, and swimming on the Belize River. Accommodations are in a two-story ranch house near Warrie Head Creek.

GUANACASTE NATIONAL PARK

Location: *Less than 2 miles from Belmopan, at the intersection of the Hummingbird and Western Highways.*
Size: *52 acres.*
Hours: *8 a.m. to 4 p.m. daily*
Fees: *$3*
Visitor Information: *Belize Audubon Society, 2-34987, or Guanacaste National Park, 8-22018.*

On Earth Day (April 22) 1990, the Belizean government officially created Guanacaste National Park in a lush parcel of forest alongside the Belize River. The park is named after a huge guanacaste tree growing near the reserve's southwestern boundary. Also known as the tubroos or monkey's ear tree, the guanacaste is a highly prized hardwood known for its resistance to insects and decay. Guanacaste lumber is the material of choice for construction of dugout canoes, feeding troughs, and rice-hulling mortars.

This particular giant (the species produces some of the largest trees in Central America) towers more than 120 feet above the forest floor and was spared the woodcutter's ax only because naturally occurring splits in its massive trunk make it unusable as timber (all other guanacaste trees in the park have been harvested). The tree's broad, sky-seeking branches support hundreds of epiphytes, including many brilliant species of orchid and bromeliad.

A short trail leads through the forest to the guanacaste tree from a visitors center operated by the Belize Audubon Society. Known as the Guanacaste Education Center, the facility was dedicated to the U.S. Peace Corps as Audubon's way of honoring the Corps' contributions to conservation and education in Belize.

Other large trees seen along the trail to the guanacaste tree include the mammee apple, bookut, ramon, quamwood, silk cotton, and raintree. Several mahogany trees have been planted near the park's visitors center as part of a reforestation program. You can hike a self-guided interpretive loop trail and view a display of native orchids at the visitors center.

Despite Guanacaste's diminutive size, it harbors abundant wildlife. Species observed here include jaguarundi, kinkajou, paca, armadillo, iguana, deer, and opossum. Resident birds include the blue-crowned motmot, black-faced ant thrush, smoky-brown woodpecker, red-lored parrot, black-headed trogon, and squirrel cuckoo, among more than 50 confirmed species. Swimming is encouraged in the nearby Belize River or Roaring Creek.

What's Worth Saving?

In 1994 a preliminary biological survey carried out by Bruce and Carolyn Miller—working with the Wildlife Conservation Society—recorded a glimpse of Tapir Mountain's biological treasures. Among other findings, this "snapshot" survey confirmed the presence of numerous mammals, at least 129 bird species, and more than 15 tree species within the reserve's tropical moist forest. Notably, the team recorded the presence of several migrant birds—including the wood thrush and Kentucky warbler. The Millers concluded that such reserves play a key role in ensuring the future survival of neotropical migrant birds. Conservationists have focused much attention on these neotropical migrant bird species that spend summers in North America and winters in the

Getting There

Accessible by bus, taxi, private car, or package tour. Restrooms, drinking water, and picnic facilities are available; cooking and camping are not permitted. The well-maintained trail network throughout the park follows a graceful curve of the Belize River at its confluence with Roaring Creek. Call ahead if you're interested in information on guided tours.

TAPIR MOUNTAIN NATURE RESERVE

Location: Wedged between Roaring Creek and Upper Barton Creek in the northern foothills of the Mountain Pine Ridge, about 10 miles west of Belmopan.
Size: 6,828 acres.
Hours and Fees: Not open to the general public. Qualified scientists and other researchers can make arrangements to visit by appointment with the Belize Audubon Society (see below).
Visitor Information: Belize Audubon Society, 2-34987, or Pook's Hill Lodge, 8-12017.

Tapir Mountain (formerly Society Hall) Nature Reserve is an intact block of tropical forest, home to all manner of flora and fauna. It has been kept this way because of the determination and foresight of its conservation-

tropics. Many species of these amazing songbirds have been declining as a result of habitat loss in both their winter and summer homes. Bird life in the area is so rich that even casual visitors not interested in birding take notice.

Diverse wildlife populations are also encountered in the Tapir Mountain Nature Reserve and surrounding areas, including the Central American or Baird's tapir—Bellze's national animal—for which the reserve is named. According to 1997 data from the World Conservation Monitoring Centre the species is listed as "vulnerable" throughout its range in Central and South America, meaning the tapir faces a high risk of extinction in the wild in the medium-term future.

minded landowner. Svea Dietrich-Ward had for many years sought a way to permanently save this area. In 1986, the German-born conservationist entered a long-term lease agreement with the Belize government on the condition that the property's natural resources be protected. Soon after, officials proclaimed it a "nature reserve." (In Belize, this designation is a subcategory of the National Parks System Act, specifying that such lands be preserved for scientific research and education.)

Perhaps the greatest threat to Tapir Mountain is illegal hunting within the reserve's boundaries by nearby residents. Another encroachment is by farmers engaged in slash-and-burn agriculture. This is compounded by the lack of access for land managers to monitor and prevent such deforestation.

In the last few years the reserve has benefited from the presence of the Ray and Vicki Snaddon family, which established its resort, **Pook's Hill**, on Tapir Mountain's northeast corner boundary. The Snaddons, who come from South Africa and Great Britain, have kept watchful eyes on this remote nature reserve while operating what is—in my estimation—one of Belize's best lodges for natural history tourism.

The Tapir Mountain area consists of undulating limestone karst dotted with sinkholes, exposed rock outcrops, small streams, and bubbling springs. Ancient Maya garbage "middens," consisting mostly of shells, potsherds, and bones, are concealed by a dense forest of climbing vines, palms, and scores of other tree species. In some of the valleys and low-lying portions of this reserve, the forest canopy crests at nearly 100 feet.

Getting There/Outfitters

Because of its protected status, access to the Tapir Mountain Nature Reserve is limited to scientists and other researchers (contact the Belize Audubon Society, which manages the reserve). Immediately adjacent to Tapir Mountain is the Pook's Hill 300-acre private nature reserve and lodge, a recommended overnight destination.

THE CAVES BRANCH REGION

For those with a special interest in caves and a unique outdoor experience, we recommend a visit to the Caves Branch area along tributaries of the Sibun River, about 45 minutes southeast of Belmopan. The limestone hills and valleys of the region are honeycombed with caves, a number of which were used for sacred rituals and burials by the ancient Maya.

Even for experienced travelers who have been to many of the large Maya ruins, it's hard to imagine the deeply spiritual ceremonies held underground here by the priests of the Maya. Only until you stand quietly in an utterly dark cave, absorbing and processing the archaeological evidence of blood-letting ceremonies, animal sacrifices, and shamans, can you begin to appreciate the power of Xibalba, the sacred netherworld of Maya gods.

The caves are found within of one of Belize's most ecologically diverse natural areas, punctuated by citrus orchards and small farms. Some visitors see jaguars in close proximity, and more often there are sightings of howler and spider monkeys, Baird's tapir, white-tailed deer, coatimundi, kinkajou, river otters, boa constrictors, and bats. Some 214 bird species have been identified locally. High tropical forest canopy, thicket areas, and marsh/riverine areas make up the three general habitat types found here, all excellent for birding.

Outfitters

Ian Anderson's Caves Branch Adventure Company, Box 356, Belmopan, 8-22800, caves@pobox.com, brings visitors directly inside the extensive below-ground realm of the Caves Branch region. Anderson and his guides are still discovering dryland crystal caves and new passages off of five extensive underground river caves systems. In all, there are at least 36 dry "crystal" caves in the area (guests of the Caves Branch Camp have a chance to enter six of these venues), known for their sparkling array of calcium carbonate crystals. Anderson's team takes visitors into all five of the region's underground river systems. Featured trips include a float through Belize's longest (over 7 miles) river cave system; a cave rafting trip in the security of large inflatable rafts; a "crystal cave" expedition, where visitors scramble for miles beneath the surface through narrow passageways that connect cathedral-sized caverns; overnight jungle treks; horseback excursions; and after-dark jungle and river safaris. All outings are reasonably priced (several are available without a minimum number of participants) and the groups are always kept small enough to give everyone the best experience. Also offered are day trips by vehicle to the Cahal Pech and Xunantunich ruins as well as to the Belize Zoo and the Community Baboon Sanctuary. Recommended.

Slickrock Adventures (800-390-5715) offers Caves Branch daytrip cave floats using inflatable and hard-shell kayaks and riverboats (see Chapter 4, Special Interests). Tours of these and other caves are also available from **Pacz Hotel & Tours**, 2 Far West Street, San Ignacio, 92-2110, which can arrange area mountain bike trips, horseback riding, and jungle treks. On any cave trip, be sure to bring good hiking shoes, an extra pair of old tennis shoes for the mud and water, long pants, flashlight, long-sleeved shirts, and insect repellent.

Getting There
The Caves Branch area is located from 10 to 20 miles south of Belmopan, along the Hummingbird Highway, north of Blue Hole National Park. There is frequent daily bus service from Belize City via Belmopan and from Dangriga. Contact the Z-Line, 2-73937 in Belize City and 5-22160 in Dangriga, for information. Cars can be rented in Belmopan, Belize City, San Ignacio, and Dangriga. (See Appendix A.)

Where to Stay and Eat in the Caves Branch Region
Caves Branch Jungle Lodge, at Mile 41.5 on the Hummingbird Highway, 300 yards northwest of the Blue Hole; $20 and up, food extra; 8-22800, caves@pobox.com. Camping, bunkhouses, private cabañas, and excellent family-style meals on a 58,000-acre estate, owned by Caribbean Investments Ltd. and managed by expatriate caver Ian Anderson. Visitors participate in the adventure of floating on inflated truck-tire inner tubes into and through an underground network, while Anderson and the other guides point out such natural cave features as stalactites, stalagmites, rimstone dams, flowstone, and calcite soda straws, as well as archaeological wonders. About 25 miles of birding and walking trails begin just outside the compound. Also on the estate are five above-ground "blue holes" (collapsed cave formations filled with water). The area's flora is outstanding, including 160 varieties of epiphytes, bromeliads, and ferns (orchids grow in the enclosed outdoor showers!). Recommended.

ST. HERMAN'S CAVE AND
BLUE HOLE NATIONAL PARK

Location: *About 12 miles southeast of Belmopan on the Hummingbird Highway.*
Size: *About 200 acres.*
Hours: *8 a.m. to 4 p.m. daily.*
Fees: *$3.*
Visitor Information: *A visitors center is a few hundred miles north of the park on the Hummingbird Highway. The Belize Audubon Society, 2-34987, manages the park, also supported by the Eden Conservancy.*

A well-marked sign guides visitors to the entrance trails of Blue Hole National Park and St. Herman's Cave. (This Blue Hole is not to be confused with the more famous offshore Blue Hole located near Half Moon Caye.)

The Belize Audubon Society maintains a visitors center just off the Hummingbird Highway for the Blue Hole National Park and St. Herman's Cave (both attractions are within the boundaries of the park, connected by an undisturbed stand of tropical forest and a short trail). All visitors must check in at the center, where a small admission fee is collected.

The centerpiece of the park is an amazing sight: a deep rectangular pool of churning sapphire water formed by the collapse of an underground river channel. A Caves Branch Creek tributary wells up from an unseen source and travels for about 100 yards before plunging mysteriously down a siphon that carries it into yet another cave beneath the mountain. The dome-shaped chamber where the water is sucked underground creates an unusual echo-chamber effect as liquid swirls beneath it. This tranquil setting is a good spot for swimming, picnicking, and birding. The sparkling pool is about 25 feet deep and moves fast, so bathers should be careful. Some foreigners swim nude here, although this practice is actually illegal in Belize and it offends most Belizeans. There are no overnight camping facilities here or anywhere in the park. Note that during rainy periods the water may turn murky green instead of the usual luminous blue.

The same Caves Branch Creek travels through nearby **St. Herman's Cave** which is accessible from the Blue Hole via a well-maintained forest pathway called the **Nature Trail**. Fauna recorded in this area include jaguar, ocelot, jaguarundi, tapir, peccary, anteater, gibnut, coatimundi, deer, and kinkajou. Once you arrive at the cave, a flashlight is handy for exploration, along with a good pair of waterproof boots, with a decent sole for traction.

The hike to St. Herman's Cave from the Blue Hole is about 1.5 miles and takes about 45 minutes along an interesting and moderately strenuous jungle trail. The most direct route, however, is from the **Blue Hole Visitors Center** located about 1 mile north along the Hummingbird

Highway, from which it's an easy 15-minute walk from the St. Herman's entrance. The trail to St. Herman's begins immediately behind the center and curves to the right along a dirt road next to a citrus plantation.

St. Herman's was used by the Maya during the Classic period, A.D. 100 to 900, and the concrete steps leading into its mouth are laid over stone steps carved more than 1,000 years ago. Ancient pots used to collect "virgin water" from cave drippings, along with spears, torches, and other artifacts, have been removed by archaeologists for study.

OTHER CENTRAL BELIZE CAVES

A small cave a few miles southeast of Over-the-Top, off the Hummingbird Highway, is **Petroglyph Cave**, named for the ancient rock drawings left by indigenous people centuries ago. Permission from the Department of Archaeology, 8-22106, fax 8-23345, must be obtained to enter this cave. I suggest that you ask department officials to recommend an experienced local guide as well.

A fairly large cave that is open to the public but not as accessible as St. Herman's is **Ben Lomond Cave**, located in the limestone hills fringing Southern Lagoon, about 25 miles southwest of Belize City and not far from Five Blues Lake National Park (see below). It can be reached only by taking a boat to the lagoon and then hiking through dense coastal bush. A stream flows from the cave's wide mouth. Not visited by the author is **Manatee Cave**, located in the same area off the Coastal Highway west of Southern Lagoon. This is a difficult cave and definitely *not* for beginners.

I strongly recommend hiring a local guide with caving and wilderness evacuation/first-aid experience before entering either Ben Lomond or Manatee Caves. Contact **Tony Rath** of **Naturalight/ Pelican Beach Resort**, 5-22004 or trath@btl.net., for suggestions.

FIVE BLUES LAKE NATIONAL PARK

Location: *About 32 miles south of Belmopan.*
Hours: *Dawn to dusk, daily.*
Size: *4,050 acres.*
Fees: *Donation requested.*
Visitor Information: *81-2005 (Over-the-Top community phone).*

About 10 miles south of Caves Branch on the Hummingbird Highway is St. Margaret's Village and Over-the-Top Camp, near the crest of a ridge on the Belize and Stann Creek District borders. On the same side of the highway as the popular Over-the-Top Restaurant is a small sign marking the turnoff (at Mile 32) onto an unpaved road heading north 4 miles to Five Blues Lake National Park. The park's crown jewel is a small, 200-foot-deep lake surrounded by steep karst limestone hills. It's called Five Blues because of the various shades of blue reflected by the sky during the course of a day.

Even if you do not make it to Five Blues Lake during your visit to Belize, you will see many spectacular examples of chalk-white karst formations along the Hummingbird Highway as it winds through the limestone hills between Caves Branch and Dangriga. This lush area is changing quickly, however, as immigrants and developers are establishing farms and plantations along the route at a rapid rate. The Hummingbird Highway corridor has become one of the primary battlegrounds in the struggle to balance the needs of Belize's steadily growing population and fragile economy with calls for environmental preservation and a boost in natural history tourism. Your visit to the parks and other attractions in this region will give more economic clout to those who would rather protect and display the inherent beauty of central Belize's forested hill country than destroy it in favor of subsistence farming and large-scale agriculture.

Five Blues Lake National Park is a remarkable testament to private-sector conservation efforts in Belize. It is one example of helpful local involvement in the management of protected areas by residents and business owners in nearby villages. Largely through the efforts of the Association of Friends of Five Blues, a grassroots community group, the original 885-acre park has expanded to include 4,050 acres of tropical forest and an extensive cave complex.

The park's trails—**Gibnut**, **Howler Monkey**, and **Jaguar**—wind through the jungle and along one side of the spectacular lake. One trail ends at an interesting cave with an unusual entrance in the side of a tall limestone cliff. At Five Blues Lake you can enjoy a picnic lunch, take a swim, or arrange for a serene boat ride across the water. With your local guide, I also recommend a short trek past the lake into a Maya cave system located within the protected area. The ancient Maya reportedly used the deep pools of the lake as sacrificial wells. A visitors center and dive platform were added to the park in 1998.

Where to Stay and Eat in Five Blues Lakes

Over-the-Top Restaurant, at Mile 32 in Over-the-Top; 81-2005. Contact Francis and Gloria Reid at the Over-the-Top Restaurant to arrange lodging, meals, or accommodations. The telephone number listed here is also the village's one and only community phone. The Reids can coordinate with Barbara Borland and the **Woman Rising Bed & Breakfast Group** that works in association with the Friends of Five Blues. This group of about 10 local women provides basic rooms in their homes (or separate rustic guest facilities) on a rotating basis and at a modest cost. Meals are provided for a small fee.

Palacio's Resort, just outside St. Margaret's Village toward Dangriga, no phone. Offers a restaurant, lodging, swimming, and horseback riding.

Tamandua Jungle Experience Cabañas, on the Five Blues Lake entrance road, Box 306, Belmopan; 8-23182. A private 170-acre wildlife sanctuary and fruit orchard with meals and tours available. Look for the sign at Over-the-Top, near Mile 32 on the Hummingbird Highway. Conditions are rustic: There's no electricity and reservations are recommended. These are the closest accommodations to the park.

NORTHERN BELIZE

8

COROZAL, ORANGE WALK, AND BELIZE DISTRICTS

Northern Belize is not a priority destination for most visitors, even though it has much to offer, including nature reserves, Maya ruins, and jungle lodges, along with such outdoor recreation opportunities as sailing, birding, fishing, swimming, and windsurfing. And since you may very well begin and/or end your trip at Belize City's international airport, we urge you to spend at least one or two days exploring the attractions easily accessible to the north of that area.

The northern coastal strip of Belize has a distinctive cultural personality, since it was the first part of the country settled by Europeans. The vast majority of the nation's people live in the three districts of the north: Corozal, Orange Walk, and Belize. This includes most of the Creole, Mexican, mestizo, and European-descended population.

The climate is warm and humid; much of the terrain is a swampy savanna that is crisscrossed by waterways. Geologically speaking, this coastal plain is fairly young, formed as a limestone seabed before the oceans receded and mainlands uplifted. A few karst formations and ridges provide texture, as well as thermal currents for hawks and other raptors. Nature lovers can find plenty of wading birds in the region's numerous wetlands, and anglers can hook a wide variety of fish in the broad, nutrient-rich rivers.

This area is the most cultivated in the country, particularly in the northeast, where sugarcane is king, and in the northwest, where Mennonite farmers have recreated a landscape straight out of the American Midwest. True, northern Belize lacks the dramatic scenery and abundant wildlife of the offshore islands and interior mountains. Yet it also offers many unique and worthwhile natural and archaeological destinations, including the Shipstern Nature Reserve, Lamanai ruins, New River, Crooked Tree Wildlife Sanctuary, Belize Zoo, Río Bravo Conservation Area, Monkey Bay National Park, Altun Ha ruins, and the Community Baboon (Howler Monkey) Sanctuary. All are described in this chapter except the archaeological sites, which are found in Chapter 10.

COROZAL DISTRICT

Today's bucolic Corozal District (which borders the Mexican state of Quintana Roo) masks a turbulent past. A series of massacres of mestizos and whites by enslaved Maya throughout the Yucatán peninsula led to a long, bloody retaliation in the mid-19th century known as the Caste Wars. Thousands of people, Maya and mestizos alike, fled to safety across the Río Hondo into British Honduras; today their Spanish-speaking descendants make up the majority of the population. Their farming expertise was welcomed by colonial authorities and, as a direct result, Corozal is today one of the country's most extensively cultivated areas (primarily sugarcane). The main city, Corozal Town, and surrounding areas are a good escape

© Tony Rath

Corozal Town's waterfront as seen from Chetumal Bay

from the sometimes hectic pace of travel in other parts of Belize. Corozal is also the gateway to Belize for travelers coming from Cancún and other points in Mexico. Except for the sticky summer season, there are near-constant trade winds off the water, and extremes of precipitation and temperature are unusual.

The word *Corozal* is modified from the Spanish name for the cohune palm tree, which ancient Maya considered to be a symbol of fertility. This area—along with most of northern Belize—has always been relatively prosperous because of its fertile soil and benign climate.

COROZAL TOWN
Location: *About 95 miles north of Belize City and less than 10 miles south of the Mexican border.*
Population: *About 10,000 (1999 estimate).*
Visitor Information: *Menzies Travel, Vince Murray, and Jal's Travel Agency (see below) in Corozal Town. Also try the Belize Tourist Board, (800) 624-0686, or Belize Tourism Industry Association, 2-77213.*

Corozal Town consists of a mixture of clapboard wooden houses and concrete block buildings. All are built on foundations of the Maya ceremonial center of Santa Rita. In 1955, Hurricane Janet destroyed much of the town, which until then featured mostly adobe (mud-and-straw brick) buildings.

The Corozal District was originally settled in 1849 by refugees from a Maya massacre in nearby Bacalar, Mexico. For a good visual description of this history, see the fine mural by Manuel Villamor Reyes in Corozal Town's municipal building. (If the town hall is closed, the Reyes mural can be seen through windows on the ground floor.) In 1986, the painting was restored and updated to show the economic exploitation of immigrant workers in the district during the 1850s and 1860s.

Surrounding Corozal Town's Central Park are a modern Catholic church, a library, the city hall, an Adventist church, and government offices. There are also several old brick "pillboxes," used as defensive fortifications by the British during the last century.

Although Corozal Town is built along the shoreline of Chetumal Bay, the water immediately adjacent to the city is polluted. There is a long stretch of beach here, linked by a clean, lawn-covered park that is landscaped with rain shelters, picnic tables, playgrounds for children, and sea grape and palm trees.

Corozal provides a good base for visitors for a couple of days because the town has the area's best accommodations and services. In addition, we recommend Corozal Town as a base of operations for sportfishing enthusiasts looking to hook a huge tarpon or other game fish without having to share the rich waters on the Belizean side of Chetumal Bay with many other fishers.

Things to See and Do

The economy of the entire Corozal District centers on the sugar industry. The old **Aventura Sugar Mill**, about 7 miles south of Corozal Town, started operation in the 1800s. Although the processing plant is no longer in use, its chimney stands as a symbol of an industry that generates an estimated 80 cents out of every dollar earned here. The foundation of an old **Spanish colonial church** is also on the site. Raw sugarcane is now processed at two other area mills: **La Libertad** and **Tower Hill**. Tours of the mills now operating are available by prior arrangement; the facilities usually shut down from July until December.

About 7 miles to the north of Corozal Town and less than 2 miles from the Mexican border (off the right side of the main road to Chetumal) is picturesque **Four Mile Lagoon**. Locals use this as a favorite picnicking spot and weekend hangout. It is recommended for foreign visitors, too, especially those interested in sailing, fishing, swimming, windsurfing, and kayaking, all well-suited to these calm waters.

Besides the small ruin of **Santa Rita**, now surrounded by the modern roads and buildings of Corozal Town, a small yet interesting coastal Maya site known as **Cerros** is a quick boat ride across Corozal Bay. More fully described in Chapter 10, Archaeological Sites, Cerros is a late Pre-Classic trading center—reached after a short, pleasant walk on a trail cut through tropical forest—boasting tombs, ball courts, and a magnificent temple. The temple offers a fine view back across the bay to Corozal Town, Sarteneja, and Chetumal. Note: Women travelers should go in a group or with a guide.

Guides

Skilled boatman **Manuel Hoare**, 4-22744, is recommended as an excellent area guide to Maya ruins, Shipstern, and Chetumal. If you are coming from Sarteneja, on the tip of the Shipstern Peninsula, we recommend boatman and fishing guide **Fernando Alamilla**, 4-32085, who also gives a good tour of Cerros. Bicycles may be rented from **Leslie's Travel**, 4-22377, in Corozal Town.

Getting There

From the United States, you may wish to consider flying to the Yucatán and taking a bus or shuttle flight to Chetumal, just north of Corozal, since commercial airfares from the U.S. to Cancún can be half the cost of airfares from the U.S. to Belize. Information on transportation options from Cancún is available from **Menzies Travel**, 4-22725; **Tony's Inn**, 4-22055; and **Vince**

Murray, 4-22784, or Vince@btl.net. Good service is also reported by travelers using **Jal's Travel Agency** in Corozal Town (and Belize City, 2-45407), where tours and airplane tickets are available.

From within Belize, the **Venus**, 4-22132, and **Batty**, 4-23034, bus companies both run regularly between Corozal Town and Chetumal, 10 miles to the north. In 1999 Venus had early morning express buses to Belize City, as well as an hourly morning schedule south from Corozal Town. Batty had afternoon express buses to Belize City as well as regular, nearly hourly afternoon service to points south. The express trip from Corozal to Chetumal takes about 20 minutes and to Belize City around 3 hours.

Tropic Air, 4-22725, tropic@cbtl.net, offers twice-daily flights to San Pedro (on Ambergris Caye) from Corozal with connecting flights to both the municipal and international airports in Belize City. **Maya Island Air**, 4-22874, mayair@btl.net, also serves the San Pedro route with several flights daily. Other airlines occasionally offer service here.

Where to Stay in Corozal Town

Caribbean Village Resort, south end of town; $30; 4-22725, fax 4-23414. Proprietors Henry and Joan Menzies are local agents for Tropic Air and operate a full-service tour/transportation company. They offer thatched-roof cabañas (with private baths), full RV hookups ($17), and camping ($5). Recommended.

Corozal Central Guesthouse, 22 Sixth Ave., one block south of the Venus Bus Station; $20; 4-22784, Vince@btl.net. Owner Vincent Murray is wired on the World Wide Web, offering free e-mail and computer access for guests, along with kitchen facilities, clean rooms, and a good deal of information about the Corozal area.

Hok'ol K'in Guest House, south of town, on the water; $45; 4-23329, fax 4-23569, maya@btl.net. Run by a former Peace Corps worker. Meals and well-priced tours available. Friendly and helpful. Recommended.

Hotel Maya, on the south end of town on the Corozal-Orange Walk Highway; $30; 4-22082. Great view of the bay and good Mexican bar and restaurant. An agent for Maya Island Air, which flies daily to San Pedro.

Nestor's Hotel, 123 Fifth Ave.; $15; 4-22354. Popular among experienced, budget-minded travelers; has bar and restaurant.

Tony's Inn & Beach Resort, far south end of town; $75; 4-22055, fax 4-22829, http://www.belize.com/tonys.html. The Tony Castillo family offers upscale, air-conditioned rooms, a private beach and marina, and many tour and water sports options for guests. There's a gift shop, bar, restaurant, swimming pool, and car rental service on the premises.

Where to Eat in Corozal Town
Crises Restaurant, North Ninth Street on the bay. Serves above-average Belizean cuisine and is recommended for its home-style atmosphere.

Hailey's Restaurant and Bar, at the Caribbean Village Resort. Good food and friendly service. Recommended.

Jack and Fanny's Wonderful Chinese Restaurant, on the corner of 5th Avenue and 3rd Street. The best Asian food around. (In fact, I have heard uniformly negative comments about Corozal's other Chinese restaurants.)

Smugglers' Den, at nearby Consejo Shores, serves both drinks and food (the fare is Belizean, with an emphasis on such tasty local snacks as

Chetumal

Overshadowing the northern edge of the Corozal District is the large Mexican city of Chetumal, capital of the state of Quintana Roo. Traffic is nearly non-stop at the Santa Elena border here, in large part because Mexico's lower prices make this a popular shopping trip for hundreds of Belizeans. Chetumal offers plenty of places to stay and eat, and you can take buses or planes to other parts of the Yucatán peninsula, including Cancún and Cozamel (both about 220 miles north). About 25 miles north of the city is the scenic Bacalar Lagoon (also called Las Lugunas de Siete Colores), which has a variety of cafés and accommodations.

The Belize consulate in Chetumal is at 226-A Avenida Alvaro Obregón (983-22871). Nationalities requiring a visa to visit Belize can usually obtain one here. The border is open from 8 a.m. to 5 p.m. daily. Allow at least 20 minutes for the crossing, more during rush-hours.

garnachas and *salbutes*). A nice place to picnic and swim on sunny days. Houses available for rent.

Tony's Inn, south of town, includes the Vista del Sol Restaurant (expensive) with a patio that overlooks Chetumal Bay. For a treat, try the chocolate freeze. Tony's also features Corozal's only tiki bar on the beach, the Y-Not.

THE SHIPSTERN NATURE RESERVE

Location: 3 miles south of Sarteneja.
Size: Almost 22,000 acres.
Hours: 9 a.m. to 12 noon and 1 p.m. to 4 daily, overnight camping allowed for registered visitors.
Cost: $5 entrance fee includes a tour of the visitors center and the butterfly center, and a guided walk on the Chiclero Botanical Trail. Other guide fees are $5 per hour and the transportation cost to Xo-pol Pond is $18.
Visitor Information: Casper Bijleveld, ITCF, fax 4-32247, itcf@papiliorama.ch.

Sticking out like a hitchhiker's thumb into the northern end of Chetumal Bay, the Shipstern Peninsula is one of the least developed areas in all of Belize. Until relatively recently, it could only be reached by private boat (now there is an all-weather road). A few thousand mostly Spanish-speaking people live in this vast expanse of hardwood forests, savanna, and mangrove swamp. Most of the population is concentrated in the isolated fishing village of Sarteneja, which perches on a small patch of dry ground near the peninsula's northeastern tip.

San Estevan, Progresso, Chunox, and a few other small settlements—situated between huge sugarcane fields—punctuate the lush landscape en route to Sarteneja. However, the peninsula's main attraction is its large nature reserve, named after the abandoned village of Shipstern. This nature sanctuary—managed by the International Tropical Conservation Foundation of Switzerland—is in the vicinity of the government's large Freshwater Creek Forest Reserve and its boundaries take in a large portion of the Shipstern Lagoon before sweeping west to the coast near Condemned Point. A wardens' quarters, guest house, visitors center, butterfly center, and the Chiclero botanical trail of the Shipstern Nature Reserve are 3 miles south of Sarteneja.

Shipstern Nature Reserve's boundaries encompass northern hardwood forests, saline lagoon systems, freshwater lagoons, and mangrove shorelines that are little-disturbed by humans. Shipstern is an infrequently visited showcase for four of Belize's main interior ecosystem types: savanna, lagoon, river, and canopy forest.

ITCF

Collared peccary

Shipstern Nature Reserve is considered an exceptional example of a heterogeneous forest regenerating from devastating tropical storm damage. (Most of the mature trees were destroyed by Hurricane Janet in 1955.) With assistance from one of Shipstern's wardens—who also serve as visitor guides—it is possible to see the transition from different forest types, particularly as you approach lagoon and savanna areas.

Flora and Fauna
The flora and fauna have made a remarkable recovery during the past four decades, and hundreds of plant and animal species have been recorded here, including scores of migratory birds from North America that winter in Shipstern. The moist forest of the Shipstern Peninsula, still largely untouched, is the only protected area in the country that includes the more seasonal hardwood trees, as well as vast saltwater estuaries that are an especially important habitat for many wading and fish-eating birds. Bird-watchers can expect to see several species of flycatcher, toucan, warbler, wading birds, ducks, and parrots. Among the birds recorded here are the Yucatán jay, reddish egret, wood stork, black catbird (rarely recorded on the mainland), American coot, great white egret, and roseate spoonbill. All five species of Belize's native cats, along with tapir, paca, coatimundi, white-tailed deer, peccary, and armadillo, roam the Shipstern forests and savanna. Jaguar signs and tracks are seen frequently.

Reserve Accommodations

Overnight accommodations originally built for scientists working at the Shipstern Nature Reserve are now being shared with visitors. Keep in mind that the focus here is on observing nature, not indulging in cozy amenities. The reserve features large, screen-sided observation towers on sturdy metal frames strategically placed for excellent wildlife observation. Simply called "tree tops" by the staff, one is located at the end of an access road where the dense forest gives way to a seasonally wet savanna fringed by buttonwood, black poisonwood, and other trees. Here Shipstern wardens are in the process of constructing a freshwater pond using rainwater collected from the observation platform's roof. This strategy has worked before at Shipstern as a magnet for fauna—affording excellent viewing at sunrise, at dusk, and during spotlight checks at night. Warden Aldana reports seeing white-tailed deer here frequently, and the elusive Baird's mountain tapir has also been seen. Visitors can also arrange with Shipstern wardens to camp here.

Another "tree tops" observation tower is located on a bank of **Xo-pol Pond**, a prime place to watch birds and crocodiles. This is part of the most recent addition to the Shipstern Nature Reserve, the 660-acre Chacan Choc Mol.

Recommended Hikes

The nature trail around the banks of **Xo-pol Pond** is a haven for wood storks, roseate spoonbills, American coots, great white egrets, northern jacanas, and many other birds (as well as Morelet's crocodiles). Located about 11 miles west of Shipstern's main compound, a well-informed Shipsten warden will take you to Xo-pol for a modest guiding and transport fee.

Another recommended guided hike is along the **Chiclero Botanical Trail**, located in the forest near the headquarters building. A warden will explain the traditional medicinal and ceremonial uses of dozens of trees along the path. The excursion is included in the reserve's $5 entrance fee, along with a visit to Shipstern's visitors center and a complete tour of the butterfly breeding/education facility.

Butterfly Breeding Program

The reserve's butterfly breeding and education efforts remain a primary program at Shipstern, and visitors can view a display of food plants required by specific species and of the different life stages of butterflies. Most of the latter are brilliantly-colored members of the order *Lepidoptera*, which are eventually reintroduced into the wild after getting a head start in the reserve's breeding and rearing enclosures. Visitors may see giant swallowtail, postman, and zebra, among other colorful varieties.

Saving the Wood Stork

Raising and showing butterflies to visitors is not the only work underway at Shipstern. An intensive, round-the-clock vigil near American wood stork nests keeps the four wardens busy on rotating shifts from February through July every year!

"People from Sarteneja kill them to eat them, so we have to be there," Warden Juan Aldana explained. The program has been quite successful, too. From an estimated 60 breeding pairs in 1991, this astounding 24-hour "nesting watch" helped increase the population to some 300 breeding pairs in 1996. Visitors who visit the wood storks' nesting caye may stay overnight at the small observation outpost, with advance approval from Shipstern's wardens.

The Shipstern Nature Reserve is also an active and unique place for ecological research in Belize through an ongoing cooperative research agreement between the reserve and the University of Neuchâtel in Switzerland. During my last visit, one researcher was establishing permanent botanical transects in order to better track the evolution of the forest, while a colleague made an inventory of both fruit- and insect-eating bats (10 species had been identified).

Getting There
Shipstern Nature Reserve can be reached by private car or via taxi from Sarteneja (see page 206).

Where to Stay in Shipstern
Shipstern Nature Reserve Lodging—For lodging in the "tree-tops" or guesthouse at the Shipstern Nature Reserve, contact reserve headquarters

in advance by fax, 4-32247. It costs $10 per night to stay at Shipstern's guest house, any of the "treetops," or at the facility near the wood stork nesting site. The tent camping fee is $5 (bring your own tent). Modestly priced meals are also available at the Shipstern Nature Reserve.

SARTENEJA

Location: Northern tip of Shipstern Peninsula, on Chetumal Bay.
Population: About 500 (1999 estimate).
Visitor Information: Belize Tourist Board, (800) 624-0686.

The village of Sarteneja, northeast of the Shipstern Nature Reserve, was almost completely washed away in 1955 by Hurricane Janet. The tin-roofed, cinder-block settlement has been rebuilt several times in its history, always around a well located, massive piece of seemingly solid stone. Legend has it that this particular well, once used by seafaring Maya, has never gone dry. *Sarteneja* is a Mayan phrase meaning "water between the rocks."

The Maya apparently abandoned the original village about 1700. During the mid-1800s, Yucatán settlers fleeing the Caste Wars reestablished Sarteneja, which became widely known for its skilled boatbuilders. To this day, Sartencja's fishermen sail as far south as Guatemala and Honduras in the beautiful handcrafted sailing vessels they call "lighters." The fishers sell their catch in Belize City, San Pedro, or Chetumal on the way home, then turn around and start another fishing expedition a few days later. They often pick up sand and coconuts on the cayes they visit, which they sell on the mainland. Every Easter a huge, festive sailing regatta is held in Sarteneja harbor and prizes are awarded for the fastest and most elegant boats.

Although more than 350 Maya sites have been pinpointed on the Shipstern peninsula, only one ancient structure has been excavated. Visitors reportedly can tour the small ceremonial site near the village by asking the landowner's permission and paying a small entrance fee. While the world's archaeologists organize themselves, local residents continue to dismantle many of the old buildings to make modern houses of their own.

The native shrimp, lobster, and conch are fished during a carefully controlled season by the more than 90 percent of Sarteneja residents who earn their living from commercial fishing. After the lobster and conch season, another controlled commercial season allows the harvest of snapper and grouper.

Things to See and Do

A couple of nearby cayes and reefs offer snorkeling possibilities here, but they are difficult to reach without a chartered boat. Birders are advised that the area's murky lagoons are important feeding grounds for such unusual waterbirds as the flamingo and the spoonbill, as well as manatees and crocodiles.

Outfitters
Fishing: A growing number of foreign sportfishers are now plying the waters off Shipstern in search of barracuda, grouper, snook, yellowtail, and particularly tarpon. I recommend Sarteneja-based fisherman, boatman, and guide, **Fernando Alamilla**, 4-32085, for a memorable and likely productive fishing trip in Chetumal Bay or nearby waters.

Tours: An adventurous option for visitors is a guided boat tour of the recently established **Bacalar Chico National Park and Marine Reserve** across the bay near Ambergris Caye. Local guide **Alamilla**—who is said to have come up with the idea for the park—can take you there. If he's unavailable, contact restaurant owner **Israel Cruz**, 4-32031, for other options. Tours to nearby areas, including night trips into the jungle to observe some of the forest's unusual nocturnal wildlife, can be arranged in Sarteneja by simply asking around town for a knowledgeable guide.

Getting There
An all-weather road to Sarteneja branches off the Northern Highway at a main bridge over the New River just north of the main market in Orange Walk Town. The trip by car takes about 1 hour from Orange Walk Town and around 2 hours from Belize City, in good weather. **Venus**, 2-73354, has an afternoon bus to Sarteneja from Belize City, with a stop in Orange Walk Town en route. A Sarteneja bus from Belize City's Magazine Road station runs several times in the afternoon with a 20-minute layover in Orange Walk.

As of 1999, the main difficulty with bus transportation to and from Sarteneja—besides the fact that frequent stops along the way make the trip rather long—is that all return buses from Sarteneja depart around 3:30 or 4 a.m. One option is to hire a boat (most operators charge $75 for the one-way transport) from Sarteneja to Corozal, thus avoiding the bleary-eyed Sarteneja bus departure.

Where to Stay and to Eat in Sarteneja
Cruz's Restaurant, on the waterfront; 4-32031. Owner Israel Cruz has information on the village's (limited) lodging and boat charter options.

Diani's Hotel, on the main street; $15; 4-32084. Eleven simple rooms and a restaurant. Owner Pedro Cruz also runs a general store.

Shipstern Nature Reserve supports several informal guest houses and bed-and-breakfasts in the area. Inquire at the reserve headquarters for referrals.

ORANGE WALK DISTRICT

Slightly inland from Corozal but still influenced by the breezy, balmy coastal climate, Orange Walk District is one of the least-visited areas in Belize. This is because most accessible parts of Orange Walk are cultivated in the form of sugarcane and citrus plantations, as well as Mennonite farms of corn, sorghum, rice, and vegetables. The coast is swampy and much of the pristine wildlife habitat is either privately owned or inaccessible.

Worthy destinations here include the Programme for Belize Lands **Río Bravo Conservation Area**, Maya ruins of **Lamanai** (described in Chapter 10, Archaeological Sites), and the **New River Lagoon** (Belize's largest lake). In the far northwest corner of the district is **Aguas Turbias National Park**, which has no services and limited access. For more information about this remote park, which borders wilderness areas in Guatemala and Mexico, contact the Belize Audubon Society.

A good base for visitors is **Orange Walk Town**, a bustling mercantile center on the banks of the **New River**. Major roads from here lead in four directions and link the more than 20 villages of the district, consisting mostly of Spanish-speaking mestizos, English-speaking Creole, and German-speaking Mennonites.

ORANGE WALK TOWN

Location: About 65 miles northwest of Belize City.
Population: 16,000 (1999 estimate).
Visitor Information: Try Caribbean Holidays, 3-22803, a travel agency on Beytias Lane, where you can also book international flights. Also check with the Belize Tourist Board, (800) 624-0686, and Belize Tourism Industry Association, 2-77213.

Settled largely by refugees from the mid-19th-century Yucatán Caste War, Orange Walk Town has the badly eroded ruins of two forts, Mundy and Cairns, that recall the scene of bloody conflicts between Belizean settlers and the district's earlier occupants, the Icaiche Maya. These indigenous residents pressed an unsuccessful series of attacks in a bid to rid the area of intruders. The final battle took place on September 1, 1872. One of the last remnants of this standoff is the old flagpole in front of the Orange Walk City Hall, site of one of the old British forts.

Before settlement by Mexican mestizos occurred in the late 1880s,

207

the Orange Walk District was dominated by loggers for more than a century. During that time the timber taken from the region was floated down the New River into Corozal Bay (also called Chetumal Bay).

Now agriculture reigns supreme. Sugar has been the most important crop for many decades (surpassing chicle and corn earlier this century), and Belizean rum (distilled at the Cuello processing plant under the "Caribbean" label) is a lucrative market for the cane that is harvested here. Other cane is rendered into molasses and, of course, processed sugar. The region is also an important producer of citrus, papaya, and beef cattle.

The best gift shop in Orange Walk Town is **KU's**, 26 Liberty Avenue, which sells ceramics, wind chimes, and cotton boxes. There are several gas stations, pharmacies, and convenience stores.

Outfitters

Several local hotels and travel agencies arrange tours to Maya sites and boat trips along the district's inland waterways, which are home to a wide variety of flora and fauna.

For a recommended trip down the New River to the Maya ruin of Lamanai, contact **Jungle River Tours**, 20 Lover's Lane, 3-22293, fax 3-22749. Brothers **Antonio** and **Herminio Novelo** are among the best Belizean guides for archaeology as well as natural history. The Novelos provide a superb day trip of birding on the New River and sightseeing at the ruins.

For larger groups interested in an excellent New River/Lamanai trip, we recommend contacting **Maya Mountain Lodge & Tours**, near San Ignacio, 92-2164, fax 92-2029, jungle@mayamountain.com. Budget travelers may wish to try **Lamanai Maya Tours**, located next to the New River toll-bridge, 3-23839. Day trips are also arranged by **Chan Chich Lodge**, near Gallon Jug.

If you are interested in seeing 75 of Belize's more than 300 native species of orchids, **Carlos Godoy** offers a tour that will bring you face to face with Belize's national flower, the black orchid—and much more. Godoy greets visitors at a small house on the east side of the northern highway in the village of **Trial Farm**, just north of Orange Walk, 4 Trial Farm Road, 3-22969, and guides them down the New River to see some of the exotic species that thrive in Belize. Operating under a government permit, he gathers and propagates orchids and bromeliads that would otherwise be destroyed by logging and farming. For the serious orchid enthusiast, Godoy can also facilitate the procedures involved in exporting these delicately beautiful flowers. He also runs recommended birding, botany, archaeology, and boat trips on the New River to Lamanai and other destinations.

Getting There

Buses from Belize City to Orange Walk Town run daily at about 1-hour intervals. Check with the Venus or Batty Brothers bus services for fares and schedules. A private car or express bus can make the trip from Belize City in a little over an hour; local buses take slightly longer. There is frequent service from Chetumal and Corozal Town, and much less frequent connections can be made for Sarteneja and villages en route to the Shipstern Peninsula. All through-buses stop for about 20 minutes in Orange Walk Town, where passengers can buy food and change money. There is no scheduled air service.

Where to Stay in Orange Walk Town

Some hotel locations are very noisy. Be advised that there are at least a dozen rowdy brothels in Orange Walk, fronting as hotels and/or restaurants. Cocaine and marijuana are sometimes sold openly here, despite severe government penalties. Unless you want to risk spending time in a Belize jail, resist the temptation to buy illegal drugs.

Chula Vista Hotel, in the adjacent village of Trial Farm; $20; 3-2365. Restaurant, bar, and seven clean, basic rooms.

D'Star Victoria, south end of Belize-Corozal Road; $25 and up; 3-22518, fax 3-22847. Best hotel in town, with 31 rooms, a bar, swimming pool, disco, and other amenities.Can be noisy at night.

Mi Amor, 19 Belize-Corozal Rd.; $25; 3-22031, fax 3-23462. My favorite: clean rooms (with fans or air-conditioning), private baths.

New River Park, near the New River toll-bridge south of town; $40 and up; 3-23987, with bar and restaurant. Only lodging for visitors at the put-in and take-out for the popular New River/Lamanai ruins trip.

Where to Eat in Orange Walk Town

Orange Walk has many Chinese restaurants, but get a recommendation from a local before picking one, since Chinese food in Belize is of variable quality. At last report, **Lee's Restaurant**, west of the plaza at 11 San Antonio Road, was a favorite. Many hotels also serve decent food, notably the **D'Star Victoria**.

The Diner, 37 Clark St., serves pretty good Belizean and international food at all three mealtimes. Steaks and desserts recommended.

HL's Burgers, downtown. A favorite among locals for American-style fast food.

INDIAN CHURCH (LAMANAI)

Indian Church is a small village immediately northwest of New River Lagoon and about a mile southwest of the ancient Mayan city of Lamanai (see Chapter 10, Archaeological Sites). Although there's not much to see in this impoverished community of mostly Spanish-speaking farmworkers (many of them Guatemalan refugees), there are several places to stay while touring the area. Howler monkey and archaeology research is ongoing at nearby Lamanai.

Where to Stay in Indian Church

Lamanai Outpost Lodge, a 20-minute walk or 10-minute canoe ride from the Lamanai ruins; $100 and up; (888) 733-7864, tel/fax 2-33578, lamanai@btl.net. Overlooking the 28-mile-long New River Lagoon, this impressively landscaped, cabaña-style retreat offers guided canoe tours, swimming, birding, a medicinal plant trail, massages, and even a spotlight "river safari" at night.

Tours to the nearby **Lamanai ruins, Mennonite farms, Crab-catcher Lagoon, Colonial Sugar Mill,** and **Indian Church** are available as part of the lodge's packages. The facility was constructed using largely local materials and labor, in a manner that minimizes negative environmental impact. Among the amenities are a pontoon boat for cruises on the lagoon. A fine restaurant and bar are open to non-guests. Ask about "herbal" and birding tours.

From Belize City the lodge may be reached in about 2.5 hours, by either auto or auto/boat combination. Driving from Orange Walk Town, take Yo Creek Road to San Felipe and turn left for the final 12 miles to Indian Creek.

Other Options

Not visited by the author are two modest accommodations in Indian Church: **Doña Blanca's** and the **Gonzalez Guest House** (both 3-23369, community phone). Ask locally about **Xochil Ku,** a nearby butterfly educational center operated by local residents.

RÍO BRAVO CONSERVATION & MANAGEMENT AREA/PROGRAMME FOR BELIZE

Location: About 75 miles northwest of Belize City.
Size: About 250,000 acres.
Hours: Open by appointment or prior arrangement only.
Cost: None.
Visitor Information: Programme for Belize, 2-71248, or Box 749, Belize City, pfbel@btl.net.

A nonprofit group called Programme for Belize has, since its formation in 1988, achieved remarkable success in protecting a major portion of the northwest corner of Belize as relatively pristine lowland jungle. Thanks to their intervention, this forest remains one of the largest tracts of undisturbed subtropical habitat in the region. From its inception, the sponsoring group's primary objectives have been to create a model of appropriate economic development and to provide funding for conservation, education, and scientific and management training throughout the country for the lasting preservation of Belize's natural heritage and biological diversity.

In the early 1990s, Programme for Belize acquired 26,892 acres in the Río Bravo area. This purchase connects two blocks of land that, together with other acquisitions, comprise the **Río Bravo Conservation and Management Area**. The Programme has thus converted about 250,000 acres into a single unit that facilitates management; assures the future for an extensive, wildlife-rich tract of tropical forest; and secures a vital habitat corridor along Irish Creek. Programme for Belize has raised several million dollars from corporations, foundations, and individuals to purchase and administer these lands, which are surrounded by another 450,000 acres of largely intact forest and savanna.

The government-approved management plan for the Río Bravo Conservation Area allows for the development of low-impact agriculture, forest product propogation and harvesting, and tourism based on natural history and archaeology. (There are at least 60 ancient Maya sites on Programme for Belize land, including **La Milpa,** third-largest in Belize, where a royal tomb was discovered in 1995.) A fundamental long-term goal for the Río Bravo area is to pay for its conservation through sales revenues derived from its renewable natural resources. Programme for Belize believes lessons learned at Río Bravo will serve as a model for the region.

Private contributors continue to be key to the success of this large-scale conservation project. Through the Massachusetts Audubon Society, contributors are invited to donate $50 to "adopt" an acre of tropical forest, something many

© Tony Rath

Tourists at La Milpa

211

schoolchildren have done as class projects throughout the United States and Europe. The Society sends a certificate to donors indicating how many acres the individual or group has helped protect.

Most of the Río Bravo area is a nearly untouched subtropical haven where howler monkeys, spider monkeys, king vultures, gray foxes, more than 80 species of bats, and 110 species of orchids now enjoy a permanent refuge. Some 200 species of trees have been identified here along with all five Belizean species of cat: margay, jaguarundi, jaguar, puma, and ocelot. At least 344 species of birds have been identified as either year-round residents or migrants that frequent the area (out of a total of about 540 species identified to date in Belize).

The Río Bravo Conservation and Management Area covers the northeastern part of the Petén wilderness, a large, biogeographically distinct expanse that extends into southeastern Mexico and northern Guatemala. Nick Brokaw and Elizabeth Mallory have identified more than a dozen floristically distinct vegetation types in Río Bravo, including upland forest, palm forest, swamp forest, riparian forest, and second-growth. A research facility has been strategically located for easy access to these distinct habitat types. It provides training in archaeology, forest management, and ecology while concurrently monitoring the reserve's biological diversity. Outreach to villages surrounding the Río Bravo area has involved local residents in chicle harvesting, handicraft production (culminating in sales to foreign visitors), guide training, and environmental education.

Chan Chich Lodge

Visitors wishing to see Programme for Belize lands are best off staying in Chan Chich Lodge, near the settlement of Gallon Jug. This is a luxurious and expensive group of elegant cabañas set in the middle of a Classic-period Maya ruin, which was being systematically looted before Chan Chich's construction. The accommodations were built for Belizean businessman Barry Bowen (the lodge's owner) by Tom and Josie Harding, who now manage Chan Chich. Ancient Maya monuments border the resort's grounds on all sides, giving the impression that the cabañas are original Maya homes. Their plush interiors, however, give a different impression. Polished and oiled woodwork, colorful drapes, a full bar, pool, and gourmet dining combine to make Chan Chich one of Belize's finest lodges. Indeed, it has received a top ranking in at least one world survey of jungle accommodations. On-site ammenities include a bar, a reataurant, a hot tub, and a pool.

By prior arrangement with Programme for Belize, 2-71248, fax 2-75616, tourists can visit the nearby **La Milpa** and **Laguna Seca** archaeological sites. Other activities include superb birding (Chan Chich means "little bird" in Mayan), jungle walks, canoeing, horseback riding, guided nature/archaeology tours, and simply relaxing. An escarpment west of Gallon Jug is a favorite of king vultures, white hawks, crested eagles, and other raptors. This area may be the best in Belize for spotting jaguars and other cats. There are nearly 10 miles of trails here.

Getting There

Unless the weather has been dry, it is best to fly to Gallon Jug rather than attempt the rough dirt roads into the area. Javier's Flying Service, 2-45332, flies here three times each week, charging around $100 for the 30-minute round-trip from Belize City.

Gallon Jug is approximately 3½ hours from Belize City via Blue Creek Village (turn south on the marked road immediately west of this Mennonite community near the Mexican border). Be sure to inquire locally about road conditions before heading out, since the road may be impassable when wet. Note that the Iguana Creek Bridge Road, from the south, is no longer open as far as Gallon Jug.

Where to Stay near Río Bravo

Chan Chich Lodge, near Gallon Jug; $140 ($90 off-season); in Belize 2-75634 or fax 2-76961, in U.S. (800) 343-8009, info@chanchich.com, www.chanchich.com. Book well in advance, as rooms fill up quickly. Meals, day trips, and drinks cost extra. (For more information, see text above.)

Río Bravo Research Station, near Gallon Jug; $70 and up; 2-75616, fax 2-75635. Nature trails and tour guides, as well as educational facilities. Day visits cost about $20 and include a 2-hour tour. Accommodations are rustic, but clean and comfortable.

BELIZE DISTRICT (NORTH)

The Belize District is located in the heart of the country, roughly midway between the northern and southern borders, along the Caribbean coast. Most of its population is concentrated in Belize City, with a few farming and fishing communities in the north and west. Most visitors pass through Belize City (covered in Chapter 5) at some point during their stay, but many are oblivious to the district's outlying attractions, each an easy day trip from the country's biggest population center. In contrast to the congestion of Belize City, there are virtually pristine nature reserves and protected areas less than an hour's drive away that teem with wildlife. For the traveler interested in an "up close and personal" look at Belize's exotic flora and fauna, the rural Belize District offers several must-see destinations. (For information on destinations in the southern portion of the Belize District, see Chapter 9, Southern Belize.)

CROOKED TREE WILDLIFE SANCTUARY

Location: 33 miles northwest of Belize City and 3.5 miles west of the Northern Highway.
Size: 3,000 acres.
Hours: Dawn to dusk daily.
Fees: $4.
Visitor Information: Belize Audubon Society, 2-34985 or 2-35004.

Crooked Tree Wildlife Sanctuary, a wetlands area on the northern boundary of the Belize District, is one of Belize's prime destinations for nature-lovers. Visitors from temperate-zone countries can easily see more birds in a single day than they are likely to see back home in a year. Even before you cross the causeway that connects to the freshwater island where **Crooked Tree Village** is located, you are liable to spot the American coot, northern jacana, snail kite, least grebe, white ibis, olivaceous cormorant, and rough-winged swallow. More than 250 different bird species have been recorded within the sanctuary, but the richness and variety of habitats here suggest that many more may be waiting to be "discovered." **Revenge Lagoon**, **Spanish River**, and **Black Creek** are some of the many excellent birding spots within the sanctuary's boundaries.

Not only is the variety of bird life tremendous at the Crooked Tree wetlands, especially later in the dry season (March through May), but the aggregate number of waterfowl is astonishing. Huge flocks of birds congregate here, taking advantage of the area's abundant food resources and safety as a resting spot on spring migration routes. The rare jabiru stork nests within the sanctuary, and the limpkin, with its black body and strange-looking neck, is another frequently observed inhabitant. You may delight in identifying an elegant green-backed heron, sleek blue-winged teal, multicolored black-bellied whistling duck, ungainly wood stork, or brilliant Yucatán jay.

For the best experience while visiting the Crooked Tree Sanctuary, contact manager **Donald Tillett** through the **Belize Audubon Society** in Belize City, 2-35004. I also recommend that you allow at least a full day to visit Crooked Tree, and that you hire a local guide.

Conservation at Crooked Tree

Crooked Tree Wildlife Sanctuary was established voluntarily by the area's 750 residents in November 1984, with substantial financial assistance from the Wild Wings Foundation. But local residents and the Belize

Audubon Society have made the most significant contributions to the success of Crooked Tree. During the early years, Audubon's management was accomplished exclusively by dedicated volunteers, mostly community residents.

"Crooked Tree Village has always been interested in conservation," village chairman Rudy Crawford pointed out in a 1997 interview. "When the Audubon Society came around, the idea of a wildlife sanctuary readily appealed to residents." Crawford believes that the subsequent sanctuary has succeeded because, first, the village is a family-oriented community with a long-standing conservation ethic, and second, Crooked Tree has responded to the demand for tourism-related businesses. While tourism is the village's fastest-growing industry, its mostly Creole residents still engage in subsistence farming, livestock raising, and fishing.

Visiting Crooked Tree by Land

The sanctuary's well-maintained visitors center and museum are situated at the beginning of the long causeway, which—together with the entrance road—runs between Crooked Tree Village and the paved Northern Highway linking Orange Walk and Belize City. You are required to check in at the visitors center before you explore the sanctuary ($4 entrance fee). If it is not open when you arrive or if the village bus fails to stop here, most Crooked Tree lodges will collect this fee and pass it on to the sanctuary. You may also pay on your way out.

The visitors center itself has informative displays that are designed to test your knowledge of the sanctuary's birds, as well as of the general natural history of the area. The sanctuary manager and wardens are happy to answer questions and assist in your explorations.

Several marked nature trails emanate from the village and, in fact, the majority begin simply as the meandering unpaved roads of Crooked Tree. One is appropriately named after the northern jacana, a delicate bird that flashes yellow wings when it flies and is light enough to tread confidently on water hyacinth as it forages for small fish and mollusks. Other trails bear the names of birds you may also see in the course of a half-day stroll through this tranquil village: **Trogon, Limpkin,** and **Kiskadee.**

Crooked Tree's managers are planning to build a ¾-mile-long boardwalk connecting the sanctuary's Spanish Creek to the ancient Maya ruin of **Chau Hiix,** which has been under excavation in recent years. Chau Hiix is the Mayan name for one of Belize's lesser-known cats, the jaguarundi.

David W. Steadman of New York's State Museum in Albany has compiled an impressive list of birds seen near Chau Hiix, including the crested guan, great curassow, ocellated turkey, bare-throated tiger-heron, azure-crowned hummingbird, scissor-tailed flycatcher, white-crowned parrot, yellow-lored parrot, and rufous-browed peppershrike. These are only a fraction of some 235 species he recorded in the Crooked Tree area.

Visiting Crooked Tree by Boat

I recommend hiring a boat and guide for a half-day trip south from Northern Lagoon, to Spanish Creek, up Black Creek, and to the Chau Hiix ruin. Fortunate visitors also have an opportunity to see black howler monkeys, iguanas, coatimundis, and Morelet's crocodiles, among other fauna. I also suggest that, if necessary, you remind your guide to periodically kill the engine and float quietly among the birds and other animals. Boat trips can be arranged through either the highly recommended **Paradise Inn** (see below) or **Jex Tours**, 21-2032. The latter is located on the main entrance road to Crooked Tree Village.

The greatest concentration of wildlife can be seen during April and May, when the water level is lowest. Mornings and evenings are peak activity times year-round. As you travel along the shore of **Crooked Tree Lagoon**, you will see Belize's largest contiguous stand of remaining logwood. Crooked Tree, one of the first non-Maya villages founded in Belize's interior, was established because of its accessibility to this commercially valuable timber, still exported in small amounts. On the way to **Spanish Creek** your guide can also point out distinctively

Crooked Tree Wildlife Sanctuary's visitors center and museum

216

Your Donation at Work

Donations to Crooked Tree Wildlife Sanctuary are encouraged and graciously accepted. This financial assistance keeps both the sanctuary and the Belize Audubon Society going. The Crooked Tree Wildlife Sanctuary turns over 10 percent of its entrance fees to the community for local service projects.

By supporting the sanctuary through the Belize Audubon Society, visitors can be part of current management activities, such as an annual May census of jabiru storks—one of the world's largest birds—accomplished with the help of local guides who volunteer their time and expertise. Belize Audubon is also carrying out a study of jabiru nesting behavior, the fledglings' growth period, and preparations for leaving this flagship species at a couple of targeted nests within Crooked Tree.

shaped bullet trees. These trees are used to make boat gunwales; its wood is so hard that bullets cannot penetrate it. Along this portion of the shoreline, the master of hovering flight, the snail kite, searches for the abundant land snails that cling to logwood stems. The captured snails leave behind white, multichambered clusters of eggs, thus replenishing the food chain.

Calabash Pond, **Revenge Lagoon**, **Western Lagoon**, **Southern Lagoon**, and **Jones Lagoon** are other wild places encompassed by the Crooked Tree Wildlife Sanctuary. Crocodiles and several turtle species can be found here, as well as howler monkeys and iguanas. Some wetlands are kept off-limits in order to prevent disturbance to wildlife.

Outfitters

Visitors with a serious interest in birds should arrange their trips through **Rudy Crawford**, 2-44333, fax 2-32579, or **International Expeditions**, (800) 633-4734. Crawford arranges personalized birding trips as well as horseback and carriage rides; guided trips to the Altun Ha Maya ruins, Lamanai, and the Community Baboon Sanctuary. Rudy's son Glen is an experienced naturalist who can help visitors add new species to their

Cashew Festival

Since 1993, a Cashew Festival has been held at Crooked Tree during the first weekend each May. This celebration exemplifies community-driven conservation diversified through music, dancing, feasting, storytelling, demonstrations of cabaña thatching, folklore performances, and, of course, demonstrations of the harvesting and preparation of local cashew nuts. The festival affords a rare opportunity to learn first-hand about the variety of cultures in Belize: rich Creole, Garifuna, Maya, and mestizo traditions. Crooked Tree residents even select a Cashew Queen.

"By harvesting, processing, and selling cashews, residents have established a livelihood that enhances their natural environment, an achievement which they feel is cause for celebration," explained Tom Grasse of International Expeditions, an Alabama-based tour company that helped start the successful festival. Cashew trees are native to the area, and their delicious fruits are used to make wine, jam, and sandwich spreads; they are sold in raw and roasted form as well. Mango products are also made and sold from the enormous, centuries-old trees that dominate the village. During the festival, birding trips often yield excellent results, since low water levels in the sanctuary's lagoons concentrate and attract vast numbers of waterbirds.

checklists. Most outfitters will charge $70 and up for a guided 4-hour boat excursion, conducted on horseback if the water is low. Check with local hotels for other guides.

Travel agencies and lodges in other parts of Belize also arrange sanctuary tours. For larger groups interested in an excellent tour of Crooked Tree—and/or the nearby New River/Lamanai trip—I recommend **Maya Mountain Tours,** jungle@mayamountain.com, 92-2164, fax 92-2029, and **G&W Holiday Tours,** 25-2461 or 2-33417, gholiday@btl.net.

International Expeditions
(800 633-4734), a long-time and highly-recommended tour operator in Belize, offers a "Naturalist Quest Tour" that includes boat and land tours of the Crooked Tree area. Knowledgable local guides help birders and photographers see exotic plants, birds, and other wildlife. International Expeditions can also supply you with cashew nuts harvested by the villagers of Crooked Tree, or you can buy them from local vendors.

Getting There
Buses from Belize City run daily to Crooked Tree. Check with Venus, 2-73354, or Batty Brothers, 2-72025, for fares and schedules. A Crooked Tree community bus, Jex, 21-2032, also runs three times a

A ripe nut dangles from a much larger cashew fruit in Crooked Tree Village.

International Expeditions

day between the village and Belize City—the advantage is that it comes all the way into Crooked Tree Village instead of dropping you on the Northern Highway. Bus fare is about $3 from Belize City. Taxis can also be arranged from Belize City or Orange Walk Town during the dry season. Expect to pay $75 and up for a round-trip from Belize City, slightly less for a round-trip from Orange Walk.

Where to Stay and Eat near Crooked Tree
Bird's Eye View Lodge, on the water; $55, with breakfast; 2-32040 or fax 2-24869, birdseye@aol.com. Also has a dorm facility with shared bath ($10) and accommodates tent campers for $5 per night. Boat rentals and birding tours available.

Chau Hiix Lodge, accessible by 40-minute boat ride up the Spanish River; rates start at $575 for three nights, including all meals and other services; 2-73787 or (800) 654-4424. Small and unique; operated by American expatriate Robert Brooks. Caters specifically to birders. Independent travelers should make advance reservations.

Maruba Resort, outside the village of Maruba (half an hour from Crooked Tree) on the Old Northern Highway; $180, includes meals; 3-

22199, (800) 552-3419. This self-styled "spa" has drawn complaints from some travelers about alleged poor service, high prices, and substandard facilities. Pool and restaurant on the premises. Emphasis on health and relaxation. In fairness, some visitors love the place.

Paradise Inn, on the main lagoon; $50; 2-44333, fax 2-32579, 75512.2552@compuserve.com. Comfortable bungalow accommodations and good restaurant, first-rate tours. Ideal for birders. Recommended.

Other Options
Other overnight accommodations are provided in homes of Crooked Tree Village residents. These are simple, inexpensive bed-and-breakfast arrangements in a rural atmosphere. Try **Rhaburn's Rooms, Molly's Rooms**, or **Mary Tillett's Rooms** (each about $15). While none of these families had a private telephone as of early 1999, visitors can make advance arrangements by calling Crooked Tree Village's community phones, 2-44101 or 2-44333. All-inclusive tours of Crooked Tree are offered by International Expeditions, (800) 633-4734.

Where to Eat in Crooked Tree Village
Meals, which may include local fish, are available at local hotels and homestays, as well as the **Corner's Inn Restaurant**, in the center of the village. Also recommended is **A&B Restaurant**: Take a right at the main junction in the village.

THE COMMUNITY BABOON SANCTUARY
Location: *About 30 miles northwest of Belize City.*
Size: *18 square miles.*
Hours: *8 a.m. to 5 p.m. daily.*
Fees: *Visitors must check in first at the museum and pay a $5 registration fee, which supports management of the sanctuary.*
Visitor Information: *Community phone, 21-2001, or Jungle Drift Lodge, 14-9578, jungle@btl.net.*

The Community Baboon Sanctuary, an easy day trip from Belize City, is one of the best places in Central America to get a close-up view of a monkey in its natural habitat. In Belize, black howler monkeys are called baboons; therefore the "baboons" being protected at this unusual private sanctuary have little in common with their African cousins of the same name. They are, in fact, an endangered species found only in a few lowland forests from southern Mexico to Honduras (most howlers in Central America are golden mantled, not black).

Howlers—so named because adults (mostly males) emit a distinctive raspy, guttural growl that can be heard for a mile or more—are threatened in much of their rapidly shrinking range. The protected colony that can be seen by visitors on an easy day trip from Belize City numbered about 1,500 monkeys in 1999, and these troops make up one of the few healthy-sized populations in the region. And thanks to an innovative management scheme, the size of this group is increasing all the time.

What is most unusual about the Community Baboon Sanctuary and its interpretive museum is the fact that the project is voluntary, entirely reliant on the goodwill of interested subsistence farmers who work the lands immediately adjacent to the broadleaf jungle the howlers prefer. Although the sanctuary is both praised and admired by government offi-cials, it is completely dependent on private lands and funding for its sur-vival. Since the sanctuary's creation in 1985, the area's mostly Creole landowners have responded generously to the international scientific com-munity's concern about the primate's dwindling habitat.

The current situation is a dramatic change from only 15 years ago, when the howler monkeys were frequent targets of local Maya and Guatemalan refugees (who killed them for meat), as well as unscrupulous poachers (who sold them as pets). Both practices are now against the law throughout Belize, where only licensed hunters are allowed to legally stalk wild game. The howlers have also been hard hit over the years by hurri-canes, which destroy their treetop aeries, and by yellow fever, the same deadly disease that affects humans. But more significantly, they have been victims of deforestation. As arboreal vegetarians partial to wild fruits and flower blossoms, they need a thick forest canopy to survive.

In order to preserve this critical habitat along the Belize River, about 25 miles inland from the Caribbean, about 140 farmers have agreed to maintain corridors of tall broadleaf jungle along the borders of their fields, to refrain from cutting such favored food trees as strangler fig, breadnut, amate fig, trumpet, and hogplum, and to protect 66-foot-wide strips of forest along the riverbank. These practices not only ensure that the mon-keys will have a safe place to live, eat, and raise their families, but also help reduce erosion, minimize river siltation, and allow more rapid regen-eration of the soil after slash-and-burn agricultural clearing. The smaller plots of cultivated land are now hedged in by thick vegetation that will quickly invade the area once it loses its productivity.

Organizers began asking their neighbors to sign conservation pledges in the mid-1980s, and so far very few farmers have refused or withdrawn from the sanctuary. Locals have found that visitors help them out financially by hiring guides, patronizing businesses, and overnighting at homestays. The women of the village often prepare hot meals for tourists, and the men take foreigners on leisurely walking or canoe trips to observe the flora and

Howler monkey at the Community Baboon Sanctuary

Richard Mahler

fauna along the meandering Belize River. Also, several small stores sell food and drinks.

Like Bermudian Landing, eight other villages within the sanctuary are gradually attracting tourism business. They bear the sort of colorful names encountered all over Belize, including **Double Head Cabbage**, **Scotland Halfmoon**, and **Flowers Bank**. The howler population has expanded vigorously within all nine participating communities.

Starting in 1992, the monkey colony along the Belize River was strong enough to withstand the transfer of some of its members to the Cockscomb Basin Wildlife Sanctuary, about 80 miles to the south. A 1996 reintroduction program was successful in transferring eight howlers to the Macal River near San Ignacio. In these locations, a combination of hurricane damage, hunting, and yellow fever had wiped out indigenous troops during the past 30 years.

Another side benefit of the Community Baboon Sanctuary's success is the resurgence of other wildlife in the protected area, including the much-hunted iguana. Nearly 200 bird species have been identified, along with dozens of different mammals, including jaguars, ocelots, paca, and deer. Researchers are also coming here to study the highly endangered Central American river turtle, which is now holding its own within the sanctuary's borders.

The sanctuary is the winter home of many migratory birds that fly to

Belize every year from as far away as Canada. Colorful year-round residents include parakeets, parrots, toucans, and tanagers. Though modified by centuries of selective logging and small-scale farming, local forests still support about 100 tree species and scores of varieties of vines, shrubs, flowers, and herbs. Many wild orchids and bromeliads can be seen clinging to the trunks of tall trees.

Outfitters
The sanctuary staff can direct you to reputable local guides. Fees vary and are sometimes negotiable, but expect to pay up to $25 an hour. Guided canoe trips are also available for up to $20 an hour. **Jungle Drift Lodge** (1-49578) offers an affordable, 15-mile Belize River canoe trip, among other excursions. Also try the **M&H Rivercamp** (see below). Because the jungle trails are often overgrown and muddy, rubber boots, long-sleeved shirts, trousers, hats, and insect repellent are advised. Always check with the headquarters and obtain a map before heading out.

Knowledgeable guides can be hired in Bermudian Landing and nearby Flowers Bank for a recommended canoe trip on nearby Mussel Creek. This river and wetland complex boasts a great diversity of waterbirds, flora, and reptiles. My recent half-day guided Mussel Creek tour with **Camille Young** yielded close encounters with two troops of howler monkeys, a manatee, and over 18 bird species (including a hooded oriole and a pygmy kingfisher).

As of 1999, the only direct contact with sanctuary headquarters was by two-way radio, which is sometimes unreliable. It is possible, however, to simply stop at the office, buy a field guide, tour the sanctuary with one of the nature guides, and arrange a homestay. In Belize City, stop by the Audubon Society office at 12 Fort St., or call them at 2-34985 (base@btl.net).

Getting There
The sanctuary can be reached by private car in about an hour from Belize city via the Northern or Western Highway. From either direction, take the Burrell Boom cut-off and follow the signs to Bermudian Landing. Taxi fare is about $45 one-way from the international airport or Belize City. Note that there are only a few stores and no gasoline stations within 20 miles of the reserve. Specific directions on getting to the sanctuary by car or bus are available from the sanctuary's office, which can also make arrangements for groups interested in touring the area, as well as for overnight accommodations.

Leonard Russell's orange bus provides scheduled service between Belize City and Bermudian Landing, departing from Cairo Street, near the intersection of Euphrates Avenue and Orange Street,

The Dawsons are one of several Creole families that operate homestays for visitors to the Community Baboon Sanctuary.

in Belize City at 12:15 p.m., 4:15 p.m., and 4:50 p.m. on weekdays. The bus returns to Belize City around 6 a.m. (about $2 one way). **Jungle Drift Lodge** picks up visitors at the International Airport for about $40 (reserve ahead).

Where to Stay and Eat near Community Baboon Sanctuary

Jungle Drift Lodge, on the river only 400 yards from sanctuary headquarters; $25 and up; 14-9578, fax 27-8160, jungled@btl.net. Bungalows (with and without private bath); a two-story family cabaña; and shower, kitchen, and restroom facilities. Camping is allowed ($5), and both canoes and kayaks can be rented ($5 an hour). Fully guided canoe trips are $20 per person.

Little Eden Guest House, near the Belize River in Bermudian landing; $35; 2-82129. Two basic rooms, electric fans, shared bath, gift shop on premises. Can arrange sanctuary tours. You must share a bathroom.

M & H Rivercamp & Ranch, in Scotland Halfmoon, just north of Bermudian Landing, Box 961, Belize City; $20 for cabañas, $4 for campsites; no phone. Meals, river tours, and horseback rides available at reasonable rates.

Russell's Place, a pleasant bar and restaurant on the riverbank in Bermudian Landing, serving traditional Belizian food.

Other Options

A few informal and decidedly rustic **homestay bed-and-breakfasts** (about $15 a night) are available in the sanctuary and outlying villages. I suggest calling the Bermudian Landing community phone, 21-2001, and arranging your stay in advance. I particularly recommend the **Geraldine Joseph family, Alexandra Young, Dawson Family,** or **Helen Herrera.** Meals usually cost about $5 each. Camping is available on the museum grounds (usually for a small fee) by arrangement with the sanctuary's staff. RVs are allowed to park overnight next to the museum, also for a modest fee.

BURDON CREEK NATURE RESERVE

This mangrove and wetland ecosystem west of Belize City was protected in 1992 primarily as buffer against flooding and water pollution in the country's largest city. Urban sprawl threatens the area and tourist access is minimal. Inquire locally about boat trips along the natural and human-made canals that transect the reserve and offer wonderful birding opportunities.

Several local tour operators offer excursions through Burdon Creek as part of their package trips to the Northern and Southern Lagoons en route to Gales Point. Inquire at the Belize Audubon Society, 2-35004, for more information.

THE BELIZE ZOO

Location: About 30 miles west of Belize City and 14 miles east of Belmopan on the Western Highway.
Size: About 1,600 acres, with 28 acres devoted to animal exhibits.
Hours: Daily, except major holidays, from 9 a.m. to 4:30 p.m.
Fees: Admission to the zoo is $7.50 for adults and $3.75 for kids. Zoo memberships (starting at $25 for individuals) are available by writing to Box 1787, Belize City. Supporters receive a newsletter about the Belize Zoo's ongoing activities, and contributions are used for conservation education.

One place where you are guaranteed to see native animals in their natural surroundings is the Belize Zoo. Most of us regard zoos as anything but a natural setting; however, as you know by now, things are done a bit differently in Belize. Instead of placing its animals behind bars in severe-looking cages, the zoo's managers have created an intimate, cozy atmosphere by putting their creatures in chicken-wire enclosures beneath a shady forest canopy. Each of the animals is referred to by its own name—from Sugar, the purring ocelot, to Rambo, the keel-billed toucan—and all are well cared for.

The philosophy that permeates the zoo's exhibits is one of respect for all wildlife. Hand-lettered signs remind visitors that practices such as poaching and live capturing continue to threaten the survival of several unusual Belizean natives, including cats, macaws, and monkeys. In fact, many of the creatures held by the zoo are "pets" that were abandoned by their owners after they became too big, too wild, or too unwanted. Guides at the zoo are involved in a conservation outreach program designed to teach visiting Belizean schoolchildren (over 10,000 each year) about the natural wonders of their homeland.

At least 125 animals can be seen here, including the endangered scarlet macaw, jaguarundi, margay, jaguar, otter, black howler monkey, anteater, and great curassow. The assembly includes some 18 mammal species, 12 bird species, six reptile species, and several species of fish and insects. All live within areas that are as large and as close to their natural habitats as could be achieved by the zoo personnel.

Not long ago the zoo added two jabiru storks to its family. The jabiru is

Richard Mahler

A tour guide displays a boa constrictor at the Belize Zoo.

a flagship species for conservation in Belize. It has a huge slightly upturned bill, a bright red neck collar, stands up to 5 feet tall, and has up to a 9-foot wing span. While it is possible to see this magnificent bird in the wild in Belize, a visit to the zoo is worth it just to be sure you see a jabiru.

Such Belize-loving celebrities as actor Harrison Ford and musician/ author Jimmy Buffett made donations that enabled the zoo to move to expanded quarters in late 1991. A large waterbird aviary was opened in 1993, and future plans include a butterfly exhibit, a freshwater aquarium (with advice from the famous Monterey Bay Aquarium), and a reptile center. A biologist by training, director Sharon Matola works constantly to improve the zoo and has taken advantage of Belize's thawed relations with Guatemala to acquire both a jaguarundi and a male spotted jaguar (named C.T. Katun) from that country. In 1996 a female black jaguar (Ellen) came to the zoo from Texas, where she was born in captivity.

The zoo is an easy day trip from Belize City, as well as a good diversion en route to the Cayo District, Caracol, or Tikal.

Visitor Information and Services

There is no restaurant but a vendor sells snacks and there's a gift shop. The zoo operates a Deluxe Guest House on its property, where you can arrange tours of both the zoo and the education center. To contact the zoo during business hours, call 8-13004, or send e-mail to: belizezoo@pobox.com. Its website is www.belizenet.com/belizezoo.

227

How It All Started

The Belize Zoo was founded in 1983 by its director, Sharon Matola, after wildlife filmmaker Richard Foster's budget was cut and he was left with 17 animal "stars" that had no movies to appear in and no place to go. Matola, Foster's assistant, was told to disband the troupe of jaguars, coatimundis, peccaries, pumas, and other animals that had been trained to "act" in nature documentaries.

Instead of abandoning them, Matola boldly painted a description in front of each creature's enclosure and put a "Belize Zoo" sign in front of the compound. Success came only after she devoted thousands of hours to finding ways to feed and house the animals, while at the same time cultivating countrywide interest in their well being. Matola's credo is manifest in the way she has always run the zoo: Public awareness and education are critical to wildlife conservation. Her nature-oriented storybooks have become favorites of Belizean children who, in turn, are convincing their parents to adopt lifestyles that protect the country's environment. The zoo's educational

There are many biting and stinging insects (uncaged) at the zoo and a good repellent is strongly advised. Keep your arms, legs, and ankles covered while observing the animals, since wildlife tends to attract flying creatures that pester humans.

Getting There

The Belize Zoo is clearly marked on the Western Highway at about Mile 29. Going west from Belize City, you will encounter the Tropical Education Center first on your left, then the old zoo site on your right, and finally the new zoo a little farther along, also on the right. The visitor center, which includes an excellent gift shop and playground, is about ½-mile off the highway on a dirt access road. Taxis are easy to arrange from either Belize City or Belmopan. Expect to pay $70 and up for a round-trip. Buses from Belize City run virtually every hour throughout the day (less often on weekends *programs have made a noticeable impact on prevailing attitudes toward native flora and fauna.*

A particular favorite is April, a Baird's tapir (Belize's national animal) which thrives at the zoo. Throughout Central America, this large but shy creature is in trouble; its future survival as a species is threatened by habitat destruction and hunting. The tapir, a relative of the hippo, is the largest of all native Belizean land animals, and adults may weigh up to 650 pounds. The zoo's female tapir has endeared herself to thousands of Belizean children, who have watched her frolic in her paddock. April's pairing with a new mate (named Scotty) reflects one of the major goals of the zoo—to give every animal a partner and thus ensure that future visitors will always be able to view each species at close range. Captive breeding programs for creatures such as the citreoline trogon and iguana have also been carried out at the Belize Zoo. For iguanas, the Belize Zoo has collaborated and shared information with other captive rearing programs like the successful one at Pook's Hill Lodge adjacent to the Tapir Mountain Nature Reserve.

and holidays). Check with **Venus,** 2-73354, or **Batty,** 2-72025, for current fares and schedules. Drivers will pick you up and drop you off on the highway, from where you must walk to the zoo. The San Ignacio–Airport shuttle van will stop at the zoo on request.

BELIZE TROPICAL EDUCATION CENTER

Across the highway from the zoo is the Tropical Education Center, a sort of nature school for Belizeans operated by University College of Belize. The property was previously owned by Dora Weyer, one of the first conservation leaders in Belize and a founding member of the Belize Audubon Society. Weyer retired to the U.S. in 1989, and one of her conservation legacies is this 140-acre complex, with self-guided nature trails, visitors dormitory, lecture rooms, a library, and offices for its Belizean staff. Schoolchildren and college students who have never been in the bush come here to spend a few days surrounded by nature. Solar energy powers the entire compound. Visiting educators are welcome to visit, and birders can use the raised bird-watching deck.

MONKEY BAY WILDLIFE SANCTUARY AND NATIONAL PARK

Location: 31.5 miles west of Belize City on the Western Highway.
Size: 1,070 acres.
Visitor Information: Contact Monkey Bay Wildlife Sanctuary at P.O. Box 187, Belmopan; 23180, fax 8-23235, mbay@pobox.com.
Fees, Services, and Lodging: There is no admission fee to the sanctuary, and overnight visitors are welcome ($5–$8).

Located along the Western Highway about 2 miles west of the Belize Zoo is Monkey Bay Wildlife Sanctuary. Adjacent to the property, across the Sibun River, is Monkey Bay National Park. Monkey Bay Wildlife Sanctuary was established on Earth Day 1990 as a privately owned and operated protected area of mostly pine savanna, cohune palm, and tropical gallery forest, along with freshwater wetlands, lagoons, and river habitat. Monkey Bay National Park was legally established in May 1994 and, together with the sanctuary, comprises a 3,300-acre wildlands corridor spanning the Sibun River watershed.

Among the sanctuary's attractions are rolling jungle ridges, 2 miles of nature trails, and Sibun River frontage that includes a secluded bathing beach. The field research station and other facilities—all open to visitors—are part of an evolving permaculture that integrates solar power systems, rainwater catchment, a biogas-generating latrine, reforestation, composting, and raised-bed organic gardens.

Observers at Monkey Bay have reported seeing at least 220 species of birds within the reserve's borders, including parrots, toucans, crakes, trogons, flycatchers, and cuckoos. Other wildlife sightings include jaguar, puma, deer, peccary, crocodile, iguana, tapir, and coatimundi.

Visitors might wonder why this particular name was chosen, since there is no bay and no monkey species are listed among the native denizens. Monkey Bay retains a name given to the property at a time when black howler and white-faced spider monkeys frequented this stretch of the Sibun River. A hurricane in 1978 destroyed the tall forest canopy habitat that these monkeys favor, forcing the remaining animals to retreat to the limestone karst hills visible on the southern horizon. However, on two occasions in 1993, monkeys were again observed near the sanctuary.

"We hope that with more recovery time, the forest here will again host these two endangered species," the sanctuary's co-founder, Matthew Miller, told me. "In order to enhance this recovery process and provide an attractive and well-protected habitat, the Monkey Bay staff has actively been planting 200 acres of tropical forest trees, including mahogany, sapodilla, balsam, baboon cap, and velvet apple."

Several North American high school and university groups participate in Monkey Bay's experiential-based learning programs, and visitation from Japan is also increasing. Belizean students visit Monkey Bay regularly for guided walking tours of the tropical forest.

A large wooden field-research station at Monkey Bay (dubbed "The Barn") accommodates a classroom, library, and natural-history display room. It doubles as accommodations for visiting researchers and teachers. Monkey Bay is considered an ideal location for earth literacy and natural-history education programs, and offers homestay opportunities with families in rural villages for visitors with a thirst for cultural immersion.

Children of all ages are encouraged to visit, as are members of education and/or research groups.

Camping and Nature Programs

Monkey Bay is one of the few places in Belize where visitors are not only allowed, but encouraged to camp. Tenters are offered one of several large, thatch-covered, raised camping platforms in the savanna. Nature hiking, photography, picnicking, swimming, canoeing, and self-directed study are also available.

Monkey Bay has an "open door" policy, but it's best to call or write ahead. There are campsites ($5) and basic rooms ($8), plus a kitchen where you can get an inexpensive meal ($3 to $5).

Getting There

The well-marked dirt entrance road is about 45 minutes west of Belize City. Local buses will drop you off at the junction, and you can walk the short distance to the field station. A taxi from the international airport costs about $40.

Where to Stay and Eat at Monkey Bay

J.B.'s Kool Spot, within walking distance of Monkey Bay at Mile 32 on the Western Highway; 1-49322. This laid-back restaurant and bar (with live music on weekends) has been popular with Belizeans and foreigners since its founding years ago by a colorful (and since departed) expatriate named J.B. The current owners also rent basic cottages for about $13 a night. The Belizean-style food is good and free to young children when accompanied by adults.

SOUTHERN BELIZE

9

BELIZE, STANN CREEK, AND TOLEDO DISTRICTS

Long neglected as a tourist destination, the south of Belize is coming into its own among visitors looking for smaller crowds and more pristine outdoor attractions. Not long ago this part of the country was difficult to travel in and offered few amenities or services for those passing through. Today it boasts a solid infrastructure of hotels, restaurants, tour companies, and related services. True, conditions are sometimes a bit rough, but the area's natural beauty more than compensates for an occasional dusty road or lumpy mattress.

Southern Belize has special appeal for those interested in natural history and indigenous cultures. Offshore are seldom-visited cayes and atolls, plus some of the country's best places to dive, snorkel, fish, sail, kayak, windsurf, and study marine life. I particularly recommend areas near South Water, Tobacco, Stuart, and Curlew Cayes off Dangriga, and Colson, Pompion, and Ranguana Cayes east of Placencia. For those who can make the distant trip, Glover's Reef is one of the finest sites in the entire Caribbean for snorkeling, diving, and sportfishing.

Birders will be rewarded with many opportunities in this ecologically diverse region. My favorites include Man o' War Caye (a nesting area for the magnificent frigatebird) and both the Sittee and Monkey Rivers (wide jungle waterways with many side channels and lagoons). The Cockscomb Basin is an excellent place to see flora and fauna of the tropical forest—including the occasional jaguar—as are the various protected areas of the Toledo District. In swampy areas and beaches along the

233

coast, you may see such wildlife rarities as the Caribbean manatee, hawksbill turtle, and jabiru stork.

For those eager to learn more about the rich cultural mosaic of Belize, the southern districts are fascinating places to explore. As elsewhere in this tiny country, ancient Maya ruins abound. At Lubaantun, for example, you can see how a mortarless building technique yielded temples more reminiscent of Peru's Machu Picchu than the Classic Maya. Near Dangriga, the Mayflower site is tucked amid thundering jungle waterfalls. Among and around all such ruins, the contemporary Kekchí and Mopán Maya live 20th-century lives amidst the ghosts of their ancestors.

Southern Belize is also the heartland of the Garinagu (Garifuna) culture, representing a unique blend of African, Caribbean Indian, and European traditions. Many of the region's Garifuna music, dance, and religious rituals are openly shared with outsiders—an experience not to be missed. Other communities are equally proud of their Creole, Guatemalan, East Indian, Chinese, mestize, and Lebanese ethnicities. At least one village boasts of its pirate origins, while another traces its roots to immigrant Confederates who sought refuge after the U.S. Civil War!

The region is approached from the north to the south in this chapter.

BELIZE DISTRICT (SOUTH)

Much of the Belize District's southern area is uninhabitable swamp, with limited access and few attractions for the foreign visitor. One exception is the village of Gales Point, and the brackish lagoons that lie between this Creole community and Belize City. (For more information on the Belize District, see Chapter 8, The North.)

GALES POINT
Location: About 25 miles south of Belize City, 15 miles north of Dangriga
Population: 350 (1999 estimate).
Visitor Information: Gales Point Bed and Breakfast Association, 5-22087, or Manatee Lodge, 800 334-7942.

Gales Point offers visitors a refreshing dose of rural Creole hospitality, some unparalleled nature attractions, and a great example of community conservation. A limestone escarpment on the northwest bank of this lagoon is the site of several caves that can be explored as a guided side trip. We also recommend a boat ride up **Soldier Creek** (also called Plantation Creek), which has abundant orchids and other exotic plants.

The name Gales Point describes both a community and a narrow

▲ A horse-drawn Mennonite buggy in the Cayo District (Steele Wotkyns)

▼ Garifuna Settlement Day Parade in Dangriga (© Tony Rath)

Maya children (Kevin Schafer)

▲ Wilderness rain forest areas and pristine rivers are protected in the Bladen Nature Reserve. (Dan Dancer/Lighthawk)

▼ Belize River boatman (Steele Wotkyns)

▼ Painted cement Maya head in San Pedro (Richard Mahler)

▲ Black howler monkey (Kevin Schafer)

▼ Baird's tapir and its young (Kevin Schafer)

▲ Scarlet macaw (Kevin Schafer)

▼ Jaguar (Kevin Schafer)

▲ West Indian manatee
(Kevin Schafer)

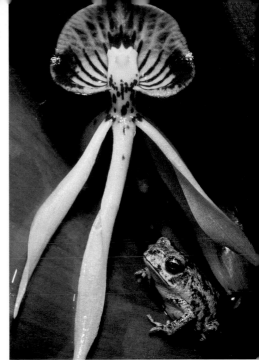

▲ Orchid and toad
(Kevin Schafer)

▼ Calliandra flower (Kevin Schafer)

▲ Maya ruins near Corozal (© Tony Rath)

▼ Heliconia
(International Expeditions)

▼ A snorkeler discovers brain cora
off the coast (© Tony Rath)

▲ Keel-billed toucan
(Kevin Schafer)

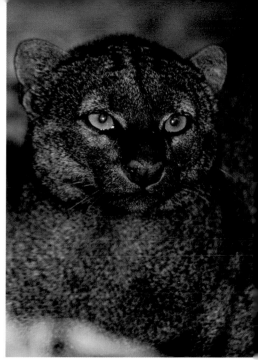

▲ Jaguarundi (Kevin Schafer)

▼ Creole children along the Northern Highway (Kevin Schafer)

▲ The Blue Hole at Lighthouse Reef (Kevin Schafer)

▼ Sea-kayaking off South Water Caye (© Tony Rath)

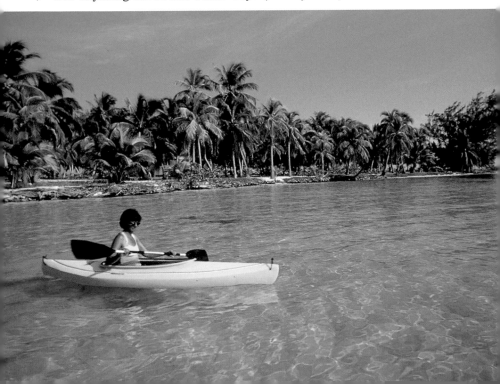

2-mile finger of land jutting up from the south end of **Southern Lagoon**. The village was founded by logwood cutters many years before Belize became a British colony and is inhabited mostly by their descendants—Creole farmers and fishers.

The lagoons and estuaries near the village are full of marine life and represent the region's most important stronghold for the Caribbean manatee. This is, in fact, the species' largest breeding ground. The reticent mammal, which looks something like a tuskless walrus, feeds on the thick grasses and other vegetation found in the lagoons. Manatees are distant cousins of elephants and often weigh over 200 pounds. Local guides are happy to take tourists to feeding areas where the gentle beasts are seen most often. The nearest feeding ground is only a few hundred yards from the village.

Gales Point Manatee Community Sanctuary

In 1992, residents created the Gales Point Manatee Community Sanctuary to protect the manatee and develop conservation-oriented tourism. This cooperative venture pools local skills and resources to provide boat trips, wildlife observation, sportfishing, and cave exploration. About 15 residents provide boating and/or guiding services, while some 20 homes are open to overnight visitors. Other residents produce and sell handcrafted items such as tie-tie baskets and hats. Cashew and berry wines, as well as mango and cashew preserves, are made and sold locally. This visitor-related activity is designed to enhance Gales Point's base of subsistence agriculture without jeopardizing its rural character and beautiful environment.

Local conservation efforts have focused on protecting endangered hawksbill turtles, since nearby **Manatee Bar** is one of the few known nesting beaches for this endangered marine reptile. With assistance and training from Wisconsin-based Community Conservation Consultants, area residents have installed wire mesh to protect nesting hawksbill turtles from predation. As a result of this community-driven work, as many as 12,000 turtle hatchlings make it into the Caribbean in a single year.

With the help of international organizations, residents have installed buoys and signs to help protect the manatee from powerboats, planted disease-resistant coconuts, and installed improved sanitation facilities to maintain water quality in the lagoon. These seemingly small efforts are critically important to the long-term viability of small communities like Gales Point, which have staked much of their future on the growth of natural-history tourism.

Gales Point Outfitters

Tour operators arranging trips to the area include the recommended **Jal's Travel** (2-45407) in Belize City, **Pelican Beach Resort**

Learning Experiences

For an unusual cultural experience, visitors may wish to enroll in the recommended **Maroon Creole Drum School**, operated by Emmeth Young, one of the best drummers in Belize. Young offers camping on his land (meals included for a modest fee) and charges $5 an hour for expert instruction in making and playing the traditional Belizean drum. You'll learn a good deal about Creole history and culture in the process. Advance reservations are preferred, since Young performs in Belize and other countries from time to time. Write him c/o Gales Point Village, Belize District, Belize, or call 5-22087.

Oceanic Society Expeditions (800-326-7491) offers trips in which participants are asked to help researchers assess the distribution and habitat use of resident manatees, and to protect hawksbill turtle hatchlings (on Manatee Bar beach) from predators. Guests stay in village guest quarters and campsites, taking meals with local residents. The nine-day expedition includes a trip to nearby **Ben Lomond Cave.**

Boat excursions from Gales Point take visitors past small cayes in the various bodies of water—particularly **Bird Island** in Northern Lagoon—that are important breeding grounds for iguanas, crocodiles, and waterbirds, including the white ibis and boat-billed heron. Aquatic flora and fauna are abundant here, since a tremendous amount of nutrient-rich runoff flows through these passageways en route from the Maya Mountains to the Caribbean. The tangled mangrove forest along the shoreline is an important nursery for young shrimp, crabs, lobster, and fish. Wildlife in the area includes deer, peccary, armadillo, gibnut, and various cats. Expect to pay $20 and up for a guided tour by boat or on land.

(5-22044) in Dangriga, and **Ricardo's Beach Huts** (2-31609) on
Bluefield Range Caye.

Scheduled boats from Belize City depart from **Blackline Marina**, on
Haulover Creek, 2-44145. Competent local boatmen include **Allen
"Passo" Andrewin** and his brother, **Mose** (5-22087).

Getting There
Gales Point is at the culmination of a dead end, 15-mile dirt road that
stretches through swampy terrain north of Dangriga. Although it is not
difficult to reach by road, the village is more frequently approached from
the north by boat via the Southern Lagoon. Small crafts can make an
inland passage from Belize City via the Burdon Canal Nature Reserve and
Boom's Creek in an hour or two, navigating a bewildering maze of waterways. An alternative is heading directly south along the Inner Channel in
open water and then following a narrow estuary across Manatee Bar into
Southern Lagoon, also called Manatee Lagoon.

Where to Stay and Eat in Gales Point
The Gales Point Bed and Breakfast Association, 5-22087 (community telephone). Offers simple homestays ($15 and up, plus meals) and
tent sites ($5), with no advance reservations required. There is one small
store in the village for basic supplies.

Manatee Lodge, at the tip of Gales Point; $150, meals included;
8-23320 or (800) 334-7942. Co-owned by the Hidden Valley Inn and
oriented toward sportfishing, the Manatee was remodeled in 1993. The
12-room facility offers boat tours to manatee breathing holes and a turtle
nesting beach, as well as birding trips. Foreign anglers are attracted to the
several species of game fish that abound in these waters, notably tarpon,
snook, and cubera. Besides guided fishing trips, guests can take off on one
of the lodge's Sunfish sailboats. Transportation arranged by the lodge
from Belize City.

STANN CREEK DISTRICT

Southern Belize has only two distinct political jurisdictions: the citrus-rich
Stann Creek District immediately below Belize City and Belmopan, and
the lightly-populated Toledo District south of the Cockscomb Basin and
Monkey River.

The easiest ways to reach the region's far-flung communities are by air
(fast but relatively expensive), boat, private car, or scheduled bus service.

Daily buses ply the bumpy Hummingbird Highway that links Belmopan with Dangriga, continuing from Dangriga to Hopkins, Placencia, and Punta Gorda via the mostly unpaved Southern Highway. (A gravel-surfaced short-cut, known variously as the Coastal Highway or Manatee Road, heads directly south from the Western Highway near Hattieville and rejoins the Hummingbird Highway a few miles west of Dangriga.)

Although paved, the 52-mile Hummingbird Highway is scenic and uncrowded, but notorious for its bone-jarring potholes and muddy bogs. Allow at least 2 hours for the drive from Belmopan to Dangriga. Along the way, you may wish to stop at Caves Branch, Blue Hole National Park, Five Blues Lake National Park, and St. Herman's Cave. There are also a couple of large citrus plantations where tours are available by appointment.

Midway along the Hummingbird Highway you enter the Stann Creek District, the more populous of Belize's two southern districts. Although Dangriga is Stann Creek's administrative center and largest town, several nearby communities are well worth a visit.

DANGRIGA
Location: 32 miles south of Belize City.
Population: 11,000 (1999 estimate).
Visitor Information: Sightseeing suggestions are cheerfully dispensed at PJ's Gift Shop and the New Riverside Café (which also has a pay telephone). Airplane tickets can be purchased at The Treasure Chest, which doubles as a souvenir store and travel agency, or at Pelican Beach Resort. Via Internet, check www.belizenet.com

The name of this busy port town was changed from Stann Creek to Dangriga some years ago to honor the proud Garifuna (also called Garinagu) people who make up the majority of its residents. The name means "standing water" in the Garifuna language, a reference to the brackish pools that form when the rain-swollen Stann Creek overflows its banks on its way through town toward the Caribbean. Dangriga was settled by European traders and farmers in the late 17th century, then became an important shipping center during colonial times.

Services
In addition to a post office and BTL office, there are three banks, several gas stations, and many grocery stores.

Things to See and Do in Dangriga
Melinda's Historical Museum, next to PJ's Gift Shop at 21 St. Vincent, 5-22266, displays Garifuna artifacts such as mahogany *badaya* bowls

Main street in Dangriga, the largest town in the Stann Creek district

used in making cassava flour. The museum is open ($1 admission) from 9 a.m. to noon and 2 to 5 p.m. daily except Thursday and Sunday.

Punta rock can be widely heard on holidays or at one of several nightclubs: the **Wrong House, Son-Flo Disco**, and **Dada's Disco**.

Outfitters

Because of its location and services, Dangriga is a good base for excursions to the southern cayes and atolls or to the nearby Gales Point Manatee Community Sanctuary, the Cockscomb Basin Wildlife Sanctuary, the Garifuna village of Hopkins, the Mayflower Maya site, and the Mopán village of Maya Center. Most of the hotels can arrange guided trips or you can contact **Rodney's Tours**, 5-22294, at the airstrip. **Pelican Beach Resort** 5-22044 arranges highly recommended day trips that are open to non-guests. Expect to pay $45 to $75 for most day trips. Be prepared to pay about $50 for a snorkel trip, slightly more for fishing or diving trips. Also recommended is **Jorge Rosado**, 5-2020, who specializes in nature and cultural history tours, in collaboration with International Zoological Expeditions.

The Garifuna

The Garifuna (otherwise known as Black Caribs) are a distinct and close-knit ethnic group of mixed West African and Caribbean Indian ancestry who arrived here in great numbers beginning in 1823, after civil unrest

239

© Tony Rath

*Chakanari dancers performing
at Christmas*

along the Honduran coast drove them north. The Garifuna legacy begins many years earlier, when shipwrecked slaves escaped to the British-controlled islands of Dominica and St. Vincent in the West Indies. These West Africans (mostly males) intermingled with aboriginal Red and Yellow Caribs (mostly females), sharing many customs and rituals as the years progressed. Their mixed-blood offspring developed impressive skills in fishing, farming, and hunting. They also remained staunchly independent, refusing to bargain with the Europeans who tried to subdue them and take over their lands. For several decades they successfully resisted colonization.

Finally, in 1795, the Garifuna chief was killed by an English soldier's bullet. His conquered people were rounded up and shipped off to the Bay Islands off Honduras, at that time a part of the British empire. Over the next 25 years, small bands of restless Garifuna wandered up and down the Central American coast, establishing settlements in what are now Belize, Guatemala, Costa Rica, and Nicaragua, as well as mainland Honduras.

On November 19, 1823, a large group of Garifuna from the Bay Islands joined about 200 others who had settled at the mouth of Stann Creek some 20 years earlier. A Puritan trading post had been built on this spot, and the traders called these structures "stands." Over time, this term was locally corrupted into "stann," and the revised name stuck. The date of the mass Garifuna landing, November 19, is still celebrated loudly and enthusiastically each year on Settlement Day, a Belizean national holiday. Because Dangriga is one of the largest Garifuna communities among the many now spread along the coastline of four Central American nations and the Windward Islands, a visit here provides an excellent opportunity to learn about a fascinating Afro-Indian subculture that is little known outside Belize.

Garifuna Culture
It is in arts and crafts that the Garifuna particularly excel. Their drummakers are revered for a perceived ability to induce the obeah magic

Settlement Day

The ideal time to come is on Settlement Day and, if possible, the week leading up to the November 19 celebration. Hundreds of Garifuna from throughout Central America and the Caribbean flock to Dangriga for the festivities. The streets are alive with dancing, drumming, and impromptu music concerts. (At other times of the year, several nightclubs and hotels offer indigenous music and dancing.) Feasts and celebrations last far into the night.

Scheduled events include a reenactment of the arrival of Garifuna leader Alejo Beni and his boats from Honduras, plus a fascinating religious ceremony in the Catholic church which combines European, African, and Carib rituals. (Most Garifuna—like most Belizeans—now consider themselves at least nominally Roman Catholic.) The ceremonies are performed in the Garifuna language, a unique mixture of West Indian, West African, Spanish, English, and French words.

On Settlement Day, Dangriga's main street (St. Vincent) is closed to traffic so that musicians, costumed dancers, and revelers can parade with abandon, carnival-style.

through the music of their instruments. Dances are performed to the beat of three drums of varying sizes, traditionally made out of carved cedar trees or sea turtle shells. Some of the younger Garifuna have incorporated these ceremonial instruments into reggae and calypso musical stylings, giving birth to a distinctive style of music known as "punta rock," now popular throughout Belize. More traditional groups that perform in Dangriga include the Turtle Shell Band, Punta Rebels, and Warribaggabagga Dancers. The chance to see a performance by these or any other Garifuna dance troupe should not be missed. Fortunately, many of the region's upscale hotels schedule visits by these dance groups once or twice each week. The local office of Island Expeditions (5-23328) presents free Garifuna drumming weekend nights at Len's Cool Spot in the Sabal neighborhood.

The Garifuna Religion

*Many outsiders, including Belize's early white colonists, have con-
tended that the traditional spiritual beliefs of the Garifuna are akin
to Haitian-style voodoo, which is only partially true. The central
focus of Garifuna religion is the mysterious and magical practice of
obeah, originating in West African traditions brought to the Americas during the 1600s. Through the use of fetishes, amulets, symbols, and rituals, followers believe spiritual energy—both positive
and negative—can be directed to individuals. Indigo crosses on the
foreheads of small children, for example, keep away bad spirits,
and the blood of sacrificed animals (usually chickens or pigs) wards
off evil. A small cloth doll stuffed with black feathers, called a
puchinga, may be buried under an enemy's doorstep to bring
about tribulation, illness, or even death.*

*At the opposite end of the spectrum, a kind of white-magic
healing ceremony and feast of reconciliation known as the dugu is
also used to rid the community of evil spirits. This ritual, rarely
observed by outsiders, takes place over the course of a full week*

In the weeks leading up to Christmas, garishly painted and masked
John-Canoe (also spelled Yan-kunu) dancers perform in the streets for
gifts of rum, money, and candy. The dance is performed only by men,
who imitate the strident movements of a white slave master. At midnight
on Christmas Eve, the town echoes with the deep blast of several hundred
hollow conch shells blown simultaneously.

These vivid community rituals are favored subjects of several well-
known Garifuna painters, residents of Dangriga, whose studios are open to
visitors. Most have adopted a kind of folk-primitive realism recalling the
simple artwork of Haiti. The paintings emphasize bright colors, flat perspective, and festive or rural themes. Artwork may be purchased from artists on
commission, but be sure of your agreement before making payment.

Benjamin Nicholas—probably the most famous Belizean artist—
welcomes visitors at his 27 Oak Street gallery, near the Bonefish Hotel.
Nicholas' paintings are on display in public buildings and offices through-

and is accompanied by animal sacrifices, hypnotic music, and non-stop dancing.

Through the intercession of a byei, *or shaman, the Garifuna believe they can communicate with the dead, thereby tapping into the power of their ancestors. Some expatriate Belizeans come from as far as the U.S. and Canada to attend special ceremonies, called* gubida, *whereby contact with the deceased is used to cure sick relatives or avenge evildoings.*

Practitioners of obeah believe they can make contact with the dead whenever certain ceremonies are performed with the accompaniment of monotonous, trance-like drumming, singing, and dancing. These performances may last all night, or even days on end, without a break. Ethnomusicologists have noted that the rhythms and call-and-response patterns of the Garifuna are very similar to those used in the religious and social rituals of West Africa, where they presumably originated. The practice of playing with sticks is also African. If you'd like to learn more, ask a Dangriga tour guide to show you around the city, which boasts a "Garifuna cathedral" among other culture-specific attractions.

out Belize. Accomplished drum-maker **Austin Rodriguez** has a similar studio at 32 Tubroos Street, where he sells baskets, masks, and reed purses, as well as fine drums (priced from $50 and up). Next door to Rodriguez is a boatbuilder who carves dories out of a single tree trunk. **PJ's Gift Shop**, 21 St. Vincent, and **The Treasure Shop**, 64 Commerce Street, are recommended for smaller handicrafts. **Mercy Sabal**, 22 Magon Street, makes and sells colorful Garifuna dolls.

Garifuna Cuisine

While visiting Dangriga, try to sample some traditional Garifuna cuisine, which vaguely resembles the "soul food" of the American South. Home-brewed cashew wine and "local dynamite" (a mixture of raw coconut milk and Belizean rum) are popular lubricants, along with chicory-flavored coffee.

Endless varieties of cassava bread—all delicious—can be purchased from the smiling housewives who make them from scratch. The preparation of such breads, using a flour made from potato-like cassava roots that have been strained and ground by hand, is a time-honored Garifuna practice which takes at least two days to accomplish. The cassava's importance to local people cannot be overstated, and in fact the word "Garifuna" roughly translates as "the cassava-eating people." Other popular dishes are *hudut*, masked plantain (also called "plantain fu-fu"), and boiled fish in coconut sauce (known as *sere*). Not to be missed are the sweet oranges and grapefruits grown on nearby citrus plantations and in backyard gardens: buy them at produce vendors or public markets.

Getting There

Several bus companies, notably the Z-Line, 5-22211, have daily departures to and from Dangriga via the Hummingbird and Southern highways. The Z-Line depot is at the south end of Dangriga, at the intersection of St. Vincent and Havana Streets. Other buses pick up passengers downtown near the Stann Creek Bridge. The 1999 fare from Belize City was about $5 (allow about 3 hours). Dangriga is about 35 miles by boat (no scheduled service) from Belize City, 105 miles via the Hummingbird Highway (through Belmopan), or 70 miles via the Coastal Highway.

Maya Island Airlines and Tropic Air have scheduled flights several times daily to Dangriga from Belize City's international and municipal

Dangriga schoolchildren listen attentively to their teacher.

Richard Mahler

244

airports. In 1999 the fare was about $45 from the former, $38 from the latter. The airstrip is at the northern end of Dangriga, next to the Pelican Beach Resort. Flying time is 20 minutes.

If you drive to Dangriga via the Hummingbird or Coastal Highways, bear in mind that the term "highway" in Belize doesn't always mean the road is uniformly smooth and well-paved. Although upgrading is always underway, virtually all Belizean roads have notoriously bad sections full of ruts, potholes, and wash-outs. You're advised to take a four-wheel-drive vehicle with at least one spare tire and plenty of gas.

Where to Stay in Dangriga

Accommodations on Glover's Reef and Tobacco and South Water Cayes, along with the research stations on Carrie Bow and Wee Wee Cayes, are easily reached by chartered boat from Dangriga. Inquire among the water taxi operators whose boats are docked near where North Stann Creek enters the sea.

Bluefield Lodge, 6 Bluefield Rd.; $25; 5-22742. Six attractive rooms, with private baths, hot water, and ceiling fans. Run by the friendly owner, Miss Louise.

Jungle Huts Motel, on Ecumenical Drive next to North Stann Creek; $30-$48; 5-22142, fax 5-23166. Cabaña-style, a/c, private baths (with hot water) and cable TV in some rooms. Recommended.

Pal's Guest House, south of the bridge, 868 Magoon St.; $22 with bath, $16 without; 5-22095. Clean and comfortable waterfront rooms with fans and cable TV. Some shared baths.

Pelican Beach Resort, north end of town on Pelican Beach, next to airstrip; $80-$150; 5-22044, fax 5-22570, pelicanbeach@btl.net, www.belizenet.com/pelican. My favorite, this is the only full-service resort in town, with a fine restaurant and bar. A two-story wooden colonial building (renovated in 1996) with high ceilings and a wide veranda. Friendly, well-informed staff arranges trips to the Cockscomb Basin, Maya ruins, Gales Point, Sittee River, Hopkins, and the barrier reef. Local tours of the town of Dangriga and nearby citrus plantations are also available.

Owned by members of the Bowman clan, a pioneering British colonial family that has contributed much to the Belize conservation movement. Your hosts are Belize Audubon board member Therese Bowman Rath and her American husband, nature photographer Tony Rath, whose photographs are on sale here. Tony's slide shows at the Pelican are not to be missed. He also manages the Belize by Naturalight Web site.

245

Riverside Hotel, 5 Commerce St. at the river bridge; $20; 5-22168, fax 5-22296. Shared baths, no hot water, clean rooms adjoining a large common area.

Río Mar Hotel, 977 Waight St.; $18; 5-22201. Clean, basic, small rooms. Trips can be arranged here to South Water and other cayes. Noise from bar and video games can be a problem at night.

Where to Eat in Dangriga

Bonefish Hotel, 15 Mahogany Road, 5-22165. A runner-up for best restaurant, with fresh seafood a specialty. Lodging here is popular with divers.

Burger King, at the Commerce Street/Vincent Street Bridge. No relation to the international franchise. Serves standard Belizean fare and OK breakfasts.

New Riverside Café, on the riverfront downtown. Helpful tourist information center, a departure point for boat trips to the cayes, and a great place to meet local guides. Also known for its delicious daily specials. Serves vegetarian dishes and fresh juices.

Pelican Beach Resort, north of town. Has the best selection, though rather overpriced. Makes a point of including a Garifuna dish in each evening's meal.

Richie's Creole Diner, on Commerce near the police station. Giant, delicious, Belizean breakfasts served with born-again Christianity.

The Ship's Mate, on Stann Creek in the center of town, next to the bus terminal. A classic fisherman's diner and hangout.

HOPKINS
Location: 8 miles south of Dangriga.
Population: 1,100 (1999 estimate).
Visitor Information: 52-2033 (community phone) or Bob and Marsha's Travel Center (fax, e-mail and local maps).

Situated on the sandy, palm-shaded inlet of a small bay south of Dangriga, Hopkins is a relaxed Garifuna fishing village. It can easily be reached by private boat or by following a 4-mile unpaved road from the Southern Highway. This route crosses a marshy landscape that is particularly rich in bird life. Even the majestic jabiru stork has been sighted here, so keep a sharp eye out as you head for the village.

In Hopkins, life is simple and unhurried. People walk everywhere, using sandy paths that parallel the beach. There was no electricity or TV here until 1992, and running water is a recent innovation. Most residents subsist on small-scale fishing and farming. Women still tend the family garden plots and sing together as they weave red baskets or grate cassava roots on wooden slats. The men hand-carve their dugout canoes and weave fishnets out of hemp cloth. Children chase each other on the broad beach and splash about in the aquamarine water.

At the end of each day, the fishers of Hopkins haul their brightly painted dories beneath the coconut palms and join their families for the evening meal inside one-room houses, many of traditional thatch-and-pole construction. Homes are clustered together, with marvelous views of a gently curving bay to the east and misty jungle mountains to the west. Happily, this is one of the few remaining Garifuna villages where the old customs and language not only survive, but are embraced daily.

At night, you may want to take in the Ayumahani Band, which performs often at the Laru Beya Bar. There are several grocery stores in Hopkins, a BTL office, and a post office. The liveliest nightspot is the Swinging Armadillo, a bar, restaurant, and guest house on the beach. (The owner also rents bicycles.)

Outfitters

The best all-around outfitter in the area is the recommended **Jaguar Reef Lodge** (see below), which has its own dive shop. Two-tank dives cost about $70 in 1999.

Many tour operators will gladly make an excursion to the village when traveling to or from the **Cockscomb Basin Wildlife Sanctuary** (an easy day trip from Hopkins). Better yet, take the quick boat ride from Dangriga with one of the locals, setting out from the Stann Creek bridge. En route you can often arrange accommodations with the boatman, since everyone in Hopkins knows everyone else.

Kayaks, windsurfers, sailboats, and bicycles can be rented easily at most hotels.

Getting There

Getting to Hopkins usually involves an inexpensive, 30-minute bus ride from Dangriga or Placencia via the Z-Line. If the daily schedule isn't convenient, try hopping aboard one of the daily supply trucks heading south from downtown Dangriga at 2 p.m. or arranging private transportation via the Southern Highway. The unpaved road is no challenge for rental cars.

Where to Stay and Eat in Hopkins

Caribbean View Hotel, on the north beach; $30; 5-22033. Comfortable and clean. Only two rooms face the sea.

Hopkins Guest House, on the beach; $25; no phone. Offers canoeing, camping, and rafting.

Hopkins Inn, in the heart of the village, near the school and church; $45 including breakfast; 5-37013, hopkinsinn@btl.net. The beach cabañas have tiled bathrooms, private verandahs, refrigerators, and coffeemakers. Breakfast is included in the rate, and the American owners, Greg and Rita Duke, offer fishing, snorkeling, and sightseeing trips. A catamaran and bicycles are available for rent. Recommended.

Jaguar Reef Lodge, a few miles south of the village; $165; 9-23452 or (800) 289-5756, jaguarreef@btl.net; www.jaguarreef.com. By far the most upscale resort in Hopkins, this Canadian-owned, cabaña-style lodge sits on one of the finest beaches in Belize and offers such amenities as gourmet meals, a well-stocked bar, big air-conditioned rooms with personal refrigerators, and daily excursions. The latter include snorkeling and sailing, river and ruin tours, kayaking and mountain biking, and visits to the Cockscomb jaguar sanctuary. There's fine swimming offshore. The lodge has a dive shop and also offers C-Breathe, a modified scuba system for snorkelers. The excellent restaurant is open to non-guests. Pick-up arranged from the Dangriga bus station or airport. Highly recommended. Reduced rates off-season.

Jungle Jeanie's, north side of village; $15; 5-37047. Offers beach huts, camping, a restaurant, and bar as well as kayak, windsurfer, and canoe rentals. Outhouse and outdoor shower. No phone. Try the veggie pasta.

Ransom's Beachside Garden, on the beach; $20; 5-22889. A cabaña-style lodge that also rents bicycles and kayaks. Glorious tropical gardens.

Sandy Beach Lodge, on the beach, south side of the village. Operated by a group of Hopkins women as a tourism cooperative; $18; 5-37006, t-travels@btl.net. The rustic lodge's several neotraditional cabañas, built with the assistance of the Barbados-based Caribbean Council of Churches, have been open since 1987 and provide an important source of income. Meals cooked Garifuna-style by local homemakers are available for $5 or less. Some rooms have private baths, others have outhouses.

Titi's Pizza, near the beach. Operated by an Italian expatriate. Try the conch or lobster pizza.

Other Options

Houses in Hopkins can also be rented for about $12 a night (try **Mama Nuñez**, a friendly midwife and wonderful cook, who also has campsites). Informal camping along the beach costs about $5 a night, with prior consent. Inquire also at **Hopkins Guest House, Sand Bar Restaurant** (run by Canadian expatriate Jean Barkman), or **Lebeya Restaurant** (operated by a Swiss woman).

Locals are happy to fire up their oil-burning stoves to make meals for casual and overnight visitors, often including fresh fish, rice, beans, citrus fruit, coconut, and the ubiquitous cassava bread. For simple local cuisine, try **Innie's, Ruthie's**, and **Iris's**, all on the main road ($4 to $10 per meal).

SITTEE RIVER AND POSSUM POINT BIOLOGICAL RESEARCH STATION

Location: 2 miles up the Sittee River from the Caribbean.
Size: About 50 acres.
Hours and Fees: Visitation is by prior arrangement only.
Visitor Information: 52-2888 or General Delivery, Sittee River Village.

About 5 miles south of Hopkins, on the banks of the wide, sinuous Sittee River, is Possum Point Biological Research Station. The 50-acre nature reserve is owned by Paul and Mary Shave, American expatriates who lease government-owned Wee Wee Caye (9 miles east) for use as a marine laboratory and education center. With a local Belizean family, the couple also oversees **Bocatura Bank Campground**, a 4-acre plot about a mile downriver from Possum Point. Although these operations cater primarily to natural-history study groups, individuals and small groups of kayakers, fishers, and birders can be accommodated on a space-available, reservation-only basis.

The Sittee is one of the biggest and most important rivers in southern Belize, and a trip up this watercourse is highly recommended. Birders can expect to see flycatchers, herons, egrets, woodpeckers, kingfishers, orioles, tanagers, parrots, and toucans along the lower reaches of the river. Its sediment-rich waters are also teeming with fish. There are several side channels that lead to wetlands and lagoons with even more flora and fauna. If you're lucky, you may see dolphins and manatees near the mouth of the river, and crocodiles and turtles upstream.

The Possum Point research station enjoys a lush setting, surrounded by broadleaf forest at a sharp bend in the river. It is named after the many opossums found here when the lab and surrounding cottages were being built in what was then thick bush. Wildlife still abounds, and birders will be especially rewarded—Possum Point has well over 100 species of "yard birds." The call of the jaguar can sometimes be heard as the cat passes through the property at night. Possum Point and Wee Wee Caye embrace studies in coral reef ecology, botany, herpetology, entomology, ornithology, and mammalogy, as well as general tropical biology.

The ruins of the 19th-century **Serdon Sugar Mill** (no admission charge) are preserved as a park not far from the village on the road to the Southern Highway. You'll notice how the jungle has quickly reclaimed some impressive machinery, including the rusty hulk of a steam engine.

A few miles south of Sittee River along the Caribbean coast, **Sapodilla Lagoon** has an abundance of orchids and water birds. Boat trips can be arranged from Possum Point to these destinations and **Boom Creek**, a jungle tributary of the Sittee River. You can also navigate a hand-dug canal to **Anderson Lagoon**, which eventually opens on the Caribbean Sea.

Where to Stay and Eat near Possum Point

Lillpat Sittee River Resort, (805) 963-2501 in U.S., lillpat@aol.com, www.belizenet.com/lillpat. This unpretentious fishing lodge on the Sittee River caters to serious fishers. Offers four days for $210 including meals and week-long packages from $1,000. If full, try the nearby Sittee River Lodge.

Sittee River Lodge, $70 including meals; 5-37066. Two cabins with private baths. Fishing tours available.

Toucan Sittee Lodge, fronts the Sittee River, Sittee River village; $25, meals available; 5-22888. Guided fishing trips arranged ($125 per day). Bungalow style; rents bicycles and canoes.

Wee Wee Caye, 52-2888. Has seven cottages, and the tiny island is a wonderful place to snorkel, swim, and relax. Paul Shave, a marine biologist, has counted 46 species of coral and 10 species of crab in the immediate area of Wee Wee Caye. He and his wife, Mary, have taken great pains to preserve the mangroves, where a number of *wowlas* (Creole for boa constrictors) make their home, feeding on lizards, iguanas, and small birds. Bring plenty of insect repellent, as the tiny island's no-see-ums can be fierce.

COCKSCOMB BASIN WILDLIFE SANCTUARY
Location: About 20 miles southwest of Dangriga.
Size: 102,000 acres.

Fees and Registration: *All tourists must pay a $5 fee at the entrance booth in Maya Center before heading into the Cockscomb. Fee: $5 per person. Cold drinks and Maya crafts are sold here; sales benefit Maya Center residents (many of whom were forced to relocate from the basin when it became a park).*
Hours: *8 a.m. to 5 p.m. daily, 24-hours for overnight visitors.*
Visitor Information: *Belize Audubon Society, 2-34987 or 2-35004, or write the sanctuary at Box 90 in Dangriga.*

This huge tract of Stann Creek District wilderness—locally referred to as "the Cockscomb"—encompasses a sweeping mountainside basin with an eastern edge that begins about 25 miles southwest of Dangriga. The sanctuary is the world's first-ever reserve established to protect the jaguar, one of the largest and most endangered felines in the Americas. It represents a dynamic evolution of nature's wonders as well as scientific research and conservation prowess.

The Cockscomb is highly recommended as a rewarding destination for the traveler who wants to actively support Belizean conservation while simultaneously reaping its benefits. This is one of the least expensive and most impressive locales for exploring Belize's lush broadleaf tropical forest. Wildlife and plant life are abundant, and the patient visitor will likely see some exotic creatures (and feel tiny winged ones that bite).

Visitor Orientation

From the combination registration hut and handicraft shop in the village of Maya Center (a mandatory check-in point located immediately west of the Southern Highway), you will travel about 7 miles on a rough dirt road to reach the Cockscomb visitors center, campground, picnic site, and guest huts. Stay alert—the road is a favored trail of many mammals in the sanctuary, including the jaguar.

There is a small parking lot at the sanctuary's headquarters, located at the site of an abandoned lumber camp that is still littered with some of the cages used by zoologist Alan Rabinowitz during his pioneering studies of the jaguar here in the mid-1980s. Nearby are a couple of campgrounds and dormitories available for overnight travelers. There are also restrooms for public use.

From here you can take self-guided tours along a number of well-maintained forest trails. Brochures, maps, and signposts help identify the various local tree and plant species, which include colorful orchids and naturally buttressed hardwoods. The pathways vary considerably in their length and ruggedness, so check with the resident manager before heading out. There are some fine swimming holes where you can cool off after (or during) a strenuous trek.

251

History

The Cockscomb Basin's human history dates back to the ancient Maya, who left a Classic-era ceremonial site called **Kuchil Balum** deep within the forest. Pockets of fertile soil in these granite mountains helped support their milpa agriculture for many generations. The last of these modern Maya were relocated during the late 1980s in the interest of wildlife habitat preservation.

The Cockscomb's powers of forest regeneration are among its most intriguing qualities. The area's lushness is particularly amazing when you consider the hurricane damage inflicted on many of its tall trees, and the collective insults of slash-and-burn agriculture and timber-cutting over long periods of time. If you hike along the entrance road, you may have trouble distinguishing what is left of an airstrip that was last used in 1984 to facilitate radio tracking during Rabinowitz's jaguar studies. The tropical forest has almost completely taken over what was once a bare piece of land. At one end of the runway a narrow trail leads to a crash site, where a small plane still hangs from the forest canopy. The passengers (a pilot, a cameraman, and Rabinowitz) were only slightly injured.

Back at the visitors center, granitic **Victoria Peak** juts up from the back of the basin. The rocky 3,675-foot summit is capped by dark quartzite and may be part of the oldest geologic formation in Central America. The tall peak has been a sailors' landmark for centuries and was first scaled by Europeans in 1888.

Outfitters

Nearly all major hotels and travel agencies in the Stann Creek District arrange day trips to the sanctuary. We particularly recommend the **Pelican Beach Resort** in Dangriga, **Turtle Inn** in Placencia, and **Jaguar Reef Lodge** in Hopkins. Such trips usually cost about $60, including transportation, a guide, and lunch.

Cockscomb Hiking Trails

Nowhere else in Belize will you find such an organized system of well-maintained trails. All are wide; most are short and level so do not involve difficult hiking. A complete trail map is posted in front of the visitors center and guest huts as well as at the main entrance road.

The **Ben's Bluff Trail** takes the more ambitious walker on a short but strenuous trek to a ridgetop from which a good part of the entire Cockscomb Basin is visible. This high point has been frequently used to track jaguar via radio telemetry. Picture a researcher slowly sweeping the antennae back and forth across the dense jungle that stretches for miles before her. Or envision the sly cat, resting in the shade of a tall tropical hardwood (probably one you are unwittingly staring at) or stalking its prey along the bank of a rushing stream.

The easier **Waterfall Trail** takes you to a bank of South Stann Creek for a refreshing plunge into clear, swift water. This swimming hole also has a picnic area beneath a shady tree. Another path heads in a westerly direction from the visitors center, past the camping area and in the direction of **Victoria Peak**. A side trail on the left, beyond the bamboo thicket, takes you well into the forest, over a narrow suspension bridge, and past a swampy area that is a rewarding observation ground for the Cockscomb's many amphibians (bring repellent to ward off mosquitoes). Yet another trail follows switchbacks up a fairly steep hill, then zigzags down an embankment to end at one of the most gorgeous waterfalls in the sanctuary. Don't be shy—jump in!

Other Services and Reminders

Cockscomb trail maps are available at the headquarters for 50¢, rubber boots may be rented for $1.50, and guides are available and hired on-site. If there are 10 or more people in your party, the Cockscomb staff will present a slide show on the sanctuary for $25. The Belize Audubon Society has produced an in-depth guidebook in association with several individuals who know the sanctuary very well. The recommended *Guide to the Cockscomb Basin Wildlife Sanctuary* is available at the Audubon office in Belize City, at the sanctuary's headquarters, and at various gift shops throughout the country, or contact Community Conservation Consultants at (608) 735-4717, ccc@mwt.net.

There are fine swimming holes in the Cockscomb, so you may wish to bring a swimsuit and towel. Long-sleeved cotton shirts, trousers, sunscreen, rain ponchos, and hats are advisable. Tuck your pant legs into your socks to repel ticks and chiggers. Without such preparations, a visit can become very uncomfortable!

The Cats of Cockscomb

Among the main attractions for any visitor, of course, are the cats of Cockscomb. Because of their mostly nocturnal habits, however, the odds are that you will not actually see one. Still, your chances are better here than perhaps anyplace else. Besides embracing one of the highest concentrations of jaguars anywhere in the world (an estimated 30 cats in 1999), the sanctuary is home to many of Belize's four other feline species: ocelots, margays, jaguarundis, and pumas. Best bets for a sighting (early and late in the day) are along the roads and riverbanks of the Cockscomb, where the felines like to hunt. Even fleeting sightings of seldom-seen animals like the puma (which should be reported immediately to the sanctuary manager) are valued by the scientific community.

How the Sanctuary Came to Be

The most recent—and perhaps the most relevant—sequence of human involvement in the Cockscomb Basin is the effort to protect it. This campaign initially focused on preserving the jaguar, an "indicator species" that can serve as a good index of an ecosystem's health. Where there are large predators like the jaguar, there are likely to be hundreds of smaller animals.

The chain of events leading up to the designation of this area as a permanent wildlife sanctuary began in 1983 with a 2-year jaguar study sponsored by Wildlife Conservation Society, a division of the New York Zoological Society. Living in what is now a restricted-access warden's building, Rabinowitz carried out an intensive field study of the jaguar's range, diet, habits, and general ecology. The U.S. scientist trapped several jaguars, recorded their vital statistics, and fitted them with radio collars. This enabled him to track the felines and thus determine the size and location of their territorial ranges. Rabinowitz lived among the local Maya, employed several of them during his studies, and chronicled his many adventures—with certain embellishments—in an entertaining book entitled Jaguar.

With strong backing from the Wildlife Conservation Society and important in-country political assistance from the Belize Audubon Society, Rabinowitz recommended that the area be set aside for official protection of the jaguar. In late 1984, the Cockscomb Basin was declared a national forest reserve with a "no hunting" clause to protect the cat. The World Wildlife Fund then provided crucial financial assistance to support the basin's status as a protected area. In 1986, after much deliberation about the trade-offs involved, the government declared 3,000 acres of the 108,000-acre area as the Cockscomb Basin Wildlife

Sanctuary/Forest Reserve. This made Belize the first country to protect an area specifically for jaguars.

Several Maya families were required to move to Maya Center, where they have shifted from milpa agriculture to craftwork. Their cooperative sells the work of local artisans at the Maya Center visitors' registration booth. Some of the men transplanted from the sanctuary are employed there as managers, caretakers, and guides. The Maya-descended Belizean now in charge of the reserve, Ernesto Saqui, is one of the best-trained and most knowledgeable nature reserve managers in Central America. You pass his modest home soon after you check in at Maya Center.

In November 1990, the Cockscomb Basin Wildlife Sanctuary was expanded to include 102,000 acres of the Cockscomb Basin. This feat was accomplished through the joint efforts of the Belizean government, Belize Audubon, World Wildlife Fund, and other groups. Management by Belize Audubon has enabled the Cockscomb to emerge as a successful model of ecosystem conservation that integrates low-impact tourism with science. Wildlife habitat and ecosystem fieldwork, such as a 1990 expedition sponsored by the Belize Center for Environmental Studies, is crucial to continued success in Cockscomb management.

By the late 1990s, the Cockscomb sanctuary had become one of the crown jewels of the Belize park system, proving that environmentalists, governments, business people, and indigenous groups can work together to provide a safe haven for wild plants and animals. If you would like to support this efforts, the sponsoring Belize Audubon Society and World Wildlife Fund welcome your donations (see Appendix B for their addresses).

Jaguars are the third largest of its genus in the world and the most powerful land predator in Central and South America. It is called "tiger" by many Belizeans, *tigre* by local Spanish-speakers, and *balum* by the Maya. The jaguar's diet includes white-lipped peccaries, armadillos, agoutis, Virginia opossums, iguanas, deer, coatis, and kinkajous. Even if they cannot see the cats, Cockscomb visitors sometimes swear they can feel the presence of these elegant and graceful creatures.

Jaguars are not known to attack humans, except when provoked. It's not as if they are incapable of succeeding in such a foray, however. They are believed to sometimes prey on the Baird's tapir, an endangered relative of the horse (locally called "mountain cow") that may attain 650 pounds when fully grown. You can sometimes see the tapir's tracks in the muddy banks of South Stann Creek. Like the jaguar, the tapir is very shy, so this may be your closest encounter.

Howler Monkeys

During the early 1990s, an exciting collaborative effort succeeded in reintroducing black howler monkeys into their former range within the Cockscomb. Hunting, logging, a yellow-fever epidemic in the 1950s, and devastation by Hurricane Hattie in 1961 are all factors that probably accounted for the local extinction of howlers. According to Rob Horwich and his affiliated organization, Community Conservation Consultants/Howlers Forever, a total of 63 howler monkeys were relocated into Cockscomb from other parts of Belize from 1992 to 1994.

Other Wildlife

Within minutes of arrival, you will realize why the Cockscomb Basin has a reputation as a birder's paradise. At least 290 species have been recorded here, including the endangered scarlet macaw, chestnut-brown Montezuma oropendola (distinguished by its bright yellow tail), Agami heron, collared aracari, keel-billed toucan, and king vulture. In 1994 the park director and a warden recorded a flock of 10 scarlet macaws flying over Maya Center, at the Cockscomb's entrance. Another group of macaws was spotted a few days later within the sanctuary. Their continuing presence suggests a healthy, well-protected ecosystem.

The basin also provides habitat for many amphibians and reptile species. A team of Belizean conservation leaders and scientists identified over 35 species that included nine snakes, 12 lizards, 14 amphibians, and a frog known as *Smilisca phaeota*, not previously recorded in Belize. The red-eyed tree frog was also identified, and one of its major breeding areas located. The team estimated that the Cockscomb provides habitat for roughly 70 percent of Belize's non-marine reptile species.

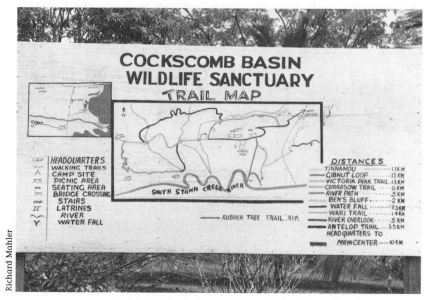

Trail sign at Cockscomb Basin Wildlife Sanctuary

During hikes through the Cockscomb, you may also come across the Central American river otter, a playful mammal that epitomizes an exuberant carpe diem lifestyle.

Getting There

The only road in and out of the Cockscomb Basin is well-marked and intersects the Southern Highway (Mile 14) at the village of Maya Center, about 25 miles south of Dangriga. The Cockscomb's headquarters are about 7 miles up the dirt road. Walking there from the Southern Highway is possible, but no services exist en route and it can be very hot and dusty. The road has been improved in recent years but is sometimes impassably muddy during very wet weather, even for those on foot. Four-wheel-drive vehicles are recommended. Several buses pass the entrance each day en route from Dangriga or Placencia; check locally for exact times.

Where to Stay and Eat near the Cockscomb

Those who do not wish to spend the night at the sanctuary can choose from a variety of accommodations in Maya Center, Dangriga, Placencia, Sittee River, and Independence. Tours can be arranged from these locations, or you can be dropped off by one of the public buses that pass the entrance (ask to be let off at Maya Center) and walk in.

257

Victoria Peak: No Longer Belize's Highest Point

*A 1996 survey determined that **Doyle's Delight**, on the main divide of the Maya Mountains, stands about 13 feet taller than Victoria Peak, the Cockscomb mountain previously believed to be the highest point in Belize. A four-member team from the Youth Environmental Action Group reached the top of Doyle's Delight after a 6-day April ascent and found it to be 1,124 meters (or 3,688 feet) above sea level. Located an air distance of 35 miles southwest of Victoria Peak, the mountain was reported to be "cool, damp, and windy" at its summit and covered with many palms, oaks, and ferns. Reaching the top required an 80-mile Land Rover trip through thick tropical forest, followed by an arduous climb over steep ridges and across treacherous creeks. The first known successful ascent of Doyle's Delight was made by British forces in 1987.*

Cockscomb Wildlife Sanctuary, Box 90, Dangriga; rustic, with dorm-style rooms, $10-to-$15 a night. Campsites, $1.50 a night, are available for rent in three campgrounds near the Cockscomb headquarters. Some of the dorm accommodations have electricity (from solar panels), and the newer unit has bathrooms and showers. Dorm reservations are strongly recommended—camping is first-come, first-served—especially from November through April. Reservations are made by contacting the sanctuary, the **Belize Audubon Society** office in Belize City (2-34987; Box 1001, Belize City), or the **Pelican Beach Resort** (5-22024) in Dangriga, which maintains radio contact with Cockscomb. There is fresh water, but you must bring your own food and other provisions (a kitchen is available for $2 a day). Showers and outhouses are available at no charge. Remember, insect repellent is a must! A rain poncho is also advised.

Nu'uk Che'il Cottages and Campground, immediately west of the Maya Center registration office; $20 for basic rooms, $8 for campsites; 5-23131 or 5-22666. Sanctuary manager (and avid conservationist)

Ernesto Saqui and his wife, Aurora, operate this lodge. The modest Aurora (one of the Cayo District's five famous García sisters) is a Maya healer who sells herbs, tinctures, salves, coffees, teas, and handicrafts in the **H'men Herbal Center** next to the guest house. For $1.50, Aurora will give you a guided tour of her medicinal herb garden. Nu'uk Che'il Cottages also offers transportation to Cockscomb, Placencia, and other communities. A restaurant and day-trip tour service may have been added by the time of your visit.

SEINE BIGHT AND MAYA BEACH

Location: 4 to 6 miles north of Placencia.
Getting There: Seine Bight and Maya Beach can be reached either via the daily Z-Line bus that runs between Placencia and Dangriga, or by private car or bicycle. Seine Bight is a pleasant 2-hour walk up the beach or dirt road from Placencia. Maya Beach is a couple more miles farther north—the bus stops here, too. Round-trip taxi fare to Placencia is $20. In 1998 a shuttle began serving the entire Placencia Penninsula (see following section).

Even smaller and more laid-back than Hopkins, the 700-resident Garifuna community of Seine Bight (and adjacent village of Maya Beach) is about 30 miles south of Dangriga, and about 10 miles from the Cockscomb turnoff, on the Placencia Peninsula. Until the mid-1980s, the village could be reached only by boat (a 4-hour trip from Dangriga by dugout canoe). Since then, daily buses and private auto traffic have dimmed its status as one of Belize's most isolated coastal communities. Nevertheless, the peninsula still feels like—as one visitor put it—"the island you can drive to." With more than 14 miles of adjacent beaches, this has the look and feel of the idyllic tropical paradise that so many people dream about.

Seine Bight is said to have been founded by pirates in 1629 and later inhabited by French fisherfolk deported by the British from Newfoundland when England took control of northeastern Canada. Like Hopkins, the residents occupy small palm-thatch houses atop high stilts (to keep away insects, rodents, snakes, and floodwaters). Daily duties follow traditional Garifuna patterns: Women take care of children and subsistence gardens, while the men hunt and fish. Souvenir hunters will want to check out **Lola's Art**, a gallery and café featuring local craftwork, at the north end of the village.

Where to Stay and Eat in Seine Bight and Maya Beach

Blue Crab Resort, on the beach in Seine Bight; $40; 62-3544, kerry@btl.net. Six rooms with varying amenities. Meals, diving, fishing, snorkeling, and interior daytrips available.

Green Parrot Beach Houses, in Maya Beach; $125; 62-2488, greenparot@btl.net. A Canadian couple opened this complex in 1995, offering A-frame bungalows built by local Mennonites. Recommended especially for those planning long stays or traveling with children. A good restaurant is on-site. Day trips, $30 to $65, include snorkeling, diving, Maya ruins, river tours, and the jaguar preserve plus reef fishing (at about $200 a day). Kitchens in all rooms. Power and water are off 9:30 p.m. to 7:00 a.m.

Hotel Seine Bight, in Seine Bight; $85; 62-3544, mikepam @btl.net. Aromatherapy, massage, pool and gourmet cuisine (16 main course choices each day!) amidst jungle-style ambiance. Some of the two-story suites have their own private balconies; day trips are easily arranged. Luxurious, small, European-run. Drumming and dancing in evening. Known for its distinctive interior design and architecture.

Nautical Inn, a short distance north of Seine Bight; $100; tel/fax 62-2310 or (800) 688-0377, nautical@btl.net. Upmarket restaurant, bar, dive shop, canoeing, volleyball, and air-conditioning. Built in a style that recalls New England more than the tropics. Uneven service.

Serenity Resort, south end of Maya Beach; $85; 62-3232, serenity@btl.net. Bungalow-style lodge with a/c in newer section. Can arrange tours, snorkeling, and diving. Restaurant on site.

Other Options

Low-budget options along this stretch of coastline include **Auntie Chigi's Place** (no phone, write Edna Martínez, Seine Bight Village). For local food, try **Vern's** in Seine Bight (bring your own alcohol), or **Kulcha Shack**, which has Garifuna drumming and dancing at night.

PLACENCIA

Location: Southern tip of Placencia Peninsula, about 30 miles south of Dangriga.
Population: 380 (1999 estimate).
Visitor Information: Belize Tourist Board, (800) 624-0686.

Straddling a sandy, palm-forested spit of land at the tip of an 11-mile-long peninsula, Placencia (also spelled Placentia) is one of the oldest continuously inhabited villages in Belize. Its residents brag that their small settlement was founded by English buccaneers in the early 1600s, and artifacts discovered beneath their homes suggest this was the location of several fierce battles between British and Spanish sailors. There is also ample evidence that Placencia was a Maya fishing camp long before the Europeans arrived. For the last few centuries it has been home to a close-knit cluster of mostly Creole families whose ancestry includes Garifuna warriors, freed African slaves, and Scottish pirates. Today the village seems to share only four last names: Leslie, Cabral, Eiley, and Burgess.

Much of Placencia's charm can be attributed to its scenic locale. A long and gently curving beach—arguably the prettiest in Belize—graces the village's windward side. A few hundred yards opposite this wide strip of talcum-powder sand is **Placencia Lagoon**, a placid waterway harboring abundant marine life. Since the southernmost tip of the settlement borders the Caribbean, the illusion is that of being on a tropical island, with only the north connected to mainland Belize. Before a dirt road was hacked through the swamps, Placencia might as well have been an island, since the only access was by boat.

A young resident of Placencia on "Main Street"

© Tony Rath

One unusual feature of Placencia is its main "street," a concrete sidewalk that stretches for about a mile through the center of town. (Vehicles are relegated to a single unpaved road that skirts the western edge of the village.) Placencia's unhurried ambiance is reminiscent of Caye Caulker, with smiles and friendly exchanges the norm among locals and visitors alike. With a wide range of inexpensive and reasonably good restaurants and bars to choose from, visitors will not lack for food and drink.

Along the 3-mile Placencia beachfront, dozens of guest houses, campgrounds, and lodges snuggle beneath the palm trees. The azure water is surprisingly deep here, and dolphins occasionally frolic close to shore. (The depth and tricky currents can make swimming hazardous at times.) Soothing trade winds usually keep biting insects at bay.

Placencia's one-room post office, a stone's throw from the pier, also dispenses airline and bus tickets. Janice, the friendly and well-informed postmistress, will happily place phone calls and find you a room or camping spot. If you want to charter a boat, reserve a tour, or sample some cassava bread, this is a good place to start.

Outfitters

One of the better boatman and tour guides is **Casey Eiley**, who can take you fishing or on a natural history tour, 6-23161. I also recommend **Samuel Burgess Guide Service**, next to the B&J Restaurant. For trips up the Monkey River, about $45, look for **Dave Dial**, 6-23156, at his Shell Gas Station or Tourist Trap Lodge. **Darrell Garbutt** is a recommended guide, although there are many others who do a fine job. (You may wish to pack your own lunch as restaurant food in Monkey River Town is expensive.) The best birding is early morning.

The tarpon and bonefish opportunities hereabouts are superb. Several resorts and businesses now cater exclusively to anglers, and there are a number of topnotch fishing guides based in Placencia. Among Placencia's better fishing-guide services are **Kingfisher Sports**, 62-3104 or (512) 826-0469, which takes its *Kingfisher V* to wherever you want to go; **Pow Cabral**, 62-23132, whose wife operates **Carol's Cabañas** north of the village; and **David Westby**, 62-3234.

Recommended catamaran and snorkeling trips are offered by **Dave Dial**, based at the Shell gas station. His company charges about $20 for a half-day snorkel trip, or $35 for an all-day excursion. For diving, try the well-equipped **Rum Point Inn**, 62-3239, rupel@btl.net or **Placencia Dive Shop**, 62-3227, pds@btl.net, affiliated with Kitty's Resort (also offering snorkel and river trips). Expect to pay at least $65 for a day of diving, $200 if you charter a boat. Also recommended: **Seahorse Dive Shop** at the end of the pier, 6-23166, seahorse@btl.net.

Kayaks are rented by several businesses in Placencia and it's possible to paddle from here to the barrier reef—or up the Monkey River as far as the Maya Mountains, many miles from the coast. I recommend **Ranguana Lodge**, 62-3112, **Kitty's Place**, or **Kevin Maderia**, 62-3178.

Bicycles can be rented at several area lodges, including Deb 'n' Dave's, Kitty's Place, Singing Sands, and the Rum Point Inn. Some resorts let their guests use bikes for free, others charge $10 to $15 per day. Because it is flat and tree-shaded, this is a terrific area for cycling.

Interior day trips to the Cockscomb Basin Wildlife Sanctuary and Maya ruins cost about $60 and can be arranged through local hotels and guides.

Local outfitters that specialize in manatee watching, birding, camping, and other nature-oriented activities include **Southern Guides** (62-3277) and **Placencia Tours** (62-3186). Expect to pay about $60 per person for day trips, except caving expeditions ($100 per person and up).

Here, as elsewhere in Belize, it's best to arrange prices for tours and services before you set out on your trip.

Things to See and Do

There are several popular nightspots in the village, where an inexpensive bottle of local rum goes a long way. Favorites include the **Cozy Corner, Dockside Bar, Mike's Caribbean Club** (packed at happy hour), **Tentacles, Sonny's, Lagoon Saloon** (with live music on weekends), and **Kingfisher Bar**. Live music, drumming, and dancing are sometimes available weekend nights at the **Cozy Corner** and **Flamboyant Restaurant**. Cozy Corner also operates a small, moderately-priced hotel.

By and large, Placencia is an informal place where you can easily fit in by doing nothing. If you change your mind, it's an excellent departure point for such lesser-known southern cayes as Colson and Pompion and the Silks, or the interior nature parks and Maya ruins. Birding and beachcombing are especially rewarding here, and the nearby lagoon is an important breeding area for saltwater crocodiles, marine turtles, and manatees. You won't find much lobster or conch in the waters around Placencia, but some of the best snook, tarpon, and other sportfishing is available within a short boat ride.

Getting There

The hub of activity in Placencia—such as it is—can be found at the very tip of the peninsula, where the pier, marina, gas station, bus stop, pay phone, and fishing co-op are all located. A passenger ferry called *The Hokey-Pokey* leaves here for nearby Independence (a 50-minute trip for about $10), from which Tropic Air (at Big Creek) and bus connections go both north and south. (In recent years convenient daily bus and plane service has come to Placencia, so there's little reason to make this shuttle unless you want to make faster connections.)

Both the James and Z-Line bus companies have buses heading north or south from (separate) stops in Independence. It's about $4 to Dangriga (2 hours) and a little less to Punta Gorda (3 hours). You'll pay your fare on board; departures are early morning and midafternoon.

The Placencia airstrip is immediately north of Kitty's Place, about 2 miles from the village, and served by Tropic Air. Flying time from Belize International is 50 minutes and the 1999 one-way fare was about $65. A taxi usually awaits deplaning passengers or you can arrange with your hotel to be picked up. I recommend some patience here; Placencia does not operate at an urban pace.

Inquire locally about direct boats from Placencia and Independence to Honduras. Once-a-week boats operated by **Charles Leslie**, 6-23104, and **Manuel Zabaneh Jr.** (6-22131) reportedly make round-trips to Puerto Cortés for about $40 per passenger. The trip takes between 3 and 4 hours. Inquire at the BTL office, 62-3160, about occasional passenger boats from Placencia to Guatemala. Exit formalities are taken care of at the immigration office in Big Creek.

A shuttle service runs vans up and down the Placencia peninsula for a fee much lower than that charged by local taxis. One-day passes are $6 ($3 for half-day) with unlimited on/off privileges.

Where to Stay in Placencia

Clive's Campground, at the north end of the sidewalk; $4; no phone. Clive also rents a few basic cabins.

D&L Resort, in the center of town; $25; 62-3243. A relatively modest five-room hotel.

Deb & Dave's Last Resort, on the back road into the village; $20; 62-3207, debandave@btl.net. Budget rooms, shared baths, ceiling fans, garden setting. Co-owner Dave Vernon is an excellent guide and operates Toadal Adventure Tours (hikes, bikes, kayaks, and floats).

Jaguar Inn, $80; (800) 663-0775 or 62-3330. Offers several cabañas in a garden setting, with a nice bar/restaurant on the premises.

Kitty's Place, on the far north side of the village next to the airport; $100 and up; 62-3227, fax 62-3226, kittys@btl.net. Fishing, sailing, diving, and jungle tours; accommodates campers and long-term visitors. My first choice among moderately-priced, full-service hotels. Guests have several room options at this rambling, informal location. Excellent restaurant, cabañas, and beach. Offers lodging on French Louis Caye ($50 per person).

Luba Hati, 15 minutes north of village; $150; 62-3402, lubahati@btl.net, www.lubahati.com. European-style resort with 7 rooms, Franco's Italian restaurant, and bar. Swimming beach, sauna, massage, fishing, diving, inland day trips. Sea kayaks and bicycles available at no charge.

Robert's Grove, on 8 acres north of the village; $150; (800) 565-9757, 62-3565, info@robertsgrove.com. American-owned, luxury 13-room resort open (Nov–June) since 1997. Bar, restaurant, 50-foot pool, tennis court, fishing/snorkeling boat, private beach, and pier. Arranges day trips and excursions.

Rum Point Inn, 2 miles north of Placencia, past the airport; $225, includes meals; (800) 747-1381 or 62-3239, rupel@btl.net. This recommended luxury lodge is operated by Corol and George Bevier, early supporters of Belize's environmental movement and very knowledgeable tour guides. Their son, Wade, is a photographer, diver, and naturalist active in the Audubon Society. He also maintains an E-6 photo-processing lab and knows a great deal about local marine fauna. The Rum Point compound includes a gourmet restaurant (served family style after Corol "blows the conch"), a well-stocked library, 10 dome-shaped cottages, and a two-story, air-conditioned complex built in 1997. The featured attraction here is a well-equipped NAUI/PADI dive shop and a 42-foot custom dive boat, the *Auriga*, which prowls 400-square-miles of prime underwater habitat. Kayaks, Hobie-cat sailboats, and bicycles are available for rent, and a swimming pool was added in 1998. Interior day trips available ($60 and up).

Sea Spray, north end of the village; $16; 62-3148. Can arrange day trips and tours.

Tradewinds Hotel, $50; 62-3122. Cabañas and well-appointed rooms along 5 acres of beachfront.

Turtle Inn, north of the village; $112; 62-3244, turtleinn@btl.net. Seven beach bungalows and a beach house available. You can also rent diving and snorkeling equipment here from the inn's **Hawksbill Dive Shop** (scuba certification offered). Sportfishing and other day trips start at $45. An inclusive meal program at the lodge's restaurant is about $60 per day. Skip White, the American owner, is an expert on adventure travel in Belize, having explored the backcountry here since 1984. Recommended.

Where to Eat in Placencia, Maya Beach, and Seine Bight

Restaurants in Placencia tend to close early, so it's a good idea to be at your table by 8 p.m. Note that here, as elsewhere in Belize, many businesses are closed from noon to 1 or 2 p.m.

Alfredo's, on the main sidewalk, near the center of the village. Specializing in Italian dishes.

Chili's, on the south point, near the main dock. Excellent breakfasts.

Daisy's Ice Cream Parlor, in the center of town. Serves Placencia's finest homemade ice cream.

The Flamboyant Restaurant (formerly Jene's), opposite the Seaspray Hotel. One of the friendlier social centers along the walkway. Delicious, reasonably priced meals are served under the filigree shade of a flamboyant tree.

The Galley, on the edge of the village, next to the soccer field. Some insist that this is the best food in Belize.

Green Parrot Resort, up the road in Maya Beach. Worth the trip for a truly gourmet meal.

"John the Bakerman" Whylie, behind Wallen's Market. Excellent pastries.

Kitty's Place, about 1.5 miles north of the village, next to the airstrip. Terrace dining with a view of the Caribbean.

Miss Lilly, behind Hortense's Market. Sells delicious homemade cassava and coconut bread from her front door.

Pickled Parrot, in "downtown" Placencia behind the Orange Peel Gift Shop. The Parrot has decent food, a pleasant palapa-roof bar, and pizza specials on Friday night.

The Rum Point Inn, immediatley north of the airstrip. Family-style meals, reservations required.

LAUGHINGBIRD CAYE NATIONAL PARK
Location: *About 12 miles southeast of Placencia.*
Size: *About 10,000 acres.*
Visitor Information: *Friends of Laughingbird Caye, 62-3239 or c/o Rum Point Inn, General Delivery, Placencia, Belize.*

A small, coconut-studded island, Laughingbird gets its name from the large number of laughing gulls that once used it as a rookery. Overuse by humans caused the gulls to abandon the island completely, although a few have returned since 1990, along with brown pelicans, green herons, and melodious blackbirds. In recent years this has been a popular destination for day-tripping picnickers, snorkelers, divers, and sea kayakers, who place Laughingbird on their regular route. The government has taken steps to minimize this disruption, but in the interest of conservation you may wish to drop anchor elsewhere. The island gets so crowded on some days that it's difficult to find a place to sit down. Sadly, the coral is deteriorating, and many of the fish have gone elsewhere. If you do stop here, be sure to use a mooring buoy to minimize coral damage.

Laughingbird Caye, the southernmost island in the Inner Channel, is only about 120 yards long and 10 yards wide. Its unusual shape, an angular oval atoll on a continental shelf, is called a *faro*. Like true atolls, faroes are steep-sided and widely separated from other land formations. The national park that includes this faro encompasses more than 10,000 acres of the surrounding marine area.

Getting There/Outfitters

Day trips to Laughingbird Caye National Park and the nearby Silk, Abigal, Tarpon, Bugle, Colson, Scipio, and Lark Cayes can be arranged in Placencia among the many boat charter operators. Wippari Caye, Little Water Caye, and Ranguana Caye have had overnight accommodations in recent years; with Nicholas, Lime, and Hatchet Cayes slated to host resorts before 2000. Many of the cayes on the southern part of the reef also have part-time fishing camps, and a handful have full-time residents. Expect to pay about $40 for a snorkel trip to Laughingbird from Placencia.

BIG CREEK, INDEPENDENCE, AND MANGO CREEK

Location: About 40 miles by road south of Dangriga and north of Punta Gorda.
Size: The three villages encompass about 30 square miles.
Visitor Information: Belize Tourist Board, (800) 624-0686.

The small villages of Big Creek, Independence, and Mango Creek dot a 7-mile branch of the Southern Highway directly across the lagoon from Placencia.

Big Creek has been developed as an important port servicing the deep-water cargo ships that come here to load bananas, mangos, pineapples, citrus, and other cash crops. Until the late 1980s, shallow-draft boats and barges had to shuttle small loads of these exports to Puerto Barrios in neighboring Guatemala. Dredging has made this a major industrial center for Belize. There are virtually no tourist attractions.

Immediately north of Big Creek are the tiny settlements of Independence and Mango Creek (many people now consider all three villages as the same community and use their names interchangeably).

Getting There/Outfitters

The Hello Hotel (a Z-Line bus stop), $45, 62-2428, is owned by Antonio and Beth Zabaneh, who also own the adjacent grocery and are experts on boat trips that can be arranged from here to Glover's Reef, Guatemala, and Honduras. (For those leaving Belize, the necessary passport stamp can be obtained from the village police station.) The slightly cheaper and faster James Line bus stops a short distance away, in front of María's Restaurant.

Where to Stay and Eat in Big Creek

Billbird Hotel, $60; 6-22084. Formerly Toucan Inn, a remodeled barracks for employees of Big Creek's largest banana company. The Billbird is known for its Irish food and the English pub atmosphere of its **Tipsy Toucan** bar.

María's, next to the James Line bus stop. Serves simple Belizean and Guatemalan food.

MONKEY RIVER TOWN

Location: About 10 miles south of Big Creek (technically in the Toledo District).
Size: The village encompasses about 20 acres and has about 300 residents.
Visitor Information: Belize Tourist Board, (800) 624-0686.

This sleepy Creole fishing village is about 15 miles by boat southwest of Placencia, tucked behind mangrove forests at the mouth of the slow-moving Monkey River. This lowland waterway drains the Bladen and Swasey watersheds, which now enjoy protected status as important sources of irrigation water and sanctuaries for wildlife.

The **Paynes Creek/Monkey River Wildlife Sanctuary** and **Punta Ycacos Reserve** encompass over 24,000 acres between Monkey River Town and the tiny coastal villages of Punta Negra and Punta Ycacos. The area, home to numerous howler monkeys, jaguar, and tapir, is gradually being developed for natural history research and tourism. An overgrown dirt road (impassable in wet weather) connects the north side of Monkey River Town with the Southern Highway, about 15 miles away. Another jungle river to explore is **Golden Stream**, south of Monkey River Town.

Over the years, Monkey River Town has been hard hit by disasters: a blight destroyed the banana industry (since revived), the government stopped subsidizing local rice growers, and trappers sold most of the local crocodiles for their skins. During March and April the village briefly comes alive again with a celebration centered around the iguana egg-laying season. People from throughout the area descend on Monkey River Town to eat freshly killed iguanas (usually cooked in a stew) and their eggs, which are considered a delicacy. Efforts are now under way to develop forms of low-impact tourism and park management that would provide jobs for residents while preserving the environment.

Outfitters

For a fee of about $40, guides from Placencia, Big Creek, or Monkey River Town will take a visitor by powerboat through a series of mangrove islands and up the largely uninhabited Monkey River for several miles. Here many species of birds and, yes, even monkeys (black howlers) can be seen. Occasionally you'll spot crocodiles and turtles sunning themselves on the river's sandy beaches, while the iguanas thrash about in overhanging trees. (There were once spider monkeys along the river, but a yellow fever epidemic wiped them out during the 1950s.) If you wish, your boatman may stop and escort you along jungle trails where the tracks of many wild animals can be seen.

Lucky visitors may see the animals themselves: deer, ocelots, peccaries, tapirs, coatimundis, agoutis, and even jaguars.

Among the best local guides is lifelong resident **Darrell Garbutt,** 62-2014, a former fisherman and iguana hunter who will take visitors on a jungle hike and share his astounding knowledge of the jungle river environment. Darrell is an expert at identifying water birds and animal tracks.

Tours of the Monkey River usually depart Placencia about 7:30 a.m., returning at 2:30 p.m. Bring sunscreen, a hat, and a zoom lens (if you plan to photograph wildlife). I also recommend **P.I. Tours** (62-3209) and **Placencia Dive Shop**. Expect to pay about $50, including lunch, for the day trip from Placencia.

For those with a true spirit of adventure, I recommend Seattle-based **Monkey River Expeditions,** (800) 500-2175 or (206) 660-7777, mre@halcyon.com, which runs guided, 3-day trips up the Monkey River (camping gear provided), combined with a night in Monkey River Town and two nights camping on Ranguana Caye. Additional nights are spent in Placencia and with a rural Maya family after a tour of the Lubaantun and Nim Li Punit ruins.

South of Monkey River Town to Punta Gorda is a relatively pristine jungle coastline now under government protection. Very few people live here and there are virtually no services. You can hire a boat and guide, however, in Monkey River Town, Placencia, or Punta Gorda. Several coastal rivers and lagoons offer excellent birding and fishing.

Where to Stay and Eat in Monkey River Town

Alice's, 62-2014. The best restaurant in Monkey River Town, where you'll find savory Creole cuisine and the village's only telephone. I recommend the fish balls with fried plantains (and, of course, beans 'n' rice). Camping is possible, by permission, on a sand spit at the edge of the village.

Bob's Paradise, a mile north of Monkey River Town on a coconut-studded beach called English Town; $100; 6-12024. American-run bar, restaurant, and three-unit cabaña complex. Accessible only by water.

Enna's Hotel, $25; 6-12033. William and Enna Anderson operate this eight-room hotel. Serves simple, wholesome meals.

The Monkey House, $100; 6-12032, watch@btl.net. A small bed and breakfast.

Sunset Inn, $25. In 1998 this 9-room hotel and café was opened by the Wellington Garbutt family. They also offer guide services (snorkeling, birding, camping, hiking, and river trips).

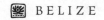

BLADEN NATURE RESERVE
Location: *About 20 miles southwest of Placencia.*
Size: *97,000 acres.*
Visitor Information: *Access to the Bladen Nature Reserve is strictly limited to qualified scientists, archaeologists, and other designated researchers. Permission must be obtained in advance from the Belize Audubon Society, which manages the Bladen, at 2-35004 or 2-34987.*

The 1990 designation of the **Bladen Branch** (of the Monkey River) watershed area as a nature reserve set a significant benchmark in the race to protect the earth's most biologically diverse ecosystems—broadleaf moist tropical forests—before humans destroy them. Protection of this Toledo District wilderness, sprawling across the Maya Mountains' rugged foothills, helped set the stage for an even bolder action in which Bladen became part of a vast protected area that includes **Chiquibul National Park** and the nearby **Cockscomb Sanctuary**; together the reserve encompasses some 450,000 acres of tropical forest.

The Bladen Nature Reserve provides refuge for at least 194 bird species and at least 300 plant species, in addition to such creatures as the Baird's tapir, white-lipped peccary, mountain lion, iguana, jaguar, southern river otter, greater bulldog bat, white-tailed deer, brocket deer, and Central American spider monkey. The Bladen's important birds include the king vulture, mealy parrot, slaty-breasted tinamou, ornate hawk eagle, Philadelphia vireo, and rufous-capped warbler. The area contains uninvestigated Maya ruins, steep granite mountains, conical limestone outcrops, sinkholes, caves, underground streams, and waterfalls. Within the reserve's boundaries is **Richardson Peak**, one of the highest mountains in Belize.

The Bladen may someday become the core of a much larger protected area through its possible designation as a United Nations (UNESCO) Biosphere Reserve. The government has considered protective declarations linking the Chiquibul east to the Maya Mountain Divide. Whatever the outcome, one thing is certain: The Belize government has set an international standard in protecting the existing pristine watershed. As one Belizean put it, "The Bladen is a little gem, and it shines."

TOLEDO DISTRICT

Heading south from the citrus and banana plantations of the Stann Creek District, travelers enter the most sparsely populated and least developed region in Belize. The Toledo District is (barely) connected to the rest of the country by a single dirt road—the Southern Highway—and one

Ancient Maya in the Bladen Wilderness

The upper Bladen Branch watershed shows traces of the past presence of ancient Maya. In the early 1990s, surveys by archaeologist Peter Dunham and a team from Cleveland State University turned up four previously unknown Maya sites. These settlements provide new evidence for a 1,000-year-old trading network in the Bladen. According to Dunham, up to 7,000 people may have inhabited the Bladen valley. A flood plain in the area called Quebrada de Oro ("the passageway of gold") contains other Maya ruins that archaeologists have never excavated. Participants in a late 1980s field study found 18 roughly rectangular mounds here, now overgrown by vegetation. An abundance of breadfruit trees suggests that the Maya cultivated this species at Quebrada de Oro, as they did at Tikal.

There appears to have been some looting of the Quebrada ruins and at another more western site in the Bladen. In addition, just prior to the Dunham expedition, looting at one of the four newly discovered ruins resulted in the destruction of an ancient structure at this site. Unregulated visitation remains one of the biggest problems facing the reserve's managers and those concerned with protecting these and other Maya sites throughout Belize.

One of Dunham's teams made a stunning ornithological discovery in 1994 in the Bladen—they watched a rare harpy eagle for 40 minutes as it perched in fig trees as close as 65 feet from its onlookers. This huge flying predator, which feeds on monkeys and sloths, had not been seen in Belize for 20 to 30 years prior to this date.

commercial airstrip at Punta Gorda. Public transportation consists of a few daily buses and a half-dozen daily domestic airline flights (Maya Island and Tropic). There is also daily boat service to and from Guatemala. Change is coming slowly to the Toledo District but coming nonetheless. One example of this is the ongoing improvement of the Southern Highway, which is being systematically widened and paved all the way to Dangriga, beginning in Punta Gorda.

Still, much of the area is without electricity, indoor plumbing, hot water, or roads. In fact, the majority of its residents are subsistence farmers—including about 11,000 Kekchí (sometimes spelled Ketchi) and Mopán Maya—living in wooden, thatched-roof huts or small cement-block houses. The per capita annual income here is estimated at less than $800. Obviously, a trip to the Toledo District is not for everyone. Although there are a growing number of accommodations with modern amenities, most lodges and guest houses are decidedly rustic.

Travel within the area is most manageable during the dry season (February through May) but can be problematic the rest of the year. This part of Belize averages well over 100 inches of rain annually; therefore, its many rivers and creeks can be difficult to ford during a downpour. There are few gas stations, grocery stores, or restaurants. In short, tourist services are minimal. Yet a visit to the Toledo District is a must for those who wish to get a firsthand look at the Kekchí, Mopán, and Garifuna cultures, and to experience small-scale tourism as a strategy for ecosystem conservation. The district also features Belize's only true rainforest and some of its most unusual ancient Maya ruins and sacred caves.

There is no better time to visit the Toledo District than the present, in part because development pressures are already changing its look and character. Many logging concessions have been granted by the Belize government in the Columbia and Maya Mountain forest reserves, and one Malaysian firm (Atlantic Industries) is logging pristine rainforest at the rate of 1,200 acres per year. Local Maya villagers, members of the Belize Audubon Society, and international conservationists have complained that logging companies are violating terms of their contracts by harvesting trees outside designated areas and destroying critical wildlife habitat, among other alleged offenses. Both the government and the logging companies have denied the charges. Meanwhile, in the Caribbean about 20 miles east of Placencia, Dover Technology of Houston has sunk Belize's first offshore oil well, which is said to have leaked petroleum products into this sensitive marine ecosystem.

You can register your opposition to environmentally destructive practices in southern Belize by e-mailing the Kekchí Maya Council at kebtol@btl.net or the Belize Audubon Society at base@btl.net.

Environmental activism in the district has increased following the apparent murder in December 1998 of Julian Cho, a 36-year-old spokesperson for Maya rights and a vocal critic of local logging practices.

On the positive side, work began in 1997 on a plan to protect the Punta Gorda area's endangered howler monkey population. By the time you read this, a nongovernmental reserve for the howlers (similar to the Community Baboon Sanctuary in north-central Belize) may be open to visitors in the "greenbelt" surrounding Punta Gorda. Also, inquire locally about the status of Santa Cruz Falls, Agua Caliente, and other new or proposed national parks in the district.

A word to the wise should be sufficient—if you want to see southern Belize in its full pristine glory, go now! One final caution: It should be noted that malaria and cholera were recurring problems in rural areas of the Toledo District as recently as 1998.

VISITING MAYA VILLAGES

One of the greatest challenges facing the Belizeans of Toledo is the need to ensure that local people—in this case mostly Kekchí Maya, Mopán Maya, Garifuna, and Creole—benefit from increased tourism and are given incentives to protect the natural and cultural resources of the region. Natural habitat degradation has been especially heavy here, mainly because of new road construction and the collective impact of forest destruction by commercial logging and the kind of slash-and-burn (milpa) agriculture practiced by a growing native Maya population and Guatemalan immigrants.

At least two noteworthy locally initiated projects are underway in Toledo, seeking to combine tourism, sustainable agriculture, cultural revitalization, and environmental conservation: the **Toledo Host Family Network/Indigenous Experience Program**, 7-22470, and the **Maya Guest House & EcoTrail Program**, 7-22119. These two programs both encourage foreigners to visit traditional Maya villages, but in fundamentally different ways. The Host Family Network places tourists in the actual homes of the Maya, where guests observe and participate in daily village life. In contrast, the Guest House Program arranges visits to many of the same villages, but tourists stay in structures that are separate from Maya homes and built specifically for use by foreigners. Under both schemes, visitors eat meals prepared by local residents and take outings guided by villagers. (Although the Maya of Belize converse among themselves in their own languages, most are also fluent in English, which is not the case in neighboring Guatemala, Honduras, or Mexico.)

"We don't look at these programs as rivals," says Hawaiian immigrant Alfredo Villoria, of San Pedro's Dem Dat's Doin' farm and one of the founders of the homestay endeavor. "We think they are complementary.

273

Some folks want to stay in a guest house and some want to stay with families. We let them exercise that choice."

Maya Guest House Program

Since 1991, several rural villages have constructed small guest houses, designed and marked nature trails, and started introducing travelers to Maya customs. As of 1999, communal guest houses were completed and operational in seven communities: **San Pedro Columbia**, **San Miguel**, **Santa Cruz**, **San José**, **Laguna**, **San Antonio**, and **Blue Creek**. A sixth facility is scheduled to open in Barranco, on the coast. Accommodations and meals are basic, and there is no electricity or indoor plumbing, but the overall experience cannot be duplicated. Reservations are recommended.

Laguna Village completed its guest house ahead of the others and offers the widest range of activities for tourists, including guided nature walks and exploration of a Maya ceremonial cave with ancient paintings.

"These people are very quiet, gentle, and vulnerable," North American visitor Louise Foster observed, in an account of her Laguna experience published in *The Belize Review*. "They are excited about reviving their traditions and sharing them with outsiders."

Laguna is a Kekchí agricultural center located about 10 miles from Punta Gorda. The population is descended from immigrants who originated in the Alta Verapaz highlands of Guatemala and came to Belize to escape brutal oppression. The Kekchí have a strong tradition of cooperation, particularly in farming and building.

Laguna's thatch-roofed guest house accommodates up to eight visitors and includes a veranda, a separate bathhouse, and outhouses. Guests are treated to a spectacular view of the rainforest-covered, limestone karst hills nearby. Since the lodge does not have a kitchen, visitors receive their meals in small groups at different households each day. Guides take guests on carefully tended footpaths, where the native medicinal plants are marked in various languages. A recommended stop is the arts and crafts center, where tourists can buy handmade baskets and other Maya craftwork directly from the village cooperative.

The Maya Guest House Program is coordinated through the Toledo Ecotourism Association, which has an office in the Belize Tourist Board information center on Front Street in Punta Gorda. The program was initiated by American expatriate William "Chet" Schmidt, who owns and operates Nature's Way Guest House/Belize Adventure Travel in Punta Gorda. Schmidt has worked with local villagers to devise a system that integrates ecosystem conservation, appropriate-scale tourism, and environment-friendly farming. Its intention is to minimize stress levels on the natural and cultural resources, while employing the maximum number of villagers. Part of the profits are used to support sustainable agriculture, a

What to Bring

When visiting the Maya villages of southern Belize, be prepared for very basic living conditions in communities that seldom have more than 200 residents. Your visit will be more comfortable if you bring a flashlight, high-traction shoes (treated with water repellent), rain gear, a swimsuit, a hat, sunscreen, a long-sleeved shirt, and cotton pants. Most local Maya are happy to have photographs taken of them if you ask politely. In return, it's appreciated if you show them pictures of your hometown, family, and house or apartment. As everywhere, they also like to receive a copy of the photos you take of them. If the Maya have items to sell, it's polite to buy something, or trade something that you have brought.

community fund, local government, and the construction of clinics. Accommodation rates are about $10 a night, plus about $3 for each meal and $5 for guided tours.

The Guest House Program was originally designed to incorporate an important strategy—controlling tourists' access. In an attempt to minimize stress levels on the natural environment and not overburden local Maya with massive infusions of outsiders, organizers can arrange for individuals and small groups to be cycled in and out on a rotating basis. Each village thus gets its share of tourists, but the overall demands on local people and resources are kept low.

Toledo Host Family Network

Catering to overnight visitors who wish to stay in the actual homes of villagers, the Toledo Host Family Network involves residents of **San Antonio, Santa Cruz, San José, Na Luum Ca, San Pedro Columbia, Silver Creek**, and **Santa Elena**.

After contacting village officials (or Dem Dat's Doin'/Toledo Information Center) and paying a $5 registration fee, tourists are introduced to a Maya family that will provide meals, a hammock (with sheet), illuminating conversation, and involvement in such daily activities as tortilla preparation, corn farming, "chopping bush," and land tilling. Guided trips are offered to nearby ruins, caves, and nature trails. Visitors pay their host families at a rate of about $5 a day for room and $2 per meal. Some of the money goes to host families and the rest is used for community service projects such as potable water systems and health clinics. In order to find out who coordinates the homestay in a particular village, ask for the name and address of the local *alcalde* or chair. Residents can point the way.

Keep in mind that conditions are primitive by the modern standards of the industrial world—you'll use outhouses (supplied with corncobs, not toilet paper) and wash yourself in nearby rivers, just like the Maya. There's not much to do at night and many houses lack electricity. (A favorite entertainment is watching rented videos in one of the few TV-equipped homes.) The Maya homestay experience isn't for everyone, but your reward is getting to meet some of the warmest, friendliest people in Belize. A good information resource is *Maya Atlas: The Struggle to Preserve Maya Land in Southern Belize* (North Atlantic Books, Box 12327, Berkeley, CA 94712).

PUNTA GORDA
Location: About 100 air miles southwest of Belize City and 15 miles north of the Guatemala border.
Population: About 4,500 (1999 estimate).
Visitor Information: Belize Tourist Board, on Front Street; Toledo Ecotourism Association, 7-22119; or Toledo Visitors Information Center, 7-22470, at the main wharf.

Even in the Toledo District capital of Punta Gorda, some 200 miles south of Belize City, the pace is slow. In the middle of this sprawling town, chickens roam freely between clapboard houses and patches of uncut vegetation. Freshly caught turtles and fish are dressed on the shoreline. Wheelbarrows full of produce roll along the broad streets. Uniformed schoolchildren play in front of unpretentious churches. Adults gossip on street corners as they go about their errands. There is virtually no traffic to dodge and the silence at night can be deafening.

If you fly to "P.G.," as the community is known locally, a spectacular view of the Caribbean and, on clear days, the mountains of Guatemala and Honduras will greet you as you walk from the airport to downtown— which happen to be only a few steps apart. The five tree-shaded principal streets of Punta Gorda run parallel to the coast and are unpaved. This tranquil façade belies a colorful and sometimes violent history.

Culture and Economy
Although P.G. is still an important fishing port (especially for sport anglers), it has been converted into a market town by gradual improvements in transportation and the influx of peasant farmers from nearby Guatemala.

There are also many traditional farms along the coast, primarily growing cassava, beans, maize, and rice. The town itself has an interesting ethnic mix that includes Maya, Garifuna, Creole, East Indian, Chinese, European, and Lebanese residents.

According to a recent census, almost 50 percent of Punta Gorda's population is Garifuna. These people have had a difficult time keeping their unique culture alive, and the modern world provides few financial and social incentives for them to do so. Their rich and varied language is not taught in the schools, and the difficulty of finding steady employment is ever-present. Farming once was a part of the Garifuna culture in the Toledo District, but today such traditions as the baking of cassava bread are practiced by only a few families. Many families have at least one member now living in the U.S. or Canada and remitting income.

Until 1994 a large number of British soldiers were stationed in P.G., which bolstered the local economy. Although the Brits are mostly gone, U.S. taxpayers continue to support a large Voice of America radio station south of the town, which beams programming throughout Central America. The facility is for sale, but still operated by the U.S. Information Agency. You can see the flashing navigation lights atop the compound's 200-foot-tall antenae.

Things to See and Do

Nightlife in P.G. is limited to a handful of bars and restaurants, or you can look overhead and see one of the most amazing starscapes in the country.

Wednesdays and Saturdays are market days, and you'll find the hand-crafted wares of Maya artisans from local villages as well as Guatemala. An amazing array of exotic fruits and vegetables is also on sale. The outdoor market is on Front Street, with booths spilling over onto adjacent Queen Street. Local handicrafts made by the **Fajina Craft Center**, 7-22470, are a particularly good value—they are of high quality, priced fairly, and their sale supports a local "self-empowerment" organization of Kekchí and Mopán women. Look for tie-tie baskets, jippy-jappa baskets, slate carvings, handwoven textiles, and embroideries. Among the more unusual craft items are reproductions of ancient Maya symbols on handmade paper.

Punta Gorda is a good base for trips to Toledo's more than 30 Maya villages and several major ruins (see Chapter 10, Archaeological Sites, for details), along with jungle rivers, caves, diving, kayaking, snorkeling, and sportfishing. Excursions can also be made to the southern end of the barrier reef and Glover's Reef, although the islands are so far offshore (40 miles) that it may be easier to head for them from Placencia or Dangriga. Local lagoons and 19th-century sugar mills round out the attractions.

Outfitters

Charter by Land/Sea, at 12 Front Street, 7-72070, schedules boat and interior trips from its office. Diving is the specialty at **Orange Point Marina**, operated by an American expatriate, with four 26-foot sailboats to charter. **Requena Boat Charters**, 12 Front Street, 7-22070, arranges fishing, snorkeling, and nature-observation trips and provides very good guides. They offer daily water-taxi service to Guatemala as well.

Timeless Tours (Box 11, Punta Gorda) runs 7- to 12-day camping excursions to cayes and jungle rivers aboard its 38-foot schooner *Juanita*, based in P.G. harbor. In Indian Creek, try **Belize Lodge & Excursions Ltd.** (2-70843), which offers river, caye, and forest trips as well as Maya ruin tours.

Antonio Chun operates his **Chun Bus** from Punta Gorda to San Antonio every Monday, Wednesday, and Friday, returning on Tuesday, Thursday, and Saturday. The fare is about $2 one-way, $4 round-trip. For information, call Chun at 7-22666. From San Antonio, you can usually catch a ride as far as Pueblo Viejo, one of the most remote villages in Belize.

Sailing, fishing, and diving are specialities of **Sea Hunt Adventures** (7-22845, seahunt@btl.net). Services include a complete dive shop and a two-bedroom cottage for rent on the waterfront. Sailing charters (MacGregor 26s, with or without a skipper) are available from **WindSong Charters** (303-893-3739; windsong@windsongcharters.com). **Paco's Boat Service**, 3 Clement St., 7-22246, makes trips to cayes, Guatemala, and Honduras.

Visitor Information

The **Toledo Visitors Information Center**, open daily from 8 a.m. to 11:30 a.m., except Thursday and Sunday, 7-22470 or fax 7-22199, is operated next to the main pier by Alfredo and Yvonne Villoria of Dem Dat's Doin'. Besides providing extensive information on Toledo attractions, the Villorias can help arrange inland tours and boat charters. The center maintains a message center, bulletin board, and paperback book exchange as well. Information is dispensed free of charge.

Another P.G. resource is the **Toledo Explorer's Club**, 7-22986, 46 José María Nuñez Street, which answers visitors' questions and arranges custom-guided camping expeditions to remote villages, rivers, caves, and cayes. Basic accommodations are provided in the group's "clubhouse."

Getting There

As of early 1999, Maya Island Airlines had four daily flights to and from Belize City to Punta Gorda; Tropic Air had two flights on the same route. The plane trip from Belize City takes about 90 minutes (with two stops) and costs around $65 (one-way).

The Z-Line bus runs twice daily to and from Dangriga and Belize

City, (53 Main St., 7-22165), and the James Line bus makes the same trip every day (arriving and leaving from P.G.'s main square). The trip to Belize City ($11) takes about 10 hours (Dangriga 5 hours, $8), via the rough Southern and Hummingbird Highways. A number of local buses and supply trucks carry passengers on semi-weekly schedules to surrounding villages, with the heaviest traffic on Wednesdays and Saturdays (Punta Gorda's market days). You can also simply flag down a passing vehicle; most will give you a ride. The turnoff from the Southern Highway is about 15 miles west of P.G. at a Shell gas station.

Getting from Punta Gorda to Puerto Barrios, Guatemala

The long-running passenger ferry between Punta Gorda and Puerto Barrios, Guatemala, permanently suspended service in 1997. Competition from faster, inexpensive water taxis put the old boat out of business.

Requena's Charter Service offers much faster (1 hour) daily 9 a.m. boat service to Puerto Barrios for about $10 one-way, one of the best bargains in Belize. If there are enough passengers (usually eight), some operators, such as **Paco's Boat Service**, will make a trip when Requena's boats fill up. You can also try bargaining your way onto one of the supply boats that shuttle between Barrios and P.G. Cruise ships occasionally dock in Punta Gorda as well. At least once a week there is a private water taxi directly to Livingston, Guatemala, which has an immigration/customs office. Ask around at the municipal wharf.

No matter how you depart, you must have your passport stamped before embarking; the Belize immigration office is at the foot of the municipal wharf. In 1999 there were no exit fees for Belize or entry fees for Guatemala. Boat connections to Honduras can be made from Puerto Barrios. Quetzales, the Guatemalan currency, can be obtained at **Grace's Shop**, from arriving water taxi passengers, or the money-changer who meets boats in Puerto Barrios. The bank in P.G. does not handle quetzales, nor are Guatemalan visas available here or in Puerto Barrios.

In early 1999, Maya Island Air (800-521-1247) offered Monday and Friday flights to and from Puerto Barrios at 10:20 a.m. ($35 one-way, $65 round-trip). Make inquiries in advance, since these flights have been subject to suspension in recent years.

Where to Stay and Eat in Punta Gorda

Mahung's, 11 Main St.; $14; 7-22044. A good value, small rooms with shared baths.

Nature's Way Guest House, south end of town at 65 Front St.; $15; 7-22119. A P.G. institution that provides many tour options and much

Fallen Stones Butterfly Farm

One of the most unusual attractions in the Toledo District is the award-winning commercial butterfly farm operated by English lawyer Clive P. Farrell and tropical plant specialist Ray Harberd. Farrell, who operates butterfly parks in the U.K. and Florida, developed this operation after a similar farm of his shut down at the Shipstern Nature Reserve in northern Belize. Located in a stunning hilltop setting near the ancient Maya ruin of Lubaantun, Fallen Stones primarily raises two species, popularly known as the blue morpho and the owl butterfly. The farm negates the need to capture these gorgeous insects in the wild, and it also returns a certain percentage of butterflies to the surrounding forests.

A tour of the facility ($5) brings you into breeding cages where dozens of butterflies feed, mate, and lay their eggs on plants that will not thrive outside the rainforest. It's an amazing experience to have these iridescent, neon-blue creatures land on your fingers and even the tip of your nose! Raising butterflies is a

information about the Toledo District. Quarters are basic: clean rooms with bunks and shared baths. Proprietor Chet Schmidt, an American expatriate married to a Belizean, can arrange visits to Maya villages and a remote campsite down the coast, and has a reliable boat for trips up jungle rivers and to offshore cayes. Recommended.

Punta Caliente Hotel, 108 José María Nuñez St.; $13; 7-22561. Next to bus stop, with restaurant and laundry.

St. Charles Inn, 23 King St.; $16; 7-22149. Comfortable rooms in good location.

Seafront Inn, north end of town; $30; 7-22682, seafront@btl.net. Comfortable and homey, also serves meals (including many vegetarian dishes).

labor-intensive process, and thousands of caterpillars (kept in muslin-covered cups in a separate room) must be fed daily by hand. A 2-acre plantation of food plants is maintained a few steps from the enclosure, and other fruit and nectar sources have been developed nearby. As a result of this activity, Fallen Stones has hired and trained many local Maya, whose handed-down knowledge of butterfly habits is invaluable.

When they reach their chrysalis (pupa) stage, the dormant insects are carefully packaged and shipped by air to the U.S. and Europe, where they emerge as brand-new butterflies within a few days of arrival. Because blue morpho and owl butterflies typically live only a couple of weeks, there is a constant need for new pupae. The next time you visit Butterfly World in Coconut Creek, Florida, you'll know where those particular butterflies came from!

The Fallen Stones Jungle Lodge, *managed separately, offers comfortable bungalows ($80 and up), fine meals ($35 a day), and excellent guided tours of the nearby forest and Maya ruins.*

Expat owners Larry and Carol Smith are diving and snorkeling outfitters. Recommended.

The Traveler's Inn, located above the Z-Line bus station at 53 Main St.; $70; 7-22568. The most upscale place in P.G., with air-conditioning, TV, and a restaurant. Operated by the Zabadeh family, Z-Line's owners.

William Tate's Guest House, near the post office at 34 José María Nuñez St.; $20; 7-22196. Air-conditioning, cable TV, owned by P.G.'s postmaster. Rooms without air-conditioning have lower rates. Recommended.

Other Options

The best breakfasts in town are served at **Granny's** and **Nature's Way,** both on Front Street. A local favorite for Belizean dishes is **Lucille's,** on

Front Street, and many travelers rave about **Punta Caliente**, at 108
José Nuñez Street, near the Z-Line bus station.

I have heard consistently negative comments about the food and
rooms at the **Mira Mar Hotel**, at 95 Front Street.

Where to Stay and Eat near Punta Gorda

Dem Dat's Doin', $15; 7-22470. A basic room is for rent at the San
Pedro Columbia permaculture farm of Alfredo and Yvonne Villoria.
Home-cooked meals are available for a modest fee and, for $5, you
can take an extensive tour of the Villoria's unusual operation. Using
relatively simple, low-impact technology, the couple (who immigrated
here from the U.S. in 1980) are almost completely food and energy
independent. They grow fruits and vegetables (including such oddities
as "flying potatoes"); capture invertebrates for scientific use; raise fish,
chickens, and pigs; collect solar energy and rainwater; and generate
methane gas (for cooking and refrigeration) through a "digester" fueled
by animal wastes. Their frangipani and ylang-ylang flowers are pressed
into perfume, and other plants are sold in a small nursery. The Villorias
have transferred much of their knowledge to their Maya neighbors, and
the results are impressive. I highly recommend a visit! Reservations are
strongly recommended.

Fallen Stones Jungle Lodge & Butterfly Farm, $80; 7-22167. About
45 minutes from P.G. near the Lubaantun ruins and the village of San
Pedro Columbia. For those who want to experience the rainforest—with
considerable creature comforts—I encourage you to try this lodge. Birding and nature tours available.

Other Options near Punta Gorda

If you have a special interest in rainforest ecology, you can stay at one
of six bungalows in the comfortable **International Zoological Expeditions** field station and lodge near Blue Creek, maintained as the private
Blue Creek Wildlife Sanctuary, $130, including all meals; 800-548-
5843; ize2belize@aol.com. A special treat is IZE's canopy-level sky-walk
that zigzags its way through the 100-foot-high forest "ceiling" (home to
more than 80 percent of rainforest organisms, including
scores of bird species). Non-IZE guests pay $12.50 for use of the sky-walk.
Guides can be hired (about $40 per day) for jungle hikes, cave exploration,
and tours of Maya ruins. Check the IZE Web site at www.ize2belize.com.

Although several prearranged tours, guest houses, and homestays are
available, it's also relatively easy to find accommodations in the interior
on your own. Many residents will take you in and feed you for about $10 a
night (or less). Other options include **Bol's Hilltop Hotel** (no phone or

Punta Gorda's Colorful History

P.G. is believed to have been founded by Puritan traders in the 17th century, then occupied off and on by English pirates and Spanish soldiers, who gave it a name that translates as "large point," a reference to the bluff upon which Punta Gorda sits. Throughout most of the colonial era, P.G. was primarily a fishing village. In 1867 a group of disaffected Civil War Confederate Army veterans and their families settled on unoccupied land nearby and tried to re-create their Deep South lifestyle around a group of sugarcane plantations. Chinese, Creole, and East Indian laborers were brought in to cut the cane and clear the forest. Over the next 40 years, a dozen sugar mills were built. But by 1910, the Toledo Settlement, as it was known, had failed, and most of the Americans returned to the United States. The name and townsite (plus many descendants of the conscripted laborers) remain.

electricity) in San Antonio and **Oh's Travelers' Farm & Lodge,** 7-22119, in San Pedro Columbia, where you can get basic roms ($14) and meals.

In 1999, new lodges were scheduled to open at Golden Stream, Nim Li Punit, and Moho Caye. Contact **Belize Lodge and Excursions** at 2-70843 or (800) 633-4734.

HOKEB HA CAVE
Recommended interior destinations include the Maya's sacred Hokeb Ha Cave (also called Blue Creek Cave), a 5-mile-long underground river system. The water flowing from this passageway is crystal clear and perfectly suited to a refreshing swim on a hot day. During the dry season it's possible to hike all the way through the cave to a nearby Maya community. Access to Hokeb Ha is by a well-marked riverside trail from Blue Creek Village, about 21 miles west of Punta Gorda. Guests at the nearby jungle lodge operated by International Zoological Expeditions can easily arrange tours through IZE, which strongly advises against entry into the caves without an experienced guide. Recommended local guides include **Bobby Polonio** and **Alfredo Romero,** who also offer treks to sugar mill ruins and chicle camps.

KAYAKING THE UPPER MOHO

The Toledo District's kayaking options include the remote **Upper Moho River**, which drains a wilderness watershed in the southern Maya Mountains. From December through April, **Island Expeditions**, (800) 667-1630 or (604) 452-3212, offers a six-day trip using inflatable kayaks. Costs start at about $1,000 per person. Inquire locally about float trips down the Río Grande, navigable for 12 miles in season.

TEMASH-SARSTOON NATIONAL PARK AND COLUMBIA FOREST RESERVE

If you want to see some of the tallest and oldest mangrove forests in all of Central America, a trip up the Río Temash fills the bill. This river and the neighboring Río Sarstoon are two of four major watercourses that drain into the Caribbean from the Toledo District. In 1992 the government protected much of the southeast Belize watershed through its creation of the 42,000-acre Temash-Sarstoon Nature Reserve, which later became a national park. Residents of the five villages surrounding the park are actively involved in its management, thanks to the Belize government's insistence on community responsibility in the oversight of protected areas.

As you speed southeast from Punta Gorda in a hired boat—there is no public transportation in the area—you will pass such scenic coastal landmarks as **Orange Point,** the **Moho River,** and **Mother Point**. The tall forest canopy along the coast contrasts with brighter green cascades of mangrove and forest stands that have been disturbed by the periodic hurricanes that batter the mainland.

I recommend that you hire an experienced boatman and guide for this adventure. The need becomes apparent as you maneuver past dangerous sandbars and tangled mangrove thickets. In this instance, a well-informed local is also extremely helpful to the amateur naturalist once you're past the verdant tunnel entrance of the Temash's delta. Comfrey palm swamp is found around the estuary of the river, possibly the only place in the country where this habitat type exists in such abundance.

The entire area is officially classified as a tropical wet-transition to subtropical forest and harbors much wildlife. Even the usually short palmetto palms tower overhead here. The deeper you penetrate this wide river, passing **Conejos** and **Sunday Wood Creeks,** the bigger the trees become. The tangle of vines and understory is almost impenetrable. And then you begin to see the river's premier natural attraction—black mangrove trees that tower above the Temash, sometimes reaching more than 100 feet.

It's believed that giant anteaters and white-faced capuchin monkeys may inhabit this area, which would be the northern limit of their range. Birds not found in other parts of Belize—including the rarely seen scarlet macaw and chestnut-bellied (or agami) heron—have also been seen here.

The presence of ospreys and local anglers attest to the Temash's richness as a fishing area. Large snook and tarpon cruise in the river, which reportedly reaches a depth of more than 100 feet. Sportfishing guides in Punta Gorda and other coastal towns can arrange excursions to visit this rich aquatic environment.

Farther north, the Columbia branch of the Río Grande drains the nearly 103,000 acres of uninhabited wilderness known as the **Columbia Forest Reserve**, one of the last remaining large tracts of intact forest in Central America. Recent explorations of the reserve have revealed sinkholes up to 800 feet deep and ¼-mile wide, plus many sacred Maya caves containing ancient artifacts. Access is difficult, however, and prior permission from the Department of Forestry is required.

OFFSHORE CAYES
Eight miles northeast of Punta Gorda, **Moho Caye** is blessed with sandy beaches, coconut palms, and spectacular views of the Maya Mountains. A nature-oriented lodge was scheduled to open here in late 1999, operated by **Belize Lodge & Excursions Ltd.** (2-70843). The lodge's operators offer tours of offshore as well as inland attractions, including seldom-visited Mayan ruins and jungle habitats.

Wild Cane Caye, a few miles northeast of Moho, boasts a rich heritage of Mayan and colonial history. The ancient Maya used the lush island as a settlement and trading center. Later settlers planted a wide variety of tropical fruit trees, still enjoyed in their respective seasons.

The nearby **Port Honduras Cayes** are a major spawning area for fish, which in turn attracts an unusual number of sea birds. These islands are very small, and many are completely submerged at high tide. Further offshore is the **Sapodilla Cayes Marine Reserve**, a marine-life sanctuary at the southern tip of Belize's barrier reef. Access is by chartered boat.

ARCHAEOLOGICAL SITES

10

Neither archaeologists nor government officials know exactly how many ancient Maya sites there are in Belize, but certainly the number is in the thousands. The remnants of Maya occupation—ranging from microscopic vegetable pollen found in the dust of potsherds to sky-scraping temples poking through the forest canopy—are found from border to border. Such artifacts are even commonplace on the offshore islands. It is now widely acknowledged that Belize was once at the very heart of the lowland Maya civilization.

Experts speculate that this relatively small territory may have easily supported as many as 1 million or more Maya, several times the area's total present population of about 255,000. In 1997, one prominent archaeologist speculated that 2 million Maya may easily have lived within the present borders of Belize a dozen centuries ago.

Despite their clear domination of the area for hundreds of years, precious little is known about these early residents. Formal excavation of the largest ruins is relatively recent, and much of the early archaeological work is now regarded as amateurish and slipshod, though important nonetheless. Many important sites have remained virtually untouched, and others have received only cursory field research. Even Caracol, the country's biggest known Maya complex, saw no serious investigation until the mid-1980s.

PRESERVATION AND EXPLORATION

Although many foreign agencies and universities are now helping the Belizeans study and preserve their Maya patrimony, many precious artifacts have already been lost to looters, farmers, collectors, and the vagaries of nature. A great threat continues to exist, as impoverished and/or unscrupulous people plunder sites in the hope of finding valuables that can be sold for prices that start at about $50 per pot (equal to more than a month's salary for many a Belizean).

Unlike Mexico and Guatemala, Belize has lacked sufficient funds to restore its major Maya cities, and only a handful of caretakers are looking after them. Access to many locations is difficult and only improving slowly. In some cases, the ruins are on private property.

Yet underdevelopment has its advantages. Even during the peak tourist season, it is not uncommon to find yourself alone at one of Belize's Maya ruins, or in the company of a single resident manager. If you are patient, you may find that you're surrounded by wildlife.

COLLECTING ARTIFACTS

Keep in mind that under Belize law, all "ancient monuments" (defined as those structures over 100 years old) and "antiquities" (human-made articles crafted more than 150 years ago) are the property of the government. Their removal, destruction, or possession is expressly forbidden without the permission of federal authorities. The collecting, buying, and selling of such artifacts is also illegal, and anyone engaged in such activity is subject to stiff fines and a jail term. Nevertheless, looting continues to be the single biggest threat to the integrity of sites here, as elsewhere in the Maya world.

Be advised that a thriving business exists in imitation artifacts, and many travelers spend good money on cheap fakes. Trading in these items is not illegal, but without proper documentation the items may be seized by customs officials when leaving the country.

WHEN TO GO AND WHAT TO TAKE

Because of the sites' varying degrees of isolation, it is best to visit during the drier months (February through May). Remember that it can rain at any time and place in Belize, and waterproof boots or shoes are advisable. Lightweight, comfortable clothing should be worn, and a hat or raincoat may be useful. It is also a good idea to bring along insect repellent, sunscreen, and drinking water.

Few of the Maya sites allow overnight visits, and only a handful have restrooms. All visitors must register and fees are usually between $1.50 and $5 per person, although these are not always collected. Children under 12 are admitted free, as are all Belizean nationals on Sundays. For further information, call the Department of Archaeology in Belmopan at 8-22106, fax 8-23345.

OUTFITTERS

A handful of U.S.-based tour companies specialize in trips to Maya ruins. We particularly like **Far Horizons**, operated by archaeologist and conservationist Mary Dell Lucas, who has lived in Belize and helped excavate several sites. Trips organized by Far Horizons are led by well-informed archaeologists and deliberately kept small to minimize disruption of research teams and rural communities. Part of each trip fee funds the archaeology project visited. Based in Albuquerque, New Mexico, Far Horizons can be reached at (800) 552-4575 or (505) 343-9400, journey@farhorizon.com. See Chapter 4 for other outfitters.

ADVANCE READING

For travelers with an interest in the Maya history of Belize, we suggest some background reading before setting out (see Appendix B for suggested books). The best local guidebook is *Warlords and Maize Men: A Guide to the Maya Sites of Belize*, which contains detailed travel instructions and maps, plus photographs and archaeological histories for each location. Another good resource is *The Belizean Bullet*, an infrequent publication of the Department of Archaeology that provides detailed information about ongoing research. The internationally distributed *Archaeology* magazine also reports often on Maya sites in Belize. For general background, read *The Maya*, by Michael D. Coe (see Appendix B for other suggestions).

PRINCIPAL SITES

Ancient Mayan archaeological sites in this chapter are listed by district, in what is roughly a descending order of their size and accessibility.

CAYO DISTRICT

CARACOL

Until 1992, this largest known Maya site in Belize was one of the most difficult to reach. Located in the Cayo District's rugged backcountry, Caracol is in the middle of the remote Chiquibul National Park, only 7 miles east of the Guatemalan border. The complex—which covers at least 55 square miles—is a bumpy 2- to 3-hour journey (in good weather) by four-wheel-drive vehicle from San Ignacio via the Mountain Pine Ridge community of Douglas DeSilva (formerly Augustine), about 30 miles distant.

Caracol's central core covers 30 square miles of thick, high-canopy tropical deciduous forest and comprises a Classic-period complex that includes many pyramids, five plazas, and an astronomical observatory. The main plaza is linked by causeways to a number of outlying ruins.

Overall, the network of structures is at least three times denser and 85 percent larger than nearby Tikal. Although estimates of Caracol's ancient population are being revised upward, in 1999 it was estimated that 180,000 or more people lived in this area at the city-state's peak, around A.D. 700. The site has ruins of an estimated 35,000 buildings, with more discovered each year.

History

Caracol (Spanish for "snail"; a reference to the numerous land-snails found here) remained unknown to the outside world until the early 1930s, when a local woodcutter stumbled upon its mysterious mounds while searching for mahogany and chicle. Loggers cut timber in the area over the next two decades—crushing many valuable artifacts in the process—and it was not until 1950 that archaeologists began mapping Caracol. The ruin was mistakenly considered a small site and left to loggers, looters, and army patrols for some time. It began receiving considerable attention in 1985, after Diane and Arlen Chase began making annual research pilgrimages from the University of Central Florida.

In 1986, while planting a plot of corn at the site, Caracol caretaker and guide Benjamin Panti made a major discovery. He chanced upon a well-preserved stone ball-court marker that contained a carved hieroglyphic record of a military victory by an underdog leader, Lord Water of Caracol, over the mighty warlords of Tikal, some 60 miles to the northwest. This A.D. 562 conquest was apparently the culmination of many years of fierce fighting between the two powers. Caracol did its best to humiliate the royalty of Tikal and the neighboring city-state of Naranjo (conquered by Caracol in A.D. 631) during Caracol's 140 years of domination, possibly even sacrificing its high-ranking captives in public executions.

Excavations at the outskirts of Caracol suggest that the ancient Maya were not divided exclusively into elite and peasant classes, as previously believed. By studying ancient garbage, archaeologists believe that the city's apparently

Richard Mahler

Carved stela at Caracol

sizable middle class apparently had access to jade, polychrome pottery, ritual vessels, and even fancy burial tombs. Experts conclude that Caracol grew rapidly for quite a while before suffering a period of decline, possibly caused in part by an equalization in social power that destroyed the influence of Maya royalty.

Clues contained in the hieroglyphic texts of carved stone monuments now unearthed at Caracol may eventually help the Chases determine why the Maya fled. "We know that when they finally left, they left fast," Diane Chase told an Associated Press reporter in 1993, noting that buildings were burned and the body of a child was abandoned on the floor of a palace.

Another riddle not yet solved is why a city as large as Caracol was built on a plateau that has almost no reliable water supply during four or five months of relatively dry weather each spring. Maya engineers managed to overcome the limitations of nature by painstakingly building reservoirs, aqueducts, paved plazas, and gardening terraces that optimized use of rainfall. Nevertheless, their ingenuity does not explain the reason for locating such a large population here in the first place. Even today, perhaps 3,000 years after Caracol's founding, visitors are advised to bring with them all the water they will need during their stay. (A Maya reservoir fulfills the needs of the research team during its February to June encampment.) It is speculated that Caracol may have been a good location for trading with other Maya communities spread throughout present-day Guatemala, Honduras, and Mexico, or that such prized plants as cacao grew here.

Another major discovery at Caracol was the bones of a woman in a royal tomb at the top of the highest pyramid. The find suggests that, in the absence of a male heir, females may have periodically ruled Maya city-states, although this skeleton also could be that of a ruler's wife or close relative.

The most visually striking structure here is *Ca'ana* ("sky palace"), a temple towering 140 feet above the plaza floor. It is 2 meters higher than El Castillo at the site of Xunantunich, previously regarded as the tallest human-constructed building in Belize. (Modern hotels in Belize City now compete for this honor.) Visitors can climb to the summit of Ca'ana and enjoy a sweeping view of the Vaca Plateau's tall forests, which extend for as far as the eye can see. Looking west and southwest from the temple, dozens of unevaluated building mounds up to 70 feet in height are evident all the way to the horizon.

In the first four years of digging, Caracol yielded 54 burial tombs, twice as many as have been found in all the decades of searching at Tikal. The project's directors estimate there are as many as 4,500 structures at the core of Caracol, compared to 2,300 mapped in the site center of Tikal. The archaeological richness of this site, one of the five largest Maya cities anywhere, is expected eventually to result in a much better understanding of the civilization, particularly since many of Caracol's tombs and monuments clearly indicate the year of their initial construction.

The Belizean government has expanded the Caracol Archaeology Reserve to the borders of the surrounding (and much larger) Chiquibul National Park. The region's high-canopy forest, much of it in pristine condition, is an important habitat for several species of cat and the endangered howler monkey, plus such rare birds as the keel-billed motmot. Endangered ocellated turkeys and other large birds strut among the ruins with impunity, though they have vanished from most of the rest of Belize. A variety of orchids, vines, and trees (many as tall as 120 feet) are found in the area. One enormous ceiba tree, at least 700 years old, towers above the epicenter of Caracol. The Maya considered ceiba trees sacred because they connected the underworld, the earth, and the sky, thus their colloquial name: World Tree.

Road Conditions

A check of road conditions from the Forestry Department's western division in Douglas DeSilva is advised prior to any rainy season visit to Caracol. Forestry officials grant access based on road conditions, since the last 30 miles into Caracol are rough—especially during or after wet weather. Most lodges will make such inquiries for their guests.

Getting There/Outfitters

High-clearance four-wheel-drive vehicles are recommended. The nearest gas station and mechanic are in San Ignacio, about 65 miles from the site. There is no public transportation to Caracol, and few taxis will make the trip. Rather than attempting a visit on your own, I recommend checking with local resorts for guided tours to the site. **Chaa Creek, Maya Mountain Lodge, Blancaneux Lodge, Hidden Valley Lodge,** and **Mountain Equestrian Trails** are among the recommended operators. Since road improvements were made in 1992, tour companies no longer schedule regular horseback trips to Caracol. Such trips can be arranged, however.

Where to Stay and Eat in Caracol

There are no overnight accommodations at Caracol and camping is allowed only with special permission from the Department of Archaeology. The nearest campground is in Douglas DeSilva and the nearest lodges are in the Mountain Pine Ridge. Remember to bring your own food and water. A solar-powered telephone is available for emergency use only.

Fees

The $5 visitor's fee is payable upon registration at the site.

Guides

On-site workers are fairly knowledgeable about the archaeology and wildlife of the area—some, like Benjamin Panti, have worked here for many years—and they will provide guided tours when archaeologists or lodge-provided guides are not available. Fluency in Spanish is helpful. When researchers are encamped, archaeologist-led tours are given at specified times. Check with tour operators or hotels for the current schedule.

XUNANTUNICH

In contrast to remote Caracol, Xunantunich (the Maya "x" is pronounced like a cross between an English "sh" and "z") is one of the most accessible ancient Maya sites in Belize. The ruins are near the confluence of the Belize and Mopán rivers, on a naturally occurring limestone bluff above the Western Highway, about 7 miles west of San Ignacio.

This is a Late Classic period ceremonial center of impressive height but relatively small size. It is just across the Mopán River from the Maya village of San José Succotz and only a few miles east of the Guatemalan border. The temple complex, occupied from about A.D. 700 until at least A.D. 1000, is surrounded by forest that is gradually being whittled away by local farmers.

Because of its commanding presence and proximity to populated areas, Xunantunich has been visited by a lengthy parade of archaeologists stretching back to 1894. In 1959, experts speculated that the site had been partially destroyed in an earthquake during the Late Classic era and reasoned that this incident may have shaken the faith the Maya had in their leaders, who claimed an intimate relationship with the gods. In recent years, however, this theory has been discredited by some archaeologists.

Dominating the topography of Xunantunich ("maiden of the rock") is a spectacular 135-foot monolith known as **El Castillo** (The Castle). In typical Maya fashion, the corbel-vaulted temple at the summit is actually built on the rubble of several earlier temples constructed one atop the other over the centuries. Visitors can climb nearly to the top of this impressive tower, which affords a sweeping view of the steamy forest and overlooks the three adjacent plazas and various corbel-arched buildings that surround them.

Visible on the east side of El Castillo's lower temple is a stucco frieze, restored in 1972 and again in 1998, showing symbols of the sun, moon, Venus, and days of the week. Also included is a headless man, apparently decapitated for some long-forgotten transgression against the royal rulers. Originally the frieze continued all the way around the structure, and its highest point was probably topped by a roof comb. An excavated stairway continues to a small chamber in the upper temple

Richard Mahler

Detail of restored Maya frieze, Xunatunich

of El Castillo. Near the structure's base is a wide terrace that once supported several smaller temples.

The grass-covered mounds surrounding the three primary plazas are the remains of ancient residential buildings. On the west side, near the restrooms, is a flat, narrow rectangle believed to be a ball court, used in a deadly form of soccer developed by the Maya hierarchy. Also visible is a room with a built-in stone bench and some walls bearing ancient Maya graffiti.

Judging from the jewelry, tools, semiprecious stones, and weaving materials found here, archaeologists believe Xunantunich was once an important and well-ordered city. No one is sure why this site was abandoned, or why it flourished so late in the Maya epoch.

The University of California-Los Angeles and University of Pennsylvania were recently is involved in an eight-year field study here. On the west side of El Castillo, the team uncovered a spectacular plaster frieze. Thirty feet long, the frieze was made between A.D. 800 and 900, a time when most other Maya cities were collapsing. Archaeologists are also uncovering small homesites and farms along the length of a *sacbé*, a very old Maya road.

Fees/Guides

The $5 admission fee is collected by resident caretaker Elfego Panti, himself of Maya descent and very knowledgeable about the history of Xunantunich.

He is happy to point out structures of interest and is familiar with local wildlife and plants. Drinking water and restrooms are also available near his office, along with a small museum.

Getting There

Heading west about 10 minutes from San Ignacio on the Western Highway, the tower of El Castillo is suddenly visible on the western horizon. As you enter the village of San José Succotz, look for a sign and bus shelter marking the turnoff on the right-hand side of the highway. You will cross the Mopán River on a tiny, hand-cranked ferry (that handles two cars at a time) secured to a steel cable. There is no charge, as this is a public right-of-way. Follow the dirt road for about one-half mile up the hill to a small parking lot, then walk into the Xunantunich plaza. The access road can be very slippery when wet. If you decide to proceed on foot, it takes about 40 minutes to walk up the hill from the ferry.

Besides passenger cars and package tours, visitors can take taxis to the Xunantunich ruins from Benque Viejo or San Ignacio for about $10. An alternative is to take a bus from either town and ask the driver to stop at the ferry crossing. Xunantunich is an easy half-day trip from the resorts of the Cayo District or the hotels of San Ignacio.

EL PILAR

El Pilar is a 100-acre, Middle Pre-Classic and Late Classic-era ceremonial center under ongoing study by the University of California–Santa Barbara and Belize's Department of Archaeology. Occupied for at least 1,500 years, El Pilar (the name derives from the Spanish word for "springs") is one of the largest unconsolidated Maya ruins in the country, situated near the Belize River, about 12 miles northwest of San Ignacio.

Particularly intriguing is a causeway that extends from the eastern half of the ruin across the border into Guatemala. The 25 identified plazas and 12 pyramids are approximately triple the number found nearby in either Xunantunich or Baking Pot. In contrast to neighboring sites, El Pilar remains largely the same as when archaeologists found it, providing a rare sense of discovery for visitors. Highlights include a standing temple, an underground corbeled tunnel, and examples of "elite" Maya architecture. Parking and picnicking facilities are available.

The ruin sits astride an undulating series of forested ridges that rise morethan 900 feet above the surrounding countryside. The management plan for El Pilar Archaeological Reserve calls for protection of the surrounding vegetation and wildlife, as well as the involvement of local residents and guides in park management. This is one of the finest birding locations in western Belize. The reserve currently has a total of five well-tended trail systems, ranging in length from one-tenth of a mile to

1.5 miles. The longest hike ends at Chorro, a waterfall and an adjacent Classic-era ruin, where you can take a refreshing dip.

A caretaker is on hand to show visitors around and archaeologists are at work from February to June. For information about the archaeologists' efforts, contact the BRASS/El Pilar Project, 1002 Huntridge Dr., Austin, TX 78758; 102402.2332@compuserve.com. A trail guide can be downloaded from the El Pilar Web site: www.sscf.ucsb.edu/~ford/pilar.

Getting There/Outfitters

Drive to the nearby village of Bullet Tree Falls and continue north on Bullet Tree Road across the Mopán River. Watch for the El Pilar road sign. The site is 7 miles north of the village. Because the road is unshaded, walking is recommended only for experienced hikers (who carry plenty of water). Transportation by vehicle, horseback, and mountain bike can be arranged from San Ignacio (try Eva's) or Bullet Tree Falls (inquire at Be Putke Cultural History Center). Particularly recommended is **Parrot Nest Riverside Treehouses**, in Bullet Tree Village. Expect to pay about $25 for a half-day tour, $40 for a round-trip taxi from San Ignacio. There is a scale model of El Pilar at Be Putke and local handicrafts for sale.

CAHAL PECH

The ridgetop ruin of Cahal Pech, practically within the town limits of San Ignacio, underwent extensive excavation and restoration during the early 1990s by San Diego State University, the University of Oregon, Canada's Trent University, and the Belize Department of Archaeology. Some visitors may be surprised—and put off—by the overlay of limestone plaster on much of these ruins, but some archaeologists insist that such restoration is historically accurate. Others disagree.

Cahal Pech derives its Mopán Maya name, "place of the tick," from the large number of bovine parasites found here when the area was used as a cattle pasture. The ruins were not mapped until 1950 and were periodically looted until a complete survey was made in 1988.

This ceremonial complex of what was once a medium-size Maya settlement and political center consists of 34 structures spread across several acres. There are seven courtyards, plus a central plaza, a number of ball courts, stelae, family tombs, and temple pyramids. The tallest building is 77 feet high. The site reportedly functioned as a kind of royal castle, standing guard over the nearby confluence of the Mopán and Macal Rivers. Cahal Pech is believed to have been closely associated with nearby Buena Vista and Xunantunich, both of which date from the same era.

Preliminary analysis indicates that Cahal Pech was occupied during the Late Classic period from at least 900 B.C. until A.D. 1100, reaching its greatest strength around A.D. 600. Notable findings here include an altar, a mosaic mask, and what appears to have been a sweat lodge. Research supports the theory that the famous Classic Maya "collapse" of the ninth century came neither swiftly nor easily, at least at Cahal Pech. Based on new evidence of lingering squalor and decay, it appears that the breakdown of the civilization dragged on for as long as 100 years, until the early tenth century.

Getting There
Visitors are welcome at Cahal Pech, which is a pleasant 20-minute walk (or 5-minute drive) west of downtown San Ignacio. Look for a sign pointing to the ruins at a point where the Western Highway makes a sweeping turn just west of San Ignacio. The site is on the south side of the road, out of view in a cluster of trees. It is currently under excavation by the Belize Valley Archaeological Reconnaissance Project.

Fees/Services
A worthwhile museum and visitors center are at the entrance to the site, open daily from 8 a.m. to 4 p.m. An informative, free pamphlet about Cahal Pech is distributed here, and the $5 admission fee is collected. A hardback book about the site, published by San Diego State University, is sold at the museum and various bookstores around Belize.

On top of a hill, a few hundred yards from the ruin, is the Cahal Pech Tavern, a popular bar, restaurant, and dance hall that's worth a visit. Vendors sometimes sell drinks and snacks near the entrance to the ruins.

PACBITUN
Located on a dirt road near San Antonio Village, about a 45-minute drive south of San Ignacio, Pacbitun (meaning "stones set in the earth") is one of the most enduring Middle Pre-Classic Maya ruins in the country. Archaeologists believe it was first occupied in 1000 B.C. and abandoned around A.D. 900. The location was known for many years by local residents but not registered by the Belize Department of Archaeology until 1971. Trent University excavated and partially reconstructed this ceremonial site during the 1980s. Findings include a number of Maya altar stones and ball courts, as well as ancient musical instruments, such as ocarinas, fashioned out of carved and molded pottery. Pacbitun has at least 24 temple pyramids, the largest standing 60 feet tall. Two thousand years ago this was apparently a wealthy trading center with fancy homes, elevated walkways, a ball court, and raised irrigation causeways reaching a half-mile long.

Getting There
The Pacbitun site is on private farmland, but owner **Fidencio Tzul** welcomes and guides visitors for a small fee. His family home is located at the

well-marked turnoff to Pacbitun one-half mile east of San Antonio. The ruins are about 3 miles farther down the side road. Tzul will be happy to answer any questions. There have been persistent rumors that the Belize government will one day purchase Pacbitun and relocate the Tzul family, so access may have changed by the time you read this. Inquire at Tanah Maya Art in San Antonio about guided tours of Pacbitun.

BELIZE DISTRICT

ALTUN HA

The ancient Maya ruins of Altun Ha are 31 miles north of Belize City on the old Northern Highway that passes through Maskall. (The new Northern Highway continues in a more westerly direction toward Crooked Tree Lagoon, reconnecting with the old highway at Carmelita.) The site of Altun Ha, located 6 miles from the sea, was an important Maya trading and ceremonial center. Here the sun was a focus of study; Maya priests were buried within one of the tallest structures, known as the **Temple of the Sun God**. Altun Ha means "stone water" in Maya, and this name refers to nearby Rockstone Pond, an ancient water catchment ingeniously dammed and lined with clay for irrigation purposes. Near this pond stands a temple in which archaeologists found artifacts the Maya obtained from the faraway city of Teotihuacán, on the outskirts of present-day Mexico City.

During its seventh-century apogee, Altun Ha became a focal point for offerings of such valuables as jade jewelry and carved pendants, as well as copal resin. At the top of the **Temple of the Masonry Altars**, such precious items were smashed into small pieces and cast into an intense fire. The precise origin and purpose of such sacrificial offering remains unclear.

Thirteen structures surround two main plazas at the site. The two tallest temples, Temple of the Sun God (the structure depicted on Belikin beer bottles) and Temple of the Masonry Altars, rise 60 feet above the grassy plaza floor. Altun Ha covers an area of about 5 square miles and includes an extensive swamp north of the plazas. It's believed that up to 10,000 people lived here during the Classic period of Maya civilization, as late as A.D. 1000.

Visitors interested in birds are likely to be rewarded here. Brilliant green Aztec parakeets often streak by in tight formation, level with the tops of the temples. Ringed kingfishers rest on the summit of the Maya structures before returning to the nearby Rockstone Pond to fish. There are also trails into the forests for birders driven by the constant chorus of calls that echo around the two main plazas.

Altun Ha was first excavated by A. H. Anderson in 1957 and by
W. R. Bullard in 1961, who undertook some of the most extensive
fieldwork conducted at any Belizean ruin. This rich ceremonial center
remained archaeologically quiet until 1963, when quarry workers
unearthed an elaborately carved jade pendant. This discovery triggered an
intensive archaeological excavation from 1964 to 1971, spearheaded by
David Pendergast with support from Canada's Royal Ontario Museum.

Perhaps Altun Ha's most famous historical footnote is Pendergast's
discovery of a huge jade head replica of **Kinich Ahau, the Sun God**, in
one of the last tombs to be excavated. The effigy was made in about A.D.
600 and was owned by an elderly priest. At the time of its discovery, this
priceless relic was the largest of its type ever recorded in the Maya
world—almost 6 inches tall and weighing nearly 10 pounds. On rare occasions this Kinich Ahau replica is taken on exhibition tours with other artifacts; eventually it will be displayed in Belize's long-planned National
Museum. Jade found at Altun Ha probably came from Guatemala's
Sierra de las Minas, since this stone does not occur naturally in Belize.

Getting There
From Belize City, take the Northern Highway about 20 miles and turn
right just north of the village of Sand Hill, at the junction of the old
Northern Highway (the sign is marked "Maskall and Orange Walk").
Proceed about 11 miles and turn left (just past Cowhead Creek) at the
sign for the 2-mile connecting road to the Altun Ha parking lot. The drive
from Belize City takes approximately 45 minutes. There is no regular bus
service to the site, although it is possible to hire a taxi or hitch a ride with
a truck that brings goods to market in Belize City from the village of
Maskall, which is located about 10 miles north of Altun Ha. This is a
popular day trip from hotels in San Pedro, Belize City, and Caye Caulker,
as well as from cruise ships.

Fee
An admission fee of $5 is collected at the visitor registration center.

Outfitters
G & W Holiday Tours has an office at the International Airport, 25-
2461, gholiday@btl.net. Winston Seawell is a wealth of information about
Belize, has reliable transportation, and gives an informative tour of Altun
Ha. **S & L Travel Services & Tours** (2-77593, sltravel@btl.net) is a
good choice for some of the best Belizean guides. If you're coming by
water from Ambergris Caye, your boatman will likely serve as your
guide—and many are excellent. Make arrangements through hotels and
travel agencies.

Where to Stay and Eat near Altun Ha

There are no accommodations at Altun Ha, but camping is allowed with permission from the caretaker, who also permits overnight RV parking.

Several low to moderately priced guest houses are available in nearby Crooked Tree Village; I recommend these for visitors who want to see both Altun Ha and the Crooked Tree Wildlife Sanctuary. **The Paradise Inn** (2-44333) is my favorite.

Maruba Resort & Jungle Spa at Mile 40.5 on the old Northern Highway; $110; 3-22199, in the U.S. (713) 799-2031. Maruba Resort boasts a restaurant and bar, an open-air Japanese-style hot tub, swimming pool, massages, cabaña-style accommodations, birding, horseback riding, tours of Altun Ha and Lamanai, and scuba or snorkeling trips. Although not recently visited by the author, some guests have made allegations of consistently poor service and unjustly high prices at Maruba.

MARCO GONZALEZ

This is a late Pre-Classic era (A.D. 1100 to 1300) residential and sea-trading center that was active for hundreds of years. Located in the thick mangrove swamp at the south end of Ambergris Caye, its ruins have been studied by the Royal Ontario Museum and York University. It's believed that most buildings were constructed of seashells, particularly conch. Pottery, obsidian, and jade, as well as basalt grinding tools, stelae, and temple mounds, were unearthed here. Access to Marco Gonzalez, which has been heavily looted, is by foot and bike trail from the town of San Pedro.

SAN JUAN

Excavated by a Texas archaeological team, this small site is at the north end of Ambergris Caye (now the Bacalar Chico National Park headquarters) and dates from the Pre-Classic period. It is one of about a dozen Maya sites pinpointed on the island, all largely abandoned by A.D. 1000 as trading patterns shifted to overland routes. Many of the other cayes and atolls have similar sites and middens, the equivalent of Maya trash heaps. The site is accessible by boat from San Pedro.

CHAU HIIX

This is a small Classic Maya site currently under excavation near Crooked Tree Village, about 35 miles northwest of Belize City. The forest-covered site is accessible by trail from the village, and there is much wildlife (including jaguars and spider monkeys) in the area. Archaeologists believe Chau Hiix was occupied before and during the arrival of Spanish clerics in the 16th century. It is being studied by an Indiana University team.

COLHA

The Colha site is located on the Rancho Creek Farm, about 7 miles north of Maskall on the (old) Northern Highway, roughly 40 miles northwest of Belize City in the Belize District. Permission of the landowner is required to see this small ceremonial site. Colha shows occupation as early as 2400 B.C., making it one of the oldest Maya sites. It is under excavation by the University of Texas, which is also exploring the nearby Blue Creek site.

ORANGE WALK DISTRICT

LAMANAI

While the towering temples of Xunantunich and Caracol are impressive by any measure, a different kind of beauty awaits visitors making the scenic journey to Lamanai, which is translated as "the submerged crocodile." These intriguing ruins are about 70 miles northwest of Belize City, on a patch of high ground that looms over the west bank of the shimmering New River Lagoon, the country's biggest lake.

Lamanai is unusual in that it was occupied longer than almost any other known Maya site, from about 1500 B.C. (or earlier) until at least A.D. 1650—and for varying intervals to the present day. As an important trading center and ceremonial site, its history extends from the formative years of the civilization until well after Franciscan friars arrived from Spain in the 1540s to convert Lamanai's "heathens." The city enjoyed its greatest strength during the Pre-Classic era of A.D. 200 to 900. Lamanai's major pyramid—referred to as the **Southern Temple** or **N10-43**—was completed around 100 B.C., then modified several times before A.D. 600.

Some of Lamanai's ruins are among the oldest surviving buildings from the Classic period, dating back to 700 B.C. Pollen samples show that corn was being cultivated here at least 800 years earlier. There are over 700 buildings in the complex, which is believed to have supported as many as 35,000 people. Only about 5 percent of the known structures have been excavated.

Thanks to records kept by early Catholic missionaries, we know that Lamanai is a Spanish corruption of *Lamanain*, the original Maya name for this place (most other sites were named by their European discoverers). The term is fitting, since the lagoon nearby was—and is—perfect crocodile habitat. Many representations of the reptile have been found here, including ceramic decorations and plaster masks, some of which may be seen in the excellent on-site museum. A figure wearing a crocodile headdress, found in many forms throughout the area, is thought to represent one of Lamanai's important rulers.

Ruin of the old sugar mill at Lamanai

Richard Mahler

Although it is possible to drive here (about 2 hours from Belize City), many visitors prefer to visit Lamanai by boat up the New River, exactly as the ancient Maya did. After navigating through miles of constantly dividing tributaries and closed-in landscape (full of water-birds and their predators), a pyramid-shaped temple (N10-43) suddenly looms 112 feet above the New River Lagoon. When the temple's crown was placed in about 100 B.C., this was probably the tallest building in the Maya world. At the apex of its considerable power, this well-situated city-state is said to have had a wide trading influence that extended over much of present-day Guatemala and Honduras, plus all of Belize.

The site's central core covers about one square mile, with residential structures and smaller buildings spread over another thousand acres. Vegetation makes it difficult to get an adequate perspective on the ground, so a hike to the summit of one of the temples is a good idea: three are over 100 feet tall.

In one section, accessible by a short path, are a few crumbling walls that remain from a 16th-century Catholic mission, one of the few reminders of Spanish occupation extant in all Belize. Attempts at conversion to Christianity began here in 1544 and the Spanish remained until 1641, when the Maya rebelled and burned their church to the ground as part of a regional uprising that included Lamanai's sister city of **Tipú**, on the Macal River (largely destroyed when a citrus plantation was put in). A second chapel was built at Lamanai using stones from one of the Maya's most sacred temples, which contributed to the friction between Europeans and Indians. In fact, a Maya stela (still visible) was erected in front of this church after its destruction. A figurine found in the ruins of the second church has gaping jaws at either end with a god coming out of one of these mouths. It is thought to be a Maya warning along the lines of, "Beware, this could happen to *you*!"

Virtually no one lived here when the British loggers arrived with their Jamaican slaves in the 18th century to extract mahogany and other trees.

Chinese and East Indian laborers were imported about ninety years later
to work in the local sugarcane fields, but they did not react well to the
demanding climate and debilitating diseases; most of the plantations were
soon abandoned. The ruin of a 19th-century sugar mill, with ficus-
strangled flywheel and boiler, is still visible. It was built in 1866 and
burned by the Maya (along with other European constructions) the
following year. A corroded molasses storage chamber, now home to bats,
lies a short distance from the abandoned mill.

Because of the ruin's protected status as an archaeological reserve,
the number of howler monkeys and other endangered mammals living
here has been on the rise. In 1993, researcher Hal Markowitz of San
Francisco State University began a long-term study of the behavioral
ecology of howlers here. Volunteers may work alongside the primate
experts through arrangement with Oceanic Society Expeditions (800-
326-7491). Participants help in all aspects of non-invasive data collection
and stay at the nearby Lamanai Outpost Lodge. OSE also offers
Lamanai trips in which participants help researchers identify and record
birds. The goal is to collect as many tropical bird songs as possible for
laboratory study.

Vegetation here is lush. Common trees at Lamanai include the guanacaste, mahogany, rubber, cohune palm, poisonwood, and ficus. The
adjacent lagoon, fed by a maze of underwater springs and aquifers, is
teeming with fish and virtually unpolluted. Waterbirds thrive here. On the
western bank stretch miles of swampy savannas that are an important
habitat for jaguars and other cats.

The wide array of artifacts found suggests that Lamanai's residents
were enthusiastic and successful merchants. One ancient pottery vessel
contained several small offerings floating in pools of liquid mercury.
Other oddities include an unusually small Maya ball court and an extraor-
dinarily preserved carved stone monument that now lies under a protective palm thatch. It is believed that this stela escaped destruction because
it apparently fell face-forward to the ground during a Maya fire ceremony
and was therefore left unmolested for fear the event itself portended evil.
The stone's outstanding depiction of the Lamanai priest-king Lord Smok-
ing Shell (whose reign began about A.D. 608) clearly shows his open-
mouthed-serpent headdress and other accoutrements. He holds a
ceremonial bar in his arms, symbolizing his royal authority.

The museum at Lamanai contains incense burners (censers), burial
urns, and chalices discovered here, along with eccentric flint carvings,
tools, and many ceramic objects. If you are fortunate enough to visit while
the well-informed Maya curator Nasario Coo is on-site, you can obtain a
thorough account of Lamanai's fascinating history. Coo may provide a
guided tour if his schedule allows.

Getting There/Outfitters

Public transportation to Lamanai is limited to taxis (from Orange Walk Town), rental cars, supply trucks, and hired boats. A dirt road, occasionally impassable during the wet season, extends to the site from Orange Walk Town via the village of San Felipe. Watch for the signs directing you to Indian Church Village and/or Lamanai.

Most visitors arrange a day trip through local hotels, travel agencies, or package tour operators, traveling from as far away as San Pedro, Belize City, and San Ignacio. I recommend **Jungle River Tours** (3-22293) or **Carlos Godoy Tours** (3-22969), which both offer fine New River/Lamanai archaeological tours.

Another approach is to drive as far as Tower Bridge, Guinea Grass, or the Mennonite community of Shipyard, then head up the New River by locally hired boat. (There is no public transportation to Guinea Grass or Shipyard.) Boats can usually be rented on the spur of the moment in any of these riverside villages or can be arranged in advance through large hotels, such as the **D'Victoria** (3-22518) in Orange Walk Town, or the **Maruba** in Maskall (3-22199).

The boat trip is very pleasant, affording opportunities for swimming and other water sports along the way. Many orchids and other flowering plants are visible in the trees overhead. Hollowed-out trunks along the riverbank provide a daytime home to a small, fish-eating bat. Many kinds of birds and animals live along the banks of the lagoon and are easily glimpsed en route to Lamanai. The **Crooked Tree Wildlife Sanctuary** is only 8 miles to the east, and many species are present in both locations. Jabiru stork, snail kite, northern jacana, squirrel cuckoo, blue-crowned motmot, limpkin, cormorant, and night heron, along with huge flocks of parrots, are among the birds recorded near Lamanai. You also may see crocodiles, although the noise of powerboats tends to scare them away.

Where to Stay and Eat in Lamanai

Lamanai Outpost Lodge, 2-33578, (888) 733-7834, amanai@ btl.net; one-half-mile away from the ruins in Indian Church accommodations (and restaurant). Rooms are also available in Orange Walk Town, about 20 miles to the northeast. Camping is not allowed at Lamanai, and no food or drink is sold here. Rustic accommodations are also available in Indian Church Village.

The site has restrooms, a picnic area, and several trails cut through the forest. Besides curator Nasario Coo, the resident caretakers can answer basic questions about the site. The structures are not well marked, however, and no literature is available. Bring your own guide or a map, as well as the usual sunscreen and insect repellent. A swimsuit is also a good idea; New Lagoon ranks as one of the best swimming holes in Belize.

CUELLO

Cuello is located on private land, and permission is needed to visit this ancient site, a minor ceremonial center and settlement area about 4 miles southwest of Orange Walk Town on Yo Creek Road. Arrangements can be made by calling the **Cuello Rum Distillery**, the site's owner, during business hours at 3-22141. Tours of the distillery, which bottles sugarcane spirits under the "Caribbean" label (and is the second-largest rum producer in Central America), can also be scheduled. Permission can usually be obtained by simply showing up; the facility is open Monday through Saturday. Ask to speak with Hilberto or Oswaldo Cuello. Their biggest concern is that visitors not disturb their cattle, which are pastured near the ruins.

Although not well developed for visitors, Cuello is one of the most exciting discoveries in the Maya world. Before the exploration of this site in 1973 by Cambridge University (and later Boston University), most experts believed the Maya civilization had its start around 600 B.C., which was the earliest date of any previously known settlement. Applying state-of-the-art carbon dating techniques to ancient maize fragments and wooden posts, it was determined that occupation by the Maya began here around 1000 B.C., possibly even earlier. Thus, the "start date" of the civilization was pushed back substantially. Subsequent findings at the Colha and Pulltrouser Swamp sites in northern Belize have set that date back to as early as 1500 B.C.

Other findings at Cuello raise more unanswered questions: Why did a mass slaughter of at least 32 individuals take place here about 400 B.C.? Why were earthenware pots placed over the heads of the deceased in some of Cuello's burial chambers? Did the Maya originate their pyramid-plaza architectural style here, as many have suggested?

One certainty is Cuello's continuous occupation for thousands of years, until as recently as A.D. 1500. The site has yielded evidence that the Maya may have been able to build the strength of their city-state empire partly through the development of more productive strains of corn, their principal crop.

Actually, there is not a lot for the casual visitor to see at Cuello, except for a reconstructed Pre-Classic-era temple. Norman Hammond and his Cambridge research team continue to conduct research at the ruin, but they fill in excavated areas after completing their studies. Still, this is an important historical site for anyone who is a serious student of the Maya.

Getting There

Cuello can easily be reached by taxi ($6) or private car via Yo Creek Road, which begins in Orange Walk Town as Baker's Street. No information or guides will be found at the site, although the Department of Archaeology can provide background materials in Belmopan.

About 25 miles down the same road are traditional and modern Mennonite farms and settlements that fan out from Blue Creek Village. By heading through August Pine Ridge and San Felipe, you will eventually reach the Mexican border crossing (pedestrians only) at La Unión. This is also the route for those driving to Chan Chich Lodge, the Programme for Belize lands, and the Río Bravo Conservation Area.

NOHMUL

Nohmul is a major ceremonial center spread among privately owned sugarcane fields near the village of San Pablo, about 7 miles north of Orange Walk Town. Permission from the property owner is required before visiting. The site—located on a limestone ridge and dominated by a pyramid atop a massive acropolis—consists of two groups of buildings incorporating 10 plazas and connected by a raised causeway (*sacbé*).

Nohmul (Maya for "great mound") was occupied first during the Pre-Classic era (350 B.C. to A.D. 250) and again during the Late Classic period (A.D. 600 to 900). At its height, the community was the seat of government for an area encompassing 8 square miles and including the nearby settlements now known as **San Esteban** and **San Luis**.

The dominant ceremonial structure at Nohmul, a large limestone-block rectangle, was built during the late Pre-Classic era with several modifications in subsequent years. Interestingly, this acropolis seems to have lost its religious significance over time and to have been converted into residential quarters by the end of Nohmul's Maya occupation.

Thomas Gann first recorded the large mound as a Maya site in 1897 and conducted digs here over the next 39 years. He and his wife found jade, seashells, chert, obsidian, pottery, and human bones. Much of this material was removed from burial tombs and sent to the British Museum in London. Neglect, looting, and the use of ancient buildings as road construction material took their toll on Nohmul before full-scale excavation could begin in 1982.

Getting There

Nohmul is about 1 mile west of the village of San Pablo, which straddles the Northern Highway midway between Orange Walk Town and Corozal Town, both about 8 miles distant. The site's owner, **Esteban Itzab**, should be contacted before proceeding to the ruin. He lives in the house directly across the street from the community water tower.

There are no facilities or services. Buses pass through the village hourly en route to Orange Walk Town or Corozal Town. Nohmul can also be easily reached by private car or taxi from either of these communities in about 20 minutes. Part of the ruin can be seen from the Northern Highway.

LA MILPA

A mostly unrestored ceremonial center, these ruins (said to be the third-largest Maya site in Belize, after Caracol and Lamanai) are on private property within the protected **Río Bravo Conservation and Management Area** in northwest Belize. Located near a biological field station in the middle of the 250,000-acre Río Bravo tract, La Milpa (sometimes called Las Milpas) comprises more than 85 structures scattered throughout thick forest. Two dozen courtyard groups have been counted, plus an elaborate system of reservoirs and causeways. Four pyramids rise to around 70 feet and a "great plaza" here has been judged to be one of the civilization's biggest. There are many other constructions, including two ball courts, believed to be associated with ritual sacrifice as well as recreation.

Stelae and other artifacts indicate major occupation during the Early and Late Classic periods, although the Maya were still a force in the area until the early 19th century, when they attacked nearby mahogany camps. La Milpa was "rediscovered" in the 1930s but extensive mapping did not get under way here until 1990, after extensive looting in the 1970s. Thanks to ongoing study by Boston University, a better picture of La Milpa is gradually emerging. In 1996, the unlooted tomb of a Maya ruler called Bird Jaguar, who died in about A.D. 450, was found by archaeologist Norman Hammond. Bird Jaguar was among the first Maya lords to undergo ceremonial burial (the ritual included placement of a cherry-sized jade bead in his mouth).

Getting There/Where to Stay

La Milpa is located in a remote area, about 15 miles east of the Guatemala border, inaccessible by road during wetter months. Most visitors arrive by private plane via the **Gallon Jug** airstrip and stay at **Chan Chich Lodge**, 2-75634, located in the plaza of another Maya ruin. Lodge bookings and archaeological tours are arranged through Programme for Belize offices in Belize City and the U.S. Arrangements should be made as far in advance as possible. (See Chapter 8, Northern Belize.)

Visitors who have obtained a permit from Programme for Belize can drive to the site in about 4 hours from Belize City (during dry weather) via Blue Creek Village in the Orange Walk District. Overnight visitors are housed (with advance permission only) in the dormitory of the Río Bravo Project's field station. Meals and guide services can be arranged there (2-75616).

COROZAL DISTRICT

CERROS AND CAYE COCO

About 20 miles northeast of Cuello, on an uninhabited stretch of Caribbean coastline overlooking Corozal Bay, are the ruins of Cerros (also known as Cerro Maya, or Maya Hill). During the dry season, the site can be reached by a dirt road via Chunox, Progreso, and Copper Bank, but it is more commonly visited by boat from Corozal Town, Sarteneja, or Consejo Shores. On a clear day, especially at sunset, the profile of the ruins is clearly visible from the opposite side of the bay.

Cerros is a late Pre-Classic era (350 B.C. to A.D. 250) complex with virtually no construction after A.D. 100. Experts believe it was an important center of maritime commerce, probably handling much of the seagoing trade headed up the nearby New River to Lamanai and the Río Hondo to the Yucatán. Its early demise may have been caused by a gradual Early Classic period shift in Maya trading patterns in favor of overland routes between the lowland and highland city-states. During this time, inland population centers such as Tikal and Caracol became established. Cerros was later used as a pilgrimage site during the post-classic period.

Although the archaeological reserve is small (53 acres), it includes three large structures that loom above several plazas and a few pyramid-like buildings. The tallest temple is 72 feet and provides a sweeping view across the water. Cerros probably reached its peak around the time of Christ's birth. During this period it appears to have shifted from an economy dependent on fishing, hunting, and farming to one reliant on the importation of pottery, salt, jade, and obsidian by dugout canoe. It was almost certainly linked to the many smaller trading sites on the Belizean cayes and atolls farther south.

Ancient ball courts, quasi-religious tombs, elegant residences, farming terraces, and boat canals have been found at Cerros, indicating that its social structure was once highly developed. Surrounding the site is a human-constructed drainage canal that was nearly a mile long, 20 feet wide, and 6 feet deep. The immediate area has been uninhabited for some time, and part of the original complex is now underwater as a result of a rise in sea level over the last 2,000 years.

Some of the buildings at Cerros display large painted stucco masks, up to 13 feet high, that depict images of humans and animals. Unfortunately, because salt-air speeds erosion and no money is available for restoration, most of the masks have been plastered over to prevent further decay. The pyramid known as **5C**, however, still has four masks: two identified as the sun and Venus, the others unknown. Some feel that the presence of these large friezes demonstrates that the divine Maya elite were in power by the end of the Pre-Classic era, or about A.D. 250.

Not far from Cerros, in Progresso Lagoon, is Caye Coco, a small island with a Post-Classic Maya site now being excavated. Discovered in 1996, the ruin is unusual in that it is only 700 years old, built about four centuries after much of the Maya civilization collapsed. This has already been ranked as one of the largest Post-Classic sites known. Teams from the State University of New York at Albany and Earthwatch Institute are sorting the findings. Contact Earthwatch for information (800-776-0188, www.earthwatch.org).

Fees and Services
Largely unrestored, much of Cerros appears to the casual visitor as little more than a series of low mounds, with only the tallest ceremonial structures hinting at past grandeur. Cerros remains without accommodations or services, and camping is not allowed. A caretaker will collect the $2 entrance fee and provide an informative tour of the ruin.

Getting There
The roundabout road from Corozal Town passes by pastoral lagoons and mestizo fishing villages, but this route cannot be recommended during wet weather.

By easily chartered private boat at the Corozal Town public pier, Cerros is about 5 miles (20 minutes) across Corozal Bay and slightly longer from Sarteneja. Transport can be arranged by Corozal's **Caribbean Village Resort** (4-22725) or boatman **Manuel Hoare**, 4-22744; or Sarteneja boatman **Fernando Alamilla**, 4-32085. Expect to pay at least $75 for the round-trip and be sure to reconfirm any reservations. Because of the ruin's close proximity to the mouth of the New River and adjacent wetlands, insect repellent and long-sleeved clothing are advised.

SANTA RITA
Amateur archaeologist Thomas Gann, a turn-of-the-century British physician living in Corozal, was perhaps the first European to recognize Santa Rita and Cerros as ancient Maya sites. Located directly across the bay from the latter ruin and northeast of the Corozal Town center (now encircled by private homes and businesses), Santa Rita flourished off and on from at least 1800 B.C. until the arrival of the Spanish in the

1530s. Some might convincingly argue that since part of the present-day town is built atop Santa Rita, human habitation has continued here without interruption since at least 18 centuries before the birth of Christ!

Gann theorized that Santa Rita was one of an important series of coastal towns strategically located so that signal fires could be used to send messages up and down the Yucatán peninsula. Although this theory has never been conclusively proven, there is plenty of evidence that Santa Rita was in fact one of the region's most powerful Maya communities and even regained some of its prominence after the disintegration of the civilization as a whole. Its strategic placement within a few miles of the Río Hondo and New River trade routes was one key to its long survival.

Santa Rita's location, on a limestone plateau overlooking the Chetumal and Corozal bays, immediately attracted the attention of Spanish conquistadors, who seized the city-state under the leadership of Alfonso Davila in 1531 from the Maya lord Nachacan. Although they were eventually routed by the Maya, the Spanish simply relocated farther north (at what is now the Mexican city of Chetumal) and managed to sever the remaining trade routes that fueled Santa Rita's prosperity. Within a few years the community was almost completely abandoned. The modern town of Corozal was subsequently established on the ruins' foundations in 1858 by survivors of the famous massacre at Bacalar, Mexico.

Despite its long and impressive history, only one visible structure remains at Santa Rita: a 55-foot-high, partially restored pyramid-shaped tomb, where two important burials were excavated. This site includes several chambers and an offertory niche. One of the rulers found buried here wore a kind of gold earring reserved only for the highest noblemen, another hint of Santa Rita's importance not only as a city, but as a terminus for trade with other rich communities. Not incidentally, the discovery of gold objects here is believed to have prompted the first attack by the Spanish.

Like nearby Cerros, Santa Rita appears to have been an agricultural center long before the seagoing trade boom hit. Once its boats got under way, however, Santa Rita found eager markets for the prized commodities gathered or cultivated nearby, including cacao, vanilla, honey, and spices. Unlike Cerros, Santa Rita thrived through the Classic period and was still stockpiling turquoise and gold from the Aztecs long after more-distant Maya cities had collapsed. Relics from Santa Rita's tombs are said to have included pottery made in the Andes mountains of far-off Peru.

Gann uncovered several burial sites, along with sculptured friezes and stuccoed murals. Much of this material has subsequently been lost—Indians deliberately destroyed six murals in 1900 before Gann could copy them—but some of the doctor's meticulous notes and drawings survive. Among important discoveries made here over a seven-year period beginning in 1979 was a skeleton adorned with jade and mica ornaments. Many of these findings are now held in the Archaeology Vault in Belmopan.

Sadly, since the founding of Corozal Town some 150 years ago, a good part of Santa Rita has been systematically looted, paved over, or built upon. Hundreds of ancient structures and artifacts here have been lost forever.

Getting There/Fees
The last ancient building at Santa Rita, known as **Structure 7**, is an easy walk or car ride from the plaza of Corozal Town. Local residents will be happy to point you in the right direction: Turn left at the Hilltop Bar and follow the road to the Coca-Cola bottling plant. No services are available at the site, although the caretaker (who once lived in one of the tombs) is very helpful and knowledgeable. He collects a $2.50 fee during Santa Rita's hours of admission, 8 a.m. to 5 p.m. daily, except Sunday. Be sure to lock your car, as some visitors have reported thefts during their visit. Women are advised not to visit the site alone.

STANN CREEK DISTRICT

MAYFLOWER
This is a fairly recent "discovery" (1976) about 20 miles east of Dangriga on upper Silk Grass Creek. The remote Classic Maya site is being surveyed by Yale and Tulane Universities. A half-hour hike leads to two impressive waterfalls: **Antelope** and **Hummingbird**. You can hire a local guide to tour the unrestored ruins or arrange a trip through the **Jaguar Reef Lodge** (5-22044) in Hopkins or **Pelican Beach Resort** (800-289-5756) in Dangriga. Among the 16 structures is a pyramid and a 100-foot stone wall.

TOLEDO DISTRICT

LUBAANTUN
Lubaantun is modern Mayan for "place of the fallen rocks," which aptly describes this Late Classic ceremonial center, noted for an unusual style of construction that is unique to southern Belize. The large pyramids and residences observed here are made of crystalline limestone blocks with no

Lubaantun

Belize Tourist Board

visible mortar binding them together, not unlike constructions by the Inca civilization in the high Andes of Peru and Ecuador. This means that every hand-cut stone was carefully measured and shaped to fit together with the adjoining stone. (Remember, the Maya had no stone tools and used the wheel only in toys.) The effect of their masterful dressed stonework looks a bit like marble. Some speculate that the Maya had destroyed the nearby forest, making it impossible to fuel the high-temperature limestone kilns needed to created mortar. The forest long ago renewed itself, and today's Lubaantun visitors include pumas, ocelots, deer, coatimundi, and parrots.

Unlike most other Maya ceremonial sites, the buildings that were then placed on top of these pyramids were made from perishable materials, such as tree limbs and palm fronds, and obviously no longer remain. We can only guess at what they looked like.

The austerity of this site—Lubaantun is now essentially a stone acropolis—is reminiscent of Quiriguá, located about 100 miles away in southeast Guatemala, and there may have been close contact between the two city-states. Curiously, Lubaantun has yielded impressive stone architecture, but virtually no carved stone stelae and only a handful of painted pottery vessels. Yet nearby **Nim Li Punit** and **Uxbenka** have plenty of sculpted rock monuments but no large masonry structures. This suggests to some authorities that a diverse social organization once prevailed in this area and that each site served a distinct purpose.

At Lubaantun, 11 large pyramid-platform structures are built around five main plazas and three ball courts. The tallest of the pyramids rises 45 feet above the jungle. There are 13 smaller plazas and a number of other structures, including a large stadium that may have been used for the observation of sacred ceremonies. Several burial tombs have reportedly been found here as well.

It is believed that carvings and other types of building decorations commonly fashioned out of stone at other Maya sites were made out of wood from Lubaantun, located in one of the most rain-soaked and densely forested corners of Belize. One theory persists that Lubaantun was an important religious, administrative, political, and commercial center, yet only for a brief time—two centuries at most, but perhaps as few as 20 years. No one knows what led to abandonment around A.D. 900, or why the hilltop site was not leveled before construction began, in the traditional manner. Instead, workers simply filled in gaps with stones and mortar.

It is thought that the greatest wealth of Lubaantun came from the harvest and trade of wild cacao—the modern source of chocolate—which was so highly prized by the Maya that they used it as a form of currency. The area is still considered prime cacao-growing country, and the 1970 discovery of a ceramic musician wearing a cacao-pod pendant lends credence to the notion that the prized beans were grown here in the eighth century. Cacao, used to make a drink prized by Maya royalty, was probably traded for jade and obsidian.

The best-known discovery at Lubaantun is the remarkable **Crystal Skull,** supposedly unearthed in 1926 by Anna Mitchell-Hedges (daughter of archaeologist F. A. Mitchell-Hedges) on her seventeenth birthday. This artifact demonstrates superb artistry and workmanship; it is perfectly carved from an 8-inch cube of pure rock crystal and shows virtually no tool marks. The treasure appears to have been modeled after a specific human head, but the identity of that individual—and the Crystal Skull's significance—remains unknown. Some believe the skull was brought from somewhere else for a "staged" birthday discovery at Lubaantun; others are convinced it is linked to the lost continent of Atlantis. Archaeologist Norman Hammond believes the skull is not a Maya creation. The relic remains in Canada and its aged owner reaffirmed during a 1996 visit to Lubaantun that she has no intention of returning it to Belize.

Getting There

Lubaantun perches on a ridge immediately north of the Columbia River, about 1.5 miles by dirt road past the village of San Pedro Columbia (turn right at the church and left after you cross the river bridge). This route is about a 45-minute walk. A steep short-cut path leads to Lubaantun from the banks of the Columbia; ask one of the local boys to show you the way. Yet another option is taking the public bus (which runs Monday, Wednesday, Friday, and Saturday) to San Miguel to the Lubaantun turnoff, which is marked by a directional sign to the ruins. The last mile of road is slippery when wet.

Accommodations and Services

Accommodations and service are available in San Pedro Columbia through both the "indigenous experience" homestay and guest house program (see Chapter 9, Southern Belize, for details). The operators of **Dem Dat's Doin'**, Alfredo and Yvonne Villoria, rent a room at their San Pedro permaculture farm by advance arrangement. You can also overnight at **Fallen Stones Jungle Lodge** (1.5 miles away) or **San Antonio Village** (5 miles distant). Camping at the ruin is not allowed.

Several hotels and travel agencies in the Toledo and Stann Creek districts arrange tours to Lubaantun and other nearby Maya ruins. There are restrooms and a picnic area here but no drinking water, food, or literature. The setting is peaceful and birds abound. A Maya caretaker, **Santiago Coc**, answers questions and collects the $1.50 entrance fee. Santiago is very knowledgeable, having worked with archaeologists here in 1970.

NIM LI PUNIT

Located about 25 miles north of Punta Gorda off the Southern Highway, this Late Classic ceremonial center remained hidden from outsiders until oilworkers stumbled upon it in the early 1970s. Since then, excavations have revealed 25 stelae, at least eight of which are carved, including the tallest (at 31 feet) carved stone monument in Belize. The site's name is Maya for "big hat" and refers to a headdress-adorned figure on the tallest stela.

Archaeologists believe Nim Li Punit may have been affiliated with nearby Lubaantun, which flourished around the same time and is architecturally similar. Digging did not start here until 1983, after the site had been badly looted. Nevertheless, an impressive stele and royal tomb were uncovered in 1986. UCLA archaeologist Richard Leventhal continues to oversee excavations.

There are several tall structures (up to 40 feet high) around two plazas and the remains of a fairly large settlement. More than two dozen monuments have been identified at Nim Li Punit, many of an unusually long and low design. One building, for example, is only 9 feet high but 215 feet long. It is believed that the site may have been a funerary cult center that acted as a kind of service community to the local elite, who were probably headquartered in Lubaantun. The true function of Nim Li Punit and its relation to other Maya centers remains unclear.

Although it is small, Nim Li Punit has hieroglyphic texts and many interesting carvings on its ceremonial stelae. As is the case at many Maya sites, there is an enormous ceiba tree (next to the caretaker's hut) and many flowering plants. The friendly resident caretaker, **Placido Pec**, will answer questions, direct you to the guest registry, and collect the $1.50 entrance fee.

Getting There/Services
Nim Li Punit is about ½-mile northeast of the Southern Highway at Mile 75 near the Maya village of Indian Creek. It is not directly accessible by public transportation, although daily Z-Line and James Line buses pass by on their way to and from Punta Gorda and Dangriga (the drivers will pick you up and let you off here).

A well-marked track leads visitors to the site from the highway in about 20 minutes. The trailhead is not far from a handicrafts stand and Whitney's Grocery Store (if you pass Whitney's Lumber Mill, heading south, you've gone too far). The nearest accommodations are in Silver Creek and Big Falls. I recommend **Rav's Guest House**, next to one of the only known hot springs in Belize. You can also stay in Punta Gorda (25 miles south), San Antonio (10 miles south), or one of the Maya villages participating in the regional guest house and homestay programs. Several hotels and tour operators in the region make trips here, often in combination with Lubaantun. A new lodge was slated to open near Nim Li Punit in the fall of 1999.

The ruins overlook a mixture of second-growth jungle and milpa plots. Local Maya use the nearby streams to bathe and are friendly to tourists, sometimes approaching them with handicrafts for sale. Except for a small sun/rain shelter, there are no facilities at Nim Li Punit. (See Chapter 9, Southern Belize.)

UXBENKA
Local Maya have known about Uxbenka—"the old place" in their local dialect, also spelled "Uxbentún"—for centuries. But the outside world only learned officially of the small site's existence in 1984, when reports of looting filtered back to Belmopan. On further investigation, archaeologists learned that indeed this was a very ancient settlement and, yes, parts of it were being carted off for private sale.

One of the seven carved stelae found here dates from the Early Classic period, the earliest archaeological date yet recorded in southern Belize, but most of the sculpted stones are too badly eroded to read. An additional 13 uncarved stelae have been unearthed at Uxbenka, which also features a couple of unexcavated pyramids and a small plaza, plus some overgrown structural mounds. There's been virtually no restoration work here and, in truth, there's not much for the casual visitor to see.

The site perches on a ridge overlooking the foothills and valleys of the Maya Mountains. The nearby hillsides have been faced with cut terrace stones, a form of agricultural masonry not found outside the Toledo District. The Uxbenka caretaker lives nearby in Santa Cruz Village and may or may not be present when you visit. A map of the ruins was produced with help from the British Army, but you'll have to ask around in order to find a copy.

Getting There
Uxbenka is on the outskirts of Santa Cruz Village, about 3 miles west of San Antonio and 20 miles from Punta Gorda. Besides private vehicle, you can get here on the Wednesday/Saturday bus that shuttles between Punta Gorda and Pueblo Viejo, or take the P.G. bus to San Antonio and hitch a ride (or walk) the rest of the way. Other transportation for visitors is by arranged tour from Punta Gorda or via the supply trucks that come through the area once or twice a week. There is a guest house in San Antonio and overnight accommodations can be arranged with Maya families in Santa Cruz. Camping is not permitted.

Nearby Attractions
Be sure to check out the soothing waterfall and swimming hole just east of Santa Cruz. Several caves are also worth visiting in the hills to the north, near San José Village. A local guide is helpful in finding these destinations.

GUATEMALA

TIKAL
The famous ancient Maya ruin of Tikal is located about 50 miles (2 to 3 hours) northwest of the Belize border in Guatemala. Set in a lush high-canopy tropical deciduous forest, the site encompasses at least 3,000 buildings, including a handful of impressively tall temples that loom above the forest. At its peak some 1,500 years ago, Tikal was home to an estimated 100,000 Maya. Yet this city-state was virtually forgotten by the outside world until its "rediscovery" in 1848. Because it is so close to Belize, many travelers make a side trip to Tikal, which is one of the most impressive in the entire Maya world. For a detailed discussion of Tikal and other nearby ruins, see the author's *Guatemala: Adventures in Nature*, (Santa Fe, N.M.: John Muir Publications).

Getting There
If traveling to Tikal on your own, you can obtain Guatemalan visas and/or tourist cards either in Belize City or at the frontier, and formalities at the

J.W. Smith

The plaza at Tikal

border are straightforward. (If you travel from Belize to Tikal in a package tour, paperwork and fees are usually taken care of by the operator.) The border is open daily from 8 a.m. to noon and 2 p.m. to 6 p.m.; crossing during off-hours is sometimes possible for an extra fee. Belize's land-border entry tax is 75 cents.

The international boundary runs along the east bank of the Mopán River between the towns of Melchor de Mencos, Guatemala, and Benque Viejo, Belize. If you are driving a vehicle, be sure to have your registration and insurance papers in order, and expect to pay a few dollars to have the car fumigated with insecticide on the Guatemalan side (this is required by law and is one reason almost no Belizean companies allow their rental cars to enter Guatemala).

Bus passengers usually have to stop on the Belize side of the crossing and walk or take a taxi a few hundred yards into Melchor de Mencos, where Guatemalan buses (about five a day) pick up westbound passengers. The same thing happens going the opposite direction, although there are some bus companies that drive their vehicles in both countries. Belizean taxi drivers often intercept passengers as they descend from buses on the Guatemala side and take them all the way to San Ignacio, for a fee of about $7 per traveler. Melchor's Palace Hotel operates a $20 round-trip shuttle to Tikal, leaving at 10 a.m. and returning about 6 p.m.

Another moderately priced option is to take a taxi (about $15 round-trip) from San Ignacio to the border and ask around for a reputable van driver to Tikal (about $50 round-trip).

Corruption of border officials has long been a problem at Guatemalan border crossings and travelers continue to complain about being asked to pay non-existent "taxes" for passing in and out of Guatemala. A polite request for a detailed receipt or outright refusal to pay such *mordidas* is sometimes effective, but not always practical. The INGUAT (Guatemala Tourist Commission) office at the Flores/Santa Elena airport encourages tourists to file formal complaints about border bribes and corrupt officials are sometimes removed as a result. Meanwhile, the Belize government sometimes assesses a $3.75 "protected areas tax" as you leave the country, providing funds for worthy conservation activities.

Services
If you simply want a quick glimpse of Guatemalan life, Melchor de Mencos is the place to find it. There is a colorful market where handicrafts are sold and a bank where Belize dollars can be exchanged for quetzales (moneychangers at the border offer slightly better rates). The hotels are inexpensive, and several offer reasonably priced tours to local Maya ruins, including Tikal. Try the **Hotel Palace** on the Mopán River, which has a restaurant, a travel service, and a car rental agency. Operator Marco Gross also owns the **Arts & Crafts of Central America** store in San Ignacio, 9-22823, where reservations for the Melchor Palace can be made. Another option is the **Hotel Palque**, also on the river.

The entrance to **Tikal National Park** is northwest of Melchor de Mencos via 2 hours of poor road, then a half-hour of paved surface to the ruins themselves. The $10 admission fee to Tikal National Park is good for the date of entry only. Because the site is so large, a good guidebook and/or map greatly enhances the experience. Well-informed, English-speaking Guatemalan guides can be hired at the site (by law, Belizean guides are not allowed to escort visitors through the ruins).

You'll need two days to take in the majority of structures here, but the highlights can be seen in a few hours. Be sure to spend some time in Tikal's **Silvanus G. Morley Archaeological Museum** ($3 admission), where many artifacts recovered by researchers are on permanent display, including relics from a ruler's tomb.

Travel Tips
En route to the park, you may be stopped by the Guatemalan military and asked to show your passport or other identification. The political situation in Guatemala is improving, but parts of the Petén wilderness are still controlled by outlaws. There are reports of tourists being robbed by gunmen

en route to Tikal from Belize, therefore you should take only as much money as you expect to need during your visit. Better yet, fly from Belize City (if you can afford it).

As tourism has increased in Belize, the number of alternative ways for getting to Tikal has also increased. Several scheduled flights are offered daily between Belize City and Flores/Santa Elena (about 40 miles south of the ruins) by Maya Island Air, Aerovías, and Aviateca. Expect to pay about $125 round-trip. Charters and day trips can also be arranged from Belize City and San Pedro for around $250 and up. From the Flores/ Santa Elena airport there are frequent minibuses to Tikal, or a car can be rented for the short drive.

Both Novelo's and Batty's bus services carry passengers from Belize City to Melchor de Mencos, dropping passengers there for connections to Tikal and/or Flores. If you are heading directly to Tikal you will need to get off at El Cruce, an intersection about 20 miles south of the ruins (and the location of a nice Maya site called **Ixlú**). From there you can take a public bus or hitch the rest of the way, but there is a risk of getting stranded. Bus schedules being what they are, you will probably need to spend a night in Flores or Santa Elena to catch the early morning public bus or a private minibus to the ruins.

Package Tours and Places to Stay

The most popular, and in many respects the easiest, way to visit Tikal from Belize is as part of a package tour. Most of the Cayo lodges arrange such trips (by van or airplane) on a weekly or even daily basis, often including the services of a knowledgeable guide. Similar tours can be arranged from Belize City, San Pedro, and other towns. Prices for package tours of Tikal vary, depending on the number of persons traveling and the duration of the trip. Expect to pay at least $80 per person, however, depending on the size of your group. Bear in mind that a one-day overland round-trip means being inside a vehicle for 5 hours or more.

Overnight visits require lodging and meals in Flores, Santa Elena, or Tikal National Park. Popular hotels in greater Flores include the **Petén**, **Posada Tayasal**, **San Juan**, and **Itzá**. Some of these places are very picturesque, situated beside the large lake that dominates this Spanish colonial town, built on the site of an ancient Maya city. Also recommended is the modern and luxurious (but environmentally friendly) **Hotel Camino Real** (800-228-3000), located about 25 minutes (15 miles) west of Tikal on the eastern shore of **Lake Petén Itzá**. This resort has many amenities, including a gift shop and pool.

There are three basic guest houses (all about $60) at Tikal National Park: the **Jaguar Inn** (502-926-0002), the **Jungle Lodge** (502-476-8775), and the **Tikal Inn** (502-926-0065). A much less expensive ($22) option is

Don David's Bungalows, about 2 miles north of El Cruce, on the main road to Tikal. American expatriate David Kutin and his family run this simple complex, which has no electricity but serves excellent meals. Call the community phone (502-926-0269) for reservations. Or try **La Mansion del Pajaro Serpiente** at El Cruce ($45, 502-926-0065). Rates start at about $40 a night. There is also one campground, which charges about $6 a night for tent, hammock space, or overnight parking. Showers and cooking facilities are included in the fee. Water is scarce, so bring your own. Several undistinguished restaurants and overpriced gift shops are also near the Tikal ruins. There is a post office, but no telephone, and electricity is only produced by generators (turned off from 10 p.m. to 6 a.m.). An overnight visit to the park is highly recommended because of the tremendous amount of wildlife, including monkeys, deer, foxes, agoutis, and cats. Birders will be particularly rewarded. Because the area has been protected since the mid-1950s, many of the animals show little or no fear of humans.

APPENDIX A
TRAVEL BASICS

BELIZE BASICS

If you have already spent time in Mexico or Central America, you're in for some surprises when you first visit Belize. First of all, almost everybody speaks English. A linguistic island in a sea of Spanish and Native American dialects, much of Belize looks and feels more like the relaxed, post-Colonial British Caribbean than Latin America. And for travelers accustomed to the extremes of poverty, overcrowding, corruption, and militarism that are typical of some destinations, the comparative tranquillity and prosperity of Belize will come as a welcome change. Its singular status as the only non-Spanish-speaking nation between Mexico's Río Grande and South America's Guyana explains some of Belize's eccentricities.

Reservations for airline tickets and hotel rooms are often needed and recommended during the "high season" in Belize, which begins just before Christmas and continues through April. It's customary to provide a first-night's payment or a credit card number to hold a room reservation.

A growing number of travel agents specialize in Belize and most of the country's larger tourism businesses can easily be reached by telephone, fax, e-mail, or Web site.

Climate

As a subtropical country that is close enough to North America to be subject to its seasonal air currents, Belize has a warm and wet summer/fall (June through November) followed by relatively cool and dry winter/spring (December through April). There is often also a dry spell in August. The driest months are February and March, although rain can (and does) fall at any time of the year. Belize is hottest in April and May. Humidity is fairly high no matter what the season. Trade winds tend to keep things less sticky along the coast, although this area is subject to sudden squalls. Winds are generally calm in midsummer (except for those pesky hurricanes).

Most visitors prefer to travel to Belize in the Northern Hemisphere's winter months. Daytime coastal temperatures during this period are in the 70s and 80s (20°-to-30°C). Even during summer months, shade temperatures seldom rise above 90 degrees F (38°C). During the "cold" spells of December and January, the thermometer sometimes falls below 55 degrees F (13°C).

Extremes are greater inland, even dropping into the low 40s in the highlands. The average temperature throughout the year is 79 degrees F. Water temperatures along the barrier reef range from the mid-70s to mid-80s.

Rainfall in Belize increases from north to south. About 50 inches a year falls near the Mexican border in Corozal, 65 inches in Belize City and the Cayo District, 95 inches in Dangriga, and 120 inches around Punta Gorda, across the Bay of Honduras from Guatemala.

Hurricanes are rare but can threaten Belize at any time between June and November. After Belize City was twice destroyed by severe storms earlier this century, a warning system was set up, and hurricane shelters were established throughout the country. You should be warned well in advance if a potentially destructive storm is expected in Belize, which seems to happen once every 15 years or so. The last big hurricane in the area, Mitch, did only minor damage in October 1998.

Cuisine

There are relatively few distinctive Belizean dishes, which is why you've probably never heard of any. The most popular meal by far is rice and beans, with or without stewed chicken and frequently spiced by habañero pepper sauce. A typical Belize breakfast might include fried jacks, a puffed pastry similar to a Mexican sopaipilla that is often smothered with tropical fruit jam, and johnny cakes, a sweet pancake. The best local recipes are compiled in the *Belize Hospital Auxiliary Cookbook*, sold at local bookstores.

Currency, Banks, and Credit Cards

Although the U.S. dollar is widely accepted—particularly on Ambergris Caye—the preferred currency is the Belize dollar, stabilized at a fixed exchange rate of $2 Belizean to $1 U.S. Coinages from 1 to 25 cents are in use.

The best rates of exchange for foreign currencies are at the borders, with Mexican pesos sometimes obtaining an especially good rate. Belizean banks charge 2 percent for the exchange of foreign currency or traveler's checks, so it may be preferable to make such transactions with merchants, hotels, or individuals, who will almost always make a straight two-for-one swap for U.S. dollars.

The Belize Bank and Barclays, among others, will draft cash on VISA and MasterCard accounts, for a fee. A maximum of $200 may be withdrawn in cash, with any higher amounts in traveler's checks (you may be asked to show your onward ticket). There are a limited number of ATMs in Belize and as of early 1999 only those maintained by the Scotia and Barclays banks would accept foreign-issued cards. Not all cards may work in these ATMs, however, and visitors should not depend on using such machines for all their cash. Money can be telexed to the larger banks in

Belize. There is no black market, as financial rates are generally uniform from one institution to the next.

All banks are open Monday through Thursday from 8:00 a.m. to 1:00 p.m. and reopen from 3:00 p.m. to 6:00 p.m. on Friday. Atlantic Bank is open Saturday mornings. After closing time, moneychangers can often be found in the vicinity of major banks. They offer fair exchange rates for most major currencies. Credit cards have long been welcome in the larger hotels and are becoming increasingly acceptable among tour operators and other businesses that cater to foreigners. The American Express agent is Global Travel, 41 Albert Street, Belize City (2-77185).

Electrical Current

Electrical current is the same in Belize as in the U.S. and Canada: 110 volts A.C./60 cycles.

Holidays, Festivals, and Business Hours

Normal business hours are 8:00 a.m. to noon and 1:00 p.m. to 5:00 p.m. Some stores are open during the morning only on Wednesday and Saturday, or evenings from 7:00 to 9:00. Few establishments open on Sundays, and regular bus and airline schedules may be canceled or curtailed. Banks, shops, and government offices may be closed on the following national holidays:

> New Year's Day–January 1
> Baron Bliss Day–March 9
> Good Friday–date varies
> Holy Saturday–date varies
> Easter–date varies
> Easter Monday–date varies
> Labor Day–May 1
> Commonwealth Day–May 24
> National (St. George's Caye) Day–September 10
> Independence Day–September 21
> Pan American (Columbus) Day–October 12
> Garifuna (Settlement) Day–November 19
> Christmas Day–December 25
> Boxing Day–December 26

A number of special events and annual festivals take place in Belize. Among the more interesting are the Baron Bliss Regatta (March 8), Crooked Tree Cashew Festival (early May), Caye Caulker Coconut Festival (late May), San Pedro Costa Maya Festival (midsummer), Belize City Festival Grand Market (mid-September), and Hike & Bike for the Rainforest (a countrywide athletic competition in late October that benefits environmental conservation).

Internet Information about Belize

Belizean hotels, outfitters, travel agencies, car rental companies, realtors, hot sauce manufacturers, conservation groups, dive shops, restaurants, boat charter companies, and even the Belize Zoo are now accessible online. Many Belizean businesses are reachable via e-mail in the format [businessname]@btl.net.

You can access the on-line edition of the excellent *Belize First* magazine at www.turq.com/belizefirst/. Audio from **LOVE-FM**, a popular Belize radio station, can be heard at www.bze.net/lovefm/. Newspapers with on-line editions include *The Reporter, Amandala,* and *San Pedro Sun.*

The most popular Web sites for general information about Belize include **Belize by Naturalight** (www.belizenet.com), **You Better Belize It** and **Belize Tourism Industry Association** (www.belizeit.com), **Belize Business Community** (www.belizebusiness.com), and **Belize Online** (www. belize.com). For information about Ambergris Caye and its outdoor recreation opportunities, check out www.ambergriscaye.com. The "forum" feature of belizenet.com is particularly helpful for travelers, hosting an ongoing question-and-answer exchange about tourism in Belize. (See Appendix B for other sites).

Language

English is the mode of instruction in all Belizean schools and is the official language of government and commerce. Spanish is widely spoken (many of the nation's newest immigrants speak little or no English) and about one-third of the people speak a Creole dialect not unlike the accented patois of Jamaica and other former British colonies of the Caribbean.

An estimated 60 percent of the population is bilingual (mostly Spanish/ English) and at least 40 percent regard Spanish as their mother tongue. The 6 percent of Belizeans identified as Garifuna speak their own language, as do the 10 percent who are Maya (mostly Mopán, Kekchí, or Yucatec). Most of the country's 6,000 Mennonites converse in an archaic Low German dialect, although most of the men (and a smaller percentage of the women) speak English and many speak Spanish.

Mail Service

Mail service is inexpensive and reliable. Cards or letters sent from Belize usually reach overseas destinations within a week (U.S. and Canada) or two (Europe, Asia, Australia). Stamps are available at many large hotels. Belize is known for its beautiful postage stamps, many of which depict the country's flora and fauna. A special department for stamp collectors is located at the main post office in Belize City. Post offices generally are open 8–5 weekdays.

Taxes and Tipping

In larger hotels and restaurants, a service charge is sometimes added to the bill. If not, tips are based on the quality of service, usually ranging from five to 10 percent, although many Belizeans do not tip at all in restaurants, and only Americans seem to tip 15 percent. Taxi drivers are tipped at the discretion of the individual, but the practice is less common than in the U.S., since taxi fares are fixed. Some hotels add a service charge of between 5 and 10 percent to your bill. If yours does not, it's polite to leave about $1 per day for housekeepers. Tour, snorkel, dive, and fishing guides expect a tip, which will vary depending on the length and type of trip.

In April 1999, the 7 percent government room tax was dropped for hotels with five rooms or less and the 15 percent value added tax was replaced by a 7 percent national sales tax. There was speculation that additional tax cuts would be forthcoming.

Telephone Service

In most large towns there is a Belize Telephone Ltd. (BTL) long-distance office where operator-assisted calls can be made. The BTL office in Belize City (1 Church St.) offers fax, telex, telegraph, and telegram service (8:00 a.m. to 9:00 p.m. Monday through Saturday). Some of the island and jungle lodges can be reached only by shortwave radio or radio-telephone, which can be problematic. Keep trying—and remember that your conversation is often being overhead by others who belong to this "party line" system.

Because public and hotel room telephones are a rarity in Belize, many travelers find it convenient to use cellular telephones. These are rented by the government telephone monopoly, BTL, for about $4.50 per day, plus a security deposit and use charges. A credit card and passport are required from foreigners who wish to set up a temporary account. Cell coverage includes Ambergris Caye and much of the area along the Northern, Southern, and Western Highways. Contact BTL at 27-7960 or sales@btl.net. At the international airport, BTL has a cell-phone rental kiosk as you exit customs.

Direct-dial calls to and from Belize are not difficult—remember to always dial 011 from the U.S. to get an overseas circuit. Belize's international country code is 501, followed by a one- or two-digit region code that varies with each district. When calling direct from the United States or Canada, dial 011-501, drop the first zero from the local number, then dial the remaining numbers. Within the country, it is sometimes necessary to dial a zero before the local number and occasionally you need only the last four digits. Remember, toll-free numbers in Canada and the U.S. cannot be accessed from overseas telephones. Most hotels are long-distance calls at a fixed rate.

Time Zone

Belize follows Central Standard Time. Daylight savings time is not observed.

Children and Families

Belize gets mixed reviews as a vacation spot for families. Many children are in heaven as long as they have cable TV, a swimming pool, and a hamburger with fries. Yes, such amenities are available in Belize, but at a price that may go beyond the range of many visitors. In Belize it is common for hotels to count children as extra adults in room and meal rates, although those under 10 sometimes are charged half-price. The same applies to local airlines and tour operators. In addition, children are often turned off by Belizean food (stewed chicken, beans, and rice) and unenthusiastic about Maya ruins and jungle treks. On the other hand, many kids rave about the Belize Zoo, nature tours (notably nighttime excursions that spotlight crocodiles), butterfly farms, canoe rides, cave tubing, sailing, and snorkeling.

WHAT TO BRING

Visitors to Belize are allowed to bring virtually anything they might reasonably be expected to need during their stay, including fishing gear and diving equipment. Light, informal clothing is recommended. Firearms are prohibited without prior clearance. Pets are allowed into the country only with proof of rabies vaccination and a certificate of good health signed by a veterinarian. Up to 200 cigarettes, 20 ounces of liquor, and one bottle of perfume may be brought in duty-free.

In contrast to most other Central American countries, Belize is a relatively expensive country to visit. Almost everything, including food, is imported and subject to substantial duty and/or value-added taxes. Therefore, it's best to bring along all the clothing, equipment, film, books, maps, diapers, and toiletries you think you'll need. If not, you can expect to pay much more than you would at home for such items, provided they are available. If you wish to make friends among the locals, bring along gifts of fishhooks and small tackle items for men, cosmetics for women, books and small toys (e.g., balloons, pens, and magnifying glasses) for children.

No matter where you travel in Belize, you'll want to carry insect repellent, sunscreen, a hat, and drinking water. It's also advisable to have an old pair of tennis shoes or Reefwalkers if you'll be on the beach and reef.

ENTRY AND EXIT REQUIREMENTS

Required for entry:
•passport
•sufficient funds (currently $50 per day minimum), and
•ticket out of the country

In recent years, the last two requirements (sufficient funds and a ticket out of the country) have not been strictly enforced, although there are occasional reports of authorities turning away individuals whose appearance was deemed unsavory and/or who carried less than $30 per day for the duration of their intended visit. Don't be surprised if an immigration or customs official asks exactly where you will be staying and precisely how much cash you are carrying, especially if you happen to be a long-haired backpacker. For stays longer than 30 days, an extension must be obtained (for a $12.50-per-month fee) from the Immigration Office at 115 Barracks Road in Belize City (822-6111).

Visas

Visas (not required for citizens of the U.S., Canada, Mexico, and most members of the EEC), may not be purchased at the border, although they can be obtained for $10 from the Belizean consulate in Chetumal, Mexico, just north of the international crossing. These documents can also be arranged at Belizean embassies in Mexico City, Washington, D.C., and other capitals, and, in some instances, through British consulates. Free transit visas are available at the border for periods of 24 or 48 hours, and visas are sometimes not needed if the visitor has an onward ticket in hand.

If visiting other countries after leaving Belize, travelers should obtain visas before arriving in Belize. Guatemala now has both an embassy and a consulate in Belize, for visitors needing a Guatemalan visa or tourist card.

Tourist Permits

Tourists are initially granted 14- or 30-day permits to visit Belize, which can be renewed for up to six months. (After six months, travelers must exit the country for at least 24 hours before returning.) As tourists, visitors may not do any kind of work (paid or unpaid) without first obtaining a permit from the Department of Labor. With domestic unemployment hovering around 20 percent, permission is not easily obtained. Work permits are valid for one year and costs range from $5 to $300 (depending on occupation).

HEALTH AND SAFETY

Immunization and Health Precautions

No immunizations are required for entry, and public health standards in Belize are generally good.

Tropical diseases are reasonably well-controlled in Belize, but mosquito-borne malaria and dengue fever are still reported. Yellow fever, cholera, and tuberculosis are rare but do occur. The cautious traveler who plans to spend extended time in the interior may want to take antimalarial drugs or obtain hepatitis A and B vaccinations, as well as oral typhoid immunization, tetanus inoculation, and a tetanus booster (usually combined with diphtheria). Ask your physician for advice or call the Center for Disease Control's "traveler hot line" at (404) 332-4559, www.cdc.gov. As of 1999, there were no reports of chloroquine-resistant strains of malaria in Belize, as there are in parts of South America and other continents. Outpatient medical attention in Belize is free at government clinics and hospitals, and there are a number of private physicians' offices throughout the country. A brand-new hospital opened in 1994 in Belize City.

The most common health problem among travelers is diarrhea, usually caused by unfamiliar intestinal bacteria and treatable with Pepto Bismol (or any medication containing bismuth), Bactrim, Cipro, or Doxycycline. If symptoms worsen or persist, see a doctor (and always drink plenty of non-contaminated water).

Since well-stocked Belizean pharmacies are sometimes hard to find, bring along your regular medications and items such as contact lens solutions or prescription eyeglasses.

Outdoor pests such as mosquitoes and biting flies are common, especially during the rainy season, and it is advisable to carry repellent at all times: Cutter's, Jungle Juice, Repel, and other preparations with a 15 percent or more DEET content. Some travelers report excellent results from Avon Skin-So-Soft lotion, citronella oil, and the consumption of garlic. Rubbing alcohol will soothe itching. Since most insects cannot fly well in a breeze, a fan is also useful. Permethrin applied to netting and clothes discourages all biting insects.

Snakes are found in much of Belize, so be careful when hiking or walking off the road. Only nine of the country's 54 snake species have enough venom to seriously threaten a human, but the roster includes the deadly tommygoff (also called fer-de-lance), as well as several varieties of coral snakes and rattlers. Scorpions, spiders, ticks, biting flies, and carnivorous ants are also fairly common.

At the seaside, on the reef and cayes, the most common problems are overexposure to the sun, scratches from sharp coral or sea urchins, and the annoying bites of such otherwise harmless flying insects as no-see-ums and sand fleas. Stepping on stingrays can cause extremely painful wounds that are potentially deadly if not treated. The scorpion fish and jellyfish are an infrequent hazard. Barracuda, eels, and sharks are common in these waters (especially the non-aggressive lemon and nurse sharks) but almost never attack humans unless provoked or drawn by bleeding wounds, including those of speared fish. Do not touch these animals—it may trigger an aggressive response.

Fair-skinned visitors should wear shirts when snorkeling (to protect their backs from sunburn) and water-resistant sunscreen. Bring along a hat, a long-sleeved cotton shirt, cotton trousers, and sunglasses for midday hours.

An altogether different sort of hazard is posed by powerboats. Several tourists have been badly injured and even killed in recent years while swimming in areas where fast-moving boats regularly travel. The most dangerous areas are off Ambergris Caye near San Pedro and in or near the "split" at Caye Caulker. Before you swim, dive, or snorkel, ask about powerboat hazards and stick to designated areas.

Food and Drinking Water Safety

Public water supplies in most large communities are chlorinated, although there have been some reports of tap water contamination. Many travelers take the added precaution of drinking only bottled water and/or other beverages. A drop of iodine or bleach can be added to each liter of local water for purification, although stronger chemical solutions such as Bactrim and Metronidazole may be needed to kill some parasites and especially virulent bacteria.

Food is generally safe in established hotels and restaurants. As in any underdeveloped country, some risk is involved in eating at roadside stands and sidewalk vendors, particularly where unrefrigerated meat, uncooked fish, and unwashed fruits or vegetables are concerned. Bottled drinks are safe.

Remember that cooking seafood does not destroy ciguatera toxin, which has been occasionally found in barracuda in Belize. Symptoms range from nausea and numbness to diarrhea and heart arrhythmia. Check locally about any reports of ciguatera poisoning, which also may occur in large red snapper, hogfish, and grouper.

Crime and Drug Issues

Several urban centers, notably Belize City and Orange Walk Town, have acquired reputations as being "unsafe" and even downright inhospitable to tourists. In each of these communities, there are persistent reports of street crime in certain neighborhoods and some degree of drug trafficking. Production of marijuana and transshipment of cocaine are big businesses in Belize, despite aggressive attempts by the United States, British, and Belize governments to squelch such illicit activity. Visitors should inquire before setting out on foot into areas that seem questionable, particularly at night. In Belize City, I recommend you go with a friend and take taxis. The most common harassment is strictly verbal, and the perpetrators will usually leave you alone if you ignore them, politely turn down their solicitation, or banter good-naturedly. Anything beyond this should be reported to the authorities immediately.

As in many other countries, it is a good idea to keep your expensive jewelry, flashy watches, and other signs of wealth at home. Tote your camera only when you plan to use it. Carry money and important documents in a money belt hidden under your clothes. Keep only as much cash in your wallet or purse as you expect to spend that particular day. Make sure you have a duplicate of valuable papers (including front pages of your passport) and keep a list of traveler's check identification numbers separate from the originals. It's also prudent to leave a copy of these items with a friend or relative back home. When going to Tikal, take as few valuables as possible.

Immediately report any theft to local police and get a written report from them. To reach the police, dial 911. For the fire department or am bulance service in Belize, dial 90. The U.S. State Department is a good source of up-to-date information about safety conditions in Belize and other foreign countries; contact the Office of Overseas Services at (202) 647-5225.

TRANSPORTATION

Arriving by Air

Phillip Goldson International Airport is at Ladyville, about 20 miles northwest of Belize City. The airport was expanded in 1998 and now has separate sections for international and domestic service. As this book went to press, there was talk that the Municipal Airport, the antiquated Belize City facility that previously handled most domestic traffic, would be closed. Immigration and customs procedures at the international terminal are straightforward and relatively efficient: You can expect to be on your way within about 30 minutes. There is a money exchange desk at the airport, along with a few gift shops, a duty-free store, cell-phone rental kiosk, and a restaurant. Taxi rates are regulated by the government and tipping is not customary: the cost is $15 ($20 for a heavy luggage or passenger load). Taxis are identified by their green license plates. A few hotels arrange private pick-up service, but there are no shuttle buses or public buses. Cars can be rented at the airport or at offices in Belize City. If you get stranded, the Embassy Hotel (adjacent to the parking lot) rents rooms for $30 to $60, double-occupancy.

When leaving the country, bear in mind that Belize bans the export of marine curios, turtles, and turtle products, as well as such national treasures as Maya artifacts and endangered plants or animals. A maximum of 20 pounds of fish may be taken out of the country, but visitors are urged to either release their catches or consume them while in Belize.

Anyone tempted to fly out of Belize with cocaine or other illegal drugs should be aware that baggage inspections are quite thorough, and even a small amount of marijuana can yield a stiff fine and/or jail term.

A $15 departure tax/screening charge must be paid for all international air departures (either in U.S. or Belizean dollars); if the individual has spent less than 24 hours in the country, there is no fee. Children are sometimes charged only $1.50. Airline overbooking is common, so it's a good idea to reconfirm international flights three days ahead and to arrive at least two hours before departure. A $3.75 "protected areas" exit tax is assessed for conservation activities.

Air Service
In 1999 Belize was served from the U.S. by three U.S. carriers and one Central American airline via the international airport near Belize City. Belize can be reached most directly from Miami (American, United, Taca), Los Angeles (Taca), San Francisco (American, Taca), and Houston (Taca, Continental). As this book goes to press, Delta is considering service to Belize.

Taca also flies to Belize from San Pedro Sula and Tegucigalpa, connecting to San José, Guatemala City, San Salvador, and Panama City. The Guatemalan airlines, Aviateca and Aerovías, have biweekly schedules from Flores/Santa Elena and Guatemala City to Belize City. A domestic carrier, Tropic, flies twice a week between Flores/Santa Elena and Belize City. Bonanza Airlines flies between Belize City and Chetumal, Mexico, with connections from there to Mérida, Cancún, and Mexico City. Jamaica Air has regular service between Belize City and both Jamaica and the Cayman Islands.

There is currently no direct service to Europe, although this could have changed by the time you read this book. Most European visitors transfer at one of the American gateway cities, in Cancún, or in Guatemala City. From Cancún there is bus and air service to Chetumal, on the northern border of Belize.

From Belize City's international and municipal airports (about 15 miles apart), frequent flights to smaller towns are offered by Tropic, Maya Island Airways, Sky Bird, Su-Bec, Javier's, and Island Air. Tropic, Maya Island, and others will also arrange charters to Mexico, Guatemala, and Honduras, as well as to destinations within Belize.

Most airlines now maintain Web sites that provide information on schedules, seating arrangements, and luggage restrictions. You can often make your own reservations via Internet and sometimes take advantage of last-minute, on-line discount prices offered by carriers eager to fill their seats. The Alliance of Central American Airlines is a coalition of five regional airlines that maintains a "webport" with a "Hot Deals" section at www.flylatinamerica.com. Web sites for some individual Belize carriers include: www.americanair.com (American Airlines) and www.flycontinental.com (Continental Airlines).

International Airlines Serving Belize
Aerocaribe Airlines
(305) 871-4262
Flights to and from Cancún, Mexico, several times a week.

Aerovías
2-75445 or (305) 885-1775
Semiweekly flights to and from Flores and Guatemala City.

American Airlines
U.S.A. (800) 624-6262
Canada (800) 433-7300
Belize City 2-32522
Daily flights from Miami with connections to other cities.
Check out "NetsAAver" discount fares on the Internet.

Aviateca
International Airport
Belize City
(800) 327-9832
Semi-weekly flights to and from Flores, Guatemala City,
and Cancún.

Bonanza Aerolineas
2-75446
Weekly flights to Mexico.

Caribbean Air
Belize City 2-2454
Honduras (504) 445-1926
Weekly flights to Roatán and San Pedro Sula, Honduras.

Continental
32 Albert Street
Belize City
U.S.A. (800) 231-0856
Canada (800) 525-0280
Belize City 2-78309
Several daily flights from Houston with connections to the rest of the U.S.
and Central America; actively supports conservation work in Belize.

TACA
41 Albert Street
Belize City
2-77363, fax 2-75213,
U.S.A. (800) 535-8780
Canada (800) 263-4039
Daily flights from Houston, Miami, and Los Angeles with connections to

New York, Washington, New Orleans, and San Francisco; also connections to the rest of Central America, including Roatán and Guatemala City.

Domestic Airlines and Air Charter Services

Note: Most of Belize's domestic flights and charters originate at the Municipal Airport in Belize City, on Barracks Road, about 15 miles east of the International Airport. In 1999 there was talk of closing the field and relocating all services to Belize City International.

Cari-Bee Air Service
Belize City
2-44253
Charters.

Javier's Flying Service
Municipal Airport
Belize City
2-45332, fax 2-32731
Charters and M-W-F flights to Gallon Jug.

Maya Island Air (formerly Maya Airways and Island Air)
231-348 or 231-362, (800) 257-8802, mayair@btl.net,
www.belizenet.com/mayair.
Scheduled service to and from San Pedro, Belize City, Big Creek, Caye Chapel, Caye Caulker, Dangriga, Placencia, Punta Gorda, plus Flores/Santa Elena and Puerto Barrios in Guatemala.

Sky Bird
Belize City
2-32596 or 2-52045, ext. 515
Daily flights between Belize City and Caye Caulker.

Su-Bec Air Service
Belize City
2-44027 or 2-62170, fax 2-30389
Charters.

Tropic Air
P.O. Box 20
San Pedro, Ambergris Caye
2-62012, fax 2-630807 or 2-62338, tropicair@btl.net
Belize City 2-45671
U.S.A. (800) 447-2931, except Texas (713) 449-5230

Daily flights to and from seven airports in Belize, plus twice weekly to Flores/Santa Elena in Guatemala. Charters available to Cancún, Mérida, Cozumel, Cayman Islands, and Roatán.

Arriving by Boat

If you arrive in Belize by private vessel, you must report your arrival to police or immigration immediately. No permits are required, but you need the usual official documents, clearance from the last port, and manifests for crew, passengers, stores, and cargo. Allowable points of entry are Belize City, Dangriga, Corozal/Consejo, San Pedro, Barranco, and Punta Gorda.

Private boats can be arranged between Corozal, Sarteneja, and other northern villages to Mexico's Yucatán. They can also be hired from Belize City, Placencia, Punta Gorda, and other places for trips into Guatemala and Honduras.

Informal water taxis provide daily service from Punta Gorda to Puerto Barrios, Guatemala, with connections there to interior Guatemala and Honduras. The crossing takes about 90 minutes, and you must have documents in order before embarking. Tickets are about $7 one-way.

A weekly ferry (actually, a large motor-powered canoe) sometimes operates between Dangriga and Puerto Cortes, Honduras. It leaves Wednesday mornings from the north side of Stann Creek, by the bridge. The trip takes about 10 hours, and you can clear immigration at the office on Commerce Street. Ask at The Hub restaurant/hotel in Dangriga for details.

Many boats ply the waters between Belize City, Caye Chapel, Caye Caulker, and Ambergris Caye. Remember to agree on your fare in advance and pay at the end of the trip. The *Andrea II* leaves the Bellevue Hotel dock (5 Southern Foreshore) for San Pedro at 4:00 p.m. weekdays, 1:00 p.m. Saturday. The return crossing is at 7:00 a.m. Trips take about 1 hour and 15 minutes to Ambergris, 45 minutes to Caulker. An efficient water taxi service operates from the Belize City marine terminal, immediately east of the Swing Bridge on North Front Street, providing regularly scheduled passenger service to Caulker and Ambergris. The one-way fare to Caulker is about $8 and to Ambergris about $12. Check with your travel agent about cruise ships that may stop in Belize.

Arriving by Car or Bus

While the Belizean road infrastructure is improving, only one (the Western Highway) is smooth and well maintained. All others vary in quality, ranging from rough dirt track to potholed pavement. Foreign aid money was obtained in 1995, however, to upgrade and pave many miles of road, including the notoriously rough Southern Highway.

Overland entry to Belize by foreigners is permitted only from eastern Guatemala (at the Western Highway crossing between Melchor de Mencos and Benque Viejo) or Mexico's Yucatán peninsula (where the Northern Highway crosses the Río Hondo at Santa Elena and Chetumal). A small Mexican crossing is sometimes open (for foot traffic only) at La Unión, a village northwest of Orange Walk. The 1,300-mile drive from south Texas to Belize takes from two to seven days, depending on the number of hours spent driving and the road conditions. Belizean buses—many purchased secondhand from U.S. and Canadian public schools—run regularly between Chetumal, Mexico, and Belize City. Seats can be reserved in advance, and ticket prices are reasonable. Passengers may pay on board. Batty Brothers and Venus are the two main companies, both charging about $8 for the 4-hour trip. From Chetumal it is a 220-mile bus ride to Cancún, where there are many inexpensive flights each day to the U.S. and Europe. You can also take a first-class bus to Playa del Carmen, which has ferries to Cancún and Cozemel.

By Bus from Guatemala

Crossing into Belize from Guatemala is bit more problematic than from Mexico. Few public buses cross the border; therefore, it is sometimes necessary to walk about 50 yards from one side to the other to buy an onward ticket and change vehicles. The crossing is open from 6:00 a.m. to midnight and is sometimes closed for the midday siesta (noon to 2:00 p.m.). Guatemalan and Belizean tourist cards are issued at the border, but visas usually are not. There is a Guatemalan consulate in Belize City, however, and a Belizean consulate in Guatemala City. (See Appendix B.)

Bus Companies

Note: Most Belize City bus terminals are near the intersection of Orange and Collett Canal Streets—not a safe area at night. All addresses and phone numbers listed are in Belize City.

Batty Bus Service
15 Mosul Street
2-72025
Points north and west.

Novelo's Bus Service
West Collett Canal
2-77372
Points west.

Venus Bus Service
Magazine Road and Vernon Street
2-73354 or 2-77390
Points north.

Z-Line Bus Service
Magazine Road and Vernon Street
2-73937 or 6-22211
Points south.

Car Rental

While it is possible to rent a private car in Belize, many travelers are put off by the high cost (typically $75 or more per day for a small car, $100 and up for a mid-size vehicle, plus about $15 a day for insurance) and limited selection (mostly Suzuki Samurais). If you're traveling to remote areas, a four-wheel-drive with spare tire and jack is advisable. Some tourists have complained about unscrupulous rental companies that have allegedly overcharged them for insurance and unnecessary repairs. Overbooking is also a problem. Only a few rental agencies will allow Belizean vehicles to travel into Guatemala and vice versa. It is possible to rent a car in Mexico and drive it into Belize, but agents will charge more if informed that this is your destination. If your Mexican car breaks down in Belize, you may have to pay for it to be towed back to Mexico for repairs and spare parts, both hard to find in Belize. Gas is expensive in oil-poor Belize (about $2.60 U.S. per gallon in 1999) and sometimes difficult to find because of spot shortages. Most rental agencies will provide a list of gas stations throughout the country, as well as maps.

Driving in Belize

International Driver's Licenses may be used in Belize, but domestic equivalents are acceptable. Drivers should carry valid licenses and vehicle registration documents if driving their own cars. If your vehicle is not going to be sold in Belize, you must obtain a temporary permit at Customs Control waiving the otherwise hefty import duty.

Third-party insurance is compulsory and can be purchased at border crossings or in major towns for about $70 a month. There is an exit fee of $2.50 per car. Visitors are permitted to use a Canadian or U.S. driver's license for 90 days, after which they must obtain a Belizean license ($20, plus photos and a medical examination report).

Car Rental Companies

Ace
12 N. Front Street
Belize City
2-31650, fax 2-31586

Alistair King
Texaco Station

Far West Street
Punta Gorda
7-2126, fax 7-2104
Four-wheel-drive available; valid driver's license required; offers tours.

Avis Rent-A-Car
International Airport or
Radisson Ft. George Hotel
Belize City
2-31987 or 2-78637

Budget Rent-A-Car
771 Bella Vista Road
Belize City
2-32435, fax 2-30237, jmagroup@btl.net
Well-run operation with a good selection of dependable cars at affordable prices. Recommended.

Crystal Auto Rental
Mile 1.5, Northern Highway
Belize City
2-31600, fax 2-31900
Rents used cars and arranges drive-away trips from Houston; valid driver's license and damage deposit required; all major credit cards accepted. Recommended.

ECO-Kar Rental
Northern Highway
Ladyville
25-2797
Conservation oriented and low cost; based near International Airport.

Hertz Rent-A-Car
2-35395, Operating in association with Safari Ltd.

Maxima Car Rental
Maxima Hotel
Hudson Street
San Ignacio
92-2265

Melmish Mayan Rentals
International Airport
Belize City
2-45221, fax 2-77681

National Car Rental
International Airport
Belize City
2-31586, fax 2-52272, www.belizenet.com
Mostly Suzuki Samurais, mostly in excellent shape.

Safari Car Rental
International Airport
Belize City
2-35395, fax 2-30268, safari@btl.net
Four-wheel-drive Isuzu Trooper specialist.

Arriving by Railroad

Belize no longer has any railroads. The few railways established during colonial days for logging and citrus have been dismantled, and today the nearest railhead is in Mérida, Mexico.

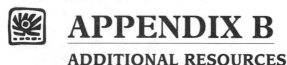

APPENDIX B
ADDITIONAL RESOURCES

TOURIST INFORMATION

An excellent source of background information is Angelus Press (2-35777, fax 2-78825, angelus@btl.net), a publisher and distributor of books, maps, and videos about Belize. Ask for their free catalogue or check out their Web site at www.belize.net.com/angelus.

Belize Tourism
Industry Association
Box 62
Belize City
2-75717, fax 2-78710, (800) 585-5081

Belize Tourist Board
Box 325, 83 N. Front Street
Belize City (800) 624-0686
2-77213 or 2-73255, fax 2-77490, BTBB@btl.net.

Belize Tourist Board
New York Office
421 Seventh Avenue, Suite 1110
New York, NY 10001 (800) 624-0686, rings in Belize;
(212) 563-6011, fax (212) 563-6033, www.belizenet.com or
bttb@btl.net

Belize Embassy
2535 Massachusetts Avenue NW
Washington, DC 20008
(202) 332-9636, fax (202) 332-6888. *Belize has consulates in New York, Miami, Washington, Chicago, New Orleans, San Francisco, and Houston.*

BELIZE ON-LINE

For a small country, Belize has a large Internet presence and a search on the country's name will yield hundreds of sites. Many hotels, outfitters, and other tourist businesses maintain Web sites and receive e-mail via btl.net, a service of the government's telephone monopoly, Belize Telephone Ltd.

For those seeking the latest information and news about Belize, the Belize by Naturalight website (www.belizenet.com) has no peer. This site tells how to get to Belize, how to get around inside the country, and what to see and do there. You will find travel details relating to hotels, tours, restaurants, car rentals, airline fares, diving, snorkeling, fishing, birding, trekking, and much more. The Belize Tourist Board offers a "virtual tour" at belizenet.com and you can read comments posted by recent visitors. The creation of Belize-based writer/photographer Tony Rath, Belize by Naturalight is loaded with stunning photos and virtual reality images. It's no wonder the site gets almost 3 million hits per month.

The Belize Online Tourism and Investment Guide has an extensive set of fact-filled pages at www.belize.com. This site includes their e-mail address (itm@belize.com); a helpful newsgroup forum where visitors can post appropriate comments or make inquiries; a thorough booklist page, with links for background information on specific places in Belize; and a handy general orientation map of the country. The Belize government has selected Belize Online as its official Internet home at www.belize.gov.bz.

Another popular Belize-oriented Web site is offered by The Turquoise Group, which posts an on-line edition of Lan Sluder's excellent *Belize First* magazine at www.turq.com/belizefirst. The tourist industry on Ambergris Caye maintains a Web site at www.ambergriscaye .com and the Belize Tourist Board at www.turq.com. Another site of interest is www.belize1.com.

An especially helpful interactive on-line publication focusing on natural history tourism and adventure travel in Belize (and neighboring countries) is *La Planeta Platica* (www.planeta.com), edited by Ron Mader (author of *Mexico: Adventures in Nature* and co-author of *Honduras: Adventures in Nature*, both published by John Muir Publications).One of Belize's weekly newspapers, *The Reporter*, receives e-mail at report@btl.net and reprints some of its pages at www.belize.com/ reporter.html.

The *Green Arrow Guide to Central America* provides information on countries throughout the region, lists tours that can be booked on-line, and answers travel questions: www.greenarrow.com. A Web site for sea-kayaking and adventure travel enthusiasts is posted at www.slickrock.com by Slickrock Adventures.

Millions of travelers now use the Internet to make arrangements for their trips and there are many one-stop or destination-specific sites online. Specialists in adventure and ecotourism include the Green Travel Network (www.greentravel.com) and Great Outdoors Recreation Pages (www.gorp.com).

RECOMMENDED TOUR COMPANIES
Belize City Tour Companies

Adventure Expeditions Belize
4 South Park Street
2-30748, fax 2-30750
Custom and individual tours; destinations include Altun Ha, Crooked Tree Wildlife Sanctuary, Community Baboon Sanctuary, Xunantunich, Belize Zoo, Lamanai, Mountain Pine Ridge, Tikal.

Belize Travel Adventures
168 N. Front Street
2-32618
Full-service travel agency.

Belize Global Travel Service
41 Albert Street
2-77185, fax 2-75213
Full service: tickets, tours, hotels.

Belize Land, Air, and Sea Tours, Ltd.
58 King Street
Tel./fax 2-73897
Charter boat, land, and diving tours.

Caribbean Holidays Ltd.
81 Albert Street
2-72593, fax 2-78007
Full service, also works with students, senior citizens.

G & W Holiday Travel & Tour Agent
Box 820
Belize City
2-31979 or 25-2461, cellular 14-8756, gholiday@btl.net
Air-conditioned van; car rental referral; archaeology tours, nature tours; historical sites; bookings for other tours, air charters, and resorts.

Jal's Travel and Tours
148 N. Front Street
2-45407, fax 2-78852
Full-service travel agency; specializes in trips to see manatees; caving, bird-watching, and Maya ruins.

MayaWorld Safaris
Box 997
Belize City
2-31063, fax 2-30263
Boat trips on New River from Orange Walk Town to Lamanai, tours Maya ruins and other sights.

S & L Travel Services
91 N. Front Street
2-75145, fax 2-77594; sltravel@btl.net
Full-service travel agency (also runs tours) with excellent reputation. Recommended.

Tubroos Tree Adventures
146 Barracks Road
2-33398, fax 2-30385
Full-service travel agency.

Cayes Tour Companies

Amigo Travel
San Pedro, Ambergris Caye
2-62180, fax 2-62192, amigotrav@btl.net
Full-service agency, scooter and bike rental, snorkeling, reef and interior tours.

Travel and Tour Belize, Ltd.
San Pedro, Ambergris Caye
26-2031, fax 26-2185
Diving, snorkeling, fishing, archaeology.

Cayo District Tour Companies

Alwyn Smith
Bullet Tree Road
San Ignacio
92-2155 or 92-3077
Taxi service and tour guide; Maya ruins, Cayo, Tikal, Mexico.

Pine Ridge Lodge
Chiquibul Road
Mountain Pine Ridge
92-3310 or (216) 781-6888
Caving, nature treks, equestrian, birding, and archaeology tours.

Windy Hill Tours
Mile 68 Western Highway
San Ignacio
92-2017, fax 92-3080, windyhill@btl.net
Affordable, all-inclusive Tikal trips; other archaeology tours.

Yute Expeditions
San Ignacio
92-2979, fax 92-2076
Trips to Tikal; birding and other natural history and archaeology tours in Cayo.

Corozal District Tour Companies

Manuel Hoare
13 G Street South
Corozal Town
4-22744, fax 4-23375
Belizean archaeology expert and boatman.

Menzies Travel and Tours, Ltd.
Caribbean Village Resort
South End
Corozal Town
4-22725, fax 4-23414
Agent for Tropic Island Air; tours in northern Belize; archaeology tours; Mexico and Guatemala guided tours.

Orange Walk District Tour Companies

Atilano Narvallez
Guinea Grass
3-22081
Boat rental; jungle river tours of Lamanai.

Godoy & Sons
4 Trial Farm
Orange Walk Town
3-22969
Specializes in orchids and bromeliads of Belize, boat trips up New River to Lamanai and beyond.

Jungle River Tours
20 Lovers Lane
Orange Walk Town
3-22293, fax 3-22201
River trips, jungle tours; Lamanai; strong Belizean archaeology expert.

Lamanai Outpost Lodge
Box 63
Orange Walk Town
Tel./fax 2-33578, (888) 733-7864, lamanai@btl.net
Windsurfing, boat trips, canoeing on New River Lagoon in Orange Walk District.

Stann Creek District Tour Companies

Allen Andrewin
Gales Point
5-22087
Jungle and boat tours; guide services.

Dalton Eiley
Placencia
6-2046, ext. 119
Natural history tours, trips to cayes, fishing, diving, boating.

David Vernon
Placencia Inland Tours
6-2046, ext. 116
Natural history, river trips, ruins, Cockscomb Basin Wildlife Sanctuary.

Jorge Rosado Tours
35 Lemon Street
Dangriga
5-2020 or 5-22119
Nature trips, reef charters and accommodations, Maya village and cave tours.

Toledo District Tour Companies

Dem Dat's Doin'
Box 73
Front Street at the Wharf
Punta Gorda

7-22470
Tourist information service, permaculture farm, bed-and-breakfast.

Julio Requena's Charter Service
12 Front Street
Punta Gorda
7-22070
*Boat trips to cayes, rivers; scheduled trips to Puerto Barrios,
Guatemala; tours to caves, ruins, indigenous villages.*

Nature's Way Guest House/Belize Adventure Travel
65 Front Street
Punta Gorda
7-22119
*Maya villages guest house and Garifuna model village contact;
boat trips to cayes.*

U.S.-Based Belize Tour Companies

Belize Services
2480 Times Boulevard
Suite 210
Houston, TX 77005
(800) 880-MAYA, fax (713) 528-6292
*Belize travel specialists, including nature, reef, and Maya ruin tours;
hotel and airline bookings; car rental; special knowledge of Corozal and
Orange Walk districts.*

Belize Tradewinds
8715 W. North Avenue
Wauwatosa, WI 53226
(800) 451-7776 or (414) 258-6687
Hotels; fishing and dive tours.

Belize Travel Representatives
5 Grogans Park, Suite 102
The Woodlands, TX 77380
(800) 451-8017 or (281) 367-3386, fax (281) 298-2335
Owner Tommy Thomson can arrange any kind of trip you want.

Explore the World
672 Las Gallinas Road
San Rafael, CA 94903

(800) 735-9520, fax (415) 454-6188
Hotel and airline booking; nature, diving, fishing, and snorkeling.

Holbrook Travel
3540 NW 13th Street
Gainesville, FL 32609
(800) 451-7111; fax (352) 371-3710.
Guided package tours of Belize and Guatemala.

Magnum Belize
Box 1560
Detroit Lakes, MN 56502
(800) 447-2931 (U.S. and Canada), fax (218) 847-0334
*Travel planners for Belize visitors at every budget and interest level;
including "jungle experience," Maya ruins, and rain forest tours.*

Ocean Connection
16734 El Camino Real
Houston, TX 77062
(800) 365-6232, fax (713) 486-8362
Diving, fishing, snorkeling, sailing, tours, hotels, airfare.

Slickrock Adventures
P.O. Box 1400
Moab, UT 84532
(800) 390-5715, fax (435) 259-6996, slickrock@slickrock.com
A variety of adventure sports combined with travel to exotic locations.

BELIZE CONSERVATION GROUPS

Belize Audubon Society
Box 1001, 12 Fort Street
Belize City
2-35004 or 2-34987,
base@btl.net, www.belizeaudubon.org

Belize EcoTourism Association
Box 1129
Belize City
25-2806, betalin@btl.netday

Belize Natural History Society
Gallon Jug

Orange Walk District
No phone

Belize Tropical Forest Studies
P.O. Box 208
Belmopan
92-3310, fax 82-3361, tfs@pobox.com

Belize Zoo & Tropical Education Center
Mile 30, Western Highway
Box 1787, Belize City
8-13004, belizezoo@pobox.com, www.belizenet.com/belizezoo

Community Conservation Consultants/
Howlers Forever
RD 1, Box 96
Gays Mills, WI 54631
(608) 735-4717, ccc@mwt.net

International Tropical
Conservation Foundation
c/o Papiliorama
Case postale 31
CH 2074 Marin-Neuchâtel
Switzerland
(032) 7534350, itcf@papiliorama.ch

Ix Chel Tropical Research Foundation/
Traditional Healers' Foundation
Ix Chel Farm
San Ignacio, Cayo District
9-23870

Programme for Belize
Box 749
Belize City
2-75616, fax 2-75635; pfb@btl.net

Slate Creek Preserve
Mile 8 Mountain Pine Ridge Road
Central Farm P.O.
Cayo District
92-3310, fax 82-3361; tfs@bcsl.com.bz

Wildlife Conservation Society
185th Street and South Boulevard, Bldg. A
Bronx, NY 10460
(212) 220-5155

World Wildlife Fund—U.S.
1250 24th Street, NW
Washington, DC 20037
(202) 293-4800

EMBASSIES AND CONSULATES (PARTIAL LIST)

Canada
85 North Front Street
Belize City
2-31060

Costa Rica
2 Sapodilla Street
Belmopan
8-22725

Guatemala
6-A Saint Matthew Street
Belize City
2-33150, fax 2-35140

Honduras
91 North Front Street
Belize City
2-45889

Mexico
20 North Park Street
Belize City
2-30193

United States
Hutson Street and Gabrouel Lane
Belize City
2-77161

SUGGESTED READING

World of the Maya

The Blood of Kings: Dynasty and Ritual in Maya Art, Linda Schele and Mary Ellen Miller. Ft. Worth: Kimbell Art Museum, 1986.

The Complete Visitor's Guide to Mesoamerican Ruins, Joyce Kelly. Norman: University of Oklahoma Press, 1982.

Guide to Ancient Maya Ruins, C. Bruce Hunter. Norman: University of Oklahoma Press, 1986.

Time Among the Maya, Ronald Wright. New York: Weidenfeld & Nicholson, 1989.

Warlords and Maize Men: A Guide to the Maya Sites of Belize, Byron Foster, ed. Belize City: Cubola Publications, 1989.

Nature and the Environment

A Belizean Rain Forest: The Community Baboon Sanctuary, Robert Horwich and Jon Lyon. Gay Mills, Wisc.: Orangutan Press, 1990.

A Guide to the Birds of Mexico and Northern Central America, Steve Howell and Sophie Webb. New York: Oxford University Press, 1995.

Belize: A Country Environmental Profile and Field Study, Robert Nicolait and Associates. San José, Costa Rica: Hnos Sucs, S.A., 1984.

Belize: An International Travel Map, Vancouver: International Travel Maps, 1995.

Belize and Northern Guatemala: The Ecotravellers' Wildlife Guide, Les Beletsky, Orlando, FL: Academic Press, 1998.

Birds of Mexico and Central America, Steve Howell and Sophie Webb. New York: Oxford University Press, 1993.

Caribbean Reef Ecology, William S. Alavizon. Pisces Books, 1994.

Checklist of the Birds of Belize, Wood, Leberman, and Weyer. Pittsburgh: Carnegie Museum of Natural History Special Publication No. 12.

Guide to Corals and Fishes, Jerry Greenberg. Miami: Seahawk Press, 1972.

Guide to Community-Based Ecotourism in Belize, Community Conservation Consultants, Gays Mills, WI. (A report on six major projects where Belize villages are actively involved in managing local protected areas.)

Jaguar: A Struggle and Triumph in the Jungles of Belize, Alan Rabinowitz. New York: Arbor House, 1986.

Jungle Walk: Birds and Beasts of Belize, Katie Stevens. Belize City: Angelus Press, 1989.

A Neotropical Companion: An Introduction to the Animals, Plants, and Ecosystems of New World Tropics, John C. Kricher. Princeton: Princeton University Press.

Macdonald Encyclopedia of Butterflies and Moths, Mauro Daccordi, Paolo Triberti, and Adriano Zanetti. Macdonald & Co Ltd., 1988.

Marine Plants of the Caribbean: A Field Guide from Florida to Brazil, Diane Scullion Littler, Mark M. Littler, Katina E. Bucher and James N. Norris. Washington: Smithsonian Institution Press, 1989.

Neotropical Rainforest Mammals: A Field Guide, Louise H. Emmons. Chicago and London: University of Chicago Press.

One Hundred Birds of Belize, Carolyn M. Miller. Washington: International Council for Bird Preservation.

Orchids of Guatemala and Belize, Oakes Ames and Donovan Stewart Correll. New York: Dover, 1985.

Preliminary Faunal Surveys at Tapir Mountain Nature Reserve, Bruce and Carolyn Miller. Wildlife Conservation Society, 1994.

Rainforest Remedies: One Hundred Healing Herbs of Belize, Rosita Arvigo and Michael Balick, Twin Lakes: Lotus Press, 1993.

Reef Fish and Reef Creatures, Paul Humann. Jacksonville: New World Publications, 1994.

Sastun: My Apprenticeship with a Maya Healer, Rosita Arvigo with Nadine Epstein. San Francisco: Harper Collins, 1994.

Snorkeling Guide to Marine Life, Paul Humann. New World Publications, 1995.

History and Culture

Creole Proverbs of Belize, Colville N. Young. Belize City: National Printers Ltd., 1989.

Hey Dad, This Is Belize, Emory King. Belize City: Tropical Books, 1984.

Inside Belize: A Country Guide, Tom Barry. Albuquerque: Inter-Hemispheric Education Research Center, 1992.

I Spent It All in Belize, Emory King. Belize City: Tropical Books, 1986.

The Making of Belize: Globalization in the Margins, Anne Sutherland. Westport, CT: Bergind Garvey, 1998.

On Heroes, Lizards and Passion, Zoila Ellis. Benque Viejo, Belize: Cubola Publications, 1989.

Profile of Belize, Society for the Promotion of Education and Research. Belize City: Cubola Publications/SPEAR Press, 1990.

Other

Belize Retirement Guide, Bill and Claire Gray. Preview Publishing, 1995. *A popular guide to "living in a tropical paradise for $350 a month."*

Birding Guide to La Ruta Maya, Dennis W. Rogers. Clincus Publishing, 1994. *Booklet with bird lists and best birding spots in northern Central America and southern Mexico.*

PUBLICATIONS AVAILABLE IN BELIZE

Belize Business & Travel Directory, Henson & Associates. Belize City: Angelus Press, 1988.

351

Emory King's Driver's Guide to Beautiful Belize, Emory King.
Belize City: Tropical Books, 1998. *Updated annually.*

Magazines and Newspapers

Amandala
(weekly; independent newspaper)
3304 Partridge Street
Belize City

Belize Currents
(semi-annual; general interest magazine)
2159 Summer Avenue
Memphis, TN 38112

Belize First
(quarterly; general interest magazine
with travel orientation)
280 Beaverdam Road
Candler, NC 28715
www.turq.com/belizefirst/

Belize Magazine
(quarterly; general interest and
conservation magazine)
14110 Perdido Key Drive #P2
Pensacola, FL 32507

Belize Natural History Society Papers
c/o Bruce Miller
Gallon Jug, Orange Walk District

Belize Report
(quarterly tourism newsletter)
Box 1881
Belize City
www.belizereport.com or editor@belizereport.com

Belize Sun
(country-wide weekly)
Box 35
San Pedro, Ambergris Caye
sanpdrosun@btl.net

Belize Times
(weekly; PUP newspaper)
Box 506, 3 Queen Street
Belize City

Belize Today
(bimonthly; free; business-oriented)
Belize Information Service
Box 60
Belmopan

Chac Nol Newsletter
(journal of the Central American Institute of
Prehistoric and Traditional Cultures)
Box 59
San Ignacio

Chamber Update
(monthly; business magazine)
Belize Chamber of Commerce
Box 291, 63 Regent Street
Belize City

Reporter
(weekly; independent)
Box 1217
Belize City

San Pedro Sun
(weekly; independent newspaper; also publishes *Belize Sun*)
Box 35
San Pedro, Ambergris Caye
sanpedrosun@btl.net

INDEX

ABOUT THE AUTHOR

Richard Mahler is a writer and broadcast journalist who has reported on conservation and nature topics for more than 25 years. The author of five published books, he has written for more than 100 magazines and newspapers, including the *Los Angeles Times, Christian Science Monitor, Miami Herald, Outside, Great Expeditions, Mother Jones, Belize First,* and *New West.* He has been a freelance correspondent for National Public Radio since 1973 and covers environmental matters for the public radio series *Living on Earth,* reporting on such issues as rainforest destruction and preservation of Native American

sacred sites. Mahler's writing and radio productions have received awards from the Associated Press, PEN USA, the Society of American Travel Writers, and the Radio-TV News Directors Association. As an advocate of natural history tourism and conservation activism, he has worked on behalf of numerous environmental organizations in the American West and Latin America. A longtime resident of New Mexico, Mahler is based in Santa Fe.